The 13th Battalion
Royal Highlanders of Canada

1914-1919

In the preparation of this work the Department of National Defence has allowed the author free access to official diaries, orders, messages, maps and other documents.

13TH BATTALION, R.H.C., SALISBURY PLAINS, FEBRUARY, 1915.

Gale & Polden.

The 13th Battalion
Royal Highlanders of Canada
1914-1919

Edited and Compiled by
R. C. Fetherstonhaugh

The Naval & Military Press Ltd

Published by

The Naval & Military Press Ltd
Unit 10 Ridgewood Industrial Park,
Uckfield, East Sussex,
TN22 5QE England

Tel: +44 (0) 1825 749494
Fax: +44 (0) 1825 765701

www.naval-military-press.com
www.nmarchive.com

Cover illustration:
Brig.-Gen. F. O. W. Loomis, C.B., C.M.G., D.S.O.

In reprinting in facsimile from the original, any imperfections are inevitably reproduced and the quality may fall short of modern type and cartographic standards.

TO THE PROUD MEMORY OF
THE 13TH BATTALION DEAD
1291 IN NUMBER
THIS BOOK IS RESPECTFULLY
DEDICATED.

Author's Foreword

IN presenting to the public this record of the 13th Battalion, C.E.F., the author would like to emphasize two points which apply throughout.

First, the reader is asked to realize that this is the story of ONE BATTALION ONLY. No effort has been made to follow the fortunes, or record the gallant deeds, of the splendid units with which the 13th Battalion was associated, except in so far as these directly affected the 13th itself. Considerations of space made this policy unavoidable.

Second, in the matter of individual mention, the author was forced to omit the account of many acts of personal courage and self sacrifice of an extremely high order. Where two or three such have been set down, ten times that number have had to be left out. Those who served with the Battalion will realize that no book of ordinary dimensions could contain a record which would do even approximate justice to individuals. Were other evidence of this lacking, a glance at the appendices of this book would carry overwhelming conviction that the half had not been told.

In conclusion the author desires to express his appreciation of the loyal support afforded him by the officers of the Battalion at whose suggestion the compilation of this book was undertaken. They furnished him with over 40 specially written reports and narratives and granted personal interviews innumerable, whenever some knotty problem impeded progress, or some difference in opinions required a careful sifting of facts. Also the author would acknowledge the unfailing courtesy and assistance of Col. F. Logie Armstrong, O.B.E., and Col. A. Fortescue Duguid, D.S.O., the former Director of Records and the latter Director of the Historical Section, General Staff, Department of National Defence, Ottawa, without whose help his task could not have been completed. A special debt is also acknowledged to those who in troublous times so faithfully kept the Battalion Diary, which is the basis of all the pages that follow.

R. C. F.

MONTREAL, February 15, 1925.

Foreword

By MAJOR-GENERAL SIR A. C. MACDONELL,
K.C.B., C.M.G., D.S.O.

"They served with fidelity and fought with valour"—CHATHAM.

THE Battalion, formed in August, 1914, from the two fine battalions of the R.H.C., went to England from Valcartier in September, 1914, and returned to Canada in April, 1919. What the Battalion did in the intervening years is well and interestingly told by our author. He has done his task well; his narrative grips one, albeit it is all too brief and too modest; and he who reads this history must read between the lines to grasp the full measure of loyalty, heroism and self-sacrifice almost daily displayed. He will realize that "when cannons are roarin' and bullets are flying the lad that would win glory must never fear dying."

It is advisable to mention a few of the milestones that led to the efficiency of the Royal Highlanders of Canada. Raised in the stirring times of 1862, they became a battalion of the Canadian Militia with its glorious traditions, (a militia that has fought for the Crown every fifteen years since 1763). First a partially kilted battalion, then a kilted battalion, they finally had the honour of wearing the Black Watch Tartan. In the South African War, members of the Battalion for the first time fought for the Empire outside of Canada and Major George Cameron won the D.S.O.

In 1904 the Regiment was affiliated with the Black Watch; this affiliation was real and fostered by the officers of both regiments, notably by Colonel Rose of Kilravock. The 13th started with its identity preserved, its Regimental Officers and glorious traditions. Tested in the furnace of the Second Battle of Ypres, it proved its worth. Compare the reports of the gallantry and losses of the 42nd Black Watch at Ticonderoga and the 13th Battalion at the above named battle.

The raising of the 42nd and 73rd Battalions from the R.H.C. added to the Regimental morale.

Then came the crowning glory, the request that they should mount the "Red Hackle." When I was promoted to command the 1st Canadian Division in June, 1917, the 13th were already a distinguished battalion with all the ear marks that indicate a good

ROYAL HIGHLANDERS OF CANADA

battalion. They had intensely patriotic officers, good *Esprit de Corps,* good discipline, traditions, and a great record which all seemed determined should not be tarnished. They were well commanded; think for a moment of their Colonels—Major-General Sir Frederick Loomis who put his efficient mark on the Battalion, Victor Buchanan, Eric McCuaig later Brigadier-General, Kenneth Perry, Ian Sinclair—hard to equal, my masters, as Battalion Commanders in a stark fight. Count their decorations, not forgetting their wound stripes; and, although he never actually commanded the Battalion, I must mention gallant, modest Clark-Kennedy, V.C., a real hero.

As battle followed battle I became thoroughly imbued with the Battalion's soundness and absolute dependability. Look up the book and see for yourself what they did. One splendid fact is outstanding, wounded officers always returned to the Battalion as soon as possible.

May I, at the risk of being too long, give my impression of a scene that is indelibly imprinted on my memory, a picture I love to recall, namely the presentation of Colours by H.R.H. Prince Arthur of Connaught. The Battalion never looked smarter, the setting for a Highland Battalion was perfect. Drawn up in line with their backs to a swift running rippling mountain stream on a meadow surrounded by well wooded hills, this battle-trained battalion of Royal Highlanders, victors on many a bloody triumphant field, proudly wearing the Red Hackle, received their Colours after a victorious campaign, from the hands of a Royal Prince, as knights of old received their spurs. The day was dark and overcast, Col. Perry asked and received permission to march past. He formed the Battalion up in column of half battalions, the Colours in the centre. Just as he gave the command "March," the sun burst out. Never have I seen a more gloriously martial sight than the 13th Battalion, Royal Highlanders, at their best, as, with pipes playing, bayonets fixed, Colours flying, kilts swinging, they passed the saluting base in the burst of sun light.

The 13th and 42nd Battalions were both towers of strength to me, hence my pride in the honour of writing this foreword.

In closing, may I congratulate the author heartily on his work.

A. C. MACDONELL,
Maj.-General.
Late Commanding 1st Canadian Division.

Contents

Chapter I.
The Outbreak of the War. June 28, 1914—September 26, 1914	3

Chapter II.
The Voyage to England and Salisbury Plains. September 26, 1914—February 10, 1915 15

Chapter III.
Over to France and Into Action. February 10, 1915—April 10, 1915 29

Chapter IV.
The Second Battle of Ypres. April 10, 1915—May 5, 1915 . 41

Chapter V.
Festubert, Givenchy and Ploegsteert. May 5, 1915—August 12, 1915 55

Chapter VI.
Messines. August 12, 1915—March 17, 1916 . . . 69

Chapter VII.
Hill 60, The Bluff and Mount Sorrel. March 17, 1916—May 31, 1916 81

Chapter VIII.
The June Show, 1916. May 31, 1916—June 13, 1916 . 95

Chapter IX.
Sanctuary Wood, Verbrandenmolen and Watten. June 13, 1916—August 31, 1916 108

[xi]

ROYAL HIGHLANDERS OF CANADA

CHAPTER X. PAGE

THE SOMME. August 31, 1916—October 9, 1916 . . . 122

CHAPTER XI.

THE WINTER OF 1916-1917. October 9, 1916—March 1, 1917 142

CHAPTER XII.

VIMY RIDGE. March 1, 1917—April 10, 1917 . . . 157

CHAPTER XIII.

THELUS, FARBUS, ARLEUX AND FRESNOY. April 10, 1917—July 16, 1917 173

CHAPTER XIV.

HILL 70. July 16, 1917—August 16, 1917 . . . 188

CHAPTER XV.

PASSCHENDAELE. August 16, 1917—November 12, 1917 . 202

CHAPTER XVI.

THE THIRD WINTER IN FRANCE. November 12, 1917—March 20, 1918 215

CHAPTER XVII.

ANXIOUS DAYS. March 20, 1918—May 7, 1918 . . 226

CHAPTER XVIII.

G.H.Q. RESERVE. May 7, 1918—August 3, 1918 . . 238

CHAPTER XIX.

THE BATTLE OF AMIENS. August 3, 1918—August 21, 1918 247

CONTENTS

Chapter XX.

The Second Battles of Arras, 1918. August 21, 1918—September 14, 1918 262

Chapter XXI.

The Canal du Nord. September 14, 1918—September 29, 1918 271

Chapter XXII.

The Beginning of the End. September 29, 1918—October 10, 1918 281

Chapter XXIII.

The Last of the Fighting. October 10, 1918—November 11, 1918 293

Chapter XXIV.

The March to the Rhine. November 11, 1918—January 4, 1919 304

Chapter XXV.

Back from Germany and Home to Canada. January 4, 1919—April 20, 1919 314

Appendices

Appendix A.
List of the Dead 323

Appendix B.
Honours and Awards 338

Appendix C.
Statistics 344

Illustrations

	PAGE
13TH BATTALION, R.H.C., SALISBURY PLAINS, FEBRUARY, 1915	*Frontispiece*
MAPLE COPSE, YPRES SALIENT, JUNE, 1916	112
A TRENCH SCENE, YPRES SALIENT, JUNE, 1916	112
IN RESERVE NEAR LENS	176
FARBUS, MAY, 1917	176
MEMORIAL CROSS, ERECTED BY THE BATTALION AT NINE ELMS, VIMY RIDGE, MAY, 1917	192
MARCHING BACK TO REST BILLETS AFTER THE CAPTURE OF HILL 70, AUGUST, 1917	208
MARCHING FROM HILL 70, AUGUST, 1917	208
AVION, SEPTEMBER, 1917	224
PASSCHENDAELE, NOVEMBER, 1917	224
WINTER, 1917-1918	240
IN THE TRENCHES NEAR LENS, DECEMBER, 1917	240
A TROPHY. AMIENS, AUGUST 8TH, 1918	256
THE DROCOURT-QUEANT LINE, SEPTEMBER, 1918	256
ENTRAINING AT BENSBERG, JANUARY 5TH, 1919	308
COLOURS PRESENTED IN GERMANY BY H.R.H. PRINCE ARTHUR OF CONNAUGHT, JANUARY 4TH, 1919	308
COMMANDING OFFICERS, 13TH BATTALION, R.H.C.	316

Maps

YPRES AND FESTUBERT	48
THE SOMME AND AMIENS	128
ARRAS AND CAMBRAI	272

The 13th Battalion
Royal Highlanders of Canada
1914-1919

CHAPTER I

The Outbreak of the War

> For all we have and are
> For all our children's fate
> Stand up and take the war
> The Hun is at the gate!
>
> Though all we knew depart
> The old commandments stand
> "In courage keep your heart
> In strength lift up your hand."
> —RUDYARD KIPLING.

I

ON June 28th, 1914, when a Serbian fanatic assassinated the Austrian Archduke, Francis Ferdinand, and his consort, Sophie, Duchess of Hohenberg, in the little Bosnian town of Sarajevo, the event was not looked upon in Canada as of outstanding interest. Bosnians, Serbs, Russians and other foreign peoples were given to political murder and something of the kind was bound to happen every once in a while, no effect being felt beyond the boundaries of the countries immediately concerned.

This particular murder, then, excited no more than casual interest. It was not even a nine days' wonder. People read about it, expressed a certain amount of pious horror and promptly forgot it in the rush of more important events connected with the summer's activities.

In mid-July foreign selling of securities became noticeable and financial circles sensed that something was wrong, but it was not until July 23rd that the situation became at all clear. On that date Austria presented an ultimatum to Serbia and the next day, when the contents of this note were made public, the world woke up with a start to realize that war was in the air.

Events now moved with bewildering rapidity, so much so that by August 2nd negotiations had broken down and the Great World War had begun. England, who had striven desperately to avert the disaster, was inevitably drawn in. Whatever may have been the desire of the British people as to taking part in the war, the appeal of the Belgian King removed all doubt from their minds. England's duty to take part with Belgium against any aggressor was clear and unmistakable. Promptly Sir Edward Grey demanded a guarantee from France and Germany that Belgian neutrality would be observed. France gave the required promise, but Germany refused point blank to do so. And so it came about that on August 4th, at midnight, England declared war against Germany.

II

As soon as it became apparent that war was probable Canada and the other Dominions rallied immediately to the support of the Imperial Government. Britain's quarrel was obviously just and the Dominions took it up without quibble or hesitation.

On July 30th Col. the Hon. Sam Hughes, Canadian Minister of Militia and Defence, presided at a special meeting of the Militia Council, after which it was announced that, in the event of war, Canada would send overseas a First Contingent of from 20,000 to 25,000 men. On August 1st H.R.H. the Duke of Connaught telegraphed this offer to the British Government and asked on behalf of the Canadian people in what further way they could be of assistance.

Meanwhile in the armouries and drill sheds of the Dominion steps were being taken to prepare units for the Expeditionary Force that was to be. In this work the 5th Royal Highlanders of Canada took the part expected of them. Formed on January 31st, 1862, the 5th Royal Highlanders of Canada had, since 1904, been affiliated with the famous Black Watch, the oldest Highland Regiment in the British Army, which in turn was lineally descended from the six "Independent Companies of the Watch" raised in 1725. With such distinguished affiliations and with a proud record of its own to maintain, the 5th responded promptly to the unexpected call. In the absence of Lieut.-Cols. Cantlie and Ross, who were in England, Lieut.-Col. Peers Davidson addressed the Regiment in the Armoury on Bleury St., calling on officers and men alike to rally to the colours for service overseas. So enthusiastic was the response to this stirring speech that a telegram was despatched to the Minister of Militia forthwith, offering a battalion of Highlanders for whatever service might be required of them.

THE OUTBREAK OF THE WAR

On August 6th the Canadian Government called for enlistments for overseas service and on Friday, August 7th, recruiting was actively begun. On that day there appeared in the Montreal papers the following advertisement, which, with no great stretch of fancy, can be considered the "birth notice" of the 13th Battalion:

5TH ROYAL HIGHLANDERS OF CANADA
ACTIVE SERVICE CONTINGENT.

MEMBERS of the Regiment and others wishing to enrol in the Contingent which will be sent by the Regiment for Active Service abroad, will make application at the Orderly Room after 9 a.m. on Saturday, the 8th instant.

D. R. McCUAIG, Major,
Regimental Adjutant.

As will be noticed in the above advertisement, the 13th Battalion had not up to this time been given its distinctive number. For some time it was still to be known as the "Active Service Contingent" of the Parent Regiment. Recruits flocked to its colours of their own accord and in addition recruiting parties were active, not in Montreal alone, but also in Sherbrooke and other parts of the surrounding country.

Major F. O. W. Loomis, who was appointed to command the new Battalion with the rank of Brevet Lieut.-Colonel, was a Sherbrooke man by birth. Born in 1870, he had joined the 53rd Militia Battalion when only 16 years of age. Twelve years later his interest and ability had earned him a commission and in 1903, on his moving to Montreal, he had transferred to the 5th Royal Highlanders. Now all his years of training were to serve him in good stead. Recruits poured in faster than they could be handled, or so it seemed, but under Col. Loomis' supervision and by the strenuous efforts of all concerned the wheels of enlistment were somehow kept turning.

Difficulties there were—serious difficulties—but these were met as they arose and disposed of as seemed best at the time. In ordinary circumstances many of the points that came up could not have been settled without reference to Ottawa, but Ottawa was having troubles of its own and requests for instructions or information often met with no response. Under such conditions Col. Loomis and his officers very wisely took things into their own hands.

ROYAL HIGHLANDERS OF CANADA

Typical of the time was the necessity of purchasing supplies and equipment without adequate authority to do so, or more bluntly, with no authority to do so at all. On this point there was no hesitation. What was needed was bought at once and permission sought afterwards. Assistance to meet these conditions was generously offered by honorary members of the Regiment, who placed at the C.O.'s disposal a sum of money sufficient to tide over this difficult time.

Meanwhile, in addition to the organization and recruiting activities, drilling of the men already enlisted was steadily carried on. A considerable number of these had had military training of some sort, either with the Parent Regiment or elsewhere, but others had had no training whatsoever and these had to be taught the very rudiments. About 65% to 75% of the recruits were Old Countrymen, the remainder native Canadians, with a small scattering of total outsiders who for one reason or another had decided to join up. In regard to the officers these proportions were reversed, all but four of those appointed being Canadian born.

To look back on those strenuous days is to marvel at the rapidity with which the unit took shape. Enthusiasm ran high and, under the stimulus of the prevailing excitement, men worked twelve, fifteen and eighteen hours a day, hardly realizing that they did so. It seems almost invidious to mention anyone by name when all gave freely of the best that was in them, but justice would not be done if some tribute were not paid to the untiring efforts of Col. Loomis, Major E. C. Norsworthy, the Second-in-Command, and Major V. C. Buchanan, the Junior Major. In addition to these the eight Company Commanders, Major D. R. McCuaig, Capt. C. J. Smith, Capt. R. H. Jamieson, Capt. K. M. Perry, Capt. L. W. Whitehead, Capt. T. S. Morrisey, Capt. H. F. Walker and Capt. W. H. Clark-Kennedy, worked with might and main, as did Capt. G. E. McCuaig, the Adjutant, and the Medical Officers, Major E. R. Brown and Capt. Douglas Morgan. Of the N.C.O.'s none rendered more valuable services than Sergt.-Major D. A. Bethune and Sergt. J. K. Beveridge.

In spite of hard work and serious attention to duty, the times were not entirely devoid of humorous incident. Few of those privileged to be present will forget the newly appointed lance-corporal who was earnestly drilling an awkward squad on Fletcher's Field. At the edge of the small plot allotted to him was a group

THE OUTBREAK OF THE WAR

of nurse-maids whose admiring, and not exactly inaudible, comments brought hot blushes to his face and confusion to his brain. Gradually his orders suffered; sharp and clear at first, they soon reflected his embarrassed state of mind. Finally, as the Colonel approached to look things over, confusion took control. "Squad!" roared the corporal, "Right! No, left! No! .... Oh, damn it! tur-r-n yer faces tae the Colonel and yer backs on a' thae blatherin' weemin."

As August wore on the ranks of the companies steadily filled and rumours were heard that soon the Battalion would go under canvas. More definite was the news that Col. Sam Hughes in person was to inspect the unit previous to its departure. This inspection was duly held on the Champ de Mars and was in many ways memorable. Men who took part in it say that it awakened in them the first real certainty that stern work lay ahead. The spot was historic and had echoed in the past to the tramp of those fighting men whose names and deeds are shrined in Canadian history. The night was wild; thunder was incessant and lightning, flashing on the bayonets and reflecting from the pools of water, seemed to convey a grim warning of what was to come.

For a few days after the review the routine of training continued. At last, however, orders were received for the Battalion to proceed to Valcartier on the evening of August 24th. All that day the Armoury was a scene of intense activity. It seemed that the thousand and one things to be done could never be done in time. Hundreds of people crowded about the doors seeking some excuse to see what was going on inside. In the interests of discipline and efficiency, however, admission was strictly limited to those who had actual business within and to the men's relatives and close personal friends who came to bid them farewell. To these tickets had been issued to simplify the duties of the guard on the door. Without this precaution there would have been chaos. Even as it was, the Armoury was uncomfortably crowded when the Battalion paraded, 1017 strong, for the march to the station.

At approximately 9.15 p.m. Col. Loomis gave the sharp commands which started the unit on its way to the war. At his orders the great doors of the Armoury swung open, the pipers struck up a martial air, company after company passed into the street and, with the Colonel himself leading, the Battalion headed for the station. Few who took part in, or witnessed, that march will ever forget it.

ROYAL HIGHLANDERS OF CANADA

Down Bleury St. and west along St. Catherine St. the Battalion made its way, the ranks almost demoralized by a cheering, swaying mob of humanity. Montreal had not yet grown accustomed to such sights; not yet did the people realize that war meant long lists of dead and wounded. That day was to come, but it was still some distance in the future, so people waved and cheered and cheered and waved without much thought of where the men they cheered were going. The men themselves were carried away by the prevailing excitement. Around them was a sea of faces and a Niagara of noise. Connected thought was out of the question. Historic as the moment was, they had little opportunity to appreciate its significance. Shouted greetings had to be acknowledged; friendly quips called for repartee and the very business of pushing through the crowded streets demanded no small amount of effort and attention.

At Peel St., where the unit swung south, the crowd was even denser than before and the skirl of the approaching pipes caused such a wave of enthusiasm that the pushing, jostling, cheering citizens nearly broke up the parade. The police were helpless and the Battalion's ranks were broken repeatedly. Under such circumstances it was a relief for officers and men to march into the comparative quiet of the carefully guarded Windsor Station, where two special trains awaited them. Once the men were on board no time was wasted. At 11 p.m. the first train steamed out, followed by the second a few minutes later. Thus, after a send-off such as the old City had probably never seen before, the 13th Battalion left Montreal.

III

Bright and early on the morning of August 25th the two trains carrying the 13th arrived at Valcartier Station, 16 miles west of Quebec. Here the unit detrained and marched two miles to camp.

Even yet few people realize how Valcartier sprang into existence almost over night. When the war broke out the site was a wilderness; the 13th on arrival found a model camp. Roads had been laid, drains and water pipes installed, showers erected and electric light brought in from Quebec; three and a half miles of railway sidings had been built, a telephone exchange was in operation, also a rifle range—3 miles long—said to be the largest in the world. Thirty-three thousand men assembled in this Camp and lived in it for over a month, while, owing to the excellence of its

THE OUTBREAK OF THE WAR

site and sanitary arrangements, there was practically no sickness at all.

On reaching camp the Battalion suffered its first experience of that Army bug-bear "conflicting orders." At first there were insufficient tents, but eventually more arrived and these were pitched on a site indicated by an officer of the H.Q. Staff. Just as this job was completed and the men, some of whom had never been in camp before, were admiring the effect, instructions were received to strike the tents and move them to a location two hundred yards away. This order was smartly carried out, but evoked considerable profanity from the hard worked rank and file. Hardly were the tents up on the new site when profanity was struck dumb by the arrival of orders to move them back again.

By night tents for the whole Battalion had been pitched in a satisfactory location and on the following day the unit took up its routine of training.

At this time the Battalion found itself in the peculiar situation of being a unit within a unit. Technically it was a part of the 12th Battalion, a force approximately 1700 strong, under the command of Lieut.-Col. F. H. McLeod. Actually it preserved its identity and carried on its own affairs, maintaining at the same time cordial relations with the other parts of the 12th Battalion, included in which was a large contingent from the Pictou Highlanders.

Training continued steadily all through the remainder of August and September. Each day the Battalion paraded to an allotted area and practised manoeuvres, or proceeded to the rifle ranges and put in a day's work at the targets. Under the instruction of Capt. R. H. Jamieson and Sergt.-Major J. Jeffery the shooting of the men showed marked improvement and, by the end of a month, was really of a high standard.

In addition to this routine of training the Battalion on two occasions took part in night outpost schemes. During the latter of these contact was established between two of the opposing patrols and, so keen were the men, that casualties of a serious nature were barely averted. Some lusty blows are said to have been struck on this occasion, but no real damage ensued.

Meanwhile those in charge of documents and records were having a strenuous time. Re-attestation of the whole force took place and men parading for typhoid inoculation had to bring their papers with them, the result being that hundreds of papers got mixed up in an almost hopeless tangle. Day and night work in the battalion orderly rooms sorted these out before the units sailed, but it was a close call. In the 13th the situation was not finally cleared up till after midnight of the last day in camp.

In connection with the anti-typhoid inoculation several "old soldiers" pointed out that this was a "voluntary" measure to which they did not choose to submit. For a while it appeared they would get their way, but the M.O. was obdurate and presented an ultimatum. "You can't be forced into this," said he, "its purely voluntary, but you damned well can't go to this war without it. Take your choice!" Faced with the awful possibility of being left behind, the "old soldiers" yielded without delay. No little amusement was caused, however, when it was found that the M.O. had not up to this time been inoculated himself. Gleefully his own alternatives were presented to him and gracefully he conceded the point. It is to be feared that the sore arm he carried for some days thereafter did not meet with the sympathy it deserved.

Another surrender to the force of public opinion was that of a small group of five or six men who had volunteered to transfer to the R.C.R. and accompany that Regiment to Bermuda. These men backed down and elected to remain with the 13th when a jeering group of their comrades gathered to "boo" them out of the Battalion lines.

During the latter period of the Battalion's stay at Valcartier, the Quartermaster, Capt. J. Handley, was a busy man indeed. Constant issues of supplies and equipment took place, including Ross rifles, bayonets, entrenching tools and web equipment, as well as Regimental transport in the form of Bain wagons, a Maltese cart for medical supplies and so on.

Horses (about sixty in number) were issued towards the middle of the month. Not long afterwards a party of men was furnished by the Battalion to lead a string of horses from the Station to the Remount Depôt, some distance away. When it became clear that this procession would pass through the Battalion lines, an informal committee was convened to study how this opportunity could best be turned to the Battalion's advantage. High officers served on this committee and gave the situation their earnest thought. No report on their deliberations has ever been published, but it is a fact that, after the cavalcade had passed, some twelve of the Battalion's

THE OUTBREAK OF THE WAR

horses seemed fresher and younger than before, while an equal number of the remounts had aged in a manner that was truly remarkable.

While on the subject of horses it is of interest to note that white horses were not permitted in the contingent in their natural state, the idea being that a white horse would be conspicuous in actual warfare and the rider subjected to unnecessary risk. Amongst the victims of this theory was a beautiful animal, the property of Major V. C. Buchanan. It was intended that this horse should be dyed a khaki colour, but something went wrong with the dye and the result was a little queer. Several attempts were made to give this new colour a name, but it was an elusive shade, defying all description. "Heifer-brindle" came, perhaps, as near as any other effort.

Social activities at Valcartier call for little comment. Two of the officers, Capt. W. H. Clark-Kennedy and Lieut. Hutton Crowdy, were married during the month and, on the occasion of these weddings, as many as possible of the 13th officers attended. Visitors' Day was another event of a more or less social character. On this day the Battalion lines were thrown open so that officers and men alike could ask their friends to come and see them. This invitation was accepted by a large number of people, many of whom came down from Montreal specially for the occasion. Every effort was made to accommodate these guests and to make them comfortable and there is no doubt that they enjoyed their visit.

Many ladies were amongst those to whom hospitality was extended and the presence of these led to several amusing incidents. One officer, for example, recalls with horror his predicament when a fair visitor spied him in the distance and rushed over to enquire the whereabouts of another officer, a mutual friend. The other officer, all unconscious of being in demand, was puffing and blowing beneath a shower not many yards distant. Firmly the first officer insisted that the mutual friend was miles away. Pointing with his stick he indicated some distant hills where, he explained, stern duty and the exigencies of the Service kept the latter at work. Meanwhile he conducted the lady back to the main road, carefully maintaining some obstruction in the line of vision to the showers. "I thought I did it awfully well," this officer tells the story, "but since then the lady has more than once referred to me as 'tactful,' so sometimes I wonder."

ROYAL HIGHLANDERS OF CANADA

Meanwhile the work of the Battalion had steadily progressed. The men had toughened and hardened from the open air life and were now as sunburned and healthy a lot as could be imagined. Constant shuffling of N.C.O.'s had taken place to insure that in each case the best man for the post had been secured. These changes were effective in stimulating the ambition of the men and in keeping those N.C.O.'s already appointed from looking on their positions as secure. Each man had to work and show ability to get promotion and work still harder to keep from being reduced again.

About this time the authorized strength of the Battalion was increased to 1100 and that of the establishment of officers to 45. About 150 men, in several parties, were absorbed from a British Columbia (East Kootenay) unit and amongst the new officers attached were a Paymaster, Capt. W. J. Taylor, of London, Ontario, and a Chaplain, Capt. A. M. Gordon, from Kingston.

Among the events of interest as the month drew to its close was a speech to all the officers of the camp by the Minister of Militia, Maj.-Gen. the Hon. Sam Hughes. The difficulties of the historian in describing an incident of this sort are exemplified in the present instance. One diary refers to this speech as "an inspiring address," while another account states quite simply that the Minister called the officers of the whole camp together and "got off a blast of hot air."

Be this as it may, the event was important as it marked the near approach of the day when the Contingent would sail. By this time the various units at Valcartier had been shuffled and re-shuffled to form the 1st Canadian Division. The 13th Battalion, Royal Highlanders of Canada, now quite distinct from the 12th Battalion, found itself one of the four battalions constituting the 3rd Infantry Brigade, under the command of Col. R. E. W. Turner, V.C., D.S.O., a veteran who had won distinction in South Africa. With the 13th in the Brigade were the 14th Battalion (Royal Montreal Regiment), composed of detachments from the 1st Regiment, Canadian Grenadier Guards, the 3rd Regiment, Victoria Rifles of Canada, and the 65th Regiment, Carabiniers Mont-Royal; the 15th Battalion (48th Highlanders) Toronto, and the 16th Battalion (Canadian Scottish), made up of units from the Seaforth Highlanders (Vancouver), the Gordon Highlanders (Victoria), the Cameron Highlanders (Winnipeg) and the Argyll and Sutherland Highlanders

THE OUTBREAK OF THE WAR

(Hamilton). This association, begun at Valcartier, lasted throughout the whole war.

In the meantime the process of equipping the 13th had continued and a Base Company, under Capt. F. P. Buchanan, had been established. All, therefore, was in readiness for H.R.H. the Duke of Connaught's great review, which, it was generally realized, was a sign that the day of departure was near indeed. This review was most imposing. H.R.H. was accompanied by the Duchess of Connaught, the Princess Patricia, Sir Robert Borden and many other notables. General Sam Hughes, who led the march past, had every reason to be proud of the force that, under his supervision, had developed so amazingly in a few short weeks. The units marched past in columns of half battalions in line, this being necessary to enable so large a force to pass the saluting point in the time available. Even the Duke of Connaught, with his many years of service and his memories of reviews in all parts of the world, was impressed by the soldierly bearing and smart appearance of these troops, who, less than two months before, had little thought that a call for active service would ever come their way. It was with emotion that H.R.H. bade them farewell and wished them God speed.

Immediately after the review preparations began for the Contingent to embark. The censorship closed down tight and for some days Valcartier was cut off from communication with the outside world. All over Canada this was correctly interpreted to mean that the Division was on the move.

In so far as the 13th was concerned the move began on the evening of September 25th. On that date, exactly one month after the arrival of the Battalion in camp, the transport, under Capt. E. J. Carthew, marched for Quebec. On the following morning reveille sounded at 3 o'clock and all ranks put in a prompt appearance. Sharp frost had occurred during the night, but hard work soon warmed the men up. After an early breakfast the Battalion paraded and marched to the station, passing on the way Maj.-Gen. the Hon. Sam Hughes, who took the salute. While the weather on this occasion was not all that could be desired, the men were in excellent spirits and kept up a lusty chorus of song. These songs were many and varied. Scotch songs predominated, as was fit and proper in a Highland Regiment, but there were English and Canadian songs as well, and songs to which no nation would lay claim without a blush. "Tipperary" was, perhaps, the most popular of all. No one knows why this trifling ditty appealed so strongly, but the fact remains that to this tune the "Old Contemptibles" poured across the Channel to their glorious end, while in all parts of the Empire the tune to this day brings to mind fleeting visions of the "original" battalions.

In spite of the weather the 13th reached the station in time to entrain at 8 o'clock. By nine, or a little after, Valcartier had been left behind and the train was slowing down at the docks in Quebec.

CHAPTER II

The Voyage to England and Salisbury Plain

> Shadow by shadow, stripped for light
> The lean black cruisers search the sea
> Night long their level shafts of light
> Revolve, and find no enemy.
> Only they know each leaping wave
> May hide the lightning and their grave.
> —ALFRED NOYES.

I

ON arrival at Quebec the Battalion, whose total strength is given as 45 officers and 1,112 other ranks, proceeded to embark on R.M.S. *Alaunia*, of the Cunard Line, which had been requisitioned by the Government as a transport. This ship was commanded by Captain Rostron, R.N.R., who previously when in command of the *Carpathia* had made a name for himself by his work in saving lives from the ill-fated *Titanic*. With the 13th on board were the H.Q. of the 3rd Infantry Brigade, under Col. Turner, two companies of the 14th Battalion, Royal Montreal Regiment, under Lieut.-Col. F. S. Meighen, and A.S.C. Details (Div'l Train). Accommodation for officers and men alike was all that could be desired and throughout the voyage no complaints on this score were recorded. The men in particular found themselves in luxury, the soft bunks and the more varied food forming a sharp contrast to the less elaborate conditions they had become accustomed to.

The Transport of the 13th was not on board the *Alaunia*, it having joined other Transport on a different vessel. Lieut. Andrew Reford, however, made arrangements with the ship's owners whereby eleven supernumerary horses, the property of officers of the Battalion, were taken over with the unit. Difficulty was experienced in negotiating this arrangement, but eventually the owners agreed to it and shelters for the horses were hurriedly constructed on the after deck.

ROYAL HIGHLANDERS OF CANADA

As soon as embarkation was completed the *Alaunia* pulled out from the dock and steamed slowly up stream to an anchorage off Wolfe's Cove. This position she maintained for the next four days, during which officers and men were initiated into the mysteries of "routine at sea." Three officers and fifty men were on duty all the time at the numerous sentry posts and other strategic locations which the "routine" indicated. Guards were mounted at 10 o'clock each morning and it was the duty of one subaltern, the "Officer of the Day," to make frequent rounds day and night and report every two hours to the "Officer of the Watch."

On the afternoon of September 30th a farewell message from H.R.H. the Duke of Connaught was read out and shortly afterwards the ship raised anchor and slipped slowly down the River. To all on board it was a very stirring moment. No one knew where the Force was going; all that was known was that it was leaving Canada for service somewhere overseas. Emotion was, of course, carefully concealed, but the man who did not feel it must have been a lump of clay indeed. On deck the pipe band burst into the strains of "Highland Laddie" and "Scotland the Brave," while the men, as soon as the pipes were silent, joined in a mighty chorus of "O Canada" and "Auld Lang Syne." Other transports were also on the move and from their decks, too, came great volumes of cheering and song.

Gathering speed the *Alaunia* proceeded down stream and in about an hour had reached a point where Quebec, with its towering Citadel, was lost to view in the gathering haze astern. Thus another of the milestones marking the Battalion's progress was passed and left behind.

II

That night Lieut. Melville Greenshields was the victim of a practical joke played by his brother officers. In the endless talks that were always taking place Greenshields had stoutly maintained his lack of belief in the value of much of the routine laid down in orders. In particular he claimed that the constant rounds of the "Officer of the Day" were a sheer waste of time and in justification of his argument he pointed out that already the routine had been relaxed to the extent that this officer was now permitted to get some sleep during his twenty-four hour tour of duty. Greenshields was on duty on this particular night and announced that he intended,

ENGLAND AND SALISBURY PLAIN

while being available at a moment's notice, to sleep soundly if no particular service were required of him. During the evening he received a "wireless" message, ordering him to see that all sentries were on the alert between 2 and 3 a.m. This, needless to say, was a "fake," as Greenshields probably suspected, but his military conscience, more acute than he was willing to admit, forbade his ignoring it. If the sentries were not alert that night, their failure was not the fault of the "Officer of the Day." He visited them regularly and, in the morning, accepted a storm of chaff with perfect composure. Always a popular officer, his sportsmanlike behaviour on this occasion advanced him still further in the regard of his comrades.

On October 1st a rumour circulated that a whole fleet of transports was to rendezvous at Father Point and there await a naval escort. Considerable credence was given to this report, but the *Alaunia* passed Father Point and at night, when the troops turned in, she was still steadily steaming to an unknown destination.

Morning on October 2nd, however, gave the secret away. When the troops awoke and came on deck they gazed on a truly wonderful scene. Anchored in a great and beautiful bay, which turned out to be Gaspé, lay a large fleet of transports and warships. In the glory of the morning sunshine and in the shadow of the surrounding hills, the sight was too magnificent for ordinary powers of description. Men felt the impressive nature of the scene, but groped in vain for words to express their thoughts. Sea power, of which they had heard so much and knew so little, lay tangibly before them in a setting which, for sheer, rugged beauty, it would be hard to surpass.

All that day the ships lay at anchor, under the protection of the ever watchful cruisers. At night one of these latter patrolled the mouth of the Basin to make sure that no enemy approached.

On the following day Maj.-Gen. Sam Hughes visited the *Alaunia* to make his final adieu. On leaving he took with him a large bundle of letters which officers and men had written to their friends. Fearing that someone's indiscretion might prejudice the safety of the whole convoy, Gen. Hughes kept these letters under his control till news reached him that the Contingent had arrived in England. Once this news was confirmed, the letters were entrusted to the mails and duly forwarded to their destinations.

At 3 p.m. on Saturday, October 3rd, the thirty-one ships left

ROYAL HIGHLANDERS OF CANADA

Gaspé Basin and formed up in three columns outside. The three columns were about a mile apart and each ship a quarter mile behind the one in front. Escort for the transports was provided by His Majesty's Ships, *Charybdis, Diana, Lancaster, Eclipse, Glory, Majestic* and *Talbot*, the whole being under the command of Rear-Admiral R. E. Wemyss, C.M.G., M.V.O. At a later date the Battle Cruiser *Princess Royal* also assisted in securing the convoy's safety. The speed of the whole fleet was not great, this being governed by the slowest vessel, which could not work up to more than about 10 knots.

On board the *Alaunia*, the fourth ship in the port line, a definite routine was at once established, the chief features of which were physical training, bayonet work, semaphore signalling and so on. Boxing and deck sports were also encouraged, while in the evenings lectures and concerts filled in the time till "lights out."

On October 6th a buzz of excitement was caused by a report that the German cruiser *Karlsruhe* was in sight on the horizon. Like so many of its fellows, this report seems to have had no foundation whatsoever. Another stir of interest was caused when it was learned that a man had gone overboard from the *Lapland*. This individual was picked up by one of the ships that followed and was popularly reported to have explained his action on the ground that the *Lapland* had run out of cigarettes and he had hoped to get some elsewhere. About this time news of the fall of Antwerp was posted, also a false report that Russia was negotiating a separate peace and that a battalion of Territorials had suffered heavy losses. This latter bulletin, which seems to have been a practical joke, caused a good deal of indignation amongst the more serious minded of those on board. On October 9th H.M.S. *Essex* passed through the lines of ships at full speed and Admiral Craddock, who was on board, signalled good wishes and God speed. Poor Craddock! he himself was destined to go down in battle before the men he signalled to had ever reached the front.

One of the problems that caused deep concern to the officers of the Contingent was the question of spies. Fear of the much vaunted German secret service put officers and men on their guard, with the result that, on the *Alaunia*, two men were arrested for suspicious behaviour. These were handed over to the authorities in England and were later publicly exonerated. A third man was discovered with a list in his possession showing all the chief ports in the British

ENGLAND AND SALISBURY PLAIN

Isles. Opposite each port was a name, apparently a code word for the port in question. For a while this case looked serious, but an enquiry disclosed that the whole affair was a lottery on the *Alaunia's* destination. The "code" words proved to be the names of those sporting members of the Battalion who had purchased tickets. This man, of course, was released on the spot.

On the evening of October 13th land was sighted and the following morning the *Alaunia* steamed into Plymouth Sound. Originally it had been planned that the whole convoy would dock at Southampton, but the presence, or suspected presence, of German submarines off Southampton had caused these arrangements to be changed. The arrival of the *Alaunia*, several hours ahead of the other ships, was the first indication to the inhabitants of Plymouth and Devonport that theirs was to be the honour of welcoming the first contingent of troops from overseas. Right royally they rose to the occasion. As each ship arrived in port it was greeted by whistles, bells and storms of cheering. The local papers in describing the event insisted that not since Drake defeated the Spanish Armada had the old town experienced such a thrill. Now another Armada had arrived, greater by far than Spain's, but this time its mission was friendly and Plymouth gave it tumultuous welcome.

If the people on shore experienced a thrill, the men on the ships did likewise. What Britisher could sail past the ancient wooden war ships that lay at anchor and refuse the tribute of at least a tiny shiver down his spine? There they lay in all their glory, a symbol of the past and a good omen for the future. Gliding past them, the *Alaunia* proceeded up-stream and came to anchor off Devonport, where she was joined a little later by the *Royal George*, carrying the Princess Patricia's Canadian Light Infantry. All day the two ships lay side by side and in the evening many friendly visits were exchanged.

The following day, October 15th, a message of welcome from Lord Kitchener was read and in the evening disembarkation commenced. When this was completed the 13th divided into two sections, one 682 strong and the other 472. These made their way through the city streets and were everywhere showered with gifts and accorded an enthusiastic reception. They entrained at different stations at 9.30 and 10.15 p.m. respectively.

After travelling all night the two sections of the 13th arrived at Patney Station at 3 a.m. and marched 10 miles over the rolling country of Salisbury Plain to camp at West Down South. This march, made with full kit, was trying, as the men had had no sleep and no breakfast. In addition, the nineteen days on board ship had softened them considerably. Despite these difficulties the sections covered the distance in approximately 3 hours and 25 minutes, a creditable performance, considering the circumstances, for their first march on English soil.

III

On the arrival of the Canadians in England, command of the Division was assumed by Lieut.-Gen. E. A. H. Alderson, C.B., a distinguished British soldier, who had won an enviable reputation in India, South Africa, Egypt and elsewhere. Under his supervision the units settled down to routine in the camps of Salisbury Plain.

West Down South, where the Royal Highlanders found themselves, was a great contrast to Valcartier. The vast, rolling plains afforded as good, or better, facilities for drill, manœuvres and sham battles when dry, but provision for the comfort of the men in the matter of showers, water supply and sanitary arrangements was not to be compared with what had existed at Valcartier. In addition the soil at Valcartier was light, sandy and excellently drained, while it is to be feared that the Canadians' recollection of Salisbury is chiefly one of mud. "Mud and rain," "rain and mud," "more rain and more mud," these phrases run like a refrain through all the letters and diaries dealing with the time. "This is a God-forsaken hole and we are getting pretty sick of it. It is raining again to-day. Nothing but rain, mud and then more rain." This extract from a letter, dated October 25th, shows that the Contingent was treated to bad weather almost from the start. On November 5th another correspondent refers to the subject again. "It has rained now for nineteen consecutive days and Winnipeg in the old days would be put to shame if it could see the mud here. It is making everyone miserable and hindering all work."

In spite of the hindrance of the mud and rain, however, it must not be inferred that the units were idle. Routine activities and drills were carried on notwithstanding the handicaps. Apart from routine, one of the first steps taken by the 13th after settling down in camp was to establish friendly relations with the Black Watch.

ENGLAND AND SALISBURY PLAIN

As has been mentioned, the 13th was affiliated with this famous Regiment through the 5th R.H.C. in Montreal. Desiring to purchase kilts, glengarries and badges of the approved Black Watch pattern, Col. Loomis detailed Capt. C. J. Smith to proceed to Scotland, where these items would be more easily procurable. In addition Capt. Smith was instructed to convey the Colonel's greetings to such officers of the affiliated Regiment as were to be found at Regimental Headquarters. Proceeding to Perth Barracks in pursuance of these instructions, Capt. Smith records that he was most hospitably received by Lieut.-Col. T. M. M. Berkeley and other Black Watch officers, while in Dundee Major John Vair presented him with 120 copies of a small Regimental History for distribution to officers of the 13th and to those men of the Battalion who would be interested in Regimental history and tradition. At a later date the Marchioness of Tullibardine, who had learned of Capt. Smith's visit and its purpose, wrote to him and expressed the wish that she be allowed to equip the 13th with khaki hose tops. This offer the Battalion accepted, with deep appreciation of Her Ladyship's interest.

On October 22nd the 13th was reorganized into a "double company" battalion. Under this system the Battalion consisted of four companies instead of eight, that is to say two of the old companies were put together to form one of the new. The command of these new companies, Nos. 1, 2, 3 and 4, was given respectively to Major D. R. McCuaig, Capt. R. H. Jamieson, Capt. T. S. Morrisey and Capt. W. H. Clark-Kennedy. These had as seconds-in-command, Capt. L. W. Whitehead, Capt. K. M. Perry, Capt. C. J. Smith and Capt. H. F. Walker. The Base Company remained under the command of Capt. F. P. Buchanan and temporarily absorbed those officers of the Battalion who, under the new arrangement, found themselves supernumerary to the authorized strength. Each of the new companies was divided into four platoons, under a lieutenant, with a platoon-sergeant as second-in-command. Each of the platoons in turn was divided into four sections, under the command of an N.C.O. This system was abandoned some weeks later, but was re-instated before the Battalion left for France and remained in force for the duration of the war.

On the day following the first try-out of the new drill the Battalion, along with other units, paraded for inspection by Field-Marshal Earl Roberts, V.C. This veteran, than whom none was more popular, reviewed the troops with care and was accorded a warm hearted welcome.

On October 25th, at a church parade, Gen. Alderson introduced himself to the men of the 3rd Brigade and he, too, was heartily cheered. Shortly before this he had announced that the "dry" canteen system would be done away with and the "wet" canteen, customary in the British Army, established. The present book is no place in which to discuss the wisdom or otherwise of this move, which aroused no small controversy in Canada. Suffice it to say that amongst the troops, who, after all, were the people most vitally concerned, the move was a popular one.

Mention of the wet canteen leads at once to the question of the general discipline and behaviour of the troops while in England. Soon after arriving the 13th had serious trouble in regard to men absent without leave. These were invariably Old Countrymen who could not resist the temptation to revisit relatives and familiar scenes, without waiting for permission to do so. Well supplied with money, these men would cut a dash as long as their money lasted and then, as soon as it was gone, slip back to camp to accept punishment for their misdeeds. Practically all of them turned up sooner or later.

Meanwhile sinister rumours as to the discipline and behaviour of the force drifted back to Canada, where they caused no little anxiety. That these rumours were grossly exaggerated is now known, but that some foundation for them existed there is no attempt to deny. How the situation appeared at the time to an N.C.O. in the 13th is summed up in the following extract from a letter. "In reply to your letter, I will try to give you some dope, taking the points you raise in order. First, discipline in ours. This is varied. It is not good compared with the Regulars, but it is quite good all the same, and I have never yet heard of a man refusing to obey an officer's order. The Canadians as a whole have a frightful name all over the country for bad discipline, but that is earned by not saluting when on leave. But after all these things are not the important part of discipline. What is important is to get orders obeyed and that is done very well indeed."

This whole question of discipline and behaviour caused, at a later date, some little feeling between the 1st Division and the men of the Contingents that followed. Some few of these latter adopted a "holier than thou" attitude and were wont to reproach the

ENGLAND AND SALISBURY PLAIN

"originals" with the bad name they had left behind them. Tradition has it that on one occasion a war worn veteran back in England on leave listened patiently to just such a tale of woe. "I can tell you," said the spotless newcomer, eyeing the veteran with disgust, "we are having a hard time to live down the reputation you fellows left in England." "Oh well," replied the veteran, "cheer up, you'll have a damn sight worse time living UP to the reputation we have in France."

To return, however, to those autumn days on Salisbury Plain! On November 2nd the Battalion paraded for a full service-dress rehearsal of a review to be held two days later by His Majesty the King. The weather was atrocious, but all were anxious that the Division should make a good showing at the royal review, so the rehearsal continued in the pouring rain for over three hours.

On November 4th the Battalion paraded for the inspection previously rehearsed. On this occasion the weather was all that could be desired. His Majesty, who was accompanied by Her Majesty the Queen, also by Lord Roberts and Lord Kitchener, inspected the Division and had many of the officers presented to him. Afterwards he complimented Gen. Alderson on the showing the Division had made.

Following the royal review came a period of some weeks during which the activities of the Battalion call for no particular comment. The weather continued to be bad and work was carried on with difficulty, but, in spite of all, the spirit of the men was good and progress in training made. As is always the case when large bodies of human beings are gathered together, strange rumours sprang up from nowhere, flourished and were believed for a season, only to fade away and be forgotten in the light of official denial or official silence. One of the most popular and persistent of these myths was that things were going so well in France that the War Office dare not publish the details for fear of stopping recruiting. Mad as this report seems in retrospect, it was widely believed at the time. One strategist in the 13th quotes it in a letter home and comments on the probable nature of the concealed successes. "In my opinion," says he, "they have probably cut the Germans' communications in Belgium." Unfortunately this opinion was wide of the mark. Four years were to intervene before the communications in question were even seriously endangered.

As November drew to a close there occurred several small in-

ROYAL HIGHLANDERS OF CANADA

cidents of interest to officers and men of the Battalion. Lieut. Gerald Lees received his captaincy as a reward for his hard work and efficient handling of his men, while Lieut. E. M. Sellon, for similar reasons, was appointed Battalion Scout Officer. Earlier in the month Lieut. L de V. Chipman had been appointed Intelligence Officer.

On the 23rd of the month Col. Loomis detailed Major V. C. Buchanan and Capt. C. J. Smith to proceed to Aldershot to discuss with officers of the 9th Service Battalion, Black Watch, some further details of Regimental custom and equipment. This trip was undertaken in a Ford car, a gift to the 13th from Lieut.-Col. Ross of the Parent Regiment in Montreal. The road proved somewhat longer than the envoys had expected, but they reached Aldershot eventually and were there most cordially received.

On November 29th the Battalion took part in a Divisional field day, which Gen. Alderson himself controlled by signals on a huntsman's horn. This method of conveying messages was new to Canadians and caused no little amusement to the rank and file. It worked well, however, and obviated the introduction of a more elaborate system.

St. Andrew's Day, November 30th, was observed in the Battalion by special privileges and by a visit from the Colonel to the Sergeants' Mess, where he partook of the hospitality provided. In the Officers' Mess flags were hung for decoration, the Lion of Scotland occupying the central place. Here the celebration, it is recorded, was in true Scottish style and this can the more readily be believed from the fact that the diarist whose account is quoted has carefully dated his entry, "November 31st."

With the advent of December weather conditions, which previously had left much to be desired, became well nigh intolerable. Under the influence of almost incessant rain the camp turned into a night-mare of mud, thick, clinging mud from which there was no escape and in which the troops lived, ate, slept and had their being. Towards the middle of the month it became clear that the health of the men could not hold out under such miserable conditions. Accordingly, on orders being received, the 13th struck camp at West Down South on December 18th and proceeded to huts at Larkhill. Living conditions were greatly improved by this move. Outside the rain continued and the mud was as bad as ever, but the huts were reasonably comfortable and afforded the troops, as well as a place to

ENGLAND AND SALISBURY PLAIN

sleep, an opportunity to dry their sodden clothes. Each hut was about 60 feet long and 20 feet wide, with one corner walled off for the sergeants. Approximately 40 men formed the complement of a hut, so that each man had room for his bedding and a little to spare, with a wide passage down the centre, this being kept clear according to one authority, "so that the drunks will not walk on anyone."

Soon after settling down at Larkhill the Battalion began to prepare for the Christmas and New Year's festivities. The first, and perhaps the most important, feature of these was that every man in the unit was granted leave at some time during the festive season, this leave varying from four to seven days in proportion to its distance from the actual dates of the two holidays. Thus half the Battalion, or thereabouts, was away from camp at Christmas, while the other half was in camp for Christmas, but away for New Year's. The two celebrations were similar in character, only the personnel being altered. On Christmas, dinner was, of course, the great event of the day. Each company prepared its own programme and, as is the custom in Highland regiments, officers dined with their respective companies. Col. Loomis, accompanied by the Sergeant-Major and piped by the Pipe Major, visited every mess and at each was accorded a rousing reception. Following his departure, each party carried on with its pre-arranged programme till well on in the afternoon. In the evening the men were free to seek such recreation as the camp provided and as suited their individual tastes.

During the early part of January, 1915, the work of the 13th was largely confined to making roads and improving conditions around the camp. This work was well in hand by the 10th of the month and the Battalion was accordingly enabled to resume its interrupted course of training. Towards the middle of the month great enthusiasm was aroused by the announcement that the Canadian Division would proceed to France early in February. Simultaneously orders were received for the Battalion to adopt the double company formation once more. This formation had been put into effect in the previous October, as already described, but had been abandoned in favour of the old eight company system some weeks later. Now it was restored and this time permanently.

With the prospect of active service not far away, the troops buckled down to work with ardour and enthusiasm. Discipline improved at once and several absentees, who apparently had kept in touch with developments, rejoined of their own accord and accepted without a murmur the heavy fines and other punishments awarded.

At about this time an outbreak of spinal meningitis in the camp threatened to postpone the date of the Division's crossing to France. Prompt measures, however, checked the disease, but not before several deaths had occurred. In the 13th three men came down with meningitis and all three died. The only other death in the Battalion during its stay in England was that of a man who was killed by falling off a cart while absent from the camp without leave.

On February 1st the 13th took part in a Brigade route march to Stonehenge, returning to Larkhill about noon. At 2 p.m. Col. R. E. W. Turner, V.C., D.S.O., inspected the Battalion and transport and afterwards expressed his satisfaction as to the unit's discipline and general appearance. Two days later Lieut.-Col. Loomis gave the Battalion a very careful inspection, in preparation for the second visit of His Majesty the King. Previous to this, orders had been received that the Division was to keep itself in readiness to move at short notice, so it was generally realized that just as the King had come on November 4th to bid the Contingent welcome he now came on February 4th to bid it farewell.

On the morning of the day in question the 13th paraded at 9.30 o'clock and proceeded to a position north of Bustard Camp, where the review was to be held. Soon afterwards the royal train steamed into a temporary platform close at hand, where His Majesty was met by General Alderson. As on the occasion of his previous visit, the King was accompanied by Field-Marshal Lord Kitchener and a numerous staff. After an inspection of the troops the royal party returned to the station platform and witnessed a march past of the whole Division. On this occasion a great improvement in the bearing of the troops was noted. At previous reviews they had made a good showing for citizen soldiers; now their whole deportment closely approximated that of well drilled regulars. Obviously the four trying months on Salisbury Plain under the guidance of General Alderson's skilled hand had not been entirely wasted. At the conclusion of the march past the troops of the Division lined the railway tracks and, in appreciation of the honour the King had paid them, gave the royal train as it steamed away a heartfelt roar of cheers.

For some days after the royal review the Battalion carried on

ENGLAND AND SALISBURY PLAIN

with routine training, waiting every minute to hear that orders to proceed to France had arrived. Divine Service for the whole unit was held in the Y.M.C.A. hut on February 7th, this marking the final appearance of Capt. A. M. Gordon as Chaplain of the Battalion, he having transferred to another unit. During his time with the 13th Capt. Gordon had worked untiringly for the welfare of the men and more particularly in the interests of those who were sick. Remembering his unselfish devotion to duty, the Battalion bade him farewell with sincere regret.

On February 10th the eagerly awaited orders for departure were at last given out. During the forenoon Brig.-Gen. R. E. W. Turner, V.C., D.S.O. inspected the Battalion and photographs were taken of various groups and individuals. In the afternoon all ranks were busy clearing up the camp and preparing kit. In the case of officers kit was strictly limited to 35 pounds and Major E. C. Norsworthy, presiding at a scale, saw to it that this limit was not exceeded. The men's kit and personal equipment was as follows:— 1 pr. trews, 1 pr. drawers, 1 undershirt, 1 shirt, 2 towels, 1 hold-all, containing soap, razor, etc., 1 balaclava, 3 prs. socks, 1 pr. boots, 1 house-wife and 1 greatcoat. In addition they carried strapped outside, 1 blanket, 1 rubber sheet, 1 mess tin and 1 haversack, the last named containing a day's ration, tobacco and so forth. Added to all these was a rifle and 150 rounds of ammunition, so that the whole weighed not much below 80 lbs. As one man tersely put it, "Once in the army you become a blinking pack mule."

At 7.30 p.m. the Left Half of the Battalion, under Lieut.-Col. Loomis, paraded and marched out of Larkhill to Amesbury Station, followed by the Right Half, under Major Norsworthy, half an hour later. The men were in great spirits and rejoiced to think that the long experience of Salisbury mud was at an end. Worse might lie before them, but this probability they were quite willing, even eager, to face. For what other purpose had they come thousands of miles across the sea? At Amesbury a number of relatives and friends had gathered to see the men off and wish them good luck. Two trains had been provided for the troops and the first of these pulled out about 11 p.m., the other following some twenty minutes later. No one knew for certain at what port the Battalion would embark, but the consensus of opinion at Amesbury Station was that the two trains were headed for Southampton. This seemed the most logical conclusion, but war takes little account of logic and soon after leav-

ROYAL HIGHLANDERS OF CANADA

ing Amesbury those on board the trains became aware from the general westerly direction they were taking that reasoning had failed them once more and that, wherever they were going, it was not to Southampton.

CHAPTER III

Over to France and Into Action

> Give us a name to stir the blood
> With a warmer glow and a swifter flood,
> At the touch of a courage that knows not fear,—
> A name like the sound of a trumpet, clear,
>
> . . . . .
>
> I give you France!
> —HENRY VAN DYKE.

I

EARLY on the morning of February 11th the men of the 13th Battalion discovered that Avonmouth was their destination. When this port was reached, somewhat before dawn, they immediately detrained and started to board the s.s. *Novian*, which was awaiting them. Embarkation of men, horses and wagons was smartly carried out, after which the men were allowed to get some sleep.

In addition to the 31 officers and 1,002 men of the 13th, the *Novian* carried the Divisional Ammunition Column, with its complement of over 200 horses. Accommodation was naturally not to be compared with that which the 13th had enjoyed on board the *Alaunia*. Three small, 2-berth cabins were available for the senior officers, while the juniors made their beds on the floor of the little dining saloon. The men were huddled in three holds, packed more or less like the proverbial sardines, while between decks were the horses.

All that day the ship remained in dock and it was extraordinary how many of the officers found urgent reasons to justify leave ashore. This was granted in most cases, there being no reason why those not actually on duty should be retained on board. Similar privileges could not be extended to the men, who stayed on board sleeping, eating, playing cards and otherwise amusing themselves.

In company with other transports and under the protection of destroyers, the *Novian* sailed at dawn on February 12th, shaping a course towards the Lizard and the Bay of Biscay. In the evening a strong wind sprang up and by morning on the 13th this had developed into a rousing gale, which compelled the torpedo boats to seek shelter and forced Captain McCormack, of the *Novian*, to turn his bows into the wind to lessen the roll of the ship, which was endangering the lives of the horses. The decision to change course and proceed out to sea was wise and seaman-like, but its necessity was unfortunate from the point of view of the troops. Sea-sickness, that scourge of the ocean, had laid hold on these latter and, being no respecter of persons, was having its way with officers and men alike. Down in the crowded holds the scene was one to beggar description. Nine tenths of the men were ill, desperately ill, and no one could help them in their misery. In the dining saloon, where the officers were quartered, matters were only relatively better. On deck the armed guard of 12 men, posted to fire on any hostile submarine, stuck grimly to their task, but were too sick to fire a shot with any chance of hitting their target. Limply they hung over their rifles, coming to attention with a feeble attempt at a click when an officer, himself too sick to notice whether they clicked or not, paid them a formal visit. And still the ship headed determinedly out to sea! One company commander, returning from a tour on deck, found his berth occupied by a very miserable subaltern, whose distress had driven him to seek some refuge other than the crowded floor of the dining saloon. Pitying his junior's condition, the company commander waived possession of the berth for several hours, but at last he himself fell a victim and was forced to claim his right.

On the following morning the wind still blew with terrific force, but after lunch it abated to some degree and the ship once more turned towards land. During the afternoon Capt. G. E. McCuaig, with a fatigue party, attempted to get some of the men up on deck for a breath of fresh air, but without appreciable results. The holds were in an awful condition, but the men were quite too sick to care. All that they asked was to be left alone.

During the voyage two men of the 13th, who had deserted from the camp at Larkhill, turned up as stowaways on the boat. How they had learned from what port and on what boat the Battalion would sail was a puzzle, for, as will be remembered, even the officers of the Battalion had been in ignorance of these details when the unit marched from Salisbury Plain. Through the mysterious

FRANCE AND INTO ACTION

channels of information at the disposal of what might be called the "semi under-world" these men had kept in touch with the Battalion's movements and, on the unit's being ordered to France, had stowed away as the surest method of not being left behind. A court of enquiry held on board ship decided that, as a punishment for their desertion, they should be handed over to the military authorities in France, to be dealt with as the latter should see fit. Accordingly they were held under close arrest until France was reached and then handed over to the A.M.L.O. The latter, however, promptly handed them back again, assuring the Battalion that he was not interested in what he called its private affairs. This action on the part of the A.M.L.O. was viewed by the stow-aways with ill concealed delight. Though well aware that they would be severely punished, the decision meant that the Battalion must take them on its strength and carry them wherever it went. As they had deserted to escape the monotony of camp life and not to avoid the dangers of active service, they faced the certainty of punishment as infinitely preferable to the alternative of being left behind.

Meanwhile the *Novian* was still being tossed by the gale, but this had lessened appreciably and the vessel was making good time towards land. Morning of the 15th found the ship slipping into the outer harbour of St. Nazaire. Owing to congestion at the docks, she anchored in the outer harbour and remained there till late in the afternoon, much to the annoyance of officers and men, who had recovered from sea-sickness and were impatient to set foot on the soil of France.

II

Finally, a berth having been cleared, the *Novian* weighed anchor and crept through the narrow entrance into the inner harbour and to the dock, where a great crowd of French civilians and poilus gave her a noisy welcome. Oranges and other articles were hurled up onto the decks in token of good will, while the men of the 13th, not to be outdone in friendliness, tossed down coins and packages of cigarettes. The French soldiers, with their long bayonets and picturesque dress, were objects of respectful interest to the Canadians. It is more than probable that these particular poilus were lines of communication troops and had never seen the front, but to the newcomers they typified the men of the Marne and the Aisne and the cordial welcome they extended assumed all the importance that similar attentions from a sixth former mean to a new boy at school.

As soon as the vessel was docked, preparations to unload the horses and wagons began, but just at this moment the stevedores of St. Nazaire, who had general charge of the arrangements, went on something resembling a strike. Nothing deterred, the Highlanders promptly undertook the work themselves. Amongst such a large body of men individuals are always to be found with some knowledge of almost any subject on earth. In this instance enquiry produced a couple of experts to work the donkey engine, which was soon hoisting the wagons out of the hold. Capt. T. S. Morrisey commanded the fatigue which had this task in hand and which, by working hard all night, accomplished it satisfactorily quite as soon as the stevedores could have done. Meanwhile another party, under command of Lieut. J. O. Hastings, was seeing to the landing of the horses. This operation was attended by some difficulty, as the horses, stiff and groggy after their knocking about at sea, had to be led down a steep incline from the level of the deck to the shore. Many of them slipped and rolled down, but this contingency had been foreseen and a pile of hay placed at the bottom to soften the final bump. Strange as it may seem, none of the horses was injured, nor did any of them seem to mind their falls. Perhaps their satisfaction in feeling firm ground beneath their feet once more outweighed any slight inconvenience they might suffer in reaching it.

Before the disembarkation of the Battalion proper, which took place the next afternoon, all ranks had issued to them the British sheep skin trench coat. At first the men were proud of these and wandered about with all the conscious importance of peacocks on parade, but eventually the fact that the coats were possessed of a diabolical smell could no longer be ignored. From the moment that this unfortunate attribute was discovered the popularity of the coats waned. What became of them is not clear. What becomes of unpopular issues in the Army seldom is clear. They vanish like snow banks in the spring, imperceptibly at first, but none the less certainly for that and, when they have gone, no man can ever tell the exact manner of their going.

Following on the heels of a strong advance party, under the command of Capt. W. H. Clark-Kennedy, the Battalion disembarked

FRANCE AND INTO ACTION

from the *Novian* and lined up on the dock for the march through the streets of St. Nazaire to the railway station. Before giving the order to march, Lieut.-Col. Loomis called for three cheers for Captain McCormack and the officers of the *Novian* who, throughout the unexpectedly prolonged voyage, had done all that lay in their power to make things as comfortable as possible for both officers and men. In spite of sea-sickness, these efforts on the part of the sailor officers had not been unappreciated by the Highlanders and the cheers were given with a right good will.

Seven o'clock in the evening found the Battalion at St. Nazaire Station, entraining for the long journey to the front. A delay was experienced in rounding up a few individuals who had seized the opportunity to slip away and accept hospitality from the French civilians, but this was not serious and shortly after 7 p.m. the journey commenced.

For two days and two nights the train crept on its way, with occasional brief stops to give the troops a chance to get some food and to stretch their legs. This latter arrangement was almost as necessary as food, for the cars were of the typical box variety, known to fame as "40 hommes, 8 chevaux," and allowed no space for even the most limited exercise. The route lay through Nantes, Rouen, Boulogne, Calais and St. Omer, thence to Hazebrouck, which was reached at 6.30 p.m. on February 19th.

The men were stiff and sore after the journey, but detrained smartly and started off without delay on a seven mile march to Flêtre. At Caestre Capt. Clark-Kennedy met the Battalion and the march to Flêtre was continued under his guidance. Rain was falling heavily by this time and the night was bitterly cold, but the men's pulses were quickened and stirred by the fact that ahead of them the black sky was lit up from time to time by brilliant flashes, while low, but unmistakably, came the rumble of the distant guns. The front, that legendary region of unspoken hopes and fears, was now within sight and hearing.

On reaching Flêtre billets were secured and the men turned in with as little delay as possible. Curiosity as to their surroundings would undoubtedly possess them in the morning; at the moment they were tired and wet and delighted to get a chance to sleep. Quiet, therefore, settled over the billets at a comparatively early hour.

Four days and five nights were spent at Flêtre, the men occupied in preparing themselves for the trenches. At this time the whole front from Switzerland to the sea was practically deadlocked. The great battles of the previous autumn had long since died down and the clash of armies that would inevitably occur in the spring had not yet begun. Trench warfare was the order of the day and it was for this type of hostilities that the Highlanders made ready. On February 20th the Battalion was inspected at Caestre by the Commander-in-Chief, Field-Marshal Sir John French, who, in the little speech that customarily follows such events, expressed himself as well pleased with the Battalion's general showing. On the following day the 13th, in company with the 14th, Royal Montreal Regiment, paraded for Divine Service in a field just near Flêtre Church, Canon Scott, from Quebec, officiating.

At 8 a.m. on February 23rd the Battalion, acting as advance guard to the Brigade, marched from Flêtre to Armentières. This town, which was reached at 2.30 p.m., was only about three miles behind the actual front, but in spite of this, shops and cafes were open and there were many civilians about the streets. This was the first shelled town that the 13th had seen and the men were much interested in the damage the shells had caused. Billets for the men were provided in the civic workhouse, while the officers occupied houses immediately opposite.

On arriving in Armentières, the 13th Battalion was attached for instructional purposes to the 16th British Infantry Brigade, under the command of Brig.-Gen. Ingleby-Williams. This Brigade was composed of battalions from the Buffs, the York and Lancs., the Leicesters and the Shropshire Light Infantry and was holding a line of trenches on both sides of the Lille Road, about three miles S.E. of the town.

Brig.-Gen. Ingleby-Williams inspected the 13th in Armentières on the afternoon of February 24th and subsequently it was arranged that two companies of the Royal Highlanders should go into the line that same night for their first tour of instruction. In accordance with these arrangements, No. 1 Company, under Major D. R. McCuaig and No. 2 Company, under Capt. R. H. Jamieson, paraded at 6.15 and 6.30 p.m. respectively and proceeded into the line, guided by men of the 16th Brigade provided for the purpose. During this movement the Battalion suffered its first casualty, Private G. W. Eadle, of No. 2 Coy., being caught by a burst of fire and instantly killed.

FRANCE AND INTO ACTION

On February 25th No. 3 Company, which as the result of the reorganization due to the double company system was now under Major V. C. Buchanan, and No. 4 Company, under Capt. W. H. Clark-Kennedy, were given a similar short tour of instruction under one of the Imperial battalions. For some days after this one or another company of the 13th was always receiving instruction in the line, while the remaining companies, billeted in Armentières, were engaged in digesting the information already gained. Each company was given three front line tours.

Describing the experience in the line, an N.C.O. writes, in part, as follows:— "We went in first with the Leicesters. We had a good place to enter the line, most of the way being protected by breastworks. When we got in I stuck my head over to see the enemy's trenches and I certainly ducked it again pretty quickly— they seemed right on top of us and were really only 60 yards away. We came out at 5 a.m. and that same night went to other trenches, this time to those occupied by the York and Lancs. We had a harder time getting in, as the communication trench was filled with water and we had to keep in the open. There was a full moon shining and the Germans spotted us and gave us a regular hail of bullets. Our fellows acted splendidly under fire and we got in without anyone being hit, much to the surprise of the Yorks, who had been watching us. These trenches were even better than the first ones, being 400 yards from the enemy. We stayed there 24 hours and coming out the moon was hidden, so we were quite safe."

It was really marvelous how much the Battalion learned in these short tours. Officers and men alike were as keen as could be and the Imperial troops were delighted to teach all that they themselves knew. The system of instruction was to attach a section of the Canadians to a platoon of the English and for everyone then simply to carry on. In this way the newcomers learned trench routine. Almost before they were aware of it, they knew about the posting of sentries, the screening of fires, the establishment of listening posts, the issuing of rum and so forth. In addition they acquired much information about ration parties, wire cutters, loop holes, ammunition, engineering material, bombs, bayonets, trench sanitation and all the scores of things that are of vital import when men gather in opposing ditches to do one another to death.

For the most part the trenches in which the 13th received their first instructions were very quiet ones. They were of the breastwork variety, that is to say built up from the ground, not dug down into it, and were comparatively dry and comfortable. All these favourable circumstances contributed to the rapidity with which the Battalion learned its lessons, but more important still was the kindly attitude of its Imperial hosts. Of the courtesy received at the hands of officers and men of the 16th Infantry Brigade, the Highlanders have preserved a lively appreciation. While this applies without exception to all units of the Brigade, particular pains in instructing the new troops would seem to have been taken by Major Bayley, Lieut. Sim and Company Sergt.-Major G. P. Munsen, of the York and Lancs, the services of these officers being gratefully acknowledged in the official diary of the 13th Battalion.

Reference to the Battalion's official diary tempts the historian to comment on a curious coincidence that came to his notice while checking the diary over. In February, 1915, the officer entrusted with the task of keeping this record makes his entries with meticulous care until he comes to February 27th. On the 27th he has neatly written the word "June," instead of "February," and on that date, June 27th, he was killed in action sixteen months later. In recording this fact there is no desire to endow it with undue significance. The entry is as described and the coincidence is of interest, or of no interest at all, depending entirely on the individual point of view.

During the time that the 13th was receiving instruction from the units of the 16th Brigade, the remaining battalions of the Canadian Division were being similarly trained by other formations belonging to the 3rd British Corps, then commanded by Lieut.-Gen. Sir William Pulteney. How carefully their behaviour under fire was being watched the Canadians little guessed, but it is a fact that keen eyes made note of what happened and reported at length to higher powers who required the information lest new and inexperienced troops be entrusted with tasks beyond their strength. To the fact that these reports were highly favourable, Sir John French, in his despatch of April 5th, has given witness.

Accordingly in the early days of March it was announced that the Canadian Division was considered fit to take over a section of the line. Little time was lost in putting this move into effect. On March 3rd the 13th Battalion formed up in the Mairie Square in

FRANCE AND INTO ACTION

Armentieres and marched, via Erquinghem and Bac St. Maur, to Sailly-sur-la-Lys, thence to billets in Rouge de Bout. These billets were in shell torn barns and were not comfortable, but the troops, excited by the prospect of holding a line of their own, were in no mood to find fault.

On the following morning the Battalion paraded in a field and was addressed by Lieut.-Gen. E. A. H. Alderson, G.O.C. the Division. Briefly, Gen. Alderson referred to the work that lay ahead and frankly he told the Battalion what was expected of it. Summed up, his instruction to the Highlanders was that, *no matter what happened,* they must hold the trenches entrusted to them regardless of the cost.

Meanwhile the position to be held by the Canadians had been selected and relief of the 7th British Division was actually under way. This move brought the Canadian Division into the line in a position extending roughly in a north easterly direction from the Sailly-Fromelles Road to the Touquet-Bridoux Road, with an overlap of some hundreds of yards at either end. On the left of the Canadians was the 19th Brigade of the 6th British Division and on their right the 15th Brigade of the 8th British Division, so that for their first experience in a line of their own, their flanks were held by troops both tried and true.

On the night of March 6th the 13th Battalion moved up into the line, replacing the 16th Battalion, Canadian Scottish, which had previously taken over from the British. Nos. 1, 2 and 3 Companies went into the front line, while No. 4 Coy. was held in Battalion Reserve a short distance back. The front line in this locality was not a trench line in the generally accepted sense of the term, but rather an irregular series of trenches and strong posts linked together to form a front. The Battalion occupied this line for three days and did a great deal of work, in conjunction with the Engineers, in repairing parapets and digging communication trenches, with a view to making the isolated posts more accessible. This work, of course, was done at night, to take advantage of the protection that darkness afforded. That the Battalion was new to trench life was evidenced by several incidents during the tour. On one occasion Lieut.-Col. Loomis, while making an inspection of the posts at night, was horrified to notice that his guide was calmly smoking a cigarette, the glowing end of which invited disaster from the German trenches across the way. A blast of wrath descended on the head of this luckless wight and no doubt convinced him that the orders regarding this particular offence were not a mere formality.

During the three days of the tour the Battalion was subjected to sporadic shelling and fairly heavy rifle fire. No officers were hit, although Lieut. C. B. Pitblado had a close call when a bullet, missing his head by the fraction of an inch, tore its way through his glengarry. The men of the Battalion were not so fortunate, Privates A. T. Knight, G. Townsend, J. A. McConochie, J. Montanelli and J. B. Twamley being killed on March 7th and Private J. Fowler on March 8th.

On the night of the 9th the Battalion was relieved and marched back to billets at Point de la Justice, in Divisional Reserve. Here the unit was held for several days, pending the outcome of the Battle of Neuve Chapelle, the roar of which was distinctly heard from the south. Had this British attack proved a success, the result would have been to involve the Canadian Division in the advance, but this consequence was not attained.

On March 13th the Battalion re-entered the trenches for another 3-day tour. The weather was all that could be desired and at nights a great deal of work was done in strengthening the position and building protection against enfilade fire. Owing to the peculiar nature of the front line the problem of enfilade was annoying. On one occasion five men in a post towards the right front were simultaneously wounded by fire of this description, Piper D. Lawson dying of his wounds shortly after. Four other privates were killed during the tour and several wounded.

What casualties were inflicted on the Germans is, of course, unknown, but testimony that the Canadians endeavoured to make themselves a nuisance is given in the following letter:— "We had one game which annoyed the Germans very much. They cook on regular stoves with chimneys and all. In the morning we could see the smoke rising and another corporal and myself would get at a loop hole each, with a third man with a periscope to watch results. We would then cut the top off their sandbags and scatter dirt all over them as well as over their breakfast. Also we would plunk their chimney on the chance of a ricochet."

At the extreme left of the Battalion front was a stream, marking the boundary between the 3rd and 2nd Brigades. This little brook provided excellent water and on one occasion, to quote another

FRANCE AND INTO ACTION

letter, "a couple of fellows were down getting a supply of water when one of them saw a fish in the stream and flopped it out. An eighteen inch pike caught in a trench!— the best fish story I've ever heard, but absolutely true. I know, because I had some of the fish for dinner, and it was fine."

At the conclusion of the tour the 13th was relieved and proceeded to billets in Rue du Bois. Here the Battalion rested for several days, "rested" being used in the Army sense, where almost any change of work is called a rest.

On the night of the 19th the Battalion moved up once more. A feature of the tour that followed was the demolition of an advanced post, known as No. 6, by a party under the command of Capt. C. J. Smith. This post, which had become valueless owing to improvements in the trenches behind it, was only about 250 feet from the German line, so that the work of demolition had to be carried out very quietly. By means of a chain of men lying in the mud, materials were passed up and the job completed in two nights' work. To the credit of all concerned this was accomplished without a casualty. During the four day tour casualties were light, although a few men were wounded and Private A. Auld killed.

Relief of the Battalion took place on the 23rd and the next day the men enjoyed a bath and change of underclothing at Bac St. Maur. On the afternoon of the 26th the Battalion marched seven miles to reserve billets near Estaires. During the march it is recorded that a new song, afterwards very popular, made its first appearance:

> "I want to go home, I want to go home
> The Germans shoot dum-dums, I don't like their roar,
> I don't want to go to the front any more,
>
> . . . . . .
>
> Oh my! I don't want to die
> I want to go home."

This little ditty, with many variations, improvements and local touches, remained in vogue throughout the whole war.

For eleven days the 13th remained at Estaires, busily engaged in drilling, route marching and practices of all kinds. On the afternoon of March 29th a party of 200 men paraded under Capts. K. M. Perry, C. J. Smith and H. F. Walker and was conveyed in wagons to a point south of Wangerie, which is due north of Neuve

ROYAL HIGHLANDERS OF CANADA

Chapelle. Here each man was provided with a pick and shovel and the party was put to work digging assembly trenches for a projected attack. This work was urgent and the men were kept hard at it till 1 a.m., when they were succeeded by a similar party from the 14th Battalion.

On April 3rd the Highlanders held a sports day, the scene of the contests being a large field close to the Battalion billets. A varied programme was run off in which Private Whetter, of the Machine Gun Section, secured the prize for the best aggregate score. No. 2 Coy. won the tug-of-war. On the following day the Battalion paraded for Divine Service in Estaires and on the 6th it was inspected by the Commanding Officer. On this occasion the men wore for the first time an issue of khaki aprons, a gift to the Battalion from W. M. Mitchell, Esq., of Bristol, England.

The next day the Battalion paraded at 6.20 a.m. and marched 16 miles to billets in Terdeghem, a village near the town of Cassel. Here, on the morning of the 10th, the 3rd Brigade was inspected by General Sir H. Smith-Dorrien, G.O.C. the Second British Army, of which the Canadian Division was now a part. General Smith-Dorrien complimented the officers of the Brigade on the work that the Division had already accomplished and added that the Canadians were soon to proceed to a lively part of the line. Just how lively the line in question was to prove the General himself had probably never imagined.

CHAPTER IV

The Second Battle of Ypres

> Tower of Ypres, a little slept your glory
> Lips again are busy with your name
> Ypres again is famous in our story
> Ypres of Flanders, wrapt in blood and flame.
> —EVERARD OWEN.

I

ON April 15th, the Royal Highlanders commenced the march towards that "lively" area of which Gen. Smith-Dorrien had spoken. From the direction taken it soon became obvious that the Battalion was headed for some part of the famous Ypres Salient, which, even at that comparatively early date, possessed an evil and sinister reputation.

Marching from Terdeghem after lunch, the 13th proceeded a distance of about six miles to Abeele, and billeted for the night. In the morning the Battalion moved back to a point where motor busses awaited it. These London busses, still bearing the signs and advertisements of pre-war days, provided the men of the Battalion with much amusement. Those unfortunates whose avoirdupois seemed a little excessive had their attention called to the benefits they would derive if only they would wear Somebody-or-other's weight reducing corsets. In turn the brawny amongst the rank and file pleaded with their tormentors to use Someone-else's Malted Milk, which the advertisement promised, "Makes Puny Men Strong."

Proceeding through Poperinghe, the omnibuses conveyed the 13th to Vlamertinghe, where the Battalion disembarked and marched through Ypres to St. Jean. Here three companies of the Highlanders went into billets as Brigade Reserve, No. 4 Coy. proceeding to St. Julien as Brigade Support.

Three days were passed in this location, during which preparations were made for taking over a part of the line. Owing to St. Jean being under direct observation from the enemy, the men were confined to billets during the day and devoted their time to care of rifles and equipment, to writing letters, playing cards and so on.

ROYAL HIGHLANDERS OF CANADA

On the night of Wednesday, April 21st, the 13th Battalion moved up into the line and took over a series of breastwork trenches from the 14th Battalion, Royal Montreal Regiment, the men little dreaming as they accomplished the relief that they were about to write a glorious page in Canadian history. Apart from an unusually severe shelling of Ypres during the afternoon, nothing had indicated that behind the German lines a blow was being prepared such as had never fallen in civilized warfare, and one which its originators hoped would carry them victoriously to Calais and the English Channel. As has been stated, however, no sign of all this had appeared when the Highlanders took over from the R.M.R. The night as a matter of fact was almost suspiciously quiet.

In view of what happened the next day, it is necessary that the situation in which the Battalion found itself be described and the disposition of the companies made clear. The Canadian Division held a line, 4250 yards in length, extending in a north-westerly direction from the Ypres-Roulers Railway to a point some fifty yards beyond the Ypres-Poelcappelle Road. The extreme left of this line was held by the 13th Battalion. Beyond the 13th to the left were French coloured troops (Turcos), while on the right flank was a battalion of their own brigade, the 15th (48th Highlanders) from Toronto. No. 1 Coy., under Major D. R. McCuaig, who had with him Capt. L. W. Whitehead, Capt. H. F. Walker, Lieut. Melville Greenshields and Lieut. C. B. Pitblado, held the left of the 13th front, from the point where it joined the Turcos to a point some 150 yards to the right of the Poelcappelle Road, making approximately 200 yards in all. The next section of the Battalion front was held by No. 2 Coy., under Capt. R. H. Jamieson, whose officers were Capt. K. M. Perry, Lieut. I. M. R. Sinclair, Lieut. A. Worthington, Lieut. A. M. Fisher and Lieut. E. M. Sellon. This section was separated from that held by No. 1 Coy. by an open gap nearly 100 yards long, through which ran a small stream. The third, and right, section of the front was held by No. 4 Coy., under Capt. W. H. Clark-Kennedy, with whom were Capt. Gerald Lees, Lieut. W. S. M. MacTier and Lieut. S. B. Lindsay.

No. 3 Coy. was in support, two platoons in trenches about 400 yards to the rear of No. 1 Coy's. position and two platoons at Battalion Headquarters in St. Julien. With the former were Major E. C. Norsworthy, O.C. the Firing Line, Capt. Guy Drummond and Capt. C. J. Smith, while with the platoons in St. Julien were Major

SECOND BATTLE OF YPRES

V. C. Buchanan, Capt. T. S. Morrisey, Lieut. C. N. McCuaig and Lieut. F. S. Molson. Lieut. J. G. Ross commanded the Machine Gun Section.

Battalion Headquarters, as has been mentioned, was in St. Julien, under Lieut.-Col. Loomis, who, in addition to guiding the fortunes of the 13th, was designated Town Commandant of St. Julien. With him was Capt. G. E. McCuaig (Adjutant) and Major E. R. Brown, the M.O. Lieut. J. O. Hastings and Lieut. C. L. Cantley, commanding respectively the Transport and Quartermaster's stores, were in Ypres on the Canal.

Such, then, was the disposition of the Battalion on the morning of April 22nd. Dawn breaking on that date revealed to the men that, in spite of work hard done by the 14th and by themselves, the trenches they were holding were rather flimsily constructed. Except for the gap already mentioned, there was a continuous parapet of sandbags, but this was too thin to be bullet proof and was chiefly useful as a screen from view. There was practically no parados, few traverses existed and no shell proof dugouts at all, this last condition being accounted for by the fact that any attempt to dig down was frustrated by the presence a few inches below the surface of water and hastily buried bodies.

In contrast to these discouraging features, the wire was excellent and the machine gun posts, on the evidence of the Machine Gun Officer, all that could be desired. Fifty to seventy-five yards away were the Germans who, during the morning and early afternoon, showed few signs of activity. An occasional rifle shot and spasmodic machine gun fire was all that indicated their existence.

About 3 p.m., however, these peaceful conditions changed and the Germans prepared to launch the blow which the previous inactivity had served to mask. The opening of their great attack was heralded by a terrific bombardment of the Canadian line and of the French line to the left. In so far as the 13th was concerned, this fell with particular severity, not on the front line, but on the trenches immediately to the rear, where Major Norsworthy and the two platoons of No. 3 Coy. were in support. After suffering severely, Norsworthy notified Major McCuaig, of No. 1 Coy., that to avoid unnecessary losses he was withdrawing his men a short distance, but that he would remain in support and would come up at once, should the companies in the line require assistance. Shortly after this telephone communication was cut, and McCuaig found himself in command of the three companies in the line.

After two hours of heavy shelling, the Germans launched a great wave of chlorine gas. This was a weapon new to civilized warfare and against it the Allies had no protection whatsoever. Rolling across the open fields this gasping horror fell with all its force on the trenches of the Turcos to the Canadians' left. Elements of the 13th also received a whiff of this hellish brew, but the poor Turcos suffered its full effects. Blinded and choking they fell in agony and perished miserably. Those who escaped the first discharge waited for no more. A horrible green death, against which courage availed a man nothing, had fallen upon their comrades and they themselves had barely escaped. So they turned and fled, and no man has been found to blame them.

Unaware of just what had happened, but uneasy because of reports from his left that the French were in retreat, McCuaig decided to visit the French trenches to investigate, giving orders to No. 1 Platoon, under Capt. Walker, to follow him. This visit revealed an alarming situation. Following the wave of gas, the Germans had launched a series of attacks and these had penetrated through the broken French lines on a front several miles in width. Continuing his investigations, McCuaig found that a remnant of the Algerians (Turcos) were holding a breastwork, running back at right angles from their original trenches, and were exchanging a brisk fire with the Germans, who had occupied a parallel hedge. As there was not sufficient cover to prolong the French line, McCuaig instructed Capt. Walker to withdraw his platoon, which had just come up, and to take a position in echelon to the Algerians in the ditch of the Poelcappelle Road. This road, as will be remembered, cut through the front line at right angles and by lining it McCuaig faced some of his forces square left, to meet the flank attacks which his observations indicated were bound to develop from that quarter.

Meanwhile, in order to steady the Turcos, who showed signs of panic, McCuaig compromised on his order to No. 1 Platoon and instructed two sections to remain where they were, while the balance carried out the original order to line the Poelcappelle Road, being reinforced by No. 3 Platoon, under Lieut. Greenshields, and subsequently by part of No. 4 Platoon.

About 6 p.m. a salvo from a battery in the rear made four direct hits on the Highlanders' trenches, causing a dozen or more casual-

SECOND BATTLE OF YPRES

ties. This occurrence showed McCuaig that his position was a desperate one, as it indicated that the Germans were firing captured guns from his left rear.

This deduction was eventually proved to be correct. Having broken through the French lines on a wide front, as already described, the Germans had swung in towards the Canadians' flank and were making some progress in the general direction of St. Julien. This brought the enemy into contact with Major Norsworthy and the two platoons of No. 3 Coy. in support, or rather the remnant of these platoons, which had suffered severely in the opening bombardment.

Inspired by the gallant leadership of Major Norsworthy and Capt. Guy Drummond, the men of the supporting platoons fought a dauntless fight. Every moment was precious and no one can estimate the value of the time that was gained by the delay this devoted effort caused to the Germans. But even sublime courage can not withstand fire and steel. Overwhelmed at last, Norsworthy and Drummond fell and such of their men as had not been killed were, with a few exceptions, surrounded and captured. Amongst the exceptions were Private Telfer and five other men, who made their way through to the front and reported to McCuaig the disaster that had befallen his supports.

The forward position was a very unenviable one. At 9 p.m. the Germans dislodged the Turcos from their advanced breastwork and drove them back in disorder. Some 200 of them, however, rallied on the Highlanders and reinforced the line along the Poelcappelle Road, also helping to construct a parados for the original front line, where, owing to the absence of proper protection, losses had been very heavy. In this work, under the direction of Capt. Whitehead and Sergt.-Major Ableson, the Turcos rendered valuable assistance.

Meanwhile a platoon from No. 2 Coy. and one from No. 4 Coy. had been added to the force lining the road, while Lieut. J. G. Ross, the Battalion Machine Gun Officer, had further strengthened this position by detailing to it two of his guns, commanded respectively by Sergt. Trainor and Lance-Corp. Parkes. These N.C.O's. took up positions on the Road itself, using as cover a few paving blocks which they managed to pry up and place in front of them.

Hardly had these preparations been completed, when the Germans pushed forward to the attack. This effort was stubborn and conducted with no little courage, but it eventually broke down before the determined resistance that was opposed to it, as did several other attacks no less courageously pushed. Fighting with their backs to the wall the Highlanders could not be overcome unless annihilated.

All night the defence was maintained under a veritable storm of rifle fire, to which, in spite of the danger of an ammunition shortage, the 13th made reply, as it was necessary to disguise from the Germans the weakness and inadequacy of the little force opposed to them.

About midnight McCuaig received a message from Lieut.-Col. Loomis directing him to use his own discretion as to his dispositions. This was in reply to a report that had been sent off shortly before dark and the delay was due to the great difficulty encountered by the runners in getting through. One of these, in fact, never got through at all, being intercepted and killed by the Germans far back of the original front line.

In accordance with Col. Loomis' orders, which left the movements of the troops in the line to his own judgment, McCuaig held a consultation with Capts. Jamieson and Clark-Kennedy, as a result of which it was decided that, if reinforcements failed to arrive before dawn, the line of the Road would be evacuated and a new line, about three hundred yards in the rear of, and parallel to it occupied. This new line provided a better field of fire than the old one and in any event McCuaig did not believe that the line of the Road could be put in a proper state of defence. A further consideration was that by the retirement the front would be shortened and thus about 100 men would be saved to fill the gaps in the line. Accordingly Capt. Jamieson was instructed to set under way the construction of the new position.

Just before dawn, no reinforcements having arrived, orders were issued for the withdrawal and this was successfully carried out, Lieut. Ross covering the movement with a machine gun, under Sergt. Trainor, and a dozen men, under Corp. W. E. Macfarlane.

Having accomplished its work, this small party was about to retire when word was passed along that reinforcements had arrived. These consisted of two platoons of No. 3 Coy., under Capt. C. J. Smith, and "B" Company of the 2nd Battalion of the Buffs, under Capt. F. W. Tomlinson, the whole under command of Major V. C. Buchanan, who, as a result of the death of Major Norsworthy,

SECOND BATTLE OF YPRES

was now Second-in-command of the 13th Battalion. The arrival of these reinforcements acted like a tonic on the weary troops in the front line and inspired the utmost confidence.

On his arrival Major Buchanan assumed the command of the firing line that up to this time had been held by Major McCuaig. The latter informed Buchanan as to the details of the situation and, after a consultation, it was decided that McCuaig, with the remains of his own company and the company of the Buffs, should re-occupy the line that had been abandoned. This move was carried out without the enemy realizing what had happened.

Shortly afterwards, at the point where the trenches crossed the Road, the Germans tried a ruse-de-guerre. A number of figures, apparently wearing French uniforms, but indistinct in the early morning light, appeared in rear of the French trenches, calling out, "We are the French." McCuaig, Capt. Tomlinson of the Buffs and a French officer were present and, receiving no satisfactory replies to their shouted questions, ordered their troops to open fire. To this the alleged French at once replied.

This incident marked the beginning of a long day of heavy casualties. Rifle fire poured in on the Battalion from three sides and the German shelling, directed by aeroplanes, was heavy and effective. About 9 a.m. casualties along the Road became so frequent that it was decided to abandon this position and retire into the trench line proper. This helped matters a little, but, as the trenches themselves had been badly battered and provided little protection against enfilade fire, the stream of wounded continued. These were passed along to the right and evacuated through the lines of the 15th Battalion. In facilitating the passage of these casualties, Capt. K. M. Perry, who improvised stretchers, using tarpaulins, wire and sticks, rendered most valuable service.

Meanwhile Lieut. Ross with his machine guns made a determined effort to cut down the enfilade fire that was causing the Battalion such heavy losses. Accompanied by Lance-Corporal Fred Fisher, who had already rendered exceptionally distinguished service, he crawled out a shallow trench and, setting up a gun, was about to open fire when Fisher was shot dead. A moment later Sergt. McLeod, who had taken Fisher's place, was killed in the same way. Leaving this particular gun, Lieut. Ross crawled to a spot where he ordered Lance-Corp. Parkes and Private Glad to set up another gun and open fire. From this location he "got the drop" on the

ROYAL HIGHLANDERS OF CANADA

most bothersome of the opposing trenches and maintained his superiority for the rest of the day.

In spite of the measure of relief afforded by this partial protection from enfilade, the day was a bad one for the men in the line. They were short of food and water and dangerously short of ammunition. In addition they were shelled continuously and were cut off from all communication with the rear. Twice during the day the enemy, supposing that the defence had been beaten down, came over to occupy the demolished trenches and twice, with rifle and machine gun fire, the Highlanders drove him back. Each time he took his revenge by calling on his artillery to wipe the 13th trenches off the map. Each time his artillery complied with a storm of shells which, they judged, would utterly subdue the stubborn defence. Each time, however, when the storm had passed, the defence failed to admit itself appreciably weaker.

All this time communication with the rear remained completely cut, while communication between the companies themselves was extremely difficult. Volunteer runners, however, maintained the inter-company communication all day. Sniped at and under heavy shell fire, they ducked and dodged and wormed their way through, carrying the messages that were so vitally important. In this work Corp. B. M. Giveen and Lance-Corp. J. J. Campbell rendered services that were especially meritorious.

About 5 o'clock in the afternoon Capt. Clark-Kennedy, of No. 4 Coy., returned to the front line after a daring expedition, as a result of which he had got through to Col. Loomis and to Brigade Headquarters. He brought back with him orders from Headquarters instructing Major Buchanan to evacuate the line he was then holding and to take up a new line, running to the rear from the point where his present line joined that of the 15th Battalion on the right.

In accordance with these instructions orders were issued to bury the Battalion's dead and evacuate the wounded. In both of these difficult tasks Capt. L. W. Whitehead rendered devoted service.

At 10 p.m., after most of the wounded had been evacuated to the lines of the 15th Battalion on the right, the companies of the 13th started to move, carrying the balance of the wounded with them, and almost immediately the Germans, sensing the move, launched a series of vicious attacks from the front, rear and left flank.

For a while these attacks rendered the situation of the Highlanders extremely precarious. Loaded down as they were with a

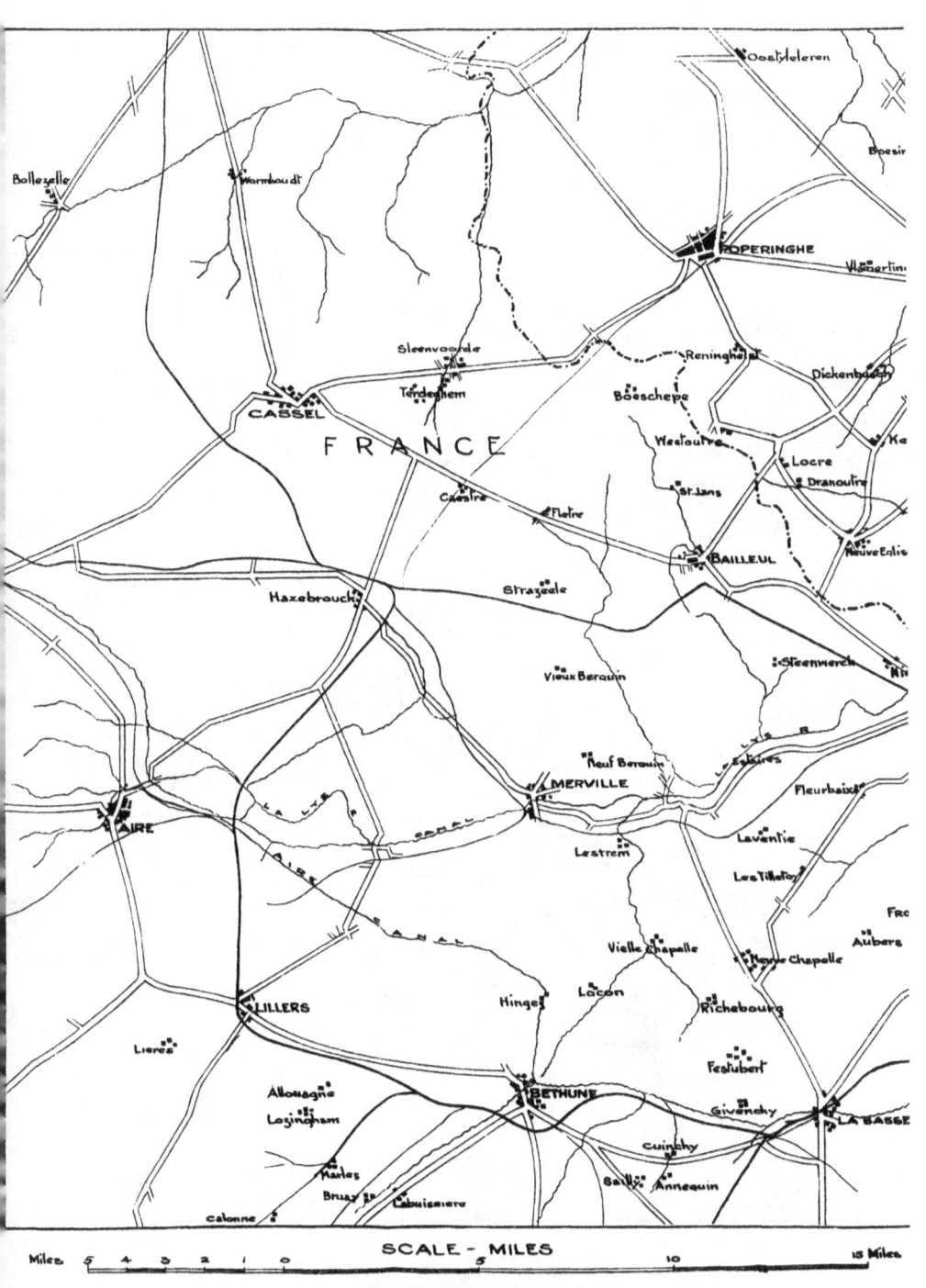

YPRES AND FESTUBERT

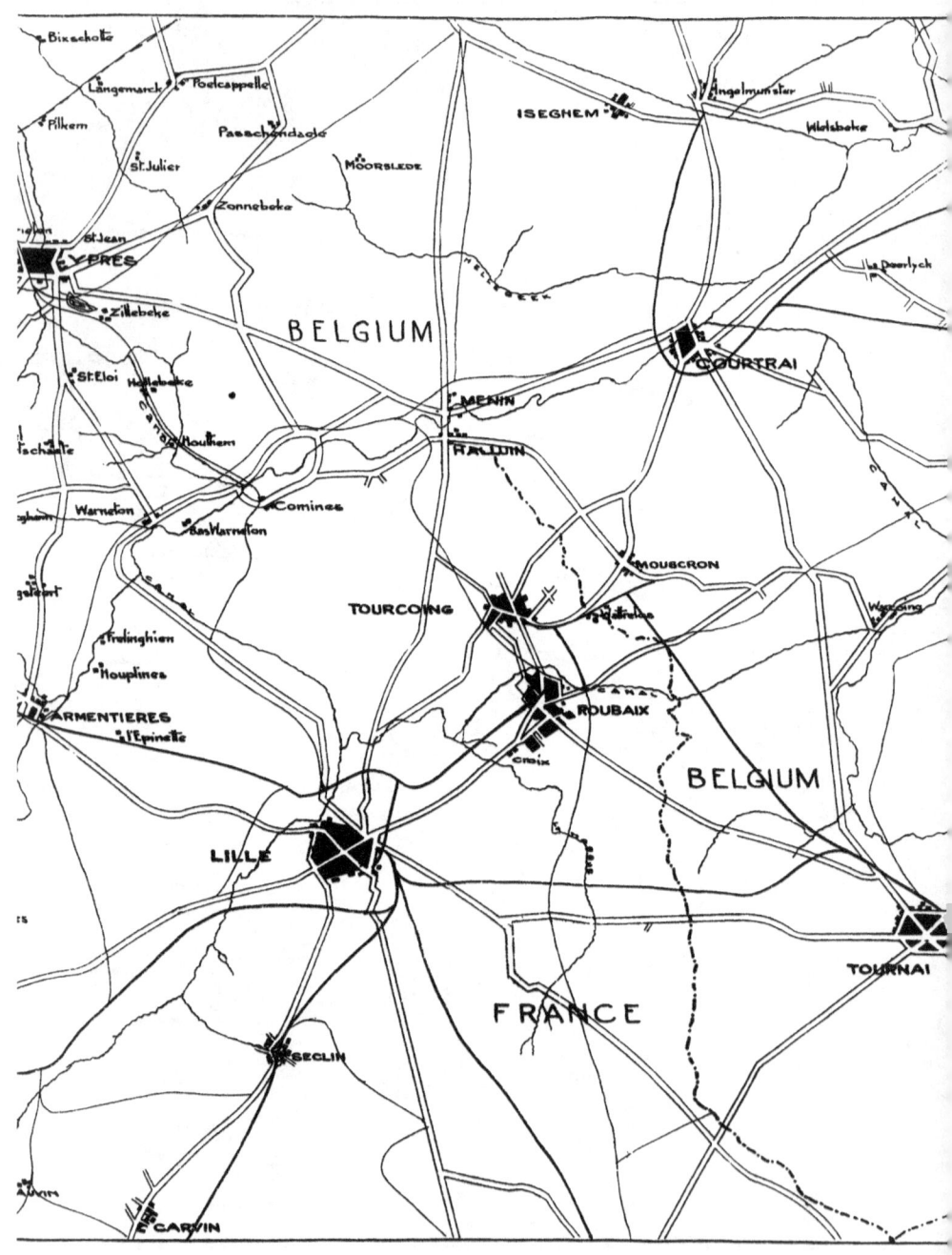

SECOND BATTLE OF YPRES

considerable number of wounded, their retreat was of necessity distressfully slow, while they had exhausted their supply of grenades and were in consequence unable to cope with the German bombing parties, who harassed them unmercifully. But for the gallant work of a small rear guard, under the command of Lieut. C. B. Pitblado, assisted by Lieut. Melville Greenshields, and supported by Lieut. J. G. Ross, it is almost certain they would have been completely overwhelmed. As it was, the attacks were eventually beaten off and the retirement painfully continued.

At this point it seems fitting to acknowledge the splendid services of Capt. Tomlinson and his company of the Buffs. From the moment of their arrival on the morning of the 23rd they rendered loyal and courageous assistance. During the retirement now being described they displayed marked courage and coolness, in fact at no time during their association with the 13th did they fail to meet any call, no matter how severe, that was made on them. The Royal Highlanders would deeply regret if by any mischance adequate recognition were not afforded to the gallantry these troops displayed.

During the night of the 23rd a fine piece of work was carried out by Lieut. J. O. Hastings and his men of the Transport Section, who came right up to the front line from Ypres and brought with them rations, ammunition and, most welcome of all, water. Lieut. Hastings personally supervised the issuing of the water, which was contained in sheepskin bags, and saw to it that each company received a fair share. In view of the heavy shelling of roads and all the difficulties, this feat of the Transport Section was considered to be worthy of the highest commendation.

Dawn on April 24th found the men of the 13th Battalion in the position to which they had retired the night before. Starting from the point where the new line pivoted on the flank of the 15th Battalion, the companies were disposed from right to left as follows: the Buffs and then the companies of the 13th in numerical order. The left flank, extending towards St. Julien, was held by No. 3 Company of the 14th R.M.R., under Major Gault McCombe. To the left of these again was a single platoon of the 13th, under Lieut. S. B. Lindsay, while his left was held by three companies of the 7th Canadian Battalion. Beyond these was a mixture of units hurriedly pushed forward to meet the menace the German break through had caused.

Soon after daybreak the Germans again used gas, which fell

with particular severity on the trenches of the 15th Battalion to the right, and followed this with another intense bombardment, wrecking the shallow trenches that had been dug and causing further losses. Under cover of this shell fire the enemy infantry worked closer and closer, endeavouring to rush the remnant of the Highlanders and administer the coup de grace.

It was at this stage of the struggle that Capt. Gerald Lees was killed and Capt. L. W. Whitehead fatally wounded. Both these officers had displayed resource and courage and their loss to the Battalion was a heavy one.

About 9 a.m. Major Buchanan decided that, as a result of the unit on his right having been forced to retire, his position was no longer tenable and orders were issued to the companies to fall back to a location some distance in the rear, taking advantage meanwhile of every bit of cover to harass and impede the German advance.

Through some unfortunate error this order did not reach McCuaig, of No. 1 Coy., nor Tomlinson, of the Buffs, till the retirement had actually begun. McCuaig, finding that his only way back was across fifty yards of open ground, realized that his chances were slim. Rallying the remnant of his company, about forty in number, he issued the necessary orders and the attempt to cross the open space began. Not many made that fifty yards in safety. The Germans had been expecting some such move and swept the open with rifle and machine gun fire the moment the retreating Highlanders broke from cover. A few got across, but the majority went down before they had covered half the distance. The Buffs, whose commanding officer had been wounded and whose numbers had dwindled to a scant fifty, remained in their position and were cut off and captured.

It was at this time that Lieut. C. B. Pitblado displayed the greatest gallantry in carrying back Capt. Whitehead, who had been mortally wounded in the head and was out of his senses. Being hit in the knee himself, Pitblado was compelled to abandon Whitehead, who was by this time quite unconscious. Subsequently Pitblado met McCuaig and the two, having seen to the retirement of the remnant of their men, were going back together when McCuaig was wounded in the knee. A few moments later McCuaig was hit through both legs and rendered helpless. Refusing to abandon his senior, Pitblado bandaged the latter's wounds under heavy fire. Just as this task was completed, Pitblado was again wounded in the leg,

SECOND BATTLE OF YPRES

which finished his chances of getting away. Lying helplessly in the open, McCuaig was hit four more times before he and Pitblado were picked up by the Germans, whose advance reached them some ten minutes later. For the courage and devotion to duty shown by these two officers during the whole engagement they were, at a subsequent date, awarded respectively the Distinguished Service Order and the Military Cross.

Meanwhile the other companies, lashed by rifle and machine gun fire and hard pressed by the German infantry, continued their slow retreat, stopping frequently to administer a stinging check when the Germans trod too closely on their heels. Heavy losses were incurred during this movement, Capt. Jamieson, Capt. Perry and Lieut. Greenshields being wounded in quick succession. Capt. Perry's wound, however, did not incapacitate him and he was able to carry on. Finally a line was reached where the retreat was ended and orders issued to "stand fast."

All day the Battalion held this line under heavy fire, while urgent messages were sent back to headquarters for ammunition and reinforcements. About 3 o'clock Lieut.-Col. Loomis arrived, accompanied by Privates Simpson and Brittan, who had carried messages back to him, and by some Pioneers with ammunition. With him he brought the glad news that relief was on the way. Until this arrived, Capt. Clark-Kennedy, with Lieuts. Lindsay and MacTier and a small party, maintained close touch with the Germans. At about dusk several battalions of British troops came up and, passing through the weary Canadian lines, carried the war to the enemy.

II

Following the arrival of the British, the 13th spent the night in reserve trenches south of Wieltje, withdrawing about a mile early on the morning of the 25th to near Potijze. Sunday, the 25th, was spent in this position and at night the Battalion was ordered to La Brique. Reaching this location at about 2 a.m. on the 26th, the men started to dig in, when orders reached them to retire across the Yser Canal to Brielen, a distance of some miles.

Thoroughly worn out as they were, this march was a trying one, but at length it was accomplished. Only a few hours rest was given them, however, when the "fall in" sounded and they were ordered forward once more to support an attack being delivered

ROYAL HIGHLANDERS OF CANADA

near La Brique. Forward they went and, having performed this particular service, moved at 3 p.m. to a point south of Wieltje, where they dug in as Divisional Reserve.

In this position the Royal Highlanders passed April 27th, under shell fire from three directions. Late in the day they moved back to bivouacs south of Brielen, moving forward again at 8 p.m. on the 28th to entrench in reserve west of the Canal. Previous to this a draft of 276 men joined the Battalion, under the command of Lieuts. Crowdy, Ives, W. D. Smith and L de V. Chipman. Of these the last named had decidedly bad luck, being hit in the ankle by shell fire within a short time of his arrival. On the same date commissions were granted to Regimental Sergt.-Major J. Jeffery, Corp. E. Waud, Lance-Corp. F. S. Mathewson, Lance-Corp. C. M. Maxwell and Private G. W. R. Simpson, in recognition of the outstanding service they had rendered during April 22nd to 24th. R.S.M. J. Jeffery was at the same time recommended for further promotion to the rank of Captain.

On the night of the 29th the Battalion moved forward about a mile to support an attack by the French. During this attack and as a result of the shelling that followed at intervals for several days, the exhausted 13th suffered a number of additional casualties.

Early on the morning of May 4th the Highlanders moved back to a position near Vlamertinghe and at 7.30 that night they bade adieu to the bloody Ypres Salient and marched, together with the other Battalions of the 3rd Brigade, via Reninghelst and Locre, to billets two miles south of Bailleul.

III

Before following the further fortunes of the Battalion proper, it is necessary to clear up some details of the Second Battle of Ypres omitted from the foregoing account in order that the continuity of the story should not be repeatedly broken.

As will be remembered, on April 21st, when the Battalion went into the line, Lieut.-Col. Loomis established his headquarters in St. Julien, of which town he was also appointed Commandant. On the afternoon of April 22nd he and his officers had just had tea when far over to the left a great green cloud was seen, pouring across the trenches of the Turcos. Gas was unknown, but it was realized that this cloud had some extraordinary significance and an account of it was at once forwarded to Brigade H.Q.

SECOND BATTLE OF YPRES

By 5 o'clock large numbers of the French could be seen retreating and by this time St. Julien itself was under steady shell fire. Just as it became dark bullets hitting all around and Very lights going up showed that the Germans had approached to within about 400 yards. Accordingly Capt. T. S. Morrisey, with a party of H.Q. details, was sent out to join other units in forming a line to defend the town north of the Poelcappelle Road.

After dark Capt. Tomlinson and a company of the Buffs arrived and these, with the two platoons of No. 3 Coy., Col. Loomis despatched to reinforce his hard pressed front line. As has been described, these units, owing to the roundabout route they were compelled to follow, did not reach the front till dawn.

At about this time a message was received from General Turner that the 10th and 16th Battalions would attack the small wood N.W. of St. Julien at midnight. This attack duly took place and the story of it is a splendid one indeed. Pressed with a dash and gallantry beyond all praise, the attack swept through the wood and drove the Germans in confusion before it. Incidentally, it relieved for the time being the worst of the pressure on St. Julien.

Meanwhile, under heavy shell fire, Lieuts. J. O. Hastings and C. L. Cantley had come up to St. Julien from Ypres with the transport containing rations and ammunition. While explaining to these officers the situation of the Battalion as far as it was understood, Capt. G. E. McCuaig was hit by a piece of shell, while at about the same time Lieut. F. S. Molson was also wounded. Both these officers had their wounds dressed by Major E. R. Brown, who was having a busy time, as casualties poured in on St. Julien from all directions.

Meantime no news reached Col. Loomis as to the fate that had overtaken his front line. He was acutely anxious and his anxiety was not relieved by the fact that small parties of all descriptions kept reporting to him with requests for information and orders. Most of the time he had little information to give, but each party he ordered on, or back, as the situation at the moment seemed to warrant.

For two days and nights this sort of thing continued, while the shell fire steadily became more intense and the German attack pushed closer and closer. At last it was seen that the town must fall and Battalion Headquarters was accordingly withdrawn. Great credit attaches to Col. Loomis for the courage and ability with which he directed operations in this shell torn town during those exceedingly strenuous days. Recognition of his services was accorded when, in the King's birthday honours list, he was awarded the D.S.O.

Mention has already been made of the work of No. 24066, Lance-Corporal Fred Fisher, at the time when he met his death, but no account of the 13th Battalion in the Second Battle of Ypres is complete without reference to the work of this plucky N.C.O. on the night previous. Coming forward from St. Julien, Fisher discovered that some of the guns of Major W. B. M. King's field battery were being fought with the German infantry close on top of them. Capture of these guns seemed imminent, but Fisher set up his machine gun in advance of the Battery, and, with the assistance of a few men from the supports, held off the enemy till the guns got away. During this encounter Fisher's small section was under concentrated fire and four of his six men were killed. Returning to St. Julien, he got four men of the 14th Battalion and endeavoured once more to push up to the front line. In coming forward he lost these men and eventually reached the front line alone. Here he continued to render valuable service up to the moment of his death. For the valour he displayed on these occasions he was recommended for, and awarded, the coveted Victoria Cross, being the first Canadian to win this honour in the Great War.

Such, then, in its main features is the story of the 13th Battalion at Second Ypres. Referring to the stand made by the Canadian Division as a whole, Field-Marshal Sir John French in his official despatch wrote as follows:—

"In spite of the danger to which they were exposed, the Canadians held their ground with a magnificent display of tenacity and courage; and it is not too much to say that the bearing and conduct of these splendid troops averted a disaster which might have been attended with the most serious consequences."

This reference, as has been stated, applies to the work of the whole Canadian Division. No one unit proved braver or more tenacious than the others. All shared alike in the glory of an amazing feat of arms. Facing overwhelming odds, the Canadian Division by its stand won the right to take its place as the equal in tenacity and courage of the famous "Old Contemptibles," whose deeds are deservedly enshrined in the proud traditions of the British Army.

CHAPTER V

Festubert, Givenchy and Ploegsteert

> The naked earth is warm with Spring
> And with green grass and bursting trees
> Leans to the sun's gaze glorying,
> And quivers in the sunny breeze;
> And Life is Colour and Warmth and Light,
> And a striving evermore for these;
> And he is dead who will not fight;
> And who dies fighting has increase.
> —JULIAN H. F. GRENFELL.

I

ON leaving the Ypres Salient, the 13th marched to billets south of Bailleul, as mentioned in Section II of the previous chapter. Accompanying the Royal Highlanders on this march was "Flora Macdonald," a goat, "found" near the position of some Indian troops in the Salient and adopted forthwith as the Regiment's official mascot.

Settling down in billets, the 13th had an opportunity to realize how much the Battalion had suffered in the recent battle. Twelve officers had gone down, while casualties in the ranks totalled 454. In other words the unit had lost very nearly half its fighting strength. Two of the four company commanders were casualties and the promotion of Major Buchanan to succeed Major Norsworthy as Second-in-command meant that No. 3 Coy. was also deprived of its wonted leader. In addition many trusted N.C.O's. had been killed or wounded, so that the whole fabric of the Battalion was badly in need of repair.

Faced with this situation, Lieut.-Col. Loomis started to rebuild his unit without a moment's delay, realizing that the time available for this work would in all probability be extremely short. Men were scarce in those days and the Colonel rightly judged that the Canadians, having proved their worth, would not wait long till they were called on to prove it again.

ROYAL HIGHLANDERS OF CANADA

Reorganization of the Battalion, then, started on the first day in billets and continued without interruption on the days that followed. A small draft of N.C.O.'s. and men was received from England and at once distributed to the companies. Capt. G. D. McGibbon also joined from the Base Company in England, while promotion from the ranks was given to Corp. J. D. Macpherson, Private S. V. Brittan, Private B. H. Rust and Private H. R. Powell. Of these, the first three had been wounded in the battle of Ypres, where all had rendered conspicuous service. News from the three wounded that their injuries would not detain them in England much longer was promptly followed by the announcement that when they rejoined they would do so with commissioned rank. Lieut. Powell immediately assumed his new duties as a subaltern with No. 2 Coy.

On May 9th General Alderson visited the Battalion and addressed the officers and men. This speech followed the lines of his order of the day dealing with the work of the Canadian Division in the Ypres Salient, in which he said:— "I would first of all tell you that I have never been so proud of anything in my life as I am of my armlet with 'Canada' on it. .... I think it is possible that all of you do not quite realize that, if we had retired on the evening of April 22nd, ... the whole of the 27th and 28th Divisions would probably have been cut off. Certainly they would not have got away a gun or vehicle of any sort. .... I know my military history pretty well, and I cannot think of an instance in which so much depended on the standing fast of one division. .... There is one more word I would say to you before I stop. You have made a reputation second to none in this war; but, remember, no man can live on his reputation. He must keep on adding to it. And I feel sure that you will do so ——."

Three days later Gen. Sir Horace Smith-Dorrien visited Battalion Headquarters and spoke in somewhat similar terms to a small group of officers. On this occasion the companies were absent on a route march, so the distinguished visitor had no opportunity to address the men. For them, and for the company officers, he left a message with Col. Loomis which expressed in fitting terms his appreciation of the services they had rendered.

These visits and messages were a source of gratification to the 13th, but nothing pleased them so much as the news, which filtered through from Scotland, that the Black Watch were adding to their

FESTUBERT, GIVENCHY AND PLOEGSTEERT

recruiting posters the simple phrase, "With which is allied the 13th Canadian Battalion, R.H.C." From the beginning the Canadians had received nothing but courtesy and assistance at the hands of the allied Regiment, nevertheless it is more than likely that the officers of the latter viewed with concealed misgivings the possibility that the untried troops from the Dominion might fail to come up to what was expected of a battalion with Black Watch traditions. If these apprehensions existed, as the Canadians suspected, they vanished in the blood and smoke of Second Ypres and for them the addition to the recruiting poster made honourable and sportsmanlike amend.

Ten days after their arrival in billets the Highlanders received orders to march once more. Parading at 7 p.m. on the 13th, the reconstructed Battalion headed south, marching all night and arriving at 2.30 a.m. at billets near Robecq. Much of this march, via Estaires, La Gorgue and Lestrem, was over new military roads which did not appear on the maps, but in spite of this the unit made reasonably good time.

May 15th was a busy day. Company inspections were ordered and much new equipment was issued to replace the losses in the recent battle. Considering the showing made at Bailleul, the good marching of the previous night and the smartness of the men at the company inspections, officers concluded that while the old Battalion would never be the same again, it was, at least, an efficient fighting unit once more. That this should be the case was just as well, for it soon became obvious that the Canadians were marching south with "dirty work" ahead.

On May 9th Sir John French had attacked the German front with the double object of securing positions on the Vimy and Aubers Ridges, which would threaten the Germans' hold on Lens, La Bassée and Lille, and at the same time preventing the enemy from withdrawing troops to reinforce their line farther south, where General Joffre and the French Army were pounding at the gates of Lens. This British attack, now known as the Battle of Aubers Ridge, had died down after several days of bitter fighting, during which the German lines had been driven back and badly bent, but never completely broken. Following the lull, the attack was now to be renewed and in the fighting to come the Canadian Division was to have a part.

Continuing their march on May 16th, the Royal Highlanders

steadily drew nearer to the scene of the new battle. On the 17th they occupied reserve trenches at Le Touret. These muddy ditches were shelled to some extent during the few hours that the 13th were in them, but no particular damage resulted and the Battalion moved back to spend the night in billets in Essars.

At 5 a.m. on the 19th "Fall in" was sounded and the Regiment advanced to Le Touret once more. Here the same muddy ditches were occupied for another period of several hours, at the end of which the Battalion, advancing as support to an attack, moved into trenches which had formed the British line previous to the opening of the battle. These were situated in front of a hamlet, which, in memory of troops who had previously occupied it, was known as Indian Village.

While in this location half the men were employed in strengthening the position, while the other half were engaged in burying dead, large numbers of whom mutely testified to the severity of the fighting in the recent advance. Incidentally, those of the Highlanders who had not previously done so, discarded their Ross rifles and equipped themselves with Lee-Enfields. The British carried these and scores were lying where they had dropped from the hands of their former owners. The exchange, therefore, was made without formality.

Meanwhile other battalions of the 3rd Brigade had taken over a section of the front and had been heavily engaged. On May 18th two companies of the 14th Royal Montreal Regiment and two companies of the 16th Canadian Scottish attacked and, despite heavy losses, pushed their assault to the boundaries of an orchard on La Quinque Rue which the enemy had placed in a state of defence. This Orchard was a veritable hornet's nest and it was at once obvious that a strong attack would be required to take it. Accordingly the companies of the 14th and 16th dug in and connected up with the Wiltshire Battalion on their right and the Coldstream Guards on the left. During the night the two companies of the 14th were withdrawn and at daybreak two fresh companies of the 16th replaced the original companies of their own battalion. The front vacated by the men of the 14th was filled by extending the Coldstream Guards on one flank and the two fresh companies of the Canadian Scottish on the other.

On May 20th orders were issued for an attack on the Orchard. Summarized, the instructions to the battalions of the 3rd Brigade

FESTUBERT, GIVENCHY and PLOEGSTEERT

were as follows: Two companies of the 16th Canadian Scottish and two companies of the 15th (48th Highlanders) were to assault the Orchard and a position extending to the right at 7.45 p.m. On the attack being carried through, the 13th Royal Highlanders of Canada were to take over the positions, consolidating and holding them. The 14th Royal Montreal Regiment was to be held in Brigade reserve. Engineer parties were to join the 13th in the work of consolidation. Simultaneously with the attack of the 15th and 16th, the 10th Canadian Battalion, of the 2nd Brigade, was to assault a fortified locality, known as K5.

In compliance with these orders, the 13th advanced from Indian Village at 7 p.m., Lieut. C. M. Maxwell being wounded by shell fire before the advance began. In this engagement the companies of the 13th were commanded respectively by Capts. K. M. Perry, E. M. Sellon, S. B. Lindsay and W. H. Clark-Kennedy, all of whom had taken part in the previous engagement at Ypres.

It was still daylight when the Battalion left its trenches and, as the only route by which the men could reach their objectives was along Prince's Road and up La Quinque Rue, or across open fields devoid of cover, losses on the way were seen to be inevitable. To reduce these as far as possible, the advance was made in single file.

Almost at once, however, the enemy spotted the move and opened a heavy fire with shrapnel. Coming up La Quinque Rue this fire struck the Battalion and men fell thick and fast. Early in the advance the Battalion suffered a severe loss when Capt. J. G. Ross, the Machine Gun Officer, was badly wounded. Before very long Lieuts. C. M. Horsey, I. M. R. Sinclair, G. W. R. Simpson, W. D. Smith and A. Worthington were also wounded. These, with numerous wounded of the other ranks, were picked up by stretcher bearers and carried back to Indian Village, where Capt. F. A. C. Scrimger, V.C., Medical Officer of the 14th Battalion, attended to their injuries. The dead it was impossible to remove till later on.

Meanwhile the companies of the 13th pushed up the Quinque Rue and reached the vicinity of the Orchard. Simultaneously the 16th Battalion launched their attack. Pushed with dash and energy, this drove the enemy to the extreme limits of the Orchard, whence he retired to a carefully prepared position in the rear.

As soon as the assault had reached its objectives, the companies of the 13th proceeded to take over. No. 1 Coy., plus one platoon of No. 2 Coy., reinforced the 15th Battalion in an old German communication trench, with their left resting on a road, which separated them from the base of the Orchard. The other three platoons of No. 2 Coy. proceeded direct through the Orchard and reported to the Officer Commanding the 16th. Lieut. H. R. Powell, commanding the first of these platoons, was ordered to place his men alongside the 16th. Powell discovered that the 16th were occupying the front of the Orchard only and that the farm buildings in the right front corner, as well as the right side of the Orchard, would have to be occupied, otherwise his right flank would be in the air and there would be a wide gap between his company and the old German trench held by No. 1 Coy.

Accordingly he ordered his men to dig in where his observations showed him that a line was necessary, informing Lieut. F. S. Mathewson, who had come up meantime, of what he was doing. Mathewson at once agreed to the plan and ordered his men to join Powell's in constructing and holding the new line. This necessitated a change in the arrangements for relieving the men of the 16th along the front of the Orchard. Word was accordingly sent back to Capt. Sellon, who arranged that No. 3 Coy. should come up and accomplish the relief in question.

Meanwhile No. 4 Coy., in support, had relieved a company of the 16th in shallow trenches to the left of the Orchard. To the left again, and somewhat in advance of this support position, was a Territorial battalion of the Black Watch, occupying front line trenches. Capt. Clark-Kennedy visited this battalion and made arrangements, as a result of which a long gap between their front and the left of No. 3 Coy's. front in the Orchard was closed.

All this time the enemy kept up heavy rifle and machine gun fire, while their flares lighted up the darkness and made the business of digging in very difficult. Shell fire was fairly heavy, which did not tend to make things easier.

Around the buildings in the corner of the Orchard No. 2 Coy. ran up against a problem which had not been foreseen, namely that the ground where they had taken their stand had once been the stable yard of the farm and was covered with a stone pavement. An advance, or retirement, was therefore desirable, but neither was possible, as even a short advance brought the men within bombing range of the new German position, while an equally short withdrawal placed the farm buildings where they blocked the field of fire.

FESTUBERT, GIVENCHY AND PLOEGSTEERT

Fortunately, at this stage, one of the farm buildings was found to contain a large amount of sand bag reinforcement. This was torn down and the bags used to construct isolated posts, which provided head cover. By morning, too, as the result of strenuous work, a trench about a foot deep had been dug in the stone pavement.

All this had not been accomplished without losses. Capt. Sellon was severely wounded about midnight and Lieut. Powell was killed. At first Powell was merely reported missing, as no one could be found who had actually seen him fall, or positively identified his body. Little hope that he had survived, however, could be indulged in. Somewhere along that hotly bombarded line it was presumed that he had fallen and, later, reports from men in hospital proved this correct. Lieut. Mathewson was also reported killed, but this was soon found to be a mistake.

Meanwhile parties of the Canadian Engineers, under Lieut.-Col. Wright, had arrived and were assisting in the work of consolidation. Col. Wright was killed while supervising the work of his men, but his splendid example was not in vain, for by day-break the position was consolidated, though the line was by no means continuous. In particular No. 2 Coy. had found it impossible to dig a trench across the road which separated the right of their three platoons from the left of the trench occupied by the remaining platoon and No. 1 Coy.

All day on May 21st the enemy kept the Orchard under heavy fire, wounding Lieut. A. M. Fisher, of No. 3 Coy. and inflicting considerable losses to the rank and file. In the afternoon they counter-attacked, but this was a weak effort and the Highlanders had little trouble in beating it back. Then, in front of No. 2 Coy., they tried a trick. All of a sudden a white flag was seen in the German trench and voices called out, "We want to surrender, come over and take us." When some of the men of No. 2 Coy. exposed themselves in answer to this request, a machine gun opened fire on them and caused several casualties, among these being Sergt. Hillier, who was killed while trying to prevent his troops from leaving their cover. Meanwhile, some of the Germans, who had also exposed themselves, were caught by the Highlanders' reply to the machine gun and amongst those seen to fall was the man carrying the white flag.

That night the Germans set fire to a large hay stack in No Man's Land, opposite the junction of Nos. 2 and 3 Companies.

ROYAL HIGHLANDERS OF CANADA

This burned for some time, the light seriously hindering the work of improving the position. In addition the enemy kept a machine gun trained on the road, where No. 2 Coy. was anxious to connect up with its remaining platoon and No. 1 Coy. A carrying party got across this road from No. 1 Coy. to No. 2 with rations, but they were unable to carry over any water.

In the meantime the light of the fire was proving of assistance to Lieut. W. S. M. MacTier, of No. 4 Coy., who had gone back to guide a detachment of the Royal Canadian Dragoons up to the Orchard from Indian Village. These troops were initiated by the Highlanders into the mysteries of work as infantry and into the details of swinging a pick and wielding a shovel. The Dragoons frankly admitted that they did not care for this sort of thing and preferred a war where they could use their horses, nevertheless they buckled to and rendered valuable assistance.

May 22nd was a fine day with a blazing hot sun, which proved trying to the men lying out with little shelter. No. 2 Coy. suffered particularly, as they had no water at all. In the afternoon, however, they got a double strand of German telephone wire across the road to No. 1 Coy. and by this means a number of bottles were dragged across with sufficient water to quench the burning thirst of the wounded and to relieve to some degree the parched throats of those who were still unhit.

Late that night, after two exceedingly trying days and nights, the 13th was relieved by the 3rd Battalion.

II

Following the relief by the 3rd Battalion, the companies of the Royal Highlanders marched independently to billets at Essars. This march was unpleasant, as the early part of it was harassed by shell fire, while the whole of it was accompanied by thunder, lightning and driving rain.

Four days were spent at Essars and the Battalion once more had time to realize the price that must be paid whenever it was heavily engaged. Roll call showed that ten officers were casualties, while losses in the ranks totalled 170.

Meanwhile the Battle of Festubert was drawing to a close. For some days attacks by British and Canadian units continued and achieved local successes in the face of almost insuperable difficulties. Courage and devotion were not lacking in these attacks, but artillery

FESTUBERT, GIVENCHY AND PLOEGSTEERT

support was, and soon it became evident that the operation as a whole must be put down as a costly failure. Aubers Ridge was not yet to pass into British hands. Accordingly, on May 25th, Sir John French issued the orders which brought the battle to a close.

On the same date the Royal Highlanders left billets in Essars and moved up to reserve trenches between Rue de l'Epinette and Rue du Bois. Two days later they relieved the 14th Battalion in the front line. On their first night in this position a wounded German was observed lying in front of No. 4 Coy's. trenches. Promptly a stretcher bearer of the 14th Battalion volunteered to go out and bring the wounded man in. While engaged in this daring piece of work the 14th man was fatally wounded and two stretcher bearers of the 13th who went to his assistance were also struck down. Four wounded men now lay where one had lain before and the trap seemed ready for further victims. Ignoring this aspect of the case, Capt. Clark-Kennedy and two of his men took up the work of rescue. Over the parapet they went and, reaching the wounded, got all four safely in without incurring any casualties themselves. Shortly after this incident Lieut. W. S. M. MacTier, of No. 4 Coy., was wounded by a rifle bullet through the ankle.

On May 29th Capt. G. E. McCuaig, who had been wounded at Ypres, rejoined the Battalion and took over the Adjutant's work from Lieut. H. D. Ives, who had been acting as Adjutant in his absence. With McCuaig came a number of new officers, amongst these being Lieuts. Bell, Moran, J. G. Walker, D. B. Donald and J. E. Christie. Of these Lieut. Bell was sent to No. 2 Coy., which was in support. Early next morning he was asleep in a dugout when a shell blew the place to bits and wounded him severely.

On the night of the 31st the Highlanders were relieved by the 2nd Gordons, of the 20th British Brigade. Relief was completed about 2 a.m. and the 13th then proceeded to Hinges, via Bethune and the tow path of the La Bassee Canal. Five days were spent in the billets and bivouacs of Hinges, during which platoon drills and company route marches were frequent. Lieuts. Peerless and Mingo joined the Battalion during this period, while commissions were granted to Private N. M. MacLean, Corp. B. M. Giveen, Private Eagle and Private F. J. Rowan.

On June 5th Lieut.-Col. Loomis and other officers reconnoitred a reserve position at Givenchy, north of the Canal, which, on the following day, the Highlanders took over from the 5th Canadian Battalion. June 7th and 8th were spent in this position and on the 9th the Battalion moved up and relieved the Royal Montreal Regiment in the front line. The following afternoon officers of No. 2 Coy., in support, were interested to observe the Prince of Wales passing their position and making his way forward. He was accompanied by a worried staff officer who was obviously remonstrating against any further advance. All protests fell on deaf ears, apparently, as the last No. 2 Coy. saw of the pair was when they disappeared up a communication trench towards the line.

This tour lasted three days and was comparatively quiet, though not entirely devoid of incident. Writing of it, a subaltern mentions that, "One night was quite lively. They had their barbed wire cut by our artillery, so all night we kept up a fairly heavy fire to keep them from repairing it. This seemed to annoy them, so they sent out a bombing party to a sap head and threw a few bombs at us. We replied with a machine gun and they went back. Then they turned a trench mortar on us and also gave us a little shelling, as well as rifle and machine gun fire. Altogether during an hour they used every implement of warfare, bar the bayonet and gas, and they didn't hit a man. It was really quite fun."

On the night of the 10th, the 4th Canadian Battalion relieved the 13th and the latter proceeded to billets in Essars. It rained during the relief and for a day after, but for the ten following days, during which the Battalion remained in billets, the weather was consistently "fine and clear." On June 15th orders were received to "stand to," ready to move at short notice, as the 1st Canadian Infantry Brigade was attacking at Givenchy and support might be required. Later this order was cancelled and the men resumed their work. Route marching, company training and battalion drill kept all ranks busy from dawn till dusk. Route marches were popular for once, however, as they invariably ended with a swim in the Canal.

Following this interval of training, the Highlanders moved up on June 22nd and relieved the 10th Canadian Battalion in the front line and support, in Givenchy sub-section B3. This tour proved to be short—only two days—but during the forty-eight hours considerable activity of a minor character prevailed. The enemy used trench mortars, rifle grenades and hand bombs with some effect, while the 13th snipers enjoyed unusually profitable shooting. A

FESTUBERT, GIVENCHY AND PLOEGSTEERT

patrol sent out to explore a vacant German trench encountered opposition, Lieut. Eagle, who was in command, and two of his scouts being wounded. Altogether 2 men were killed and 5 wounded during the tour. On completion of the tour, the 13th was relieved by the 2nd and 6th Gordons and proceeded to familiar billets in Essars, where two days were spent, chiefly in washing, cleaning and repairing equipment and in physical drill.

III

Following the conclusion of the action at Givenchy, the Canadian Division turned once more towards the north. Leaving Essars at 10.55 p.m. on June 26th, the 13th Battalion marched steadily all night and arrived at Neuf Berquin at half past four in the morning. Rain fell most of the night and the march was not particularly agreeable, but good time was made. Rain fell again during the continuation of the march that same evening, but this time the distance was shorter and billets at La Becque, near Bailleul, were reached by 11 o'clock. These were the same billets that the Battalion had occupied when refitting after the Second Battle of Ypres. Two days were spent here and on the 30th a move was made to billets one mile N.W. of Steenwerck.

July 1st, being Dominion Day, was a half holiday. A football match was organized between the two halves of the Regiment, while in addition a programme of sports was run off. Anyone strong in leg, arm or wind had a chance to distinguish himself in these, as the events included such varied items as throwing the cricket ball, kicking the football, sprints, dashes, putting the shot and a tug-of-war.

On July 2nd routine was resumed, varied, however, by a bathing parade to Bailleul. The next day Lieut.-Col. Loomis, Major Buchanan, the Company Commanders, Signalling and Machine Gun Officers reconnoitred a position which the Battalion was to occupy from Ploegsteert Wood (facing Warreton) to Wulverghem (opposite Messines). On July 5th the Royal Highlanders relieved the 1st Canadian Battalion in support, one man of the Machine Gun Section being killed by shellfire at Hyde Park Corner, while going up.

At 8 p.m. on the 9th the 13th Battalion completed relief of the 14th Battalion in the front line. One hour later two mines were exploded by the Canadian Engineers and a troublesome German post destroyed. Almost before the smoke of the explosion had cleared, a party, under the command of Capt. K. M. Perry and under the immediate control of Sergt. A. W. Ruston, went forward and occupied the craters, consolidating these and, in spite of heavy enemy fire, suffering no casualties. Four nights later the powers that be decided to blow two more mines on the Highlanders' front and again a party under Perry and Ruston consolidated. Smart work was shown in this respect, as again the party accomplished its difficult task without losing a man. One killed and ten wounded represented the total casualties of the five days. During this tour Lieut. Hugh Wallis, commissioned from the ranks of the Canadian Scottish, was posted to the 13th Battalion.

At 6 p.m. on the 14th, daylight relief being possible in this sector, the Royal Montreal Regiment took over the front and the Highlanders proceeded to billets in the Piggeries. These billets, as their name suggests, had previously been the abode of swine, but the Engineers had taken them in hand and converted them into billets. They weren't elaborate, but were comfortable and dry and quite acceptable to men whose days were often spent in much less agreeable places.

On the day following the arrival of the 13th at the Piggeries, Private E. Jolicoeur was wounded in the head by the accidental discharge of a rifle. First aid was at once given and the unfortunate man hurried to No. 1 Canadian Field Ambulance, but the wound proved fatal within an hour. The body was buried in the Military Cemetery at Hyde Park Corner.

On July 18th Holy Communion was celebrated by Canon Scott, after which the Battalion moved up and relieved the 14th in the front line. During the night a patrol, under Lieut. Rust and Corp. Wright, went out and examined the enemy wire. Continuing their investigations, this patrol advanced to within 15 yards of the German line, whence they brought back information of considerable value. During the three days of this tour the 13th did a great deal of work on the parapets. Enemy snipers were active, but secured few bull's eyes. One man was killed and four wounded.

On the 21st of the month the 4th Canadian Battalion relieved the 13th, the latter proceeding to huts at Aldershot Camp (S.W. of Neuve Eglise) in Divisional Reserve. During the week that followed large working parties were furnished by the Battalion to assist the Engineers, who were converting the "Plug Street" front into a veritable fortress. These parties were not popular, but the

FESTUBERT, GIVENCHY AND PLOEGSTEERT

men realized the value of strong positions and earned a reputation with the Engineers by their willingness and hard work. During this same week Major R. H. Jamieson, who had been wounded while commanding No. 2 Coy. during the Ypres battle, returned to the Battalion and assumed the duties of Paymaster.

On July 29th the Battalion vacated Aldershot Camp and again took up residence in the Piggeries. Working parties of two and three hundred men were supplied to the Engineers on several occasions during the next three days, while one day news was received that the Germans, not content with gas, had sprung a new form of "frightfulness" in the shape of liquid fire. Confidential reports indicated that this new weapon had been tried out against the British near Hooge, but had not been an entire success. "Jets 30 to 40 yards long issue from these flame throwers," the reports stated, "but the damage they cause is not severe. Surprise and panic would seem to be their chief danger."

Half past six on the night of August 2nd found the Battalion once more in the front line for a four day stay. Night patrolling of No Man's Land featured this tour and much valuable information was brought in. Contact with a German patrol was established on one occasion and bombs thrown by both sides. In this exchange Private E. Yorke was slightly wounded. On another occasion a new officer took out a patrol with the intention of surprising and capturing an enemy listening post thought to exist in a ruined house between the lines. In this case, however, the hunter was hunted and, surprised by a German bombing attack that came from goodness knows where, the patrol beat a hasty and not entirely dignified retreat.

At the end of this tour, the 13th was relieved by the 1st and 3rd Canadian Battalions and moved back to familiar quarters in Aldershot Huts. Here working parties were again furnished to the Engineers to carry on the business of making the "Plug Street" front exceedingly strong. On the night of the 8th Lieut.-Col. Loomis presided at a concert which the men enjoyed hugely and on the 10th he, with all the officers, N.C.O's. and 20 men from each company, attended a gas demonstration in the G.H.Q. 3rd Line trenches. After a lecture by an officer of the Scottish Rifles, all present donned gas helmets, with which the troops were now provided, and entered a trench where chlorine gas had been concentrated. None of the party suffered any ill effects and the efficiency of the helmets was clearly demonstrated, a point which up to this time had been the subject of doubt.

On the morning of August 12th Brig.-Gen. R. E. W. Turner, V.C., C.B., D.S.O., passed through the Battalion lines on his way to England to assume command of the 2nd Canadian Division, then about to join the 1st in France. As commander of the 3rd Brigade, Gen. Turner had earned an enviable military reputation and in addition had gained to an unusual degree the affection and regard of his men. Accordingly, the 13th cheered him heartily and bade him farewell with mingled feelings of regret at his departure and pleasure at the promotion that had come to him. After he had left, command of the Brigade was assumed by the Senior Battalion Commander, Lieut.-Col. R. G. E. Leckie, C.M.G., of the 16th Canadian Scottish. Simultaneously Col. Leckie received promotion to the rank of temporary Brigadier-General.

CHAPTER VI

Messines

The road that runs up to Messines
Is double-locked with gates of fire,
Barred with high ramparts, and between
The unbridged river, and the wire.

But we shall go up to Messines
Even thro' that fire-defended gate,
Over and thro' all else between
And give the highway back its state.
—J. E. STEWART.

I

ON August 15th, 1915, the 13th Battalion relieved the 10th Battalion and Canadian Cavalry Brigade in Trenches 135, 136 and 137, with headquarters at La Plus Douce Farm. This series of trenches was destined to see a great deal of the Royal Highlanders of Canada during the months that lay ahead and will be referred to frequently in the course of the present chapter. All unaware of this, however, the Battalion took over the trenches, effected some repairs to the parapets, suffered a few casualties—six to be exact—and handed over to the Royal Montreal Regiment at 6.10 p.m. on the 19th.

Billets at Courte Dreve Farm were occupied from the 20th to 24th and many working parties were supplied to the Engineers. On the 20th Major Buchanan left to command the 15th Battalion during the absence of Major Marshall, returning on the 23rd, in time to accompany his own Battalion into Trenches 135-137 on the 24th.

The relief on this occasion did not escape the notice of the enemy, who shelled the communication trenches in the vicinity of Ration Farm, wounding five men of No. 3 Coy. There were no further losses during the five day tour that followed, but on the 28th some excitement was caused when the Germans set fire to the grass between the lines. By this means they probably hoped to

ROYAL HIGHLANDERS OF CANADA

stop the Canadians from patrolling in No Man's Land at night, but if such was their purpose it failed completely of its object.

Relieved by the 14th Battalion on the night of August 29th, the Highlanders proceeded to Bulford Camp (Kortepyp Huts), near Neuve Eglise. Here on September 2nd General Plumer, commanding the 2nd Army Corps, inspected the Battalion and complimented the officers on the showing made.

On the following day the Highlanders took over Trenches 135-137 for another five day tour. Here a draft of 265 men was received from the 23rd Reserve Battalion in England. How welcome these men were may be judged by this extract from an officer's letter. "We received a draft of 265 men yesterday, which helps us a lot. For nearly four months we have been under strength, doing the work of a full battalion and, as there has been a devil of a lot of work to do, it has been mighty tough on the men. However, they have been most wonderfully willing and cheerful and, besides their fighting record, have earned the reputation with the Engineers of being the best working Regiment in the Division."

On arrival, the draft was placed temporarily under the command of Lieuts. Aitchison and Bott, who themselves had just reported from the Cadet School at G.H.Q. Later the newcomers were evenly divided between the companies. Battalion orders on the same date contained the announcement that Lieut. E. W. Waud was appointed Acting Quartermaster, vice Lieut. C. L. Cantley, transferred.

Their five day tour completed, the Highlanders handed over to the 14th once more and proceeded to billets at Courte Dreve. Large working parties were a feature of the next four days, these at one time or another being under the command of Capt. C. J. Smith and Lieuts. Aitchison, Bott, Rust, Brittan, Mingo, Macpherson, Mathewson and Greenshields, the last named now quite recovered from the wound received at Ypres.

At this time the announcement that Lieut.-Gen. E. A. H. Alderson had assumed command of the Canadian Army Corps signified to the men of the Canadian Division that a second Canadian Division had arrived in France. Simultaneously it was announced that Brig.-Gen. A. W. Currie, C.B., of the 2nd Brigade, had been promoted to Major-General to succeed General Alderson in command of what had hitherto been known in the field as *the* Canadian Division and would in future be referred to as the 1st.

MESSINES

Following this interesting announcement the Royal Highlanders entered the line for a short tour in Trenches 135-137. After three days they were relieved by the Canadian Cavalry Brigade and moved back to Aldershot Camp, whence, on September 20th, they marched to Lindenhoek and relieved the 2nd Cheshires and the 6th Welsh in the line. Headquarters were at Tea Farm. This move was made to facilitate the work of breaking in the new 2nd Canadian Division, units of which were on either side of the veteran 3rd Brigade during the days that followed.

From Sept. 20th to 24th the Battalion occupied this Lindenhoek front, being relieved by the 14th R.M.R. on the latter date and marching to billets in Locre. Proceeding on the 25th, the Battalion marched to Aldershot Camp, where the men were deeply interested in such news as reached them of British successes in the Battle of Loos. At 4.30 p.m. on the 26th they marched to Ploegsteert, "standing to" all day on the 27th and moving into the line at 7.30 that night to relieve the 6th Buffs, of the 35th British Brigade, who were proceeding south to take part in the new battle.

Six days were spent in the front line, during which instruction was given to officers and men of the 11th Lancs. Fusiliers, a unit just arrived from England. On the night of October 1st a patrol, under Lieut. B. M. Giveen of the 13th and Lieut. Gallagher of the Lancs., made an exhaustive examination of No Man's Land and the condition of the German wire. On October 3rd the Lancs. took over the front and the 13th moved to billets at Courte Dreve. At this time Capt. G. E. McCuaig took command of No. 2 Coy. and Capt. C. J. Smith assumed the duties of Battalion Adjutant.

II

On October 4th the Royal Highlanders again took over trenches 135, 136 and 137. From this time until the end of the year these trenches were held by the Battalion, alternating with the 14th Battalion R.M.R. Under the system then prevailing, four days constituted the regulation trench tour. Sometimes this was stretched to five and even six days to meet special circumstances, but four days was the accepted period in the front line, following which an equal time was spent in Brigade support, or reserve. The time out of the line, however, was not a period of rest. Working parties, consisting of every available officer and man, were called for night after night, while in the daytime work on the rear areas and preparations for the next tour kept the men from making up arrears of badly needed rest.

With almost clock-like regularity, then, the 13th during the months that followed spent four days in and four days out of the line. When in, they occupied the trenches already mentioned; when out, they were billeted at Courte Dreve, Red Lodge, or Kortepyp Huts. In the line, Battalion H.Q. was at Plus Douce Farm; two companies occupied the fire trenches, one was in support at Stinking Farm and one in Battalion Reserve at Plus Douce Farm, or Fletcher's Field.

While the sojourn of the 13th Royal Highlanders in this vicinity was not marked by any of those glorious exploits that add Battle Honours to the Regimental Colours, it ranks, nevertheless, as one of the Battalion's best feats of endurance. Properly to understand the hardships of this period and to appreciate the dogged courage by which they were overcome, a knowledge of the topography of the country is necessary. Roughly speaking, Trenches 135-137 occupied that part of the line which lay between the Wulverghem-Messines Road on the north and the Ploegsteert-Messines Road on the south. The front ran through the water-logged valley of the Douve and acted as a drain for Messines Ridge, occupied by the enemy, and for Hill 63 to the British rear. As a result of almost incessant rain, no amount of labour and revetting could prevent the trenches from falling in. Communication trenches, very necessary in a location such as this, where the enemy overlooks the country back of the front line, were practically impassable. Consequently, a network of tracks led overland through the all-pervading mud and were used by ration and fatigue parties instead of the flooded trench system.

The front line itself was a slimy ditch, where, at best, the men sank over their ankles and where, owing to the clinging powers of the local mud, an individual, once stuck, could release himself only with the greatest difficulty. It was not uncommon for men to sink to the waist in this muck and require assistance to get free. Deep dugouts were, of course, impossible, though "funk holes," dug in the side of the trench, were fairly numerous. These afforded little or no protection against missiles, but they did keep some rain off the men while sleeping.

In the memories of officers and men the endless monotony and physical hardships, the continuous fatigues and the appalling weather

MESSINES

of this period stand out so vividly as to overshadow the human enemy and all his works of destruction. Summing up warfare under such conditions, a French writer has given the following impression:—"More than attacks—more than visible battles—war is frightful and unnatural weariness, water up to the belly, mud and infamous filth—an endless monotony of misery, broken by poignant tragedies."

All during this period, however, the spirit of the 13th was in no wise subdued. Discipline was excellent and, to quote an officer, "the men had their tails up throughout." Casualties as the result of enemy action were not heavy, though each tour added a few names to the ever growing roll. Sickness, as was but natural, increased, though the total losses through illness were not serious. Influenza of a fairly severe type made its appearance, temporarily disabling several officers and a score or more of the men; other afflictions were of a similar nature and were directly attributable to the conditions under which the men lived. As a point of interest in this connection, it may be noted that when the Battalion, in November, changed over for the winter from the kilt to trousers the number of sick was appreciably increased.

On October 16th the 42nd Battalion, Royal Highlanders of Canada, arrived at the front and were initiated into the routine of trench warfare by their comrades of the 13th. The 42nd, then commanded by Lieut.-Col. G. S. Cantlie, had been raised by the 5th Regiment, Royal Highlanders of Canada, in Montreal, and was consequently a "sister" battalion of the 13th. Eventually the 42nd became a part of the 7th Brigade, 3rd Canadian Division, but pending the formation of this Division, they, with the Royal Canadian Regiment, the Princess Patricia's Canadian Light Infantry and the 49th Edmonton Battalion, served as Corps troops.

During the period that the 42nd was undergoing training by the 13th a most regrettable incident occurred when Capt. Leon Curry (42nd) and Capt C. H. Crowdy (13th) were killed by a trench mortar bomb which fell in the bay of their trench. The funeral of these two officers was held in Armentières some few days later. Both Battalions were out of the line at the time and joined, with their pipe bands, in according the dead officers full military honours.

On October 26th an aerial battle over the front line resulted in a German plane being brought down in rear of No. 4 Coy's. position.

ROYAL HIGHLANDERS OF CANADA

The pilot of this plane was dead, but an observer, severely wounded, was made prisoner and taken to Brigade H.Q. Capt. G. D. McGibbon, of No. 4 Coy., secured a trigger camera from the captured machine, which, by one of those queer strokes of fate, was also found to carry a Colt machine gun, belonging to the 14th Battalion and captured at Ypres. Following the landing of this machine the Germans shelled the wreck with high explosive, to destroy the plane and inflict casualties amongst any who might attempt to salvage it.

During November the routine already described continued. When out of the line, working parties were called for even more frequently and practically the whole Battalion, including officers, was out night after night. The nature of the soil and the steady rain rendered the work particularly exhausting, but it was urgent and could not be delayed, no matter how badly the men needed rest. The work, too, was not unattended by danger. On November 2nd the Officer Commanding the 1st Field Company, Canadian Engineers, reported that Lieut. J. E. Christie, of the 13th, had been wounded while attached to his Company, and other casualties occurred at intervals, though the total was not large.

Early in the month Lieut. P. N. MacDougall and Lieut. W. F. Peterman joined the Battalion and were given commands in No. 4 and No. 2 Companies respectively. Lieut. A. Routledge also joined at this time. About the middle of the month the Highlanders were much interested when the 7th British Columbia Battalion on the right of the 13th raided the enemy lines, inflicting losses and taking prisoners. This affair marked the revival and elaboration of a form of trench warfare employed with success by Indian battalions, near La Bassee, in 1914, and in which Canadian units from this time on were destined to become particularly adept.

Towards the end of the month, during the absence on leave of Brig.-Gen. Leckie, Lieut.-Col. Loomis assumed command of the 3rd Brigade, Major Buchanan taking over the 13th for the period of the Colonel's absence.

Early in December one of those little personal tragedies was reported when a private, absent without leave, was found drowned in the Canal near Armentières. Unimportant from a battalion point of view, this event is recorded in the diary without comment. The man's name, rank and regimental number are given and the fact that he was "found drowned." Very properly the diary has

MESSINES

no imagination. It neither speculates nor is given to conjecture. It states facts, and leaves all else to its readers. In this case the "facts" are all that is known.

Christmas arrived in due course and found the Battalion occupying its familiar front in Trenches 135-137. Nos. 1 and 4 Companies were in the front line, No. 2 Coy. in support at Stinking Farm and No. 3 Coy. in Battalion Reserve at Higginson Avenue. The weather was fair and mild and during the day there was little activity. There was no fraternizing with the enemy, such as had occurred at various points on Christmas, 1914, but, to quote a letter: "while there was no cessation of hostilities, the customary 'hate' was less intense."

Christmas dinner was, of course, somewhat of a problem. A dinner had been held on the 23rd, but everyone felt that some effort should be made to lift Christmas itself out of the rut and monotony of ordinary days. Company officers accordingly made such arrangements as were possible. In No. 2 Coy. the party was not held till 11 p.m., for reasons which the following letter makes obvious. "We had planned our dinner for 7 p.m., but about 6 a batman came in and said, 'Will you smell this meat, sir.' I didn't have to. Ugh! Our Christmas dinner! However, we waited till the rations came up at 9 o'clock and had our dinner at 11 p.m. Near our dugouts there is a farm, which, strange to say, has one room almost untouched. We blocked up the windows, etc., and had a fine place in which we cooked, not only our own dinner, but steaks and fried potatoes for the men. Then we got the whole Company in, gave them their hot meal and that day's rum as well as the next, so everyone felt fine. Then we had a sing-song and everyone enjoyed their Xmas."

Meanwhile in the front line all was quiet. In No Man's Land, however, a patrol, under Lieut. W. E. Macfarlane, and composed of Corp. A. A. Harper, Corp. E. H. Jarrett and 12 men, was busy. This patrol was out for nearly five hours. Lying close to the German line, they could at one time listen to the strains of Christmas celebrations from various directions. In the enemy trench a cornet player reminded his hearers of Christmases in pleasanter surroundings, while from the farm house, where No. 2 Coy. was feasting, came the sound of voices singing the familiar words of "Loch Lomond." Far to the rear, too, from behind Hill 63, the pipers of the Canadian Scottish could be heard hard at it.

ROYAL HIGHLANDERS OF CANADA

Shortly before midnight another patrol proceeded into No Man's Land to gather information. This party was 16 strong and was commanded by Lieut. J. H. Lovett. About 12.50 a.m. the patrol was challenged in German and fire opened on it from behind a hedge. Reply was at once made and groans suggested that one of the enemy was hit. Lovett's party suffered no losses.

Patrolling continued to be a feature of this 5-day tour. On the night of the 26th Macfarlane and his party went out at 6 p.m. and remained out till 11. Lovett and his party then took up the work and patrolled for several hours. No enemy patrols were encountered. On the following night patrols were out constantly from 6.30 o'clock till 5 o'clock in the morning. These worked in regular two hour "shifts," with an hour, or half an hour, in between. Lovett was out with seven men from 6.30 till 8.30. Corp. F. J. Reid went out with eight men at 9 p.m. and remained out till 11 p.m. At midnight Macfarlane took out eight men and patrolled till 2 a.m. At 3 o'clock this party went out again and remained out till nearly dawn. Enemy patrols, as on the previous night, were conspicuous only by their absence.

III

New Year's Eve, 1915, found the Royal Highlanders in billets at Red Lodge. The surroundings were not attractive, but every effort was made to make the occasion as agreeable as possible. Regret was mingled with all gaiety, however, as at midnight Lieut.-Col. F. O. W. Loomis, D.S.O. bade the Battalion farewell, as he was leaving in the morning to assume command of a Reserve Brigade in England. In accordance with custom the Colonel visited each hut where a celebration was in progress and said good-bye individually to all present. Col. Loomis had rendered devoted and conspicuous service while in command of the 13th and his promotion to command a brigade could not have been long delayed, nevertheless the bond between him and his officers and men was strong and deep regret on both sides featured his departure. It was with pride, however, that the Highlanders followed his career during the years that followed. From Brigadier-General he rose to the rank of Major-General, in command of the 3rd Canadian Division; he was created a Knight Commander of the Bath and a Companion of the Order of St. Michael and St. George. In addition he received from the French Government the Légion

MESSINES

d'Honneur (Croix d'officier). As each of these honours fell to his lot the Highlanders rejoiced sincerely. When he was wounded at Vimy Ridge, they felt anxiety until assured that the injury was not serious. On his departure he handed over the Battalion to Major V. C. Buchanan, who, since the death of Major Norsworthy, had filled the post of second-in-command. Buchanan's place was in turn filled by Major G. E. McCuaig, while Capt. I. M. R. Sinclair, fully recovered from the wound received at Festubert, took over command of No. 2 Coy. On January 4th Lieuts. MacDougall and Routledge were transferred back to the 42nd Battalion, R.H.C. Lieut. Routledge was wounded the following autumn and died of his wounds on October 23rd, to the deep regret of both the 13th and 42nd.

During January, 1916, the Royal Highlanders continued to alternate with the 14th Battalion in the front line and reserve, the only change being that their front was in Trenches 136-141, instead of the old familiar 135-137. Patrols were again a feature of these tours, Lieut. Macfarlane and his party combing No Man's Land at all hours of the night. Occasionally these patrols were fired at, or bombed, but no enemy patrols were actually encountered. To all intents and purposes the Canadian mastery of No Man's Land was complete.

On January 12th a diversion from the monotony of trench life was caused by a fire which broke out in St. Quentin's Farm at 5 a.m. Flames rose thirty feet in the air and the sight was made more spectacular by the explosion of a large quantity of rifle ammunition and some bombs. This farm was situated to the left of the position occupied by the 13th and was in the possession of the 16th Battalion. Fortunately few of its occupants were injured.

On January 19th the Battalion was pleased by the announcement that Major W. H. Clark-Kennedy had been awarded the D.S.O. Clark-Kennedy had left the 13th to take a post on the staff of the 3rd Brigade some months before this date, but the Highlanders still claimed him as their own and, as in the case of Col. Loomis, followed with pride the steps of his distinguished career. He held various appointments during the years that followed and became, eventually, Lieut.-Col., Commanding the 24th Battalion, Victoria Rifles of Canada. He was awarded the C.M.G., a bar to his D.S.O. and the French Croix de Guerre. Then, in 1918, during the "Hundred Days," he won the Victoria Cross. On the same date that

ROYAL HIGHLANDERS OF CANADA

Clark-Kennedy's D.S.O. was announced, further distinction came to the Battalion when Sergt.-Major Neil Osborne, Lance-Sergt. Jones, Corp. O. B. Krenchel and Private F. Ableson were awarded the D.C.M.

With the advent of February the long series of trench tours was interrupted and the Battalion proceeded to rest billets, near Bailleul. Relieved on the evening of the 1st by the 5th Canadian Mounted Rifles, the Highlanders spent the night at Red Lodge. Parading at 5 o'clock the following morning they marched towards Bailleul, arriving at their billets some five hours later. Here they remained for three full weeks, "resting," technically, but actually busily employed. On the 3rd of the month a draft of 46 N.C.O's. and men was received and allotted to the companies. On the 4th and 5th passes were issued to a large number of the men to visit Bailleul, where they might find entertainment suited to their various tastes and inclinations. On the 8th General Alderson inspected the men, who were drilling by companies. On the 9th physical drill and company practice in assault filled the morning, while in the afternoon parties of 100 followed one another in rapid succession to the baths in the Asylum at Bailleul. The next day was largely devoted to inspections. Major Buchanan gave the Battalion a thorough going over, after which the men were inspected by Field Marshal Lord Kitchener, who was accompanied by Generals Plumer, Alderson and Currie.

On the day following Major Buchanan received his promotion to the rank of Lieutenant-Colonel. News of this promotion, though expected, was received with genuine pleasure by all ranks of the Battalion. Lieut.-Col. V. C. Buchanan had served with the 13th from the beginning and at all times had commanded the respect and affection of his officers and men. Towards the latter he invariably exhibited a firm, but kindly and sympathetic interest. Of his officers he expected a high sense of duty and self sacrifice comparable to his own. As an actual instance of this, it is recorded that at about this time when new leather coats were issued from stores, a junior officer, wearing one, was interrogated by Col. Buchanan as to whether all the men of his platoon were similarly equipped. On receiving a negative reply, the C.O. ordered the junior to take the coat off and to see to it in the future that his men were equipped with any article before he drew one for himself.

MESSINES

On February 13th and 14th the men were inoculated. On the 15th and 17th the whole Battalion, including the Grenade Section, Machine Gunners, Stretcher Bearers and Signallers, practised attacking trenches.

On the latter date Brig.-Gen. R. G. E. Leckie, C.M.G. was wounded and command of the 3rd Brigade passed temporarily to Lieut.-Col. Marshall, O.C. the 15th Battalion (48th Highlanders), who continued to command until relieved by a senior officer, Brig.-Gen. G. S. Tuxford, C.M.G.

Divine Service and Holy Communion, celebrated by Major McGreer, featured the 20th. Route marches, bayonet drill, target shooting, lectures, reconnaissance and the inevitable working parties kept the men busy and filled in the time not already accounted for.

On February 22nd the Battalion vacated the rest billets near Bailleul and moved to Red Lodge, as Brigade Reserve. Coincident with this move, news began to arrive of the battle which had opened at Verdun. After five days at Red Lodge, during which working parties were large and frequent, the Highlanders moved up into the line. Trenches 136-140 were occupied on this occasion and the routine of the previous autumn and early winter was resumed. Battalion Headquarters was moved, however, from Plus Douce Farm to Fisher's Place.

On the whole the front was more active than when the Highlanders had last visited it. Artillery fire was heavier and Lieut. Macfarlane found that his control of No Man's Land was no longer undisputed. Rifle and machine gun fire and trench mortar shelling were also more continuous. On February 29th aircraft were active all morning, while both sides shelled heavily in the afternoon. On the night of March 2nd Macfarlane and a patrol established contact with an enemy patrol, whom they bombed and forced to retire. Two nights later the Battalion was relieved and proceeded to Kortepyp Huts, where several promotions were announced, Lieut. F. S. Mathewson becoming Captain, vice Capt. G. E. McCuaig, promoted; Capt. K. M. Perry becoming Major, vice Major V. C. Buchanan, promoted, and Lieut. J. D. Macpherson becoming Captain, vice Capt. K. M. Perry, promoted. At the same time Capt. E. W. Waud was transferred from No. 1 to No 4 Coy.

On March 10th the Battalion entered Trenches 136-140 for a 7-day tour. On the night of the 11th a patrol, under Lieut. Macfarlane, encountered an enemy patrol, which showed fight. The

ROYAL HIGHLANDERS OF CANADA

Highlanders' patrol was very willing and attacked without delay, forcing the Germans back with bombs and rifle fire. Two of the enemy were wounded, as were two of the 13th patrol. On the following night a German patrol was again encountered in the same vicinity. This patrol was attacked and one man wounded. A German rifle, cap and pair of mittens were picked up where the wounded man had apparently dropped them.

The 14th Canadian Battalion relieved the 13th on the night of March 17th, the companies of the Highlanders moving out independently to billets at Red Lodge, where working parties were once more the order of the day.

CHAPTER VII

Hill 60, The Bluff and Mount Sorrel

> In Flanders fields the poppies blow
> Between the crosses, row on row,
> That mark our place; and in the sky
> The larks, still bravely singing, fly
> Scarce heard amid the guns below.
> —John McCrae.

I

WHEN the trees began to bud and the increased heat of the sun proclaimed to the men of the Canadian Divisions that the spring of 1916 was at hand, the long monotony of trench tours on the Messines front came to an end. On March 17th the Corps began to move north and exchange places with the British V. Corps, which was holding the southern curve of the Ypres Salient. This move was completed on April 8th, the actual change in command of the fronts taking place four days earlier.

When spring became a reality, therefore, the whole Corps was up in the Salient, holding a position only a few miles from the spot where the 1st Division had withstood its fiery test in April of the previous year. Much water had flowed beneath the bridges since those days, but the Salient was the Salient still—a place of deservedly evil reputation, where hurricane bombardments swept out of a cloudless sky, where bloody encounters were the rule rather than the exception and where death was ever present, or just around the corner.

Soon after arrival the 2nd Division became involved in an engagement, as dour and bitterly fought as any that had marked the war up to this time. It lasted for a month, during which the contesting lines swayed backward and forward, in and out of a series of mine craters at St. Eloi. Thousands of men died in this battle and their mortal remains were swallowed up in the wreckage, ruin and indescribable mud. In the end the 2nd Division was blasted out of the positions it had held with such extraordinary tenacity, but these were so shattered and devastated that the enemy found it well nigh impossible to occupy them. The Craters, therefore, became for the most part a No Man's Land, the last resting place of many brave men and the haunt of occasional prowling patrols. For the second time the Salient had given the men from Canada a bloody welcome.

While these events were taking place on the 2nd Division's front, the units of the other Canadian Divisions had one by one been transferred northward. On March 23rd the 13th Battalion, Royal Highlanders of Canada, in billets at Red Lodge, was relieved by the 9th Royal Sussex Regiment and marched at night to Meteren, where four days were spent in company training and route marching. Much time was also devoted to repairing clothing, which badly needed attention after the hard service of the winter months. Company commanders, on the first day at Meteren, were ordered to pay particular attention to the condition of their men's feet, which, as the result of softening from months of mud and water, had caused much discomfort during the long march from Red Lodge.

Continuing the move on the morning of the 28th, the Highlanders, together with the other units of the 3rd Brigade, passed through Bailleul and on to Locre, the pipe band leading the way. A brigade march, when accomplished in the daytime, always presents an inspiring sight. On reaching the top of a hill the men could see stretching back for miles the long lines of the battalions, moving in column of route and twisting like an enormous snake in and out amongst the hills. At 2 p.m. the 13th reached their destination, which proved to be Dickebusch Huts. Here the Battalion settled down and promptly took advantage of the hours before dark to start baseball games and impromptu sports. Late in the afternoon passes arrived for two officers and seventeen men to go on leave. This brought up a serio-comic point, as the Battalion was in "trews" and several of the men stated quite flatly that they had no desire to visit England unless they could do so dressed in the kilt that was the proper uniform of a Royal Highland battalion. An appeal was made to Lieut.-Col. Buchanan and he, sensing the Regimental pride that lay behind the request, promptly ordered the Transport Officer to send back some 18 miles to the place where the kilts were stored and to bring up a sufficient number to equip all the party going on leave. The Transport had had a hard day, nevertheless the kilts were duly produced before the leave party set out at 11 p.m.

HILL 60, BLUFF AND MT. SORREL

Looking back on the war, it seems hard to realize that steel helmets were not in use from the beginning. No one had foreseen the necessity for these, but experience taught that thin steel would deflect shrapnel and save many valuable lives. Accordingly steel helmets were adopted by all the armies and the British Army in the field was equipped with them at about this time. On March 30th the company commanders of the 13th were instructed to see that all N.C.O's. and men were so equipped before moving into the line that same night.

Parading in front of Dickebusch Huts at 6 p.m., the Battalion proceeded to Café Belge, where it was met by guides of the 6th Northumberland Fusiliers, who led the way to Transport Farm, whence trench guides conducted the companies to their individual locations. The front taken over on this occasion stretched from Trench 37 left to Glasgow Cross Roads (exclusive). This position was flanked on the right by a railroad cutting, which ran through Hill 60 from the Canadian to the German lines. On the left flank was the 16th Battalion, connecting up with the 3rd Canadian Division, which, for the first time, was taking its place in line as a unit of the Canadian Corps. Nos. 1 and 2 Companies occupied the front line, supplying their own immediate supports; No. 3 Coy. was in support and No. 4 Coy. in reserve at Larchwood Dugouts. Battalion Headquarters was in dugouts in the Railway Embankment.

In this position the Battalion remained till the night of April 3rd, when it was relieved by the 14th Canadian Battalion. During the tour in the line there was considerable artillery activity and a general "liveliness" that had been missing on the Messines front, where weather and ground conditions had proved the principal enemy. Here, too, mining and counter mining work was in full swing and the front line companies were called on to supply parties to assist the Tunnellers. Contrary to expectations, this work rather appealed to the men, who liked the idea of going down into a mine shaft that led beneath the German lines.

A feature of this front which struck all ranks very forcibly was that the Germans had secured complete ascendency in the matter of sniping. Coming from the Messines front, where the ascendency had been their own, the Canadians bitterly resented this German superiority and took prompt measures to bring it to an end. New and carefully concealed sniping posts were built at night

ROYAL HIGHLANDERS OF CANADA

and picked shots detailed to them, with the result that by the end of the tour the German superiority was less noticeable. When the Canadian batteries arrived in the Salient, they were more active in retaliation and counter-battery work than their predecessors had been and greatly helped the infantry to put the triumphant Hun in his proper place. Casualties in the 13th during this tour amounted to 5 killed and 15 wounded, amongst the latter being Coy. Sergt.-Major Race, of No. 4 Coy., who was wounded on the night of April 3rd while taking out men to guide in the relieving Battalion.

From April 4th to 8th the Battalion occupied Dickebusch Huts. On April 6th the Huts were shelled, Privates Sherwood and McKay being killed and one other wounded. Further casualties were avoided by the prompt action of Lieut.-Col. Buchanan, who, at the first shell, ordered the men to vacate the huts and scatter in the adjoining fields. As a precaution in case the shelling should be repeated large working parties were employed on the 7th in digging shelter trenches, also in repairing the damage the shells had caused. That same afternoon passes to visit Poperinghe were granted to 25% of the officers and 5% of the men. In view of the fact that pay day had just occurred, those who secured passes were the envy of their less fortunate comrades.

After four days at Dickebusch Huts, the Battalion moved to Divisional Reserve in the Hop Factory, south of Poperinghe Station. Here, on the 9th, Divine Services were held for both Protestants and Roman Catholics, after which passes to Poperinghe were issued to 20% of the Regimental strength. One officer, writing home, describes the chief feature of the day in Poperinghe as follows: "To-day, Sunday, I saw a wonderful sight. We are billeted in a fair sized town, well back, and the massed fife and drum bands of the Guards Division played 'Retreat.' There were a couple of thousand troops in the Square listening—our Brigade and Guardsmen. I was never so proud of our men as when I saw them alongside the Guards. They showed the latter that the Guards aren't the only smart troops in the field." On another evening the massed pipe bands of the 3rd Canadian Brigade and the Scots Guards, under the leadership of Pipe-Major D. Manson, of the 13th, played "Retreat" and made a most creditable showing. Protection against enemy aeroplanes was afforded to the thousands who attended this concert by British scouts who circled overhead.

On April 11th bayonet exercise, musketry practice and gas hel-

HILL 60, BLUFF AND MT. SORREL

met drill took up the Battalion's time. In the evening Poperinghe was heavily shelled and a number of civilians killed. There were no casualties in the 13th. Measles broke out during the Battalion's stay at the Hop Factory, but prompt measures checked the disease and no drastic steps were necessary. On the 14th a party of six officers and three hundred men went forward at 7 p.m. to assist the Engineers in burying cable. This party worked all night and returned to billets at 3.30 in the morning.

While this was the most important feature of the eight days at Poperinghe from a military point of view, those interested in sports will recall with enthusiasm that the Battalion football team, then at its very best, achieved a notable success in defeating the team of the 1st Coldstream Guards. Rugby enthusiasts will likewise recall the hard fought contest between the officers and men, while those whose interest was more for things theatrical will not soon forget the excellent soldiers' troupe, "The Follies," which helped so materially to make the stay in Poperinghe enjoyable.

II

On April 15th reveille sounded at 6 a.m. and physical training occupied the time from 6.30 to 6.45. Holy Communion was celebrated at 9 a.m. and the day was spent in cleaning up billets preparatory to a tour in the trenches. On this occasion the Royal Highlanders paraded at 6.30 p.m., marched to R.E. Dump and proceeded thence by tram line to Woodcote House, where trench guides were waiting to show the way to the new position.

This position, known as "The Bluff," calls for some description. The Bluff itself was a long mound of earth, thrown up during the construction of the Ypres-Comines Canal. It ran parallel to the Canal on the north, or left, side. The opposing lines were astride the Canal, it must be understood, but that part of the British line taken over by the 13th was entirely on the left bank. In other words the Canal formed the Battalion's right flank. The front was not a connected line, but a series of positions joined together by roundabout communication trenches. In that side of the Bluff next the Canal were two tiny trenches, one behind the other, known respectively as "New Year Trench" and "New Year Support." Opposite these, on the side of the Bluff away from the Canal, was a longer trench, which, from its somewhat curved shape, was called "The Loop." Some distance to the left of the Loop again were

ROYAL HIGHLANDERS OF CANADA

"The Pollock" and "The Bean," two very exposed trenches, one in rear of the other. Between the Loop on the one side and the Bean and Pollock on the other ran "International" trench, which, as the result of many fierce struggles and bombardments was almost obliterated and altogether impassable. Communication between these positions was possible, therefore, only by using the roundabout communication trenches already mentioned.

At the forward end of the Bluff itself was a large crater; from there an exposed path led up to Thames Street, a deep communication trench following the top of the Bluff to "Gordon Post," whence it was possible to reach Battalion Headquarters, still further back, without going below ground. One tunnel cut transversely through the Bluff 125 yards from the front line, and another 650 yards further back; these connected with a complicated system of mine galleries and dugouts.

On the night of April 15th, when the Royal Highlanders took over this position from the Royal Montreal Regiment, No. 1 Coy., under Capt. M. Greenshields, occupied front line trenches extending to the left of the Pollock and the Bean; No. 2 Coy., under Capt. I. M. R. Sinclair, occupied New Year Trench, New Year Support and Gordon Post, with 3 small posts of 19 bombers in all in the Crater; No. 3 Coy., under Capt. H. D. Ives, took over the Loop and adjoining trenches, while No. 4 Coy., under Capt. G. D. McGibbon, occupied the Pollock and the Bean. Battalion Headquarters, as has been stated, was established in somewhat flimsy dugouts in the north bank of the Bluff.

Shortly after dawn on the 16th, Major G. E. McCuaig, who was in command of the Battalion during the absence on leave of Lieut.-Col. V. C. Buchanan, was forcibly reminded that this was an "active" sector when a sniper spotted him making a tour along the Loop and put a bullet in and out of his steel helmet, inflicting a slight wound. As a result of this tour McCuaig made a few minor changes in the dispositions of the companies, utilizing the two ends of the emergency tunnel through the Bluff to shelter parties who could be used to reinforce the front line or deliver counter attacks as might be required.

During April 16th there was artillery activity on both sides. In the morning the enemy fired about thirty rounds of high explosive into a trench on No. 3 Coy's. front, smashing in the parapet, burying a machine gun and causing several casualties, while later in

HILL 60, BLUFF AND MT. SORREL

the day an automatic trench thrower projected a series of bombs into Hedge Row, a trench held by No. 4 Coy. Here, however, the damage was slight. Casualties for the day totalled 3 killed and 6 wounded.

For the next forty-eight hours there was considerable shelling, counter-shelling and sniping. To the south of the Canal, the 2nd Division front received a severe shelling on the 17th. During the two days in question the 13th had 5 men killed and 16 wounded.

On April 19th, late in the afternoon, the enemy opened a heavy trench mortar bombardment of the Pollock, the Bean and other trenches in the same vicinity, also of the Crater, with the result that communication between Nos. 1 and 4 Companies was severed almost at once. At 7.45 p.m., after firing a large number of green signal rockets and after about fifteen minutes of extraordinary quiet, the trench mortar bombardment of the Pollock and the Bean was superseded by an intense artillery bombardment of the whole front. Simultaneously the enemy opened a heavy fire on the front of the 2nd Division to the south.

For an hour and a half the 13th front was subjected to a whirlwind bombardment, after which the barrage was lifted and considerably slowed down. At this stage a party of approximately 25 Germans effected an entrance into the Crater, the small garrison of which had suffered severely during the bombardment. With all their reserve bombs buried by shell fire and with no other means of resistance, four wounded men in No. 1 Post were made prisoner. The only unwounded man escaped and made his way to New Year Trench, reporting to No. 2 Coy. what had occurred. After cleaning up No. 1 Post, the Germans proceeded to No. 2, where they captured two or three wounded men, the others being killed. Proceeding to No. 3 Post, the enemy at last encountered opposition. Here two men were left unwounded and these put up a stubborn fight, killing the officer of the attacking party and driving off his men. Later the Germans returned with a lamp to search for the body of their officer, but were again driven off by the same two men, who threw all their remaining bombs. The anxiety of the Germans to recover the body was explained later when it was found that this young subaltern of the 123rd German Grenadier Regiment had carried into action on his person complete orders for the occupation of the Highlanders' line.

Owing to the isolated position of the Crater, details of what

ROYAL HIGHLANDERS OF CANADA

was transpiring there were quite unknown at Battalion, or even Company, Headquarters. When telephone lines were cut to all stations, except Gordon Post, McCuaig, who feared that the bombardment would be used to cover something in the nature of an attack, ordered Capt. Sinclair to send forward a strong party to defend the crest of the Bluff at all costs. This party, which was gallantly led by Lieut. A. W. Aitchison, advanced under heavy fire and suffered sharp losses. On arriving at the crest of the Bluff Lieut. Aitchison was informed by Capt. Mathewson, in New Year Trench, of what had happened in the Crater. New Year itself had been heavily shelled and none of the depleted garrison could be spared to hold the Crater. Accordingly, as soon as the Canadian artillery barrage was lifted off the Crater, Aitchison led his party forward and occupied it. For his courage in leading his party through the enemy barrage and for his work in occupying the Crater, he was awarded a well deserved M.C.

Investigation now showed that the Battalion's heaviest losses had occurred in the Pollock and the Bean during the trench mortar bombardment early in the evening. The dead and wounded of No. 4 Coy. were strewn along these trenches, which were battered beyond all recognition. Buried in the ruins of his concrete dugout was Capt. G. D. McGibbon, the Company Commander, who died shortly after being released from the wreckage which pinned him down.

Evacuation of the dead and wounded was difficult, as the mud in some places was very deep, especially near the Loop. Here a man would sink up to his thighs in a few moments. As always, though, the stretcher bearers gave unstintingly of their best and, though the evacuation of a single case sometimes took hours, no wounded man was left a moment longer than was necessary. That the Canadian Artillery retaliated successfully was proved next day when observers reported that many wounded Germans were carried out from their front line. Apparently these had been massed ready to occupy the Highlanders' line had the raid on the Crater provided a satisfactory opportunity, and had been caught by the counter barrage which the Canadian guns laid down.

Amongst the wounded in the 13th were Capt. W. F. Peterman, Lieut. F. J. Rowan and Lieut. E. W. Mingo, all of No. 3 Coy. Of these, the last named, who was hit while on a reconnaissance, showed courage in getting back with his report after being wounded. Lieut. J. H. Lovett was also wounded, while Capt. H. D. Ives, O.C.

HILL 60, BLUFF AND MT. SORREL

No. 3 Coy., was blown up and badly shocked by a bursting shell. At Gordon Post Lieut. W. E. Macfarlane was knocked unconscious by a heavy shell, which exploded within a few feet of his head. This occurred at about 10 p.m. and Macfarlane did not regain consciousness until 8 o'clock on the following morning. When he did come to, it was suggested that he go out to hospital, but he refused to consider the proposal and insisted upon doing his turn of duty that same afternoon.

At the very height of the bombardment a runner wormed his way through the barrage and reported to Battalion H.Q. with a message which, it seemed, was urgent. On opening the envelope, officers were amazed to find that it contained a routine order concerning the detailing of two men to attend a course at the Scout School. When the barrage was lifted off the 13th front at about 9.15 p.m., urgent calls were at once sent out for working parties to repair the battered trenches. These were quickly supplied by other battalions of the 3rd Brigade, under the personal command of Lieut.-Col. Marshall, of the 15th (48th Highlanders), and under the supervision of Major Fell and Lieut. E. P. Fetherstonhaugh, of the Canadian Engineers. Working at high pressure all night, these parties had the line in reasonably good shape before dawn.

Writing of the bombardment and of the defence of the Crater in a letter, an officer of the Battalion refers with pride to the splendid behaviour of the men. "It was," he says, "the most intense bombardment we have had yet. Our men were simply wonderful. Ever since our old Regiment was cut up last year we have all been saying that the new men were not a patch on the old ones. This affair showed us how wrong we were. It was the old 13th all over again—right there in a pinch."

On the following day the 3rd Brigade Staff offered to have the 14th Battalion relieve the 13th for the remainder of the regular 8-day tour. The Officer Commanding the 13th expressed his appreciation of this offer, but stated that the Royal Highlanders preferred to remain until their tour was completed. An offer of the 14th Battalion to lend the 13th several officers to replace casualties was gratefully accepted. During the remainder of the tour the front was "active," but there was no repetition of the hurricane bombardment of the 19th. Lieut.-Col. Buchanan came back from leave and took over from Major McCuaig.

On April 22nd, the anniversary of the Battalion's first great fight at Ypres, Lieut. C. M. Horsey, an original officer who had rejoined after being wounded at Festubert in May, 1915, was killed while acting in the capacity of Brigade Stokes Gun Officer. Altogether the casualties of the Battalion from the beginning of the tour up to the night of April 23rd, when it was relieved by the 14th Battalion, totalled 9 officers and 164 men. Of these, 2 officers and 36 men were killed, 8 men were missing, 2 officers and 12 men were suffering from severe concussion, while the balance of the number were wounded. In addition to these the Highlanders learned with regret that Lieut. Peerless and Lieut. Curzon Morrow, both former members of the 13th, had been killed while serving with other units.

III

When the 14th took over the Bluff Sector, the 13th moved to Dickebusch Huts, the arrival at this spot at 4 a.m. on the 24th being marked by an enemy air raid, which, fortunately, did little damage. Here the Battalion remained for over a week, special attention being paid to getting the men's feet in good condition after the mud of the trenches. On the 25th Lieut. C. D. Craig, formerly Pay Sergeant, was appointed Paymaster of the Battalion to succeed Major R. H. Jamieson. At night, on the same date, a working party of four officers and two hundred men proceeded to the front line to assist the Engineers. Similar, and even larger, parties were provided on the nights of the 26th, 27th and 30th. On April 26th a Roman Catholic service was held in the Officers' Mess, Father Killoran officiating. On the following day winter was officially admitted to be over, trousers were turned into stores and kilts were issued to the men once more.

At 7.30 p.m. on May 1st the Battalion left Dickebusch Huts and proceeded to Dominion Lines, arriving an hour and a half later. Seven days were spent in this location, featured on May 4th by a working party of 10 officers and 500 men to assist the Engineers in burying cable; on the 5th by an inspection by General Currie, who complimented the men on their steadfastness at the Bluff; on the 7th by another working party of 8 officers and 250 men to bury cable; and on the 8th by the arrival of a draft of reinforcements from England. Included in this were Lieuts. Gibson, Melrose, Roach, Prosser, Selby, Green, Brown and D. R. M. McLean.

On the night of May 9th the Battalion moved up and took over Trenches 45 to 51 from the 4th Canadian Battalion. This sector

HILL 60, BLUFF AND MT. SORREL

was on the German side of Square Wood and Armagh Wood, with the left flank on the high ground, known as Mount Sorrel, and the right flank on Hill 60. It was a particularly black night when the relief took place and the maze of old trenches, wire and uprooted trees made matters difficult, nevertheless the relief was completed at 1.20 a.m. without casualties. The fact that the front line trenches smelt most unpleasantly of high explosive, however, gave fair warning, had any been needed, that the sector was not to be regarded as a "quiet" one.

Daylight revealed the fact that the front line trenches were rather badly battered and that a long stretch of trench, completely broken down, separated the positions of the two front line companies, rendering communication difficult. The reserve trenches in Armagh Wood and Square Wood were in better condition, while in many places the long grass and the bright scarlet of the famous Flanders poppies made the scene not altogether unattractive. For the first few days of the tour the 42nd Battalion, Royal Highlanders of Canada, held the 13th's left flank. This was the first occasion that the sister battalions had served side by side.

Observation from this series of trenches was excellent and, almost for the first time in their career, the Highlanders found themselves overlooking the enemy lines. Lieut. B. M. Giveen, the Battalion Bombing Officer, was quick to take advantage of this situation, hammering the Germans with rifle grenades whenever the moment seemed auspicious.

This same officer and Major McCuaig took up a position in the front line one night to witness the action of a cement bomb, the invention of the Bombing Sergeant, which was to be propelled by a trench catapult into the enemy lines. At a given signal the Sergeant opened fire, but, after the first bomb had burst about twenty feet in front of the expectant pair and the second, which fortunately was a "dud," had landed a few feet behind them, further demonstration was called off. On the whole it seemed safer to the observers to postpone the use of this deadly weapon till such time as its trajectory could be predicted with some degree of confidence. The Sergeant was disappointed, but the officers were firm—quite firm—and could not be induced to take up a post for any further demonstrations.

On the whole this was a normal trench tour in an "active" sector. Patrols were out on several occasions and one, under Corp.

ROYAL HIGHLANDERS OF CANADA

Murney, encountered and dispersed an enemy working party. Another, under Lieut. B. H. Rust and Sergt. McKay, made a careful examination of a portion of the German front and brought in valuable information. Shelling during the whole tour was not infrequent and one afternoon part of No. 2 Coy. in reserve in Armagh Wood, was treated to a brisk bombardment. On this occasion Capt. I. M. R. Sinclair, the Company Commander, suffered his second wound of the campaign, which fortunately was not serious.

On the night of May 11th Lieut. A. W. Aitchison was making a round of his listening posts when a bullet struck him and shattered his thigh. Capt. Ramsay, the Battalion Medical Officer, improvised an excellent splint and Lieut. Aitchison was hurried back to a Casualty Clearing Station. Here everything possible was done for him, but he failed to rally and died of his wounds two days later. Referring to his death, the "Listening Post," a trench magazine, quoted the following lines, which, in the opinion of his brother officers, were singularly appropriate:

> "E'en as he trod that day to God, so walked he from his birth,
> In simpleness and gentleness and honour and clean mirth."

In spite of the fact that the Battalion was in the front line, night working parties were on several occasions furnished to the Engineers. One or two casualties occurred on these parties, which worked in rather exposed locations. Casualties for the tour numbered fifteen; six killed and nine wounded.

When the Royal Highlanders moved back, on May 17th, for a week in reserve positions, the companies and Battalion Headquarters were located respectively at Sunken Road-Verbrandenmolen, Blawepoort Farm, Woodcote House, Canal Dugouts and Swan Chateau.

Swan Chateau had once been a lovely old place indeed. War had laid a heavy hand upon it, had battered in its roof and shattered its stately trees; had dug great gaping holes in its green lawn and caved in the banks of its old fashioned moat. The swans, from which it derived its name, had perished, or disappeared, as had its human inhabitants, nevertheless it still retained more than a little of its dignity and former grandeur. Now, instead of swans, officers of a strange race swam in its moat, where shell holes had deepened the bottom. Other officers paddled about in an old punt

HILL 60, BLUFF AND MT. SORREL

and in improvised "canoes," while still others bathed under the blue sky in a bath that had been carefully lowered from the wreck of the Chateau's top storey. Through it all the old Chateau maintained a friendly, if slightly puzzled, air, as if to say, "These men are strange, and I am not accustomed to naked figures on my stately lawns, nevertheless they are a gentle race and bear the title of a 'Royal' battalion. Also they fight for France, and therefore I bid them welcome. C'est la guerre!"

During the week that the Highlanders remained in these positions, working parties at night were the undoubted feature. These, consisting of practically every available officer and man, worked under the supervision of the Engineers in, or near, the front line. At this time the Engineers were covering the greater part of the front with a network of buried cable, experience having shown that surface wires of communication were almost invariably cut just at the moment when they were most needed. It was in this task, then, that the majority of the Highlanders' working parties were employed. A great deal of work was done in Square Wood and most of those who laboured and sweated in that locality will recall the nightingale which sang sweetly as they dug beneath her favourite tree, oblivious apparently, as the men were not, to the shells which every now and again crashed in amongst the branches.

Apart from working parties, the outstanding event of the tour occurred on the night of May 22nd when No. 2 Coy., temporarily under the command of Capt. F. S. Mathewson, became involved in what might be termed a "private war" between the enemy artillery and some guns of the Lahore Division. This bombardment began when a stray shell exploded some of the Lahore ammunition, setting fire to the out-house in which this was stored. Seeing that they had located a battery, the enemy opened an intense fire with high explosive, knocking out three of the Lahore guns and wounding or killing about 50% of the Battery personnel. From the positions of the other companies of the 13th it seemed that No. 2 must be annihilated, as a veritable storm of high explosive tore the neighbourhood of Blawepoort Farm to bits. As was so often the case, however, No. 2 Coy., while having a most unpleasant time, was not suffering severe casualties. A few men were knocked out by concussion and one or two were wounded, otherwise, when the bombardment ended, No. 2 was in as good condition as before it had begun. For the whole tour, including this bombardment and

ROYAL HIGHLANDERS OF CANADA

the various working parties, the Battalion's losses were 6 killed and 18 wounded.

Late on the night of May 25th, after relief by the 8th Canadian Battalion, the 13th proceeded to Patricia Lines as Corps Reserve. In this location the Highlanders remained for a week. On May 26th they rested; on the 27th they were paid, while on the same night five officers and three hundred men, under Major Perry, proceeded to the neighbourhood of the Asylum, near Ypres, to bury cable. This party was officially thanked by the Divisional Signal Officer and the Engineers, who stated that they could ask for no better battalion to work with than the 13th. On the night of May 31st another large party, under Major McCuaig, proceeded forward and rendered equally valuable assistance.

As an offset to the hard and unpleasant work of these parties, passes to visit Poperinghe were granted to a large percentage of the men at one time or another during the week that the Battalion remained in Corps Reserve. Officers and men alike appreciated this privilege and the pockets of the hardy Poperinghers were considerably enriched by their liberal spending.

Meanwhile, on May 28th, General Alderson had handed over command of the Canadian Corps to Lieut.-Gen. the Hon. Sir Julian H. G. Byng, K.C.B., K.C.M.G., M.V.O., late commander of the IX Corps. This officer, whose Regiment was the 10th Royal Hussars, had seen a great deal of service in the Soudan and in South Africa. He had distinguished himself in France in command of the 3rd Cavalry Division of the "Old Contemptibles" and, later, had rendered valuable service in Gallipoli. His reputation in consequence of these services was such that, when he assumed command of the Canadian Corps, all ranks were satisfied that they would be led by a hand no less experienced and true than that of the General who was leaving them.

CHAPTER VIII

The June Show, 1916

In lonely watches night by night
Great visions burst upon my sight
For down the stretches of the sky
The hosts of dead go marching by.

Dear Christ, who reign'st above the flood
Of human tears and human blood,
A weary road these men have trod,
O house them in the home of God!
—FREDERICK GEORGE SCOTT.

I

NOT long after Sir Julian Byng assumed command of the Canadian Corps, the Ypres Salient, living up to its volcanic reputation, burst into full eruption once more and again a Canadian division was called on to block the German road to Ypres. This time the attack struck the 3rd Canadian Division which was occupying the line from Bellewaarde Beek to Mount Sorrel. Sharp at 8 a.m. on June 2nd, the bombardment heralding the attack began. For months the intensity of artillery fire had been increasing, until even a small attack at this time was preceded by shelling that would have been considered phenomenal a year before. In this case, however, no small attack was intended and the concentration of guns that poured shells on the Canadian lines was such as no British troops had seen before.

Along the whole Bellewaarde Beek-Sanctuary Wood—Hill 62, Hill 61—Armagh Wood—Mount Sorrel front, the Canadian line was simply obliterated. Major-General Mercer, commanding the 3rd Division, was killed and Brigadier-General Victor Williams, of the 8th Brigade, was made prisoner. The 4th Canadian Mounted Rifles suffered 637 casualties and were practically annihilated; the 1st Canadian Mounted Rifles had a casualty list of 367, which included amongst the killed Lieut.-Col. A. E. Shaw, the Commanding Officer; Lieut.-Col. G. H. Baker, of the 5th Canadian Mounted

ROYAL HIGHLANDERS OF CANADA

Rifles was killed, as was Lieut.-Col. C. H. Buller of the P.P.C.L.I. Seventeen out of the twenty-two officers of the "Patricia's" were also casualties; while the 42nd Battalion, Royal Highlanders of Canada, the 49th Edmonton Battalion, the 2nd Canadian Mounted Rifles, the Royal Canadian Regiment, and numerous other units lost heavily, either in the bombardment, or the counter attacks that developed later.

By noon, four hours after the bombardment began, the whole Canadian front and reserve system had been torn and devastated till it was well nigh unrecognizable. Then, at 1.45 p.m., the Germans launched their assault. This penetrated the broken front with little difficulty, but encountered determined resistance on reaching the support line in Sanctuary Wood, Armagh Wood and Mount Sorrel. Here the fighting was of the bitterest nature possible. Outnumbered, and at a disadvantage in every way, the Canadian units fought desperately and devotedly to prevent the enemy from penetrating through the reserve system and turning the flanks of the troops on either side. Nevertheless, when General Mercer's death was more or less established and General Hoare-Nairn, C.R.A. of the Lahore Artillery, assumed command of the 3rd Canadian Division late in the afternoon, the situation, though somewhat improved by the stubborn resistance and by local counter attacks, was still critical. Another strong attack, it seemed, must burst through the weakened lines which alone barred the road to Ypres. A counter attack with fresh troops was essential to prevent this calamity and orders were promptly issued summoning up such reserves as were available.

Far back of the front, at Patricia Lines, the 13th Battalion was enjoying a sports day when the "stand to" order was received. This arrived late in the afternoon and was followed before long by orders for the Battalion to proceed without delay to support an attack by the 14th and 15th Battalions.

In accordance with these orders, the 13th paraded at 7.30 p.m. and immediately started a forced march towards the front. Straining every nerve to increase speed, the Battalion omitted the regular halts, stopping only once, at Ouderdom, where Lieut.-Col. Buchanan ordered the men to leave their packs, thus lightening the load for the work that lay before them.

Gun flashes were by this time playing like a thunderstorm in the blackness of the sky ahead, but the Battalion did not come

THE JUNE SHOW, 1916

under enemy fire until it reached the bridge across the Ypres-Comines Canal. Here shrapnel was bursting with great regularity, the enemy clearly realizing that the point was one which reinforcements for the line would have to pass. Unable to await a pause in this shelling, the Highlanders pushed through. It was impossible to go through without casualties, however, and no miracle occurred to save the 13th from losses. Caught by a particularly heavy burst, Lieut. D. R. M. McLean was severely wounded, while the Bombing Section suffered casualties to almost 50% of its personnel.

After passing this unpleasant spot, the Battalion advanced as rapidly as the shelling and congestion of traffic allowed, until Zillebeke Trench was reached. In this trench, which ran along the shore of Zillebeke Lake, the 13th got badly mixed up with the 14th and 15th, whose attack the 13th and 16th were to support. Streams of wounded, making their way to the rear, added to the congestion until it was almost impossible to move.

From Zillebeke Trench the men of the 13th tried to find a route across the open that would bring them speedily to the position they were to occupy near Manor House. For a while every effort met with failure, the men sinking to their waists in the marsh land that intervened. Eventually, after day had broken, and after being on the move for over eight hours, a way was found and the companies distributed along the hedges in their proper positions.

The counter-attack which now took place had originally been planned for 2 a.m., but, owing to the impossibility of getting the attacking troops into position, the hour for the assault had been postponed until 7.10 a.m. On the right the 7th Battalion, with the 10th in close support, was to advance and retake the ground from Mount Sorrel to Observatory Ridge. In the centre the 15th and 14th Battalions, supported respectively by the 16th and 13th were to recapture Hill 62. On the left, and not in immediate contact with these attacks, the 49th and 60th Battalions, with the 52nd in close support, were to retake the front from Hill 62 to a point where the Royal Canadian Regiment still held its original position near Hooge.

Various changes in the plans for this counter-attack took place and it was not until approximately 8.15 a.m. that the 14th and 15th Battalions got away. Immediately these battalions came under a heavy and concentrated fire. They pushed their attack with the utmost disregard of losses, but the objectives assigned to them were impossible to attain and, after an advance of some 500 yards, they were compelled to establish a line, which ran roughly parallel to the front of Maple Copse. Elsewhere the counter-attack was but little more successful in attaining its final objectives. Inasmuch as it established links across some of the more dangerous gaps in the secondary system of defence, however, it cannot be regarded as a total failure.

All day on June 3rd the 13th Battalion worked hard digging trenches. Rations were eaten cold, as fires would have betrayed the position and invited unwelcome shelling. At dusk a general move forward was made, No. 1 Coy. moving up to the rear of Maple Copse, No. 2 Coy. to Zillebeke Village, and No. 4 Coy. to Valley Cottages. No. 3 Coy. remained in support at Manor Farm.

These company moves were carried out under a heavy enemy barrage, which caused some 40 or 50 casualties. Included amongst the wounded was Capt. J. Jeffery, M.C., an officer who, first as Regimental Sergeant-Major and then with commissioned rank, had rendered valuable service during the whole period of the Battalion's career in France. Capt. E. W. Waud was also wounded at this time, as was Lieut. W. E. Macfarlane, who had suffered previously in the Battalion's April engagement at the Bluff. Capt. J. O. Hastings, who had been the Battalion's Transport Officer from the beginning, was also a casualty on this night. While bringing the ration wagons up through the enemy barrage, his horse was killed under him and he himself severely wounded.

Previous to this the Battalion had suffered a severe loss when a shell burst among a group of four officers, who were on a reconnaissance in the front line, and killed Capt. Melville Greenshields, an original officer, who had been wounded at Second Ypres and who, throughout the whole campaign, had rendered untiring and efficient service. The same shell wounded Capt. W. F. Peterman, who had barely recovered from a previous wound received at the Bluff, in April.

During June 4th the men of the Battalion could accomplish little, owing to the atrocious weather and the necessity of exposing themselves as little as possible. At night, however, working parties were active, while No. 3 Coy. moved up and relieved No. 1 Coy. in the position behind Maple Copse. All ranks of the Battalion were pleased at news received during the day that the Commanding

THE JUNE SHOW, 1916

Officer, Lieut.-Col. V. C. Buchanan, had been awarded the D.S.O. This item was the one bright spot in a bleak and decidedly unpleasant day.

On June 5th the weather was still wet and the dugouts and trenches were in a fearful state of mud. Shelling was brisk, particularly on No. 3 Coy's. front, where considerable damage was done to the trenches and some casualties inflicted. A conference of commanding officers met at Battalion Headquarters on this date and completed arrangements for a counter-attack on the German lines at 1 a.m. on June 8th.

On June 6th the weather cleared and by mid-day the men had dried their clothes, though conditions under foot remained atrocious. There was considerable aerial activity all day, during which time the Battalion remained prepared for an enemy attack, which did not develop. At night parties were busy carrying supplies, working in the front line and strengthening the position in the rear of Maple Copse.

After a few hours of sunshine on the 6th, the weather again changed and on the 7th the men were treated to a steady drizzle of rain. This weather prevented aeroplane observation, which in turn stopped the Artillery from registering on the new German line. Accordingly the counter-attack, planned for June 8th, was postponed and at night the 22nd French-Canadian Battalion relieved the 13th, the latter proceeding to Dickebusch Village, whence busses conveyed the weary men to "I" Camp, near Reninghelst. Casualties during the tour amounted to 7 officers and 125 men, a heavy list considering the fact that the Battalion had not taken part in the actual assault.

II

Having arrived at "I" Camp, the 13th Battalion without delay prepared for the counter-attack, which had been postponed from the 8th and was now scheduled to take place early on the morning of June 13th.

On June 8th company parades were held in the afternoon to inspect rifles and gas helmets. All defective rifles were turned over to the Armourer for immediate repair and unsatisfactory gas helmets were replaced. On the following day the Battalion enjoyed the use of the baths at Reninghelst and elsewhere, while on the 10th a close inspection was made of grenade aprons, revolvers,

ROYAL HIGHLANDERS OF CANADA

Very pistols, shrapnel helmets and all equipment of this kind. Rifles were again inspected on this date and numerous promotions were announced amongst the N.C.O's. Under date of June 12th, the Corps Commander approved the appointment to acting commissioned rank of Corp. H. R. Monsarrat, Sergt. G. L. Earle, Lance-Corp. S. Reaume, Sergt. W. J. Anderson and Sergt. D. S. Grieve.

June 11th was devoted to final preparations for the counter-attack. Aeroplane photographs had been obtained by this time and a large map was prepared, showing every possible feature of the ground to be fought over. Lectures were delivered on the attack and care was taken that every officer and N.C.O. should be made aware of the part that he personally was to take, as well as of the general plan. In this way it was hoped that, on an officer, or N.C.O. becoming a casualty, someone who knew exactly what was expected would be found to "carry-on."

In general outline, the scheme of attack was as follows. The assault was timed for 1.30 a.m. on June 13th and the honour of carrying it out was assigned to the 1st Canadian Division, under Major-General A. W. Currie. For the occasion the brigades of the Division were re-shuffled to meet special requirements. Thus, on the right, Brig.-Gen. Lipsett had a brigade composed of the 1st, 3rd, 7th and 8th Battalions, while on the left Brig.-Gen. Tuxford commanded a force consisting of the 2nd, 4th, 13th and 16th Battalions. In Divisional Reserve was Brig.-Gen. Hughes, whose command included the 5th, 10th, 14th and 15th Battalions. The actual assault was to be delivered by three battalions, which, from right to left, were the 3rd, the 16th and the 13th. Roughly, these had as their respective objectives, Mount Sorrel, Hill 62, and the position to the north of Hill 62. Demonstrations and bombing attacks were to take place on the flanks of the main attack to deceive the enemy up to the last possible moment. In addition the attacking battalions were promised that on this occasion they would have no reason to complain that artillery support was inadequate. Guns of all calibres had been massed and were preparing to give the enemy some of his own obnoxious medicine.

Such, in brief, was the general plan of the attack. Each battalion elaborated on this scheme and worked out its tactics to conform with the general plan. In his operation order to the 13th, Lieut.-Col. V. C. Buchanan, D.S.O., gave instructions as follows:—

"On the night of June 11th the 13th Canadian Battalion, the

THE JUNE SHOW, 1916

Royal Highlanders of Canada, will relieve the 22nd Canadian Battalion in the support position previously occupied by the 13th on the night of June 7th. On the night of June 12th the Battalion will move forward to the trenches south of Maple Copse, preparatory to an assault. Nos. 1 and 3 Companies, the former on the right, the Battalion Bombers and two Machine Gun crews will be in the front trenches.

Nos. 2 and 4 Companies, the former on the right, the balance of Machine Gun Crews and all details will be in the support trenches.

At the hour of the assault, the Battalion will move forward in four lines, each of two half-company frontage, at intervals of 30 seconds.

The Battalion Bombers and two Lewis Guns will follow the second line. The remaining machine guns will follow the 4th line, as will details and Battalion H.Q.

Major K. M. Perry will be in charge of the first two lines.

Major G. E. McCuaig will be in charge of the 3rd and 4th lines.

Companies will be divided for supervision into parties of approximately ten men, under N.C.O's., and must keep in touch with the general line of the advance. Any men who become separated from their group will attach themselves to the nearest group.

The attack is divided into four objectives: The first objective is the present enemy front line from Observatory Ridge to, and including, Vigo Street. This objective will be known as 'Halifax.' One platoon of No. 2 Coy. in the 4th line will remain behind to ensure that this trench is cleared.

This platoon will rejoin their company as soon as relieved by the 4th Battalion.

The second objective is our old reserve line, to be known as 'Montreal.' The front line of the attack will remain in this trench to clear and consolidate it. The other lines will pass on through.

The 3rd objective, which is our old support line, to be known as 'Winnipeg,' will be our ultimate front line. This trench will be consolidated as soon as possible.

The 4th objective, which is our old front line, is to be known as 'Vancouver.'

The Battalion Bombers are divided into eight squads of eight men each. Two of these squads will move up Observatory Ridge Road and two up Vigo Street, the latter under the Bombing Officer. The remaining four squads will, as soon as the 3rd objective has

ROYAL HIGHLANDERS OF CANADA

been reached, move forward to the 4th objective, one squad to establish a block in the communication trench opposite St. Peter's St. Two squads will move up Crab Crawl and Torr Top and establish a block in the communication trench opposite the latter. Another squad will move up Pinch Cut and along the old front line to the left. They will be joined by the two squads who have come up Vigo Street and who will establish a block in the old support line on the left flank. Coloured flares will be carried and will be used to denote the progress of the attack as follows:—

On reaching the 1st objective—White Flare.

On reaching the final objective—Red Flare.

Attack held up—Green Flare.

The S.O.S. will be as usual.

In addition, messengers will be sent by Nos. 1 and 3 Companies to Battalion H.Q. as soon as they have reached the final objective.

Each man will carry 270 rounds of S.A.A., one day's rations, one iron ration, full water bottles, two grenades and five sand-bags. Every second man will carry a shovel."

Instructions were also issued as to the hour at which the artillery barrage would lift and allow the troops to advance.

On the afternoon of June 11th Major-Gen. A. W. Currie, the Divisional Commander, inspected the 13th and afterwards addressed the officers on the coming operations. At night, in accordance with the order quoted above, the Battalion moved up and relieved the 22nd Canadian Battalion in the position near Manor Farm, where the men remained all day on the 12th under fairly heavy shell fire and with no shelter from a drenching rain.

At night the 13th moved up through Zillebeke, to the trenches from which the assault was to be launched. The road up was so packed with troops and the darkness so intense that there was little time to spare when the four attacking waves were finally disposed along the muddy jumping-off trenches, between the forward edge of Maple Copse and the Observatory Ridge Road. These trenches were held by the 2nd Canadian Battalion and there was a good deal of congestion in them when the two battalions were packed together, but much good will was shown on both sides and by midnight the Royal Highlanders were lying low awaiting the hour to attack.

At 12.45 a.m. on June 13th the blackness of the night was split by a great sheet of flame, which belched from the muzzles of hundreds of guns. It was a marvelous sight and the deep-throated

THE JUNE SHOW, 1916

roar that went with it was music to the ears of the waiting battalions. Guns of all calibres, from 18-pounders to 12-inch, were employed and the German positions were torn and rent in a manner comparable to that in which the 3rd Division's front had been treated ten days earlier. As soon as this tornado was unloosed the German artillery, in response to S.O.S. signals from their infantry, laid down a counter barrage on the Canadians' front and communication trenches. Accurately placed, this counter barrage battered in some of the parapets and inflicted a number of casualties in the crowded jumping-off trenches. Accordingly the men were not sorry when the hour for the assault arrived and they were ordered forward into the open.

Climbing over the top at the zero hour, 1.30 a.m., the four waves of the Royal Highlanders began their advance. The condition of the ground was very bad and, in the darkness, the men slipped and slithered into shell holes, often eight or ten feet deep. The weather, too, was most unfavourable and rain fell heavily at intervals, but the men pushed forward most determinedly and maintained their direction surprisingly well. One feature that helped matters was that the preliminary bombardment had effectively cut the enemy wire. Here and there uncut wire was encountered, but not in quantity sufficient seriously to impede the advance.

Major K. M. Perry, commanding the first two waves, became a casualty just as he was leading the attack into the first line of German trenches. On learning of this Major G. E. McCuaig, in command of the third and fourth waves, handed these over and took Perry's place.

After capturing the "Halifax" line, McCuaig led the attacking waves against "Montreal" and "Winnipeg." By this time the opposition had stiffened appreciably and the Battalion was fighting hard to maintain the speed of its advance. On the left a strong machine gun post threatened at one time to hold up that flank altogether, but was silenced by a grenade party, who, creeping from shell hole to shell hole, outflanked it and bombed its stout hearted crew into submission. With this and some similar strong points disposed of, the attack swept forward. Bitter hand to hand fighting occurred at many points in the maze of trenches, shell holes and muddy ditches through which the attackers bombed and bayonetted their way. Pushing up a trench on one such occasion, Capt. F. S. Mathewson, commanding No. 2 Coy., rounded a traverse suddenly and came face to face with a large Hun. Both were surprised, but Mathewson, recovering his wits first, planted his fist with terrific force on the Hun's jaw. The latter went down without a word, but was not altogether the loser in the contest, as Mathewson's fist was badly shattered. In spite of the pain of this injury, the latter continued to lead his Company during the remainder of the attack and rendered valuable service.

Elsewhere Coy. Sergt.-Major Ableson, of No. 1 Coy., after having been wounded, was attacked by an unwounded German, who attempted to seize his rifle. In the struggle that followed Ableson suffered over thirty knife wounds. When discovered by the second wave of the attack he was bleeding from his head, arms, body and legs, but in spite of these injuries the German had quite failed to wrest the rifle from his determined grasp.

At another point Lieut. B. M. Giveen, the Battalion Bombing Officer, found that an enemy machine gun was holding up the advance. Realizing that this obstacle must be cleared away at all costs, Giveen led an attack against it. When most of the attackers had become casualties, he persisted in the attack himself and eventually silenced the gun. It would be a great pleasure to record that this gallant officer survived to enjoy the honour that his daring piece of work would almost certainly have brought him. Unfortunately he fell, riddled with bullets, in the very moment of his victory.

Meanwhile, at different points, other officers and men were falling fast, as the advance pushed to its final objective. Lieut. J. D. Selbie was wounded in the arm, but carried on until he was killed; Lieut. J. G. Walker was killed while bravely advancing against a machine gun, as was Lieut. A. D. Prosser. Lieut. S. V. Brittan, who had received his commission as a reward for very fine work in 1915, was also killed, after rendering strikingly whole hearted service.

Bit by bit, in spite of minor checks, the Battalion forced its way towards the "Winnipeg" line, where, except for bombing and blocking parties, the advance was to halt. In overcoming the last resistance, Lieut. W. G. Hamilton, the Battalion Machine Gun Officer, worked hard and assisted the attack materially. Later this officer took over the Bombers, whom Lieut. Giveen's death had left leaderless, and commanded them in the dangerous work of proceeding to the "Vancouver" objective and establishing blocks

THE JUNE SHOW, 1916

in the communication trenches that led forward from the front, or "Winnipeg," line. In this work many of the Bombers became casualties and Hamilton himself was wounded.

Almost on scheduled time the attack reached its objective and Major McCuaig, with no little pride in what the men had accomplished, touched off the red flare that carried the news of the Battalion's success back to those who were so eagerly awaiting it. On the flanks the other battalions were equally successful. The whole Corps, therefore, rejoiced in the fact that what had threatened to be a German triumph had been turned by the counter attack into a Canadian victory.

Victories, however, are not won without loss and in the 13th the losses were severe, though not out of proportion to the results achieved. In addition to the casualties already mentioned, Lieut. T. B. Saunders was killed while employed in the hazardous task of blocking the forward communication trenches, and at different points Lieuts. W. J. Anderson, A. G. C. Macdermot and H. H. Heal were wounded. Amongst the other ranks casualties amounted to approximately 300, of whom 67 were killed and 32 missing, presumed killed, the balance being listed as wounded. Enemy casualties were, of course, unknown. Sixty prisoners, however, were taken by the 13th, while the number of German dead, strewn everywhere in the wake of the attack, bore silent witness to the fact that enemy losses far outnumbered the Canadian.

As soon as the Battalion had fought its way into the "Winnipeg" line, and while connection was being established with the victorious battalions on the flanks, Lieut.-Col. Buchanan, who had advanced his headquarters to keep in touch with the attack, ordered up the Engineer and Pioneer parties attached to the 13th to assist in the work of consolidation. These parties toiled unceasingly and displayed no little courage in accomplishing their difficult task. Their valuable assistance was recognized by Col. Buchanan, who expressed to their commander his appreciation of the services they rendered. Similarly, the stretcher bearer party, supplied to the 13th by the 14th Battalion, Royal Montreal Regiment, was thanked by Col. Buchanan, who reported to 14th Headquarters that these bearers had acted in every way in a manner to reflect credit on their distinguished unit. The rain and terrible conditions underfoot made the work of the bearers particularly arduous, nevertheless they rapidly evacuated the wounded to Valley Cottages where Capt.

ROYAL HIGHLANDERS OF CANADA

Ramsay, the Battalion Medical Officer, worked untiringly to give the casualties first aid and make them as comfortable as possible for the long trip down the line.

All the slightly wounded were jubilant and brought back glowing tales of the success and of their own personal adventures. In a great action each individual notices aspects and incidents totally overlooked by a comrade only a few feet away. Consequently, owing to the confusing and often directly contradictory information, it is difficult for a man in the rear to gather any clear impression of what has taken place. Often the experiences of some individual, all quite genuine, would seem to imply that he had been fighting for a week instead of for a few crowded hours. It is interesting, though, after looking at a battle from the battalion point of view, to try and imagine how it appeared to some inconspicuous and unidentified member of the rank and file. Describing a conversation with a wounded private, who drifted back through his gun position soon after daybreak on the 13th, a Canadian Artillery officer writes as follows:—

"Well, you must first try and picture the chap who told me the story. We had given him a cup of tea, and he was very grateful, and we asked him what he had seen of the show. He belongs to the 13th and stands about six feet high; his kilt is covered with a brown canvas apron, and he wears a steel helmet sideways on his head. Thin streaks of black hair come down over his eyes and his face is entirely covered with mud, except where the trickling sweat has made white channels down it. Besides his regulation kit, he has a German helmet strapped on his shoulder, three belts around his waist, and carries a German rifle as well as his own. How he manages it all is hard to see, for his left arm is bound up in a sling, but he is Blighty bound and nothing can spoil his fun. ....'I was in the line that was to do the once over, and he told us to be quiet until we got the word. Me and me pal we scraped a hole in the bottom of the trench, while you fellas (the artillery) gave 'em hell. I thought it ud never stop. I takes a peek over once and ducks me bean. It sure was some sight. Them hows. of ours looked like bleedin' mines goin' up. I says to me pal, "If those is us we're all right." Just then it began to slacken, I guess you fellas was shoven' it farther back, and we gets the word. Mike was underneath me, for the hole wouldn't hold us both. I shouts to him, "Nip it, kid, we're off to Berlin." You shud a seen us hoof it over No

THE JUNE SHOW, 1916

Man's Land. It was just a bunch of holes strung together with bits of weed. Mike fell into one up to his neck, but I didn't wait. You must have blowed up his line pretty well for there wasn't a machine gun firin' at us. It only took a few minutes to get to their front line, but there was nothin' in it. 'E told us to wait for the signal to go to our old front line, and we played about, bombin' out a few buggers that was playin' possum in the dug-outs as was left. You fellas lifted again, just like a wall of flame bein' pushed back, and we beats it for our old front line. It wasn't as easy as the first, but when I gets to it, there didn't seem to be nothin' doin', so I jumps in and out again on the other side, with Mike catchin' up from behind. We runs slap up against a parapet, and Mike yells at me "Look out! they're in there!" I ups on the parapet and, sure enough, there he was. Before I could dodge, he fires at me point blank. The bleedin' bullet went between me legs. (At this stage souvenirs, kit and paraphernalia are dumped on the ground and he proudly shows us the hole through his kilt, front and back.) It never touched me. I had me mitts on for the wire, so I heaves a bomb, "Take that you b———d!" It hit his face, but didn't bust. He fired again and missed. "Take that you dirty dog!" I says, and let him have another. That got him, and he cuddled up in a corner. "I'll be back in a minit," I says, and goes down to where Mike was pastin' them into a hole in the ground. Just as I got there a head shoves up and two arms, and yells "Kamerad." I chucks a Mills in the hole and they all starts hollerin'. "All right, come out," yells Mike, and fifteen of them crawls out, and starts yellin'. "Nix on the kamerad stuff," I says, " 'op it over there, and if one of youse downs a hand, I'll blow your bleedin' heads off." Then we gets back, and 'e says, "Wot t'ell d'ye mean by goin' over there," and I says, "Lorst me way in the dark, orficer, and brings back a lump of sausage." 'E says "Well done," and I was goin' to peek once more, when one comes with Blighty written on one end of it and my name on the other. Well, I must be gettin' along. Thanks, orficer, for the fags. I'll get the nurses to feed them to me. If I let go of this (he holds up the German helmet) some begger'll swipe it. Some war!——' "

CHAPTER IX

Sanctuary Wood, Verbrandenmolen and Watten

> O guns, fall silent till the dead men hear
> Above their heads the legions pressing on;
> (These fought their fight in time of bitter fear,
> And died not knowing how the day had gone.)
>
> Tell them, O guns, that we have heard their call,
> That we have sworn, and will not turn aside,
> That we will onward till we win or fall,
> That we will keep the faith for which they died.
> —JOHN McCRAE.

I

FOLLOWING the successful counter-attack of June 13th and the strenuous day in the front line that followed, the Royal Highlanders were relieved at night by the 2nd Canadian Battalion and, on the morning of June 14th, marched back to a point where busses were waiting to convey them to Patricia Lines.

Here billets were shared with the 16th Battalion, Canadian Scottish, who had taken part in the counter-attack, and with whom, in consequence, the 13th had a new bond in common. June 15th, the first full day in billets, was spent in resting and removing the mud and blood of the recent battle from uniforms and equipment. Muster parades were held to ascertain the Battalion's losses. On the following day a party of fifty men, under Lieut. D. S. Grieve, returned to the scene of the counter-attack to search for and bury dead. The report of this party definitely shifted to the list of killed a large number of names that had, up to this time, appeared as "missing."

At 2.30 p.m. the Battalion moved to "C" Camp, near Poperinghe, and remained in this location for several days. Muster parades were again held to check the casualty returns, rifles were carefully inspected and a new draft of men received to fill the depleted ranks. Accompanying this draft, or joining almost simul-

SANCTUARY WOOD AND WATTEN

taneously, were Lieuts. A. H. Follett, and C. D. Llwyd, (No. 1 Coy.), Lieuts. G. N. Sale and H. E. Piercy, (No. 2 Coy.), Lieuts. I. P. Falkner, H. T. Higinbotham, J. D. Cameron and J. L. Atkinson, (No. 3 Coy.), and Lieuts. V. G. Gwatkin and A. C. McAuley, (No. 4 Coy.).

On June 20th Highland equipment was issued to the new draft and on the same date the Battalion moved from "C" Camp to Dominion Lines. The three days that followed were devoted for the most part to training the new draft, special attention being paid to gas helmet drill, bombing, machine gun work and the details of trench routine. Several officer promotions were announced at this time. Conspicuous amongst these were the following: To be Acting Major—Capt. C. J. Smith: To be Acting Captains—Lieuts. B. H. Rust and N. M. MacLean: To be Acting Adjutant—Lieut. C. D. Craig (Paymaster): To be Acting Transport Officer—Lieut. F. du V. Elliot.

From Dominion Lines the Battalion moved up on the night of June 24th and relieved the 7th Canadian Battalion in Trenches 53 to 58 inclusive. These were in the Sanctuary Wood sector and still showed signs of the two battles which had swept over them earlier in the month. The communication trenches had not been rebuilt and the front line was approached overland. This was rendered possible by the fact that the ground sloped sharply to the rear, the rise obstructing the enemy's view.

Sanctuary Wood was by this time a wood in name only. Such trees as stood were riven and leafless, while their fallen branches added to the maze of wire and trenches beneath. The air was heavy with a sickening odour of decay, so that the whole battered district, even by day, was a place of grisly horror and evil omen. At night weird shadows and strange sounds—the hoot of an owl, or the cough of a hidden sentry—intensified this aspect a hundredfold. War, however, is full of such fanciful things. Men who can face shell fire, gas and all the horrors of a modern engagement are supposedly immune from what the inexperienced term childish fears, yet more than one officer whose gallantry in action is unquestioned has admitted that when alone at night in Sanctuary Wood his heart would beat uncomfortably fast and that human companionship was more than ordinarily welcome.

The first two days of the Battalion's tour in this area were comparatively uneventful, but at 4 a.m. on June 27th the enemy loosed

ROYAL HIGHLANDERS OF CANADA

one of those heavy and concentrated "shoots" for which this part of the line was famous. Guns of all calibres and heavy trench mortars were used and caused great damage to the Highlanders' front line and support. In addition the enemy laid down a shrapnel barrage on all roads and paths by which reinforcements might reach the front line, paying special attention to the Observatory Ridge Road under which, in a support trench, Capt. F. P. Buchanan had his dugout.

Capt. Buchanan, one of the original officers of the 13th, had remained in England in command of the Base Company when the Battalion proceeded to France. Later he rejoined the main section and served at the front during the latter part of 1915. Illness then compelled him to return to England, but, on recovering his health, he had come back to the Battalion once more and at the time of the bombardment now being described was serving as O.C. of No. 4 Coy.

Leaving his dugout to ascertain what effect the bombardment was having and whether, or not, the enemy was using it to screen an attack, Capt. Buchanan was struck on the head by a shrapnel shell and instantly killed. During that same hour Major C. J. Smith, another original officer, was killed when a heavy trench mortar shell scored a direct hit on the steel-lined dugout in which he had established his Company Headquarters. Smith's death on this occasion seemed a particularly hard stroke of fate, as he had just received his promotion and was serving for the first time as a Major. Originally with No. 3 Coy., then as Adjutant and finally as a company commander he had worked faithfully and given of his best in a manner that was an inspiration to all who came in contact with him. So passed from the Battalion roll two very gallant officers and gentlemen.

Nor were these two alone in making the supreme sacrifice on that June day. Lieut. C. J. Roche was killed, as were some 26 of the rank and file. Other casualties included Capt. N. M. MacLean, Lieut. A. H. Follett, Lieut. W. S. Brown, Lieut. I. P. Falkner and 46 other ranks wounded. One man was listed as "missing."

After an hour and twenty minutes of intense bombardment the curtain of fire lifted and the enemy, employing a system similar to that which they had used at The Bluff in April, attempted to penetrate the Royal Highlanders' front line. On the right flank a party of about twenty Germans advanced, but were driven off by rifle

SANCTUARY WOOD AND WATTEN

and machine gun fire. Help in routing this party was given by a machine gun of the 14th Battalion firing from the right. Another party, slightly larger, pushed forward against the centre of the position and was similarly dispersed. On the left a third party, about fifteen in number, succeeded in getting close to a sap in which the Highlanders had established a forward post. Garrisoning this post at the time were Sergt. McLeod and one other man. This doughty pair, viewing with dislike the possibility of being surrounded and captured, organized a counter-attack of their own. With McLeod acting as the first "wave" and his companion as the second, the counter-attack, which was principally a bombing affair, fell upon the astonished Germans and drove them in confusion back to their own wire. The counter-attack then re-formed and returned in safety.

The check suffered by these three advance parties apparently discouraged the enemy and prevented his sending forward the main assault body, which was concealed in front of his line. The Canadians suspected the existence of such a body and confirmation was obtained from a wounded prisoner, one of a pair captured on the right flank.

During the remainder of the tour in Sanctuary Wood the Royal Highlanders were forced to work exceedingly hard to repair their damaged trenches. Several sharp bombardments on the 28th destroyed some of the repairs and inflicted further casualties, but none of these approached in severity the eighty minute shelling of the day before. To make sure that no mischief was being planned, however, Lieut. G. L. Earle, Lieut. J. D. Cameron and an N.C.O. patrolled between the lines at night, paying particular attention to the blocked communication trench which ran into the enemy lines. No unusual features were discovered.

Late on the night of June 29th the 10th Canadian Battalion took over the Sanctuary Wood front and the 13th withdrew to huts near Busseboom. Here new drafts were received and five days spent in the usual routine of a regiment in billets. During this time the new men were medically inspected and carefully trained in gas helmet drill, company drill, squad drill and trench routine. Recreation was afforded to as many men as possible by passes to Poperinghe, these being particularly welcome after July 3rd, when the Battalion was paid by Lieut. R. E. Heaslip, the newly appointed Paymaster.

At 7.30 p.m. on July 5th, the Battalion moved to Kenora Lines.

where for three days the work of training was continued. Gas helmet and squad drills were again a feature, but variety was provided by musketry instruction, route marching and a series of demonstrations in cutting wire. Attention of all ranks was called to the standing order that cameras were strictly forbidden and that no explanation would save the owner of one from summary court martial. At the same time a new order forbade the men to drink promiscuously from the old pumps and streams in which the district abounded. Much sickness had resulted from carelessness in this respect and the men were warned that they must use the regimental water carts or other authorized sources of supply.

II

Leaving Kenora Lines on the evening of July 9th, the Battalion moved forward to relieve the 2nd Canadian Battalion in reserve billets in the forward area. This relief was not entirely uneventful, as during the march up a heavy bombardment was heard on the front, while all around the Canadian guns were giving reply. Not knowing exactly what the bombardment indicated, a staff officer met Lieut.-Col. Buchanan near Swan Chateau and ordered all the companies to halt pending further instructions. Eventually the enemy raided the 4th Battalion front on Hill 60, apparently with the idea of trying out the strength of the defence at that point. Once it became clear that no further action was imminent, the Highlanders were ordered forward to complete the delayed relief.

On taking over from the 2nd Battalion, the 13th Headquarters occupied Railway Dugouts; Nos. 1 and 3 Companies occupied Woodcote House, No. 2 took over Battersea Farm, while No. 4 moved into Sunken Road. All details were in Railway Dugouts. Four days were spent in these locations, where, owing to enemy observation, it was necessary for the men to move in daylight with considerable caution. Intermittent shelling caused a few casualties and Lieut. G. V. Gwatkin suffered the loss of two fingers from the accidental explosion of a grenade. Large working parties were the chief feature of the tour. One such was employed on the Railway Tunnel under Hill 60, while nightly parties of as many as 500 officers and men worked in consolidating the front line, cleaning communication trenches and establishing dumps of materials.

At night on July 14th the Battalion moved forward to relieve the Royal Montreal Regiment in the Verbrandenmolen Sector of

MAPLE COPSE, YPRES SALIENT, JUNE, 1916.

Canadian Official, Copyright.

A TRENCH SCENE, YPRES SALIENT, JUNE, 1916.

Canadian Official, Copyright.

SANCTUARY WOOD AND WATTEN

the front line. This position was on the right of the Railway Cutting by Hill 60 and the trenches were in very fair condition. Back of the front line it was possible to move about in the open, owing to the protection afforded by abundant foliage.

On moving into the line No. 3 Coy., under Capt. B. H. Rust, took over the right front, No. 2 Coy., under Capt. J. D. Macpherson, the centre and No. 1 Coy., under Capt. J. H. Lovett, the left. No. 4 Coy. was in reserve. No. 1 Coy's. left rested on the Railway Cutting, on the other side of which was the 16th Battalion, Canadian Scottish. This cutting, over which an old bridge still remained, ran from the Canadian into the German lines. At night, therefore, the 13th and 16th co-operated in providing a stationary patrol to stop the enemy should he attempt to advance down the cutting and debouch from under the bridge.

During the first few days in this section of the line the 13th indulged in a spirited rifle grenade duel with the opposing forces. Using the high ground of Verbrandenmolen, the Highlanders "straffed" the enemy trenches in an effort to comply with orders that every German grenade was to be returned in the ratio of six for one. In the duel the 13th freely admit that the Hun carried off the honours. In some way he marked down most of the emplacements from which grenades could be fired and it was in consequence so difficult to use these that the six to one ratio was pretty well in his favour. Refusing to accept the Hun superiority in rifle grenades as in any way indicative of the general situation, the Canadians shifted their tactics and brought into play a number of Trench Mortars and Stokes guns, which broke down the enemy trenches in several places and tore large gaps in his wire. To this move the enemy replied in kind with a certain degree of success.

At 8 o'clock on the night of July 18th the enemy opened a severe Trench Mortar bombardment on the Hill 60 Sector across the Railway Cutting and on the front line of the 13th. About 8.45 p.m. rifle grenades were added to the bombardment and the enemy artillery also joined in. Retaliation started at once, but the advantage was all with the Germans. The Stokes gun crews worked courageously, but were literally snowed under. Unfortunately, too, one of the supporting 60-pounder Trench Mortar batteries went wrong at this time and crashed a series of bombs into the Highlanders' trenches.

On the right of the line Capt. B. H. Rust, commanding No. 3

ROYAL HIGHLANDERS OF CANADA

Coy., an officer whose career had been a distinguished one, received a terrible wound in the thigh, from which he died in the Dressing Station soon afterwards. In the centre the shelling was heavy, but not so severe as on the left, where Capt. J. H. Lovett had withdrawn the majority of his men from the front line, according to previous arrangement, leaving only a bombing squad to block the Railway Cutting, and machine gunners and sentries at their regular posts.

The trenches on this front were terribly broken up and Company Headquarters completely destroyed by a heavy trench mortar shell, which scored a direct hit. The lives of Capt. Lovett and a signaller were saved by the vigilance of a runner, Private Dunn, who saw the torpedo coming and gave a warning which enabled the pair to escape. Eventually the German fire lifted and the enemy, using tactics that were familiar to the 13th from previous experience, pushed forward several attacks. Of these the main one was directed against the point where the right of the 16th and the left of the 13th rested on the Railway Cutting. One small party entered a trench from which the 16th had been withdrawn and started to cross the stone arch over the Cutting. The members of this party were revealed by the light of a flare and were seen to be wearing flat caps with Red Cross brassards. Challenged by Lance-Corp. Johnson, a Russian in the 13th ranks, they made some guttural answer to which Johnson, suspecting a trick, replied with a bomb. The Germans promptly returned the compliment, whereupon the Lance-Corporal and his party drove them back across the bridge, their retreat being hastened by a machine gun which opened on them from a distance.

Meanwhile, Capt. Lovett, though nearly blind and deaf from the explosion which so nearly cost him his life, continued to direct his company with no little skill. As soon as the bombardment lifted he ordered the men who had been withdrawn from the front line forward once more and this move was speedily carried out, largely owing to the good work of Coy. Sergt.-Major Bullock, who led the men overland through the wire entanglements protecting the second line. Lieuts. C. D. Llwyd and P. E. Corbett, new officers, also showed coolness and resource in directing their men.

The speed with which the front line was manned at this point contributed materially to the sharp repulse administered to a German party who advanced against Trench 37 S. immediately adjoining the Cutting. The men of the new draft behaved well in this

SANCTUARY WOOD AND WATTEN

engagement and one of them, unable to restrain his delight at the way in which the German attack had been beaten off, leaped onto the parapet with a shout of "Try again, Fritz, there's 'Welcome' on the door mat."

While the check administered to the Hun attacks was in every way satisfactory, some uneasiness was felt owing to the fact that the party driven back across the stone bridge by Lance-Corp. Johnson's bombers, had apparently come from a section of the 16th Battalion's trenches. Fearing that the enemy might have occupied these in strength, Lovett sent over a patrol to ascertain how the situation lay. This patrol reported that the 16th still held the trench in question and had merely withdrawn the garrison during the heaviest part of the bombardment.

With this point satisfactorily settled, the attention of the Battalion was at once turned to the work of evacuating the wounded and repairing the trenches. Casualties, considering the intensity of the bombardment, were not abnormal, nevertheless, far away in Canada, fifteen homes would receive the Government telegram telling of the death of a Highlander in action, while to thirty-eight others would be sent the less dreaded notice of wounds received.

Following this engagement the 13th remained in the line for some 24 hours, at the end of which the 8th Canadian Battalion relieved, the 13th reaching billets at Devonshire Lines at 4 a.m. on the 20th. Later on this date the officers attended the funeral of Capt. B. H. Rust, who was buried in the cemetery at Poperinghe. Deep regret was felt by all ranks at the loss of this brave officer, and the service, conducted by Canon Scott, was a touching one. Afterwards Lieut.-Col. Buchanan and other officers walked around the cemetery where scores of 13th Battalion graves gave striking proof of the sacrifices the Regiment had made in helping to hold the famous Salient.

On returning to billets Capt. J. H. Lovett was forced to admit that he was feeling the effects of wounds received on the night of the 18th. His hearing had almost gone and he suffered from other painful injuries. Accordingly he was evacuated and spent the following three weeks at No. 17 Stationary Hospital in Boulogne, rejoining the Battalion as soon as his recovery was well advanced.

For the next ten days the Battalion remained at Devonshire Lines. No parades of any kind were held on the 20th, but on the 21st the Battalion had the use of the 2nd Divisional Baths at

ROYAL HIGHLANDERS OF CANADA

Reninghelst and pay parades were also held. On the following day the companies proceeded to a point where inspection of gas helmets was made by the Divisional Gas Officer. After the inspection a demonstration in the use of gas helmets was given. In the afternoon two officers and fifty other ranks from each of the companies, with parties from the Machine Gun, Grenade and Intelligence Sections, attended a lecture at Connaught Lines on the subject of "Observation from Air Craft."

On July 23rd a Protestant service was held on the Battalion Parade Ground, Major Creegan officiating, while the Roman Catholic party, under Lieut. J. D. Gunn, proceeded to the Y.M.C.A. hut in Scottish Lines, where Major O'Gorman celebrated Mass. Later on the same day it was announced that decorations had been awarded as follows: The Distinguished Conduct Medal to Sergt. A. McLeod and the Military Medal to Sergt. A. Petrie, Corp. F. J. Walker, Lance-Corp. J. E. Westerman, Private G. Gill, Private P. Costello, Private W. Somerville and Private D. Woods. All these had distinguished themselves during the operations in the Salient.

On the 24th company training, route marches, bayonet and gas helmet drills filled in the time for the men, while all available officers attended lectures by Lieut.-Col. R. H. Kearsley, D.S.O. and Major Bertram, the former speaking on "Responsibilities and Duties of Officers" and the latter on "Intelligence Concerning the Area We Occupy." Two days later Lieut.-Col. Buchanan gave the Battalion a thorough inspection, while on the same date it was announced that,— "The General Officer Commanding in Chief, under the authority granted by His Majesty The King, has awarded the following decorations:—

The Distinguished Service Order . .	Major K. M. Perry
The Military Cross	Lieut. W. G. Hamilton
The Military Medal	Corp. G. T. Cowan
	Private R. Young.

Six more days completed the stay at Devonshire Lines, all of these, except July 28th, being devoted to the customary drilling and training so frequently referred to. On the 28th all parades were called off and a sports day organized. The programme on this occasion differed in no essential from that of previous sports days, but provided none the less a real break in the routine of training and was much enjoyed by officers and men in consequence.

SANCTUARY WOOD AND WATTEN

With the arrival of August, Lieut. C. D. Craig, who had been Acting Adjutant of the Battalion, was confirmed as Adjutant and simultaneously it was announced that Capt. C. N. McCuaig had been appointed Orderly Officer of the 2nd Canadian Infantry Brigade. Capt. McCuaig was the youngest of three brothers, all original officers of the 13th. He had served as a subaltern with No. 3 Coy. at the Second Battle of Ypres, where Major D. R. McCuaig was wounded and made prisoner and where his other brother, then Captain, now Major, G. E. McCuaig, had been wounded. From that time he had remained with the Royal Highlanders until the autumn of 1915, when illness had compelled his return to England. Now he was returning to France to serve under his old chief, Brig.-Gen. F. O. W. Loomis, who picked him for his work while with the Battalion.

On the night of August 1st the 13th moved up and relieved the 1st Canadian Battalion in Brigade Support. Headquarters was established in Railway Dugouts and the companies occupied equally familiar locations in Sunken Road, Woodcote House, Battersea Farm and so on. During the stay in these positions, movement during the day was necessarily restricted, but at night the whole area came to life and large working parties toiled unceasingly in repairing the front line, building Stokes gun emplacements and carrying material. While for the most part this work was uneventful, one party ran into bad luck and suffered several casualties. During the whole of the six day tour one man was killed and thirteen more or less seriously wounded.

On the night of the 7th the Highlanders shifted to the right to support the 2nd Brigade. On this occasion two companies were located under the Bluff, in a large tunnel system which during the summer had been constructed with the emergency tunnel, which the veterans of the April show remembered so well, as a nucleus. The other companies were situated respectively in barns to the rear and at Bedford House.

Great interest was taken by the April veterans in an enormous crater, which had replaced the smaller one at the end of the Bluff where a small post of 13th bombers had so distinguished themselves. A party of officers visited this new crater and were amused to find a movie drama being enacted in its cavernous depths. Invited to take part in the scene, the officers accepted with glee and died heroic deaths, or sprang to life and performed prodigies of valour, as the progress of the picture seemed to demand. "They died with a smile on their lips," is a description which in this instance was literally true.

Two comparatively uneventful days were spent in this location, though at night the usual working parties toiled and sweated at their heavy tasks. Four casualties were added to the ever growing list, two men being killed and two wounded. This, although no one knew it at the time, marked the last of the Battalion's 1916 tours in the Ypres Salient. Great events were taking place elsewhere on the British front in which it was now planned that the Canadian Corps should participate. The Royal Highlanders, however, were quite unaware of these plans when, on the night of August 9th, they were relieved by the 4th C.M.R. and moved back to billets at Devonshire Lines.

III

After a brief stay at Devonshire Lines the 13th Battalion joined the other units of the 3rd Brigade in a march to a special training area near Watten. This move was made in three stages. On the 11th reveille was sounded at 3 a.m. and the Battalion moved off some hours later. Every man carried his full kit, including pack, steel helmet, 240 rounds of small arm ammunition and full water bottle. At 10 a.m. the Battalion reached Abeele on the border between Belgium and France, a town which the Highlanders had previously visited when moving up to Ypres in the spring of 1915.

Reveille was sounded again that same night at 11.30 p.m., breakfast was at midnight and at 2.15 a.m. the march was resumed, the early start being made to escape enemy observation and to avoid marching in the heat of the day. On this occasion the men's equipment was as on the previous day. Cook kitchens and water carts followed in the rear of the Battalion, but all other transport was brigaded and followed in the rear of the Brigade Column, under the command of an officer of the 15th Battalion. The march on this date was long and the last two hours of it trying, owing to the dust and intense heat. Billets, however, were reached and occupied about 9.30 a.m. Continuing the march at 4 a.m. on August 13th, the Battalion proceeded to its final destination, a series of hamlets near Watten. Battalion Headquarters billeted with the Comte d'Hespel in the Chateau d'Eperlecques and the companies were also adequately, if less sumptuously, housed.

SANCTUARY WOOD AND WATTEN

On settling down in Watten the Battalion began a two weeks' course of special training. On the 14th routine drills were held and a thorough inspection made of kits and equipment, special attention being paid to steel helmets and rifle covers. On the next day rifle inspection was held by the Armourer Sergeant and the following appointments were announced: To be Assistant-Adjutant—Lieut. G. W. Brown: to be Assistant Intelligence Officer—Lieut. E. McN. Grant: to be Assistant Machine Gun Officer—Lieut. H. H. Chanter and to be Assistant Bombing Officer—Capt. C. R. Chisholm.

The Battalion assembled at 8.15 a.m. on the 16th and proceeded some miles to the Second Army Training Area, N.W. of St. Omer, which had been allotted to the 3rd Brigade for special training. Here the 13th carried out an all day practice in the assault, coming in contact for the first time with Australian troops, who were training in an adjacent area. On the same date an order that all officers' kits must be reduced to 35 lbs. gave strength to a rumour, already whispered, that the Canadians were to take part in the great allied offensive on the Somme.

On August 18th the Royal Highlanders took part with the other units of the 3rd Canadian Brigade in a large scale practice in attack. The objective on this occasion was the high ground between Barlinghem and Moringhem, with a windmill as a prominent and guiding feature. The attack was carried out in waves, with all the accepted flanking precautions and with bombing squads, machine gun teams, stretcher bearers and Intelligence sections filling, so far as possible, their battle roles. During this operation the Battalion, for the first time, practised liaison with the Royal Flying Corps, the forward waves of the attack being supplied with white ground flares to outline their position when this information was called for by the Klaxon horn of a low flying plane, identifiable by a couple of long black streamers. These white flares were lit only when objectives had been reached, or when troops were presumed to have encountered an obstacle which prevented further advance. Ground sheets were used to signal all other information.

An interested spectator of these operations was General Sir Sam Hughes, who took the opportunity to watch the Brigade at work. On the following day the Battalion practised independently, advance guards and flank guards in the morning, occupation of position in the afternoon. Divine Services were held on the 20th, and on the 21st musketry, platoon drill and practice of companies in attack filled in the time. Care was taken at these manœuvres to see that each platoon practised each phase of the attack. August 22nd was again devoted to special training. In the morning the attack was practised and the "captured" trenches consolidated. Later in the day the Battalion was put through the moves following a supposed enemy gas attack. Bayonet fighting, rifle sighting and demonstrations in blocking communication trenches occupied the time on the 23rd, and the three days that followed were devoted to special training along the lines described already.

An amazing feature of all these manœuvres was the frequency with which, after a successful attack, the fleeing enemy retired in the exact direction of one of the little estaminets with which the country was so liberally provided. Time and again defending troops, utterly unaware of the direction in which they were retreating, would find themselves pushed by a vigorous attack, not only into the outskirts of one of these establishments, but right through the doorway into the taproom itself. Here the poor bewildered soldiers felt compelled to buy drinks to justify the rudeness of their intrusion. Officers too, doubtless for lack of more arid spots, were frequently forced to use these hospitable houses as unit headquarters.

On Sunday, August 27th, Church Parade was held on the Battalion Parade ground at 10 a.m. Earlier in the morning the Roman Catholic party proceeded to church at Genspeete. Company commanders were ordered to see that all Roman Catholics were present at this parade, which led the old timers to prophesy that strenuous times lay not far ahead. Late that same night the Transport and No. 1 Coy. paraded and marched to the station at St. Omer, followed by the remainder of the Battalion three quarters of an hour later. At 7 o'clock on the morning of the 28th the Battalion entrained, and, after a tiresome journey, reached Conteville Station at 4 o'clock in the afternoon. From this point the 13th marched some four or five miles to the village of the same name.

All the men had benefited physically from the fortnight of strenuous training at Watten, which was a help, as the Battalion now marched daily towards the Somme. Halloy Pernois was the destination on the 29th and La Vicogne on the 30th. Rain fell heavily during the latter move and the men reached billets soaked through and rather tired. At La Vicogne, a huge farm, the whole Battalion shook down in great piles of hay and straw, dislodging many indignant fowls and retrieving a number of eggs.

SANCTUARY WOOD AND WATTEN

Harponville was the Battalion's objective on August 31st and here the men realized that they were approaching the scene of the new battle, as the rumble of the distant guns was clearly heard, while on the horizon could be seen the line of observation balloons that marked the circumference of the huge Somme salient.

CHAPTER X

The Somme

> Burned from the ore's rejected dross,
> The iron whitens in the heat.
> With plangent strokes of pain and loss
> The hammers on the iron beat.
> Searched by the fire, through death and dole
> We feel the iron in our soul.
> —Laurence Binyon.

I

THE great engagement of the British and French Armies, spoken of as "The Battles of the Somme, 1916," was a conflict unprecedented in history. Vast armies took part in it and swayed backwards and forwards for months, locked tight in a veritable death struggle. Trenches were captured, recaptured and captured again, while the whole face of the earth for miles was so torn by concentrated artillery fire as to render familiar scenes utterly unrecognizable. Thriving and solidly built little villages melted under the storms of high explosive like butter in a hot sun, till their very site was often a matter of dispute, to be settled, perhaps, by the discovery in the churned up soil of a few loose bricks or the merest remnant of an old stone wall.

Men died in this bitter fighting by tens of thousands, but others were found to take their places and the great struggle went relentlessly on. The Germans christened the battle "The Blood Bath of the Somme" and this phrase, ugly and horrible though it be, conveys more vividly than any other a true impression of the titanic struggle. No unit came out of the Somme unscathed; few came out unshattered.

With reference to such a battle it is difficult to speak of victory and defeat; impossible to do so in a work of this kind, which deals with the actions of a single battalion. Battalions at the Somme were as platoons in an ordinary battle. Brigades and divisions were used up in the struggle for a single trench, or farm.

THE SOMME

Launched on July 1st, 1916, the British and French attack swept forward for a time and then encountered a dogged and determined resistance. Pushed with amazing courage and self sacrifice, however, the attack continued to progress and, in spite of tremendous losses, bit its way deep into the German lines, capturing thousands of prisoners and inflicting losses on the enemy which he could not but regard as extremely serious.

Such, then, in its scantiest outline, was the situation in which the Canadian Corps was now called upon to take part. Division by division the Corps came into action and fought as the Corps always fought, the 4th Canadian Division winning its spurs and proving itself in every way worthy to take its place with the veterans of Ypres, St. Eloi and Sanctuary Wood.

Arriving at the Somme, the 1st Canadian Division was soon in action, relieving the 4th Australian Division at Tara Hill on September 4th. Previous to the actual exchange of divisional command, however, units of the 1st Canadian Division were thrown into the battle under Australian direction, amongst these being the 13th Battalion, Royal Highlanders.

Leaving Harponville, the 13th proceeded on the morning of September 1st and, marching via Warloy, reached an area, known as "The Brickfields," near Albert, where the Battalion was to pass the night. Some time later transport wagons arrived with canvas covers which the men converted into bivouacs, and in which, after a hot meal and an issue of rum, they settled down for a welcome night's rest. In the morning the bivouacs were taken down, the area thoroughly cleaned up and equipment prepared for a tour in the trenches. At 2 p.m. the company commanders received orders from Lieut.-Col. Buchanan to reconnoitre the area around la Boisselle, paying particular attention to the Chalk Pits and to the roads and means of communication between la Boiselle and Pozières.

When this party returned to camp orders for the Battalion to move up to the Chalk Pits and occupy the old German front line had already been received. At night, therefore, the companies moved off, No. 1 under command of Major J. H. Lovett, who had again recovered from his wounds, No. 2 under Major J. D. Macpherson, No. 3 under Major W. F. Peterman, who had just recovered from his most recent wounds, and No. 4 under Major F. J. Rowan, who had recovered from wounds received in the previous April.

ROYAL HIGHLANDERS OF CANADA

Passing through Albert, where the leaning statue of the Virgin stood out as a blacker shadow in the blackness of the sky, the Battalion proceeded to la Boisselle, as support to the 4th Australian Division. In spite of the fact that the area had previously been reconnoitred, darkness and the absence of all landmarks made the task of finding the proper trenches unusually difficult and the move was not completed till about 1 a.m.

In the morning, at about 5 o'clock, all the artillery in the area opened up in support of an Australian attack on a locality known as Mouquet Farm. Immediately behind the 13th, as if to lend an Imperial aspect to the affair, were some South African heavy batteries, whose guns roared with right good will. Thus the Australians attacked with British troops not far away on their flank, with Canadians in support and with South Africans helping to lay down the barrage.

In spite of this array, the attack was not a success, though at first it appeared to be. Much later, when Mouquet Farm was finally captured, an explanation of the disaster that overtook the attackers on this and other occasions was forthcoming. It appeared that the Germans had a large tunnel leading into the farm from a point well to the rear. When an attack captured and swept past the farm, the enemy, making use of this inconspicuous tunnel, would pour out and with bombs, rifles and machine guns take the attackers in rear. So successful was this strategy that on several occasions no authentic report was ever received of what had happened to troops who presumably had captured the farm. They simply vanished and, when an effort was made to get in touch with them, the enemy was found to be in possession. It was not until the night of September 16th, when the 2nd Canadian Mounted Rifles definitely took Mouquet Farm, that this secret was disclosed.

Early in the morning when the 13th was occupying the position at la Boisselle, as previously described, Lieut.-Col. Buchanan received orders from General Glasstorch, of the 13th Australian Brigade, to hold two companies in readiness for an immediate move. This order was a surprise, as the 13th had previously been informed that the Australians would not require assistance, but it was promptly obeyed and Nos. 1 and 2 Companies selected. Knowing the heavy casualties to be expected in this area, Lieut.-Col. Buchanan ordered the second-in-command of each company and 20% of the specialists into reserve.

THE SOMME

Some fifteen minutes after the "stand to" order arrived and before the men had been able to breakfast, No. 1 Coy., under Major Lovett, was ordered forward. Lieut.-Col. Buchanan was averse to seeing his companies serve under a command other than his own, but there was no help for it and he took up a post at the la Boisselle cross roads to shout a word of good wishes. The Company, as it responded to the Colonel's greeting, numbered 143 all ranks. When next it passed in front of him, it totalled 1 officer and 23 men.

Owing to the fact that the companies of the 13th acted during the ensuing engagement almost as independent units, it is necessary at this point to leave the Battalion for a time and to follow the career, first of No. 1 Coy. and then of No. 2.

After the farewell to Col. Buchanan at the crossroads, Major Lovett led No. 1 forward and heard from Gen. Glasstorch that the enemy, having cut off and practically annihilated the first waves of the Australian attack, had counter-attacked and made a considerable breach in the front line. This gap Lovett was ordered to cover and guides were furnished to lead him to its neighbourhood.

Each man of No. 1 Coy. was supplied with two bombs at a dump and entry was made into the trenches to the left of the Australian headquarters, overlooking Pozières. Capt. Maxwell of the Australians and the guides under his command rendered Major Lovett every possible assistance in the advance that followed, but at last they declared that, owing to the obliteration of so many trenches in the morning's bombardment, they were by no means sure of their exact position. The general direction of their objective was known, however, and Lovett decided to advance overland, rushing small parties from shell hole to shell hole and leaving a guide at intervals to direct those still to follow.

Considerable progress was made in this manner until a stream of machine gun bullets from the rear gave warning that the advance had progressed beyond a point where an enemy post had been established. After a great deal of difficulty this gun was put out of action and the Company, continuing its advance, reached the Australian front line trench. The left of this trench was occupied by the enemy, but the right flank was connected up with another Australian unit. The work that faced the combined Canadians and Australians, therefore, was to drive the Germans out of the left section of the trench and to link up with other Australian units, presumed to be somewhere beyond.

ROYAL HIGHLANDERS OF CANADA

In the meantime No. 2 Coy. of the 13th, under Major J. D. Macpherson, had also been ordered forward. Advancing some time after Lovett, Macpherson led his men in artillery formation up to Pozières. Leaving the men to draw bombs from the dump, he reported to the Australian O.C. and was ordered by the latter to take his men into neighbouring trenches and "stand by." Heavy shelling could be heard forward at this time, but not many shells struck nearby. Macpherson was informed that No. 1 Coy. had been in Pozières and had been sent forward.

About 10 a.m. an orderly summoned Macpherson to Brigade Headquarters, where he was told that Mouquet Farm had just been captured. Map locations were given to him and he was ordered to take his company forward and occupy a position near the Farm. Being unfamiliar with the area, Macpherson asked for a guide, but this assistance, owing to shortage of men, the Australian General was unable to provide.

On leaving the H.Q., Macpherson encountered the Brigade Intelligence Officer, who offered to help get the Company into position. Accordingly a start was made, the men in single file and in fairly close touch, this formation being advisable to avoid the possibility of platoons getting separated and lost in the maze of shell holes and ruined trenches.

After advancing for about a mile, the Australian Intelligence Officer said that the front line must be near at hand and that, while the Highlanders rested, he would go forward and reconnoitre. When a long time elapsed and he did not return, Macpherson became uneasy and decided to reconnoitre for himself. He accordingly started forward and soon came across some wounded Australians in a shell hole. These could tell him little of his position, or of the state of affairs in general, but from them he learned that some Highlanders had already passed that way and concluded that the Highlanders in question must have been Major Lovett and No. 1 Coy. Proceeding a little further, Macpherson found another shell hole occupied by Australians, this time unwounded, and from these he learned for the first time that, instead of Mouquet Farm having been captured, the troops who had attacked it had been completely wiped out. Once again, however, he picked up the trail of No. 1 Coy., which had recently passed by and occupied a trench not far ahead.

Proceeding forward again, Macpherson soon found No. 1 Coy.

THE SOMME

in the Australian front line trench, and, after a consultation with Lovett, it was decided that Macpherson should bring up No. 2 Coy. and establish a line on Lovett's left, endeavouring at the same time to discover which of the very contradictory reports regarding the ownership of Mouquet Farm was correct.

Returning to his company in accordance with these arrangements, Macpherson met the Australian Intelligence Officer, who said that he had discovered a vacant trench over to the left. As this was approximately the position that Macpherson had told Lovett he would occupy, he instructed the Australian to lead on, taking the precaution, however, of holding back the main body of the Company, until a small party, under Lieut. M. A. Jaques, could explore the trench and find out where it led.

Shortly after this party had left on its reconnoitring mission, the main body heard a crash of rifle fire and the explosion of several bombs, and a moment later a man came running back to report that the advance party had run into opposition. On receipt of this news, Macpherson took a platoon and hurried along the trench to find that Lieut. Jaques, having driven the enemy before him, was establishing a block in the trench to keep them from returning. Lifting himself up on the parapet to obtain a better idea of where the trench led, Jaques discovered that Mouquet Farm was only a short distance further on. He had just reported this important item and was taking a further look around when a sniper killed him with a bullet through the head. His work all through this trying day had been of a courageous and helpful nature and his loss at this time was one the Company could ill afford.

With his position established as the result of Lieut. Jaques' observations, Macpherson wrote a detailed report to Headquarters and asked particularly that Lewis guns be sent up, so that he could protect his flank and drive off any serious attack from Mouquet Farm. Meanwhile, by occupying the trench, which was in echelon to Lovett's position, Macpherson considerably assisted the latter, who had been harassed by enfilade fire from the party of Huns driven out by Lieut. Jaques' bombers. Contact between the two trenches, once established, was skilfully maintained by a series of patrol posts under the command of Lieut. K. M. Carmichael.

About 6 o'clock in the afternoon a message from Australian headquarters told Lovett that aeroplane observation revealed what appeared to be Australian posts, isolated, but still holding out, in the immediate vicinity of Mouquet Farm. In an effort to confirm this and to establish connection with such posts, if they actually existed, No. 1 Coy. launched a bombing attack along its trench to the left, and tried hard to push its way into the Farm itself. Fully 150 yards of enemy trench was captured in this manner, but resistance stiffened with every foot of the advance and eventually the Canadians were brought to a standstill. The remainder of the night was spent in clinging desperately to what had been gained, against repeated bombing attacks by the enemy.

In the meantime, No. 2 Coy. had driven off a similar series of attacks, but had suffered sharply from enemy shell fire. At midnight, the Lewis guns for which he had asked not having arrived, Macpherson decided to make his way back to see what was the matter. He found Lieut.-Col. Buchanan in Battalion Headquarters at Pozières and learned from the latter that No. 3 Coy., under Major Peterman, had moved up and was in position somewhere to the left of the front his own company was holding. Returning to No. 2 Coy., Macpherson took with him the two machine guns he required and used these to strengthen his unprotected flanks.

Such, then, were the adventures and misadventures of Nos. 1 and 2 Companies up to the hour of dawn on the morning of September 4th. During all this time the remaining companies had not been inactive. At 2 p.m. on September 3rd, No. 3 Coy. advanced from la Boisselle, followed by No. 4 Coy. at 5 p.m. Battalion Headquarters was moved up to a position in the Cemetery at Pozières Wood and at 9 p.m. the 13th Royal Highlanders of Canada officially took over from the 52nd, 51st and 41st Australian Battalions, No. 3 Coy. moving up and digging in somewhat in advance of the position occupied by No. 4 Coy. During the night both companies were heavily shelled, but tackled with energy the work of carrying in the Australian wounded, many of whom had been lying out in the open for long weary hours, and some for days. In this work and throughout the strenuous days that followed, Lieut. T. B. D. Tudball, Sergt.-Major Mather, Sergt. McKay and Sergt. W. C. Pearce rendered service of the finest character.

September 4th was a trying day for all the companies. Shelling was almost continuous and rain in the morning did not add to the men's comfort. No. 1 Coy. had received no rations for over 24 hours, but foraged about and discovered some excellent coffee in huge glass bottles, a souvenir left behind by the enemy when the

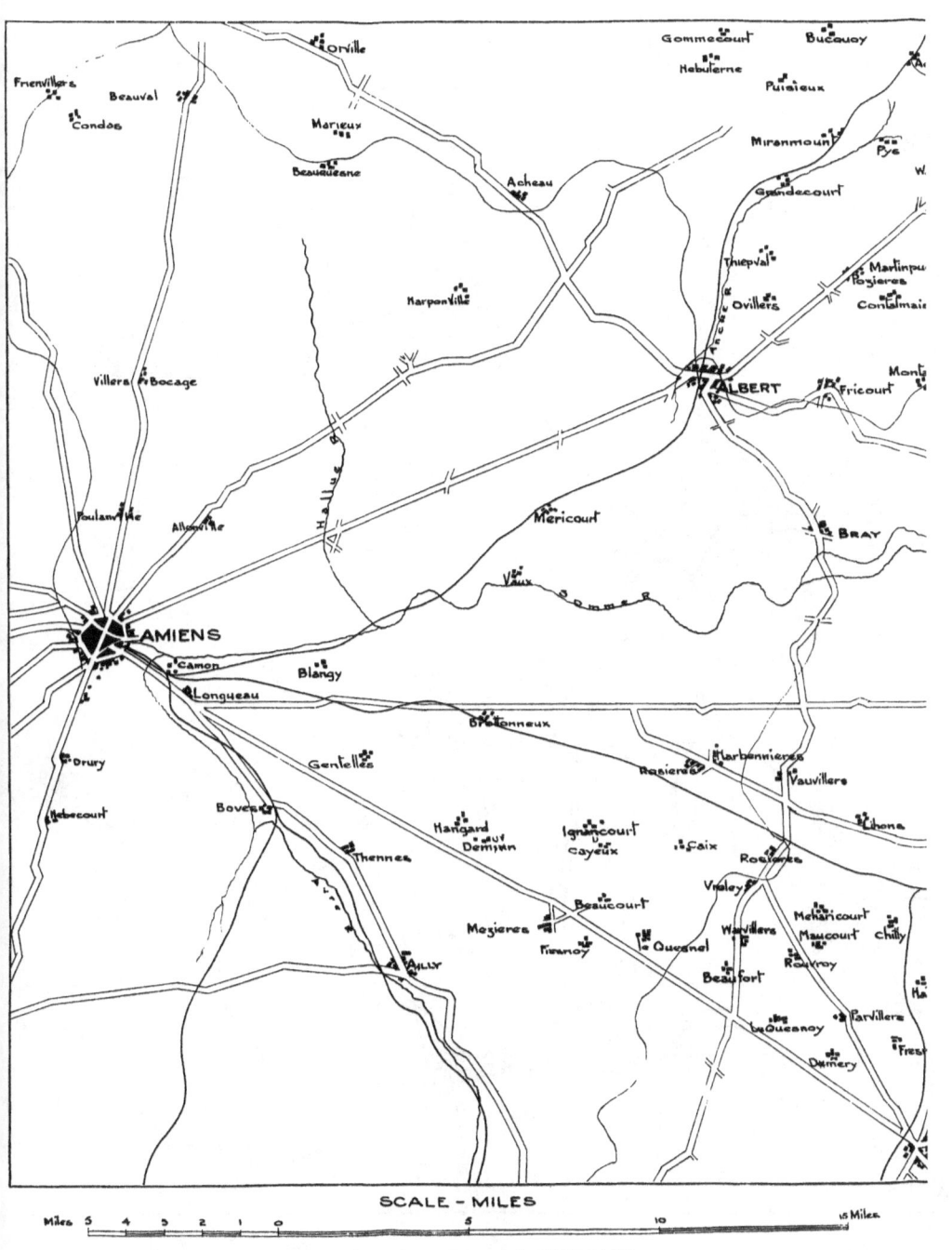

THE SOMME AND AMIENS

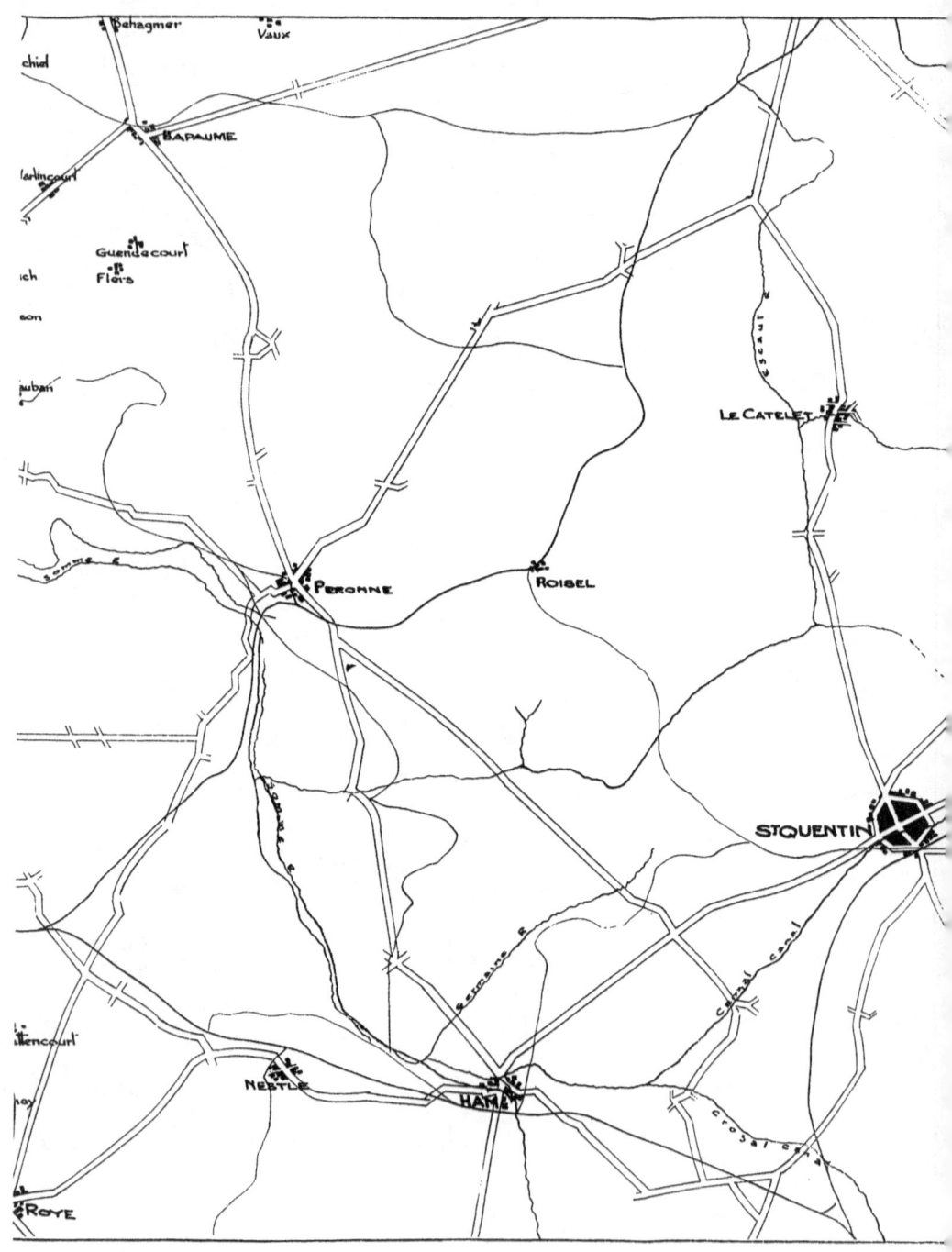

THE SOMME

Australian attack drove them out. This, with their own and German emergency rations, kept the men from feeling the absence of the regular rations too acutely.

No. 2 Coy. also suffered from shortage of food on this day, as well as from enemy shelling, which was persistent and accurate. At night connection with No. 3 Coy. was definitely established. No. 3 also connected up with No. 4 during the night so that, by daybreak on the 5th, the Battalion was acting as a co-ordinated unit once more.

At 6 o'clock in the morning a Red Cross flag appeared between the lines on No. 1 Coy's. front and German stretcher bearers began to carry in their wounded. These bearers were unmolested by the Canadians, who took advantage of the situation to remove some of their own casualties. During this "armistice," Major Lovett noticed that several wounded Germans, eluding their own bearers, slipped into his trench and surrendered. This suggested to him that the morale of the German troops opposite him might not be of the highest order and that an attempt to induce them to surrender might be worth while. Accordingly, as soon as the Red Cross Flag was withdrawn, Lovett and an Australian sergeant advanced to a position half way between the lines and tried to induce the Germans to come out. A measure of success seemed to be rewarding this move until a German officer appeared and promptly opened fire, his example being immediately followed by all his men. With a crash of rifle fire from their trenches, the Royal Highlanders endeavoured to drive the Germans under cover and give the daring negotiators a chance to escape. In this effort the men of No. 1 Coy. were only partially successful. Lovett got in, but the Australian sergeant was shot and instantly killed.

Following this incident enemy artillery fire increased and about 1 p.m. word was passed up from the right that Germans could be seen pouring up their communication trenches as if for a heavy attack. The Lahore Artillery, supporting the Canadians, also received this information and laid down a heavy barrage which apparently broke the enemy attack before it could develop. As if in reply to this, the German artillery redoubled its fire and pounded No. 1 Coy's trench heavily. By this time some sixty per cent. of the Company had become casualties and to this total, additions were being made with unpleasant frequency. Major Lovett suffered his third wound of the war, an injury which held him in a

[129]

ROYAL HIGHLANDERS OF CANADA

London hospital for the three months that followed, while Lieut. Carmichael and Coy. Sergt.-Major Bullock, both of whom had distinguished themselves throughout the engagement, were also wounded. In the evening Lieut. C. D. Llwyd, who had fought most courageously, led the weary and famished remnant of the Company back into reserve.

Simultaneously with the relief of No. 1 Coy., it was arranged that three platoons of No. 2 Coy. should be relieved by No. 3 Coy. Through some misunderstanding relief for the fourth platoon of No. 2 Coy., under Lieut. H. E. Piercy, did not arrive. In a maze of almost unidentifiable trenches, it is not difficult for an error of this sort to occur, none the less it was hard on the men of the unfortunate platoon, who for two extra days were compelled to hold their tiny bit of line. Of the one hundred and twenty bayonets which Macpherson led forward on the morning of the 3rd, about fifty remained when the action ended.

While these events were in progress on the front of Nos. 1 and 2 Companies, Nos. 3 and 4 were busily engaged in consolidating their positions. All day on September 5th they were subjected to heavy shell fire and were quite unable to obtain rations. Late in the day some water was brought up to them, but as this was strongly diluted with gasoline, it aggravated rather than assuaged their thirst and caused digestive complications which rendered the men entirely miserable. September 6th was again a day of heavy shell fire, hard work and general discomfort. At night the 14th Canadian Battalion relieved No. 4 Coy., which withdrew to Wire Trench (near la Boisselle). On the following night the 13th Battalion was relieved by the 8th Canadian Battalion and proceeded to billets in Albert, where a hot meal was served to the exhausted men as soon as they arrived.

Taking it all in all, the Battalion's first experience on the Somme had been a hard one. Thrown into a fight before they had any real conception of the area, with their flanks in the air, and under a strange command, the men of Nos. 1 and 2 Companies had acquitted themselves in a highly creditable manner, while their comrades in the other companies, many of them in their first engagement, had behaved with the coolness and reliability of seasoned veterans. Casualties had, of course, been severe. In addition to the officers already mentioned, Capt. C. R. Chisholm was wounded, as were Lieuts. A. S. MacLean, H. R. Monsarrat and H. T. Higinbotham,

THE SOMME

while amongst the rank and file 60 men were killed, 247 were wounded and 16 were missing, a heavy list, considering that the Battalion had been employed in what ranked merely as a minor phase of the great engagement.

II

September 8th, the first day in billets after a strenuous tour, was spent in resting and cleaning equipment. On the 9th the 3rd Canadian Brigade moved to Warloy, the 13th Battalion parading at 9 a.m. and reaching the new billets a few minutes before 1 o'clock. In the afternoon the baths at Rue de Guise were allotted to the men, who paraded in parties of 25 under an officer or N.C.O. On the 10th the Brigade moved to Hérissart, a short distance which was covered in a march of about an hour and a half. The next day the Brigade continued its march to the Rest Area at Montrelet-Bonneville.

Several days were spent in this area, the time being employed in all the multitudinous details that require attention when a Battalion has just emerged from a tour in the line and is preparing for another. On September 12th no orders for parades were issued, but the company commanders, at their own discretion, held rifle, gas helmet, ammunition and similar inspections. Most of the day, however, was spent in cleaning up the billets which were, without exception, the dirtiest the Battalion had ever occupied. Carried away by enthusiasm at the results achieved, a large working party was ordered to clean up the whole town.

On the following day the companies carried out independent training, as did the Machine Gunners, Bombers, Signallers and Intelligence Section. Postings on this date included the following: Major G. L. Mott to take command of No. 1 Coy.; Lieuts. E. W. Mingo and J. B. Beddome posted to No. 3 Coy. Lieut. Mingo had served with the Battalion previously and had rejoined after recovering from wounds received at the Bluff in April. On the same date as the postings mentioned above the ranks of the 13th were reinforced by a draft of men from the 1st Canadian Entrenching Battalion.

On the night of September 14th the Battalion was ordered to "stand to," as an operation of some importance was being conducted by units of the 2nd and 3rd Canadian Divisions. This attack, wherein the British "Tanks" made their first appearance, was a

ROYAL HIGHLANDERS OF CANADA

success, and support from the 1st Division was not needed. On the morrow the 13th paraded and moved to tents in the Vicogne area, proceeding from that point on the 16th and billeting in Harponville, whence, as on the occasion of the Battalion's first visit a fortnight earlier, the roar of the great Somme battle was distinctly audible.

September 17th was spent in Harponville, the men cleaning equipment and waiting hourly for orders to move. None arrived until the following day at noon, when the Battalion marched in pouring rain to the Brickfields at Albert. The only member of the Battalion who even pretended to enjoy this march was "Flora Macdonald," the Regimental goat, to whom the up hill and down dale nature of the route seemed to make some mysterious appeal. Perhaps it evoked memories of the far off Himalayas and rushing mountain torrents that poured down to the hot plains beneath. Who can say? All that one knows is that "Flora" splashed along the flooded roads and seemingly enjoyed herself immensely. In some places the roads were actually knee deep in water, so that, at 5 p.m., it was a wet and weary Battalion that built shelters out of old ammunition boxes and tarpaulins at the Brickfields.

Rain continued all day on the 19th, the men spending much time in repairing their leaky quarters. Rifles were inspected to make certain that the rain had not put them in bad condition. On the 20th the Brickfields were shelled to some extent, but no shells fell close enough to cause the Highlanders serious inconvenience. On this date a draft from the 92nd Highlanders, from Toronto, joined the 13th, bringing the latter very nearly up to strength once more.

Shelling was again a feature on the 21st, but, as on the previous day, little damage was done, although one man, a member of the new draft, was wounded in the heel. While at the Brickfields shoulder patches were issued so that men of various units could be distinguished at a glance. In the case of the 13th these consisted of a red patch surmounted by a blue circle, the former indicating the 1st Canadian Division and the latter the brigade and battalion. On the afternoon when these were issued the Brickfields presented an odd sight. Seated everywhere groups and individuals were busy sewing the bright pieces of cloth onto their tunics, as fast as Sergt. Stewart and the other tailors could cut the huge bolts of bright material into the required shapes.

On the night of the 22nd the Battalion moved from the bivouacs

THE SOMME

in the Brickfields to familiar billets in Albert. On the same date it was announced that Sergt. A. M. McLeod had been awarded the Russian Cross of St. George, 3rd Class, in recognition of courageous service, while postings included the following: Lieut. C. D. Llwyd to be Grenade Officer; Lieut. M. C. W. Grant to be Assistant Grenade Officer; Lieut. T. G. Holley to be Assistant Intelligence Officer; Lieut. E. C. Bryson to be 2nd-in-command of No. 1 Coy.; Major S. W. Gilroy to be 2nd-in-command of No. 4 Coy.; Coy. Sergt.-Major F. Spencer to be Acting Regimental Sergeant-Major, during the absence on leave of Regimental Sergeant-Major W. Chalmers.

The following day was spent in preparing for the trenches and at night the Battalion moved up to relieve the 2nd Canadian Battalion in front of Courcelette. On the whole the relief was uneventful. The Albert-Bapaume Road was crowded with ammunition limbers but, by taking to the side of the road and advancing in single file, the Battalion maintained a steady, if not rapid, rate of progress. From Pozières the men proceeded along the light railway track to a spot known as "K" Dump, thence overland for a bit and finally through some old communication trenches into the line.

During the two days that followed artillery fire on both sides was heavy, while sniping and rifle fire were, if anything, a little below normal. Courcelette was bombarded almost ceaselessly by the enemy, some parties of the 13th being caught while coming through the village and losing several men. The troops in the front line suffered appreciably from thirst, as their water bottles were soon emptied and such water as was delivered was abominably flavoured with gasoline.

At night on the 25th, the 14th and 15th Battalions moved into the front line and prepared for an attack which they were to make in conjunction with other troops on the morrow. The presence of these extra troops crowded the front line to the uttermost, but fortunately the enemy reply to the bombardment in preparation for the attack, though heavy, was not well directed and casualties were accordingly light. It had been generally understood that the attack of the 14th and 15th Battalions would take place at dawn, but it was not until 11 o'clock in the morning that the zero hour was even announced. At this time, owing to fear of listening sets, great secrecy as to the zero hour of an attack was insisted upon and the hour was never mentioned aloud in the trenches. When it was necessary to speak of it, officers were instructed to do so by code signs, but as this method had its disadvantages, they usually compromised by naming the hour in a whisper.

Shortly after noon the 14th and 15th went over the parapet and attacked. These splendid battalions pushed their assault home in a striking manner, but, as was so often the case on the Somme, where no ground was yielded without a desperate struggle, counter-attacks during the next few days prevented consolidation of all the territory originally captured.

Meanwhile the trenches of the 13th were subjected to a severe shelling, which caused numerous casualties, not only to the Royal Highlanders, but to the wounded from the attack, with whom the trenches were by this time crowded. Prisoners captured by the 14th and 15th added to the congestion, but were made use of in evacuating casualties. Shelling continued all day and showed little sign of diminishing at nightfall. Bringing up rations through this barrage was a matter of no little difficulty and danger, nevertheless the duty was satisfactorily carried out by a party under Lieut. T. B. D. Tudball, who deposited the supplies at Battalion Headquarters, whence the companies in the line were to draw them.

On this occasion Lieut.-Col. Buchanan had his headquarters in a dugout in Courcelette and had with him Major W. F. Peterman and Capt. C. C. Green, these officers acting respectively as Second-in-command and Adjutant during the absence on leave of Major G. E. McCuaig and Lieut. C. D. Craig. Having dumped the rations, Lieut. Tudball reported to Major Peterman, who approved of a suggestion that the ration party should remain at headquarters till the barrage on the road back had become less severe. During the interval that followed Lieut.-Col. Buchanan noticed that Tudball showed signs of exhaustion and gave the latter a drink of whiskey. Some time later, the barrage having eased a little, the ration party withdrew.

No one knows exactly what happened in that busy dugout at about 8.30 p.m. Who can ever describe a moment of high tragedy and disaster? All that is certain is that a shell burst in the roof and walls and ignited a supply of gasoline, the explosion and flames leaving death and ruin in their wake. All in a moment the Battalion suffered a grievous loss. Lieut.-Col. Buchanan was killed, as were Major Peterman and Capt. Green. With them perished eight of the headquarters staff, while thirty-three others, staff and runners, were horribly burned or wounded, among these being Corp. H.

THE SOMME

Day, in command of the scouts and runners on duty. With the death of the Commanding Officer and the Acting Second-in-command, control of the Battalion passed for the time being to Major J. D. Macpherson, who handed over to Major G. E. McCuaig when the latter returned from leave on the following morning.

All day on the 27th the Battalion remained in the line, enduring shelling even more severe than on the 26th. A mopping up party on this date cleared the battlefield over which the 14th and 15th had advanced on the previous day, no light task in view of the fact that many wounded had to be evacuated over terrain so churned up that the removal of a single case was often a matter calling for all the strength and endurance that eight men could bring to bear.

At one point the subaltern in charge of the mopping up discovered an enormous Hun lying on the ground. Stirring this individual gently with his foot, the officer suggested by signs that he get up and make his way to the rear. Replying in a similar manner, the German intimated that his wounds were too severe, so stretcher bearers were summoned. Owing to the weight of the wounded man, the journey back was a trying one, but at last the stretcher bearers, nearly exhausted, reached a point not far from the dressing station and laid their burden down for a moment's rest. To their almost speechless indignation the Hun thereupon rose from the stretcher, wandered about for a minute or so and, returning to the stretcher, lay down again with an air of ineffable content. The bearers, naturally, forced the Hun to walk the short distance that remained, but in view of the fact that he could probably have made the whole journey in this manner, none could deny that he had scored handsomely.

At night word reached the Highlanders that the 14th Battalion required assistance to counter-attack a position on the right. No. 4 Coy. was assigned to this duty and command for the occasion given to Lieut. H. A. Johnston. About midnight guides from the 14th Battalion arrived to lead Lieut. Johnston and his Company forward and shortly afterward the move began.

It had been arranged that the 14th Battalion would place lights facing to the rear to mark the assembly position. There is no doubt that these were placed in position, but a heavy fog fell and they were quite indistinguishable. Similarly, the few landmarks that existed in this dreary and devastated area were completely enveloped and lost to view. In the inky blackness of the dripping night and in the maze of water filled shell holes under foot, the guides, as was almost inevitable, failed in their allotted task. Time was lost wandering around trying to identify trenches and shell holes that had no individual characteristics, and the party was nowhere near the assembly point when the barrage that was to precede the attack began. Seeing that he had entirely missed his objective, Lieut. Johnston consulted with the officer guides of the 14th, who agreed with him that it was now quite useless to push on. Accordingly the venture was called off and Johnston, returning with his men to No. 4 Coy. headquarters, reported to Major Rowan the death of one of his party and the circumstances under which his mission had failed.

While these events had been taking place the 22nd Battalion had relieved the Highlanders, the latter making their way through seemingly endless mud, back past Courcelette and the famous Sugar Refinery and on to billets in Albert. So exhausted were the men after the strenuous days in the line, that billets were not reached by the main body till long after dawn, while stragglers continued to arrive in for several hours after. During the tour casualties had amounted to 28 killed, 142 wounded and 9 missing.

Meanwhile to Lieut. Tudball had fallen the sad task of conveying to Albert for burial the bodies of Lieut.-Col. Buchanan, Major Peterman, Capt. Green and Lieut. G. N. Sale, the last named having fallen in action during the progress of the tour. It was with heavy hearts that officers and men attended the funeral, which took place in Albert on the morning of the 28th. While all ranks shared in the sorrow and regret caused by the death of a beloved commanding officer, the sense of personal loss was accentuated in the case of those veterans, few in number by this time, who had sailed from Canada with the First Canadian Contingent almost exactly two years before. To them Col. Buchanan had been more than a good commanding officer. They had served under him in times of peril and trusted and looked up to him in a manner that bore testimony, more eloquent than words, to the very definite affection that existed between them.

Major Peterman, too, had been an original officer and had served the Battalion with inspired devotion. Twice he had been wounded, but on each occasion his high courage and deep sense of duty had hastened his recovery, so that he might rejoin the Regiment and continue to serve with the least possible loss of time. Capt. Green

THE SOMME

and Lieut. Sale had been with the 13th for a shorter time, but they, too, by reason of their loyal and capable service, had won a place in the regard of both officers and men.

Canon Scott officiated at the funeral and the dead received all honours that grieving comrades could bestow. Military funerals are of necessity brief and this was no exception. When the beautiful lines of the burial service had been read, the rifles spoke their farewell, the bugle sounded the "Last Post," officers and men saluted with deep respect and, turning away, left the four gallant soldiers to their well earned rest.

III

On the afternoon of September 28th the Battalion, weary after the hardships of the previous days, paraded at three o'clock and marched to Warloy, No. 2 Coy. detailing 1 officer and 6 men to march in the rear of the column to pick up stragglers. No regular parades were held on the 29th, though company commanders inspected rifles and checked shortages of kit, submitting lists of deficiencies to the Quartermaster, so that the Battalion might be made ready for the next tour in the line. On the following day Gen. Currie visited the Battalion, complimented the men on their steadiness during the recent engagements and spoke most feelingly of the loss that the Division had suffered through the death of Lieut.-Col. Buchanan.

With the advent of October the Royal Highlanders began active preparations for an attack against Regina Trench. Little could be accomplished for several days owing to inclement weather, but during this time the men bathed and received clean clothing at Warloy; were paid and practised bayonet fighting, while the companies managed to get in a two hour training period each day, as did the Machine Gun, Bombing and Signalling Sections.

On October 4th the morning was devoted to physical training, bayonet fighting and musketry instruction, but in the afternoon the weather cleared and several hours were given to the practice of battalion in attack. On the 5th the Battalion marched to Albert, this route being full of significance to the veterans who knew from past experience that a march to Albert meant dirty work ahead. The next morning a move was made to the Brickfields, where some time was spent in bayonet fighting and practising the attack. In the afternoon preparations were made for a tour in the line, but about

3 p.m. this programme was cancelled and for it was substituted an order for a large party to work on repairing roads.

On the morning of the 7th the Battalion again practised the attack, while on the same date Major G. E. McCuaig issued his operation order dealing with the engagement now imminent. Summarized, this order was as follows:

(1) The Canadian Corps is co-operating with the 3rd British Corps in offensive operations.

The 69th Infantry Brigade will be on the right of the 1st Canadian Infantry Brigade.

The 9th Canadian Infantry Brigade will be on the left of the 3rd Canadian Infantry Brigade.

(2) The objective of the 1st Canadian Division will be Below Trench, and thence Regina Trench.

(3) The 3rd Canadian Infantry Brigade will attack on a front of two battalions, the 13th Battalion on the left and the 16th Battalion on the right.

(4) The 13th Battalion will move forward in waves, No. 1 Coy. forming the right and No. 4 Coy. the left of the first two waves. No. 2 Coy. will form the 3rd wave. No. 3 Coy. will be in reserve in the support trench, and will replace the first three waves in the front line, when the latter have moved forward.

(5) The time of the assault will be notified later.

(6) No. 2 Coy. will detail mopping up parties, in case any are required.

(7) Each company will be supplied with a small candle lamp with blue glass, to put up, if possible, close to their H.Q's., facing back.

No. 2 Coy. will take up a white tape line, to establish a route back to the jumping off trenches.

The Signallers will try to establish two lines to the forward objective.

(8) Prisoners should be collected, disarmed, and sent back under escort to Battalion H.Q's. Slightly wounded men should be used for this purpose, but escorts must be adequate to handle prisoners.

(9) It is important to locate the front line definitely. Flares and periscope mirrors will be used for this purpose.

In accordance with these orders, the 13th Battalion, Royal Highlanders of Canada, paraded at 4 o'clock in the afternoon of October

THE SOMME

7th and proceeded forward. In the original operation order, quoted above, it had been announced that three companies would take part in the attack, with one in reserve, but, while passing through Pozières on the way in, the Battalion received orders from 3rd Brigade Headquarters to throw all four companies into the assault, this being considered advisable owing to the fact that the companies were much under strength as the result of recent casualties. In order to comply with these instructions, a halt was made near the Courcelette Sugar Refinery and the dispositions of the companies adjusted.

Subsequently an officer of the 15th Battalion reported to Major McCuaig that the jumping off trenches had been prepared and were all in readiness. Accordingly, the men moved forward and occupied these trenches, Battalion Headquarters being established in an old German ammunition dugout, with two entrances side by side. One of these was for boxes of ammunition and gave access to a long, slippery chute, which led down to the dugout floor. The other was the regular entrance connected with the usual stairway for human beings. Some seven or eight hundred yards away from this position was Regina Trench, the first objective of the attack, and beyond it the village of Pys, against which Major F. J. Rowan was to lead his men, should the attack on Regina prove successful.

Sharp at 4.50 a.m., Rowan, who had quite recovered from his wounds of the previous April, led the attacking waves over the parapet. It was pitch dark at this hour, but a line of telegraph poles, leading straight to the objective, gave assurance that direction would be maintained without serious difficulty.

After the waves of the attack had gone forward the small garrison left in the jumping off trenches and the officers and men of Battalion Headquarters waited eagerly for news. Some uneasiness began to be felt as time passed and no word came back, but the crash and thunder of the supporting guns was reassuring and inspired confidence. After all the practice and all the careful planning, it seemed impossible that anything could go seriously wrong.

When night faded and the eastern sky began to show a hint of dawn without any news having arrived, uneasiness gave place to acute anxiety and acute anxiety to certainty that all was not well. Suddenly, Major McCuaig and the officers in Battalion Headquarters were startled by the arrival of a huge private, who, mistaking the entrance to the dugout, rolled down the ammunition chute and sprawled on the floor at their feet. He was covered with mud from head to toe, blood dripped from a shattered arm and, even as they helped him from the ground, all present realized that such a figure at such a time could be only a messenger of disaster. Recovering his equilibrium, the private turned to Major McCuaig and delivered his report. It consisted of three words only. "Sir," said he, "we're b——d."

Unfortunately the news conveyed in this expressive, if unorthodox, manner was all too true. The attack, it appeared, had progressed smoothly over the long stretch of No Man's Land, but, on sweeping forward for the actual plunge into Regina Trench, had run into a great mass of uncut wire. Day had dawned as the men were struggling to get through this and the Germans manning Regina Trench had opened up with machine gun and rifle fire and cut the attacking waves to ribbons. Proof that this explanation of what had happened was correct was found later when scores of the Highland dead were seen hanging limply over the wires that had proved their undoing.

Only on the right flank had the wire been properly cut and here a party of the Battalion, under Lieut. Sykes, pushed forward and drove their way into the Trench. Further to the right, the 16th Battalion, Canadian Scottish, achieved success and occupied Regina Trench in some force. Failure elsewhere, however, compelled the 16th to retire and to give up the ground they had won so dearly. With them returned some 20 men of the 13th, members of the party which had succeeded in reaching its objective.

Details of the attack are extremely hard to obtain. In the 13th Battalion 17 officers and 360 men went forward and of these 13 officers and 288 men were casualties. At first it was feared that 15 officers were casualties, but at night this number was reduced to 13, when Lieut. T. G. Holley and Lieut. J. A. Plante, who had lain out all day in the German wire, got safely in and reported for duty.

Meanwhile, the small band of survivors, reinforced by the Colt Gun Sections and by a company of the 15th Battalion, 48th Highlanders, of Toronto, had manned and were holding the jumping off trenches from which the ill-fated attack had been launched. Lieut.-Col. Bent, of the 15th, offered to send up additional assistance, as soon as news reached him of the heavy losses the 13th had sustained. This offer was much appreciated by the Royal Highlanders and

THE SOMME

was in keeping with the loyal spirit of co-operation and friendship which existed between all the battalions of the 3rd Brigade, but Major McCuaig decided that the situation did not render its acceptance necessary.

When night fell once more, Lieut. C. D. Llwyd took a patrol out into No Man's Land to see if he could obtain any information about the large number of men regarding whose fate nothing definite was known. This patrol covered a considerable area, but could get little news of value. Bit by bit, however, from a score of sources, some details as to the fate of individuals were collected. Major F. J. Rowan, who led the attack, was badly wounded. Stretcher bearers started back with him, but the little party never reached its destination. Presumably all were killed by shell fire somewhere in No Man's Land. Major S. W. Gilroy and Lieuts. H. E. Piercy, K. M. Carmichael, John Grey, E. C. Bryson and A. H. Walker were also killed. The last named was a brother of Lieut. J. G. Walker, killed while with the Battalion in the previous June. In addition to these Capt. R. W. Fordham, Capt. J. D. Gunn and Lieut. E. W. Mingo had been wounded and taken prisoner, while Capt. G. C. Hamilton had been captured and Lieut. H. G. Irving wounded.

All day on the 8th, all that night and all the next day, the remnant of the 13th Battalion clung to the jumping-off trenches, suffering a number of additional casualties from shelling, which at times was severe. Among those who fell was Lieut. H. A. McCleave, who was injured while proceeding overland between the jumping-off and original front line trenches, and died of his wounds in hospital. During all this trying time, Lieut. Plante and Lieut. Holley, who had escaped from the disaster, as previously noted, together with Lieut. Tudball and Sergt. Wallace, did much by their example to inspire their men and encourage them to face with fortitude the severe strain that holding the line with such a fragmentary force entailed.

On the night of October 9th, the 2nd Brigade relieved the 3rd Brigade, and the 13th Battalion, or rather what was left of it, withdrew to billets in Albert. So reduced was the unit that practically the whole Battalion rode back from Pozières on the limbers, which the Transport Officer had thoughtfully sent forward. No. 4 Coy. consisted of two subalterns and eleven men, while the other companies were only a little stronger, the four combined showing a strength of just 100 all ranks. Surely the Battalion bore the mark of having been through that place of evil which was the Somme.

CHAPTER XI

The Winter of 1916-1917

> Out here the dogs of war run loose,
> Their whipper-in is Death;
> Across the spoilt and battered fields
> We hear their sobbing breath.
> The fields where grew the living corn
> Are heavy with our dead;
> Yet still the fields at home are green
>
> . . . . .
>
> Though here the grass is red.
>
> —M. A. Bell.

I

FOLLOWING the month at the Somme, during which the 13th Battalion entered the line on three occasions and suffered casualties in excess of the fighting strength with which it had entered that area, a move to a less strenuous district was begun. On October 10th, the first day in billets after the Regina Trench disaster, the morning was spent in resting and cleaning equipment, while in the afternoon a muster roll call was held to check the lists of killed, wounded and missing. The appearance of the Battalion on this occasion brought a lump into the throats of those who recalled the splendid unit, up to full strength, which had swung into Albert from Harponville less than six weeks before. Only in smartness and morale did the skeleton companies on this date resemble the companies of early September. No. 4 Coy., with its two officers and eleven men, presented a particularly tragic sight, but the two officers were spick and span, while the men's equipment shone as a result of the morning's labour. The Somme had shattered the 13th Canadian Battalion, but had failed to subdue the Regiment's fighting spirit.

On the following day reveille was sounded at 5 a.m., breakfast was at 5.30 and at 8.15 the Battalion, strengthened by a draft which had joined the previous day, moved off to Vadencourt, reaching

THE WINTER OF 1916-1917

billets shortly before 1 p.m. A feature of this march occurred near Warloy, when a "sister" battalion, the 73rd Royal Highlanders of Canada, under Lieut.-Col. Peers Davidson, was encountered. The 73rd belonged to the 4th Canadian Division, which had recently arrived in France and was now on its way to win its spurs at the Somme. Dividing ranks, the men of the 73rd lined the road and allowed the 13th to pass through, expressing their feeling towards the veterans by a stirring roar of cheers. Immediately following this incident the 13th halted and the men of the two battalions exchanged news and gossip concerning mutual friends at home, or experiences endured in France. A large number of men had been drafted from the 73rd while the latter was still in England, and many of these had reinforced the 13th, consequently the two battalions had even more in common than parentage and Regimental tradition.

Two days were spent with Headquarters at Vadencourt, the time being occupied in squad drill, musketry practice, bayonet fighting and practice of companies in the attack, these manœuvres being carried out at the Training Area, north of Contay, which could be reached from Vadencourt in an easy half hour's march. During these two days all the men of drafts which had reinforced the Battalion were paraded before the Medical Officer for physical examination.

Following this short interval of training, the Battalion moved on October the 14th to camps at Val de Maison. Here one day was spent, the Battalion parading for Divine Service before Major Creegan in the morning and the afternoon being devoted to resting and cleaning equipment. On October 16th the Battalion proceeded to Halloy les Pernois, where three days were spent in training, special attention being paid to bayonet fighting, company training and extended order drill. On the morning of the 20th billets were thoroughly cleaned by the men and inspected by the Medical Officer, this being the accepted and time honoured routine previous to a move. At 10 a.m. the Battalion marched and at noon the men were agreeably surprised to find that they had reached their destination, as the impression had got abroad that the march was to be a long one. Berneuil proved to be the spot selected for the overnight stop, however, and here in the afternoon the men were paid, Lieut. Heaslip acting as Paymaster, during the absence of Capt. Appleton, who was in hospital.

Continuing their march on the 21st, the Highlanders moved to

ROYAL HIGHLANDERS OF CANADA

Villers l'Hôpital and thence on the 22nd to Sibiville. During this latter march a halt was called just before reaching Frévent and the sections of the Battalion, which had been marching independently, were formed up in column with the full pipe band at the head. In this order and marching "at attention," the unit swung through the town, halting again at the other side to rest the men before climbing the long, steep hill up to Sêricourt and on to Sibiville. Moves were again made on the two days that followed, Averdoignt being the destination on the 23rd and Frévillers on the 24th. From this latter point Major G. E. McCuaig and a group of officers reconnoitred a position at Souchez, which was to be occupied by the Battalion on its next tour in the line. October 25th was a quiet day, but on the 26th the Battalion marched in the morning and reached Camblain l'Abbé about 1 p.m. The afternoon and evening were devoted to preparations for taking over the new front.

The series of trench tours that began at this time awoke in the minds of those veterans who had served in the previous year memories of the winter tours before Messines. Conditions were by no means identical, but there was enough similarity to evoke interesting comparisons. The Battalion was again under strength, weather conditions were again abominable, necessitating constant repairs to the trenches, dugouts and parapets, but the enemy seemed more active and the routine considerably more varied.

Moving into the line on October 27th, the 13th Canadian Battalion relieved the 13th Battalion, Middlesex Regiment, in an area bounded by Gobron Trench and Vincent Street. This position was on Vimy Ridge, which had been the scene of bitter fighting by the French in the previous year and which was destined to be the setting for a great Canadian triumph in the spring that lay ahead. The ruins of Souchez and Ablain St. Nazaire were overlooked from Battalion Headquarters, situated in Zouave Valley, where, owing to the protection afforded by the steep sides of the Ridge, it was comparatively safe to move about in the open even at mid-day. From the front line trenches on top of the Ridge, Lens could be seen on a fine day, but, as the ground between the opposing lines was flat, the Highlanders enjoyed no advantage of observation over the enemy trenches.

During the week of the first tour enemy trench mortars were active, causing damage that necessitated much repair work, but inflicting only 7 casualties. Much sniping also took place, while

THE WINTER OF 1916-1917

at night the Highlanders' patrols were active, scouring No Man's Land to familiarize themselves with all topographical details that might prove of future interest and value.

On October 30th a small draft joined the Battalion, the majority of these being veterans of previous engagements now recovered from wounds. A day or so later a draft of officers arrived, among these being Major K. M. Perry, D.S.O. and Lieut. W. G. Hamilton, M.C., both of whom had recovered from wounds received in the Sanctuary Wood battle of the previous June. On rejoining the Battalion, Major Perry became Second-in-Command, while Lieut. Hamilton took over his old post of Battalion Machine Gun Officer. Amongst other wounded officers who rejoined at, or about, this time, were Capt. I. M. R. Sinclair and Lieuts. W. E. Macfarlane, N. M. MacLean, W. S. M. MacTier and W. H. D. Bennett.

At noon on November 3rd the 14th Battalion took over the front and the 13th moved to reserve positions at Cabaret Rouge and Berthonval Wood. A week was spent in reserve, during which the weather was bad for the most part and a great deal of trouble caused by sudden freshets, which flooded some dugouts and floated their contents away. The terrain surrounding the positions was exceedingly bleak and bare and pitted with innumerable shell holes, which bore silent testimony to the strenuous times of the previous year. These shell holes, grass grown or water filled according to their location, were a dreary sight, but there is evidence that at least one old timer regarded them with considerable satisfaction. Explaining his attitude to a newcomer, this canny Scot let drop a pearl of wisdom, "Weel, laddie, y'see its this way. A' thae shell holes filled wi' gr-r-ass are auld shell holes. Nary a yin o' them but is months auld and if ye'll stop a meenit ye'll appr-r-eciate the signeeficance o' that, while as for-r those filled wi' watter, a mon can per-r-haps bathe his per-r-son, wi'oot some fule raisin' a hell and a' o' fuss aboot watter bein' for dr-r-inkin' purposes only."

In spite of the bad weather during this period, or perhaps it would be more accurate to say because of it, working parties at night were by no means infrequent. The rain permeated the chalky soil, causing parapets and dugouts to cave in, so there was a constant demand for repair work and construction materials, not only in the reserve area, but also in the front line. These parties were, as always, extremely unpopular, as the work was arduous, without any compensating glory or excitement. One party, on reporting at the well known Souchez Dump, found that their task was to carry large sheets of corrugated iron to a point in Zouave Valley. Each man hoisted his load onto his back and at the word of command the party stumbled forward. The route was by way of a light railway embankment, which had been built up some twelve feet high across a marsh. All went well with the party, who with bent backs were plodding dismally forward, until an S.O.S. station, hidden somewhere at the foot of the embankment, set off a series of huge rockets which missed the company by a narrow margin. Taken by surprise and considerably startled, some men stopped dead, or turned aside, with the result that a series of collisions rolled a number of men and their heavy burdens over the embankment and into the swamp below. The bitterness of the recriminations that followed is left to the reader's sympathetic imagination.

After a week in reserve, the 13th Battalion was relieved by the 1st Battalion on the afternoon of November 10th and proceeded to billets at Camblain l'Abbé. Here, on the following day, blankets were issued to all who required them and the advent of winter was proclaimed by the issue of khaki trews. On November 12th the companies paraded and proceeded to the Divisional Gas School at Maisnil-Bouché to be fitted with a new type of box respirator. At the school the men were drilled in the use of the new equipment, and afterwards, with the helmets on, were marched into a hut where the atmosphere was charged with gas, to make sure that none of the respirators were defective. Later in the day, in parties of sixty, the men paraded to the Divisional baths, where, when bathing was completed, each man was provided with clean underclothes and socks. During the afternoon the Battalion moved back about a mile from Camblain l'Abbé to Cambligneul.

On this date there appeared in orders the following promotion: Major G. E. McCuaig, Second-in-command of the 13th Canadian Battalion, Royal Highlanders of Canada, is promoted Lieut.-Colonel, vice Lieut.-Col. V. C. Buchanan, D.S.O. (killed 27-9-'16). While this promotion was merely the official announcement of what had been confidently expected, it was acceptable to officers and men alike and Lieut.-Col. McCuaig was the recipient of many congratulations and good wishes.

For nearly a week the 13th remained at Cambligneul, large parties attending courses of instruction in the use of Stokes Guns,

THE WINTER OF 1916-1917

Lewis Guns, bombs and so forth. These courses, held at the Divisional Schools at Maisnil-Bouché, occupied the greater part of the time that would under ordinary circumstances have been devoted to company training and routine drills.

It was during this week at Cambligneul that the Battalion abandoned as its official head dress the Glengarry, with the Black Watch badge, and substituted for it the Balmoral bonnet, with the famous Red Hackle. This change was no ordinary alteration of uniform, but represented a distinct milestone in the history of the Regiment, as the Red Hackle was an honour highly prized. On January 4th, 1795, the Black Watch Regiment had gained this distinction while serving against the French at Guildermausen, in Flanders, by an act of devotion and bravery involving the recapture of some abandoned guns. Through affiliation with the Black Watch, the 13th might have worn this red vulture feather from the beginning, but officers had decided that it was not fitting for a new and untried battalion, merely because of affiliation, to wear a battle honour that had been the pride and glory of the Black Watch for over a hundred years. Accordingly, permission to wear the Red Hackle had been withheld until on the bloody fields of Ypres, Festubert, Sanctuary Wood and the Somme, the Battalion had earned the distinction in its own right.

At its first parade following the issue of the Balmorals and Red Hackle, the 13th was honoured by a visit from the Corps Commander, Lieut.-Gen. Sir Julian Byng, who conducted a careful inspection. After this event the men were paid, allowing them to purchase a few extras to make them more comfortable during the next tour in the line.

On the morning of November 18th the Battalion moved up and relieved the 8th Canadian Battalion in Brigade Support, in the Carency Sector. Here four days were spent, with working parties busy the greater part of the time building dugouts, repairing trenches and carrying materials up to the front line. On November 22nd the Battalion moved forward from support and relieved the 14th Battalion, which was occupying the front line from Gobron Trench (exclusive) to Gabriel Trench (inclusive). These trenches were situated to the left of those on Vimy Ridge that the Battalion occupied during the previous tour. On the whole the tour that followed was a lively one, the enemy sending over a large number of trench mortar shells and rifle grenades, while the Canadians'

ROYAL HIGHLANDERS OF CANADA

Stokes Guns and trench mortars were also active. Machine gun fire was brisk, particularly after nightfall.

On November 26th Nos. 1 and 2 Companies of the 13th were relieved by the 14th Canadian Battalion, Nos. 3 and 4 Companies remaining in the line with the 14th to assist in consolidating the crater of a mine to be blown on the night of the 27th. This event took place as scheduled and resulted in a stirring bombardment by both sides in which trench mortars, Stokes guns, Minenwerfers, machine guns and rifle grenades all came into play. One lucky German shell exploded a large supply of ammunition stored at Liverpool Dump and altogether things for an hour or so were very busy, though, fortunately, the crater of the new mine was occupied and consolidated without much loss. In all, the casualties of the 13th for the tour were 2 killed and 5 wounded, amongst the latter being Lieut. H. H. Heal, who had rejoined the Battalion after recovering from wounds received in the previous June.

While Nos. 3 and 4 Companies were engaged in the minor operation mentioned above, Nos. 1 and 2 Companies moved to Brigade Reserve at Villers-au-Bois, whence they provided working parties that taxed their limited numbers to the utmost. Most of these parties carried material for the 176th Tunnelling Company, who were at work in the neighbourhood, and whose demands for supplies were so insistent that even the pipe band of the Highlanders was pressed into service to meet them.

On the last day of November the companies of the 13th, reunited once more, moved up and took over the trenches held during the previous tour. Here they remained for four days, which were by no means eventless. On December 1st the enemy's trench mortars were active, particularly between 5 and 6 p.m., when a heavy "shoot" caused a great deal of damage to the Highlanders' trenches. Somewhat later an enemy patrol of about 12 men was seen advancing towards one of a series of saps. Fire from a Lewis gun was opened on this group by Corp. Crossley, who alone of the gun crew had survived the previous bombardment, and several of the Germans were seen to fall.

Trench mortars were active again on the following day, one large shell scoring a direct hit on a Stokes gun emplacement and killing the entire crew. As a small offset to this misfortune, one of the Battalion snipers spotted a couple of Germans looking over

THE WINTER OF 1916-1917

their parapet and picked one off with a neat shot that was undoubtedly successful.

Patrols were active on the night of December 3rd, encountering and dispersing several enemy patrols and working parties. As a result of these little expeditions much information was obtained concerning the state of the enemy's trenches and dispositions. Casualties for the tour amounted to 20 in all, 7 men being killed, 9 wounded and 4 missing, presumed killed.

On the morning of December 4th Lieut. Appleby, the Signalling Officer, took charge of the guides to lead in the 4th Canadian Battalion, which was relieving. Unit commanders reported the completion of relief by use of the code word "Columbine" and, when all units had been accounted for, the 13th proceeded to billets at Cambligneul, halting at a spot on the Carency Road where the cook-kitchens had hot tea in readiness.

At Cambligneul the Highlanders remained for a week, carrying out a definitely prepared syllabus of training. Two large drafts were received during this period, these bringing the companies up to something approaching full fighting strength. While it is not desirable to enter into the details of each day's training, an idea of the whole may be gained from the programme carried out on December 6th, which was as follows:

7 a.m.	Reveille.
7.10 - 7.30 a.m.	Physical Training.
9.00 - 10.00 a.m.	Squad Drill.
10.00 - 10.30 a.m.	Respirator Drill.
10.30 - 11.30 a.m.	Company Drill.
11.45 a.m.	Lecture to Officers.
1.30 - 2.30 p.m.	Bayonet Fighting.
2.30 - 3.30 p.m.	Musketry.
3.30 - 4.00 p.m.	Lecture by Coy. Officers.
5.30 p.m.	Lecture to N.C.O's.

The following lectures by officers to other ranks were included in the syllabus: (1) Discipline. (2) Organization and Responsibility. (3) Trench Routine. (4) Principles of Defence in Trench Warfare. (5) Esprit de Corps.

As the week at Cambligneul drew to a close preparations were begun for another tour in the forward area. The men had benefited from the intensive training and the new drafts had been satisfactorily assimilated, consequently the Battalion was in good condition physically, while the morale and esprit de corps left nothing to be desired.

Snow fell heavily on the morning of the 12th, changing later to rain, so that the roads in many places were knee deep in mud and disagreeable for marching. Unfortunately this day had been selected for the Battalion to move forward, a plan which could not very well be changed on account of inclement weather. Accordingly, the men paraded in the morning and relieved the 7th Canadian Battalion in the Berthonval Section at about 2 p.m.

While holding the position taken over from the 7th, the 13th was in Brigade Support and working parties were kept busy. Some of these were employed at Liverpool Dump in carrying rations; others entered the front line and dug ditches to draw off the superabundant supply of rain water, while still others repaired dugouts that had caved in as a result of the floods. Reports from these parties indicated that the German artillery was more active than for some time past and had apparently been augmented, probably as a result of the conclusion of the Battles of the Somme.

After four days in reserve, the 13th Battalion took over a section of the front line, relieving the 14th R.M.R. on the morning of December 17th. About 3 o'clock in the afternoon confirmation of the increased enemy artillery fire was obtained when the vicinity of Battalion Headquarters, in Zouave Valley, was heavily shelled with whizz-bangs and 5.9's, while at the same time the front and support trenches were bombarded by a choice assortment of Minenwerfers and rifle grenades. After about an hour, in the course of which several trenches and the passage way to the Signal Station were blown in, the bombardment died down. On the following day, at the same hour, the enemy repeated this bombardment in a modified form. The Signal Station was again unfortunate and all the repairs that had been laboriously effected during the night were completely undone. In the evening the enemy's machine guns were active, while his artillery put over a few bursts of shrapnel in the neighbourhood of Souchez Dump, neither of these measures meeting with any particular success.

Brisk shelling continued on the 19th of the month, while at night, inspired perhaps by hard frost and snow which reminded them of far off Canada, patrols of the 13th were unusually active. At 3 p.m. on the 20th, the Canadian Artillery, as if to remind the Hun that he had no monopoly on the hour, opened a heavy bombardment

THE WINTER OF 1916-1917

to the right of the Highlanders' front, on an area known as Broadmarsh Crater. Somewhat later this fire was shifted a little and the whole enemy territory to the right of the Brigade front given a lusty drubbing.

At about 9 o'clock that same night a flare set off by someone in the front line revealed two individuals prowling about in the Highlanders' wire. Challenged by the men in a small crater post, to make sure they were not members of a wiring party known to be out, these individuals replied in German, whereupon the sentries in the crater opened fire. One man was hit, while the other ran to a point where he was captured unwounded. The wounded man, meanwhile, conveyed to the corporal in charge of the crater his desire to surrender, so both prisoners were brought to Battalion Headquarters. No German interpreter was available and the prisoners spoke neither English nor French, nevertheless it was discovered that they belonged to the 17th Bavarian Landwehr, a unit which had taken over the German front at 8 o'clock on the previous night.

Considering the rather severe bombardments that took place during this tour, the Highlanders' casualties were by no means heavy. Lieut. H. B. Hebron was wounded and four other ranks killed, while three other ranks were wounded, a total of eight in all.

Following the completion of this tour, the 13th Battalion moved back to Cambligneul, whence, on the following day, December 22nd, the 3rd Brigade marched out to Corps Reserve, the Royal Highlanders taking up quarters in Ruitz, a small village close to the mining town of Bruay. As it was understood that the Battalion was to remain for some time in these billets, the men proceeded to make themselves as comfortable as possible, turning their attention almost immediately to preparations for the Christmas and New Year's holidays. As a matter of fact Christmas was not a holiday in the strict sense of the word, as a stiff routine of training was carried out from 6.45 a.m. until 4 p.m. All who desired, however, were privileged to attend the celebration of Holy Communion at 8.30 a.m., while in the evening, turkey, a tot of rum and a generous issue of beer proved that someone had not forgotten what kind of fare the day was expected to bring.

In contrast to Christmas, New Year's Day was proclaimed a total holiday and fitting celebrations began on New Year's Eve. Dinner for the officers was prepared in the village school house and Capt.

ROYAL HIGHLANDERS OF CANADA

W. S. M. MacTier and Lieut. A. R. Gibson, president and vice-president of the Mess respectively, were instructed to see to it that nothing was lacking to make the dinner a memorable one. All who were present will admit that these instructions were faithfully carried out. On arrival the officers found a long table, set in approved style and gleaming with a variety of cutlery and assorted glasses that hinted most pleasingly of the gastronomic and bacchanalian pleasures in store.

Following the toast to the King, which was drunk with traditional ceremony, and the toast to the fallen, which was honoured in silence, the diners gave themselves over to an unforgettable evening of merriment and song. Sharp at midnight the haggis was brought in, accompanied by the pipers, and immediately afterwards Lieut.-Col. McCuaig, escorted by several officers, made a round of visits to convey greetings and good wishes to the men. Returning to the school house, this group rejoined the party who were drinking a toast to the confusion of the Hun. As an appropriate accompaniment the popular song "Another Little Drink" had been altered for the occasion and was being rendered:—

>"Another little scrap
>And another little scrap
>And another little scrap
>Wouldn't do us any harm!"

This expressed the spirit of the Regiment as it celebrated its third New Year away from home.

II

For nearly three weeks after New Year the Royal Highlanders remained at Ruitz, the companies training rigorously and the officers, in addition to taking part in the training, attending a series of lectures on such varied subjects as, "Great Britain's Part in the War," "Courts Martial," "Co-operation with the Engineers" and "Engineer and Pioneer Services."

During all this time the weather remained clear and cold, the frozen ground providing ideal footing for the scores of drills, practices and parades. On January 8th the following announcement was received with satisfaction by all ranks of the Battalion:—

"The General Officer Commanding has much pleasure in publishing the following honours:

The Distinguished Service Order—Lieut.-Col. G. E. McCuaig,

THE WINTER OF 1916-1917

Officer Commanding, the 13th Canadian Battalion, Royal Highlanders of Canada.

The Distinguished Conduct Medal—Transport Sergeant W. Blyth, 13th Canadian Battalion, the Royal Highlanders of Canada.

On January 20th the period of training at Ruitz came to an end and the 3rd Canadian Brigade relieved the 2nd Canadian Brigade in the left Calonne Sector, the 13th Battalion occupying reserve billets at Bully Grenay. In many ways this new sector was one of the most attractive on the Western Front. Since the early days of the war it had seen little fighting, a fact to which the almost undamaged back country bore striking testimony. Bully Grenay, where the Battalion was in Brigade Reserve, was within a couple of miles of the front line, in spite of which many houses were still standing, while the civilians went about their daily affairs, almost as if nothing unusual were happening. As a precaution against the unexpected, however, troops wore steel helmets and box respirators at all times.

In this town the 13th Battalion spent four agreeable and comparatively uneventful days. Being so close to the actual front, reveille and other bugle calls were not sounded, as it had been arranged with the civilian population that the sounding of a bugle would convey a warning of enemy gas. Probably the chief event of this short period occurred on January 23rd, when the Battalion paraded in a field adjoining the town for inspection by the Brigadier. This inspection was progressing smoothly, when all of a sudden a German aeroplane appeared overhead and seemed to take a deep interest in what was going on. Judging that a signal from the plane might bring on heavy shelling, the Brigadier cancelled the inspection and ordered the men to disperse.

On the morning of January 25th, the 13th Battalion moved up and took over front line trenches, No. 1 Coy., or "A" Coy., according to the system of naming the companies adopted at this time, occupying the position from the Double Crassier to Treize Alley and "B" Coy. that from Treize Alley to Trench 238. The other companies were in support at Maroc.

This front had certain topographical peculiarities, chief among these being the Double Crassier, a huge slag heap, about 30 feet high, which ran at right angles to the front line. The flat top of the Crassier was about 20 feet wide, and here both sides had established posts, so close together that a button could easily be tossed across the No Man's Land that intervened. Elsewhere along the

ROYAL HIGHLANDERS OF CANADA

front, which was almost half a mile in length, the distance between the two lines of trenches varied from an extreme of about 500 yards to a minimum of little more than 30 yards.

As the weather was sharp and frosty during the five days that the Highlanders occupied this area, conditions were by no means unpleasant. The 14th Battalion, on handing over to the 13th, informed the latter that the methodical Hun shelled a certain section of trench at exactly 4 o'clock every afternoon. Having encountered these extraordinarily mechanical tactics once or twice before, the 13th accepted the tip with gratitude and arranged that this particular bit of trench should be evacuated several minutes before the hour. Prompt to the moment the old Hun would open up, bang off a certain number of rounds and then settle down to finish his afternoon's nap. For the remainder of the twenty-four hours this particular section of trench was about as safe as a front line trench can be.

Half way through this five day tour the companies in the line and those in reserve exchanged places, so that on the 30th, when the Battalion was relieved and proceeded to Calonne, all had shared equally in whatever advantages, or disadvantages, the front and reserve positions offered. Casualties numbered six, 1 killed and 5 wounded.

At Calonne, where the Battalion was in reserve, the situation was most unusual, as the front line actually ran through one end of the town. In consequence of this, movement by day was dangerous, while at night streams of machine gun bullets sweeping through the streets at irregular intervals meant that safe progress was more a matter of good luck than good management. Good management, however, did enter into it, as the Royal Highlanders attended to a variety of duties during their stay in the town and provided numerous working parties at night, all these, by using reasonable precaution, coming and going without incurring losses.

On February 5th the 13th Battalion again took over the line at the Double Crassier, this time for a six day tour. As on the former occasion, the companies relieved one another half way through the tour, which was again comparatively uneventful. The cold weather caused some difficulty by freezing the majority of the water tanks in the district and the Germans aroused a little interest by projecting several phosphorous bombs into No Man's Land. Dense clouds of smoke from these drifted back over the enemy's trenches, where-

THE WINTER OF 1916-1917

upon the Highlanders, on the chance that this might screen a working party, treated the area to a few bursts of machine gun and rifle fire. Apart from these incidents, the tour was chiefly distinguished by the fact that for the first time in its history the Battalion came out of the line without having incurred a single casualty.

For the next six days the Royal Highlanders occupied reserve billets in Bully Grenay, the companies drilling and devoting a good deal of time to the training of their "specialists," i.e. bombers, snipers and so on. Pay and bathing parades were also held during this period, while working parties at night put in good work on the reserve line of trenches.

On February 17th the Battalion again took over the Double Crassier and Treize Alley front. On the following day the weather turned mild and the remainder of the tour became a nightmare of mud. Hard frozen parapets simply disintegrated and trench floors, solid as rock, changed in a few hours to glue-like man-traps with no bottom.

In spite of these unpleasant conditions, the Highlanders' patrols went out nightly and carefully noted where enemy working parties were employed and, in so far as possible, what they were doing. The patrols were really excellent and brought in a variety of interesting and valuable information. On the 21st one of the Highlanders' sentries was picked off by an enemy sniper. No idea could be gained as to where this sniper had fired from, but later in the day the battalion on the left reported that their snipers had seen him and that he had paid the penalty. In addition to the loss of the sentry, the Battalion, during the course of the tour, had a total of 5 men wounded.

At night on February 22nd, when the 14th Canadian Battalion relieved, orders were issued that the 13th, in retiring to Calonne, should proceed overland rather than by way of the flooded communication trenches, which were in such condition that the passage of a battalion through them would likely have caused them to collapse. By having troops proceed overland for a time, the communication trenches, such as they were, were preserved against any emergency. The overland route, however, proved to be in almost as bad condition as the trenches. One man actually had his boots pulled off his feet, while progress was so slow that several stragglers did not reach the billets till eight o'clock on the following morning.

ROYAL HIGHLANDERS OF CANADA

Strenuous working parties were a feature of the next six days, these numbering in strength from 250 to 500 men. Several parties carried material for the 255th Tunnelling Company—very exhausting work under such weather conditions—while others were employed in filling sandbags, wiring reserve trenches, carrying for the Trench Mortar Battery and cleaning up the district. On the first day in billets the area received a brisk shelling, one man, while standing in the doorway of his temporary home, being struck in the face by shrapnel and dying soon afterwards.

The chief incident of the tour occurred on the night of March 1st, when the 14th and 15th Battalions, which the 13th was supporting, raided the enemy lines, bombed some dugouts and captured several prisoners. Although this successful little operation did not directly concern the Royal Highlanders, officers of the 13th watched proceedings with the greatest interest, while the whole Battalion, though not "standing to," was on the alert in case of unforseen developments. Nothing unexpected occurred, however, and the 13th was not called upon. As a matter of fact the Battalion did not again enter the front line in this particular area. Spring had come and with it a call for the Highlanders' services at another part of the line.

CHAPTER XII

Vimy Ridge

England, our mother, we, thy sons, are young;
Our exultation this day cannot be
Bounded as thine;—

. . . .

Though henceforth we shall lift a higher head
Because of Vimy and its glorious dead.
—ALFRED GORDON.

I

ON March 2nd the 13th Battalion, Royal Highlanders of Canada, left Calonne and moved to Bully Grenay. Here the night was spent and in the morning the Battalion proceeded to Ruitz, a town which aroused memories of Christmas turkey and New Year's haggis, as well as of drills, parades and practices innumerable. On this occasion the Highlanders' stay was brief, the Battalion parading at 9.20 on the morning of the 4th and marching to Bois des Alleux, via Maisnil-les-Ruitz, Ranchicourt and Camblain l'Abbé, through hilly country and over a road, for at least part of the way, which had been a military highway ever since Cæsar built it to assist his campaigns in Gaul.

The attractive scenery and military traditions of the country, however, were not of such vital interest to the Highlanders as the fact that all along the route, and particularly during its latter stages, evidence accumulated that on this front something was being planned. Vast stores of shells were piled on both sides of the road; several monster guns were seen, resting till night should enable them to resume their secret progress towards the front; smaller guns were also much in evidence, while motor lorries, laden with all sorts of supplies, chug-chugged forward, and, having deposited their burdens, broke their metaphorical necks in an effort to speed back for more. None of the significance attaching to these preparations was lost on the veterans of the 13th. Something was undoubtedly being prepared, but just what no one could tell, though everything indicated a British offensive on a large scale. Confirma-

ROYAL HIGHLANDERS OF CANADA

tion of this came when the Battalion, swinging steadily along, was confronted with a huge wire "cage," whose only purpose could be to hold prisoners. This particular bit of preparation tickled the men's fancy tremendously. When and where the great attack was to take place they did not know and did not greatly care. That it was to be a success, however, they never doubted. This spirit of confidence permeated the whole Canadian Corps and grew, rather than diminished, as the weeks passed and the time for the battle approached. That vast preparations, such as they witnessed daily, could not be entirely concealed from the Hun, did not seem to lower the men's estimation of the chances of success, nor did the news that the attack was to be against the deadly Vimy Ridge, which had held firm in 1915 against French troops of the old first line regiments, troops whose courage was little short of sublime and whose bones still whitened the fields in the neighbourhood of Souchez and Neuville St. Vaast. Some indication of this perfect confidence is reflected in the opening paragraph of the operation order issued to the Royal Highlanders on April 4th, which states quite simply, "In conjunction with the Third Army, the Canadian Corps will take Vimy Ridge;" this in spite of the German boast that Vimy Ridge could not be taken by direct assault by any troops on earth.

Meanwhile, at about 4 o'clock on the afternoon of March 4th, the 13th reached billets at Bois des Alleux, about a mile and a half from the town of Mont. St. Eloy. Here two uneventful days were spent, and on the night of the 6th the Battalion moved up to relieve the 20th Canadian Battalion in Brigade support. The march up on this occasion was most unpleasant, as the roads, or what was left of them, were packed with traffic and the troops on foot were frequently forced off the highway into the muddy ditches at the sides. Even here they did not escape the penalty which is the invariable lot of pedestrians in motor traffic. As one officer rather feelingly put it: "The gilded youth of the army, or in other words, the Staff Officers, seemingly able to travel in motor cars at any speed, pursued their favourite occupation of tearing by and drenching the 'poor bloody infantry' with flying mud." In return for this delicate attention the "foot sloggers" cursed the occupants of the cars with expressive and highly imaginative profanity.

On arriving at their destination, the companies of the 13th took over a position at Maison Blanche, not far from Neuville St. Vaast. This district was distinctly dreary. As previously mentioned it

VIMY RIDGE

had been the scene of bitter fighting by the French earlier in the war. Hundreds of the gallant poilus had given their lives and been hastily buried in shallow graves dug in the white, chalky soil. Rain had washed the covering off these graves and in all directions were now visible the faded red breeches and blue tunics in which these splendid troops had met their end.

Six days were spent at Maison Blanche, the troops busily employed on working parties. Some of these assisted the 185th Tunnelling Company, others toiled at burying cables, while still others, and these possibly the most numerous, devoted their attentions to the maintenance of vital communication trenches, of which some were completely flooded and all more or less in danger of collapse.

All during this tour, whenever the weather was fine, the troops on the ground were thrilled by the vigorous fight being waged for control of the air. The enemy realized that a climax was approaching in this area and bent every effort to discover details of the blow being prepared. Similarly, the Royal Flying Corps guarded the secret preparations with all the strength it could muster, young pilots giving their lives gladly, rather than have Hun machines secure information which might nullify all the work of making ready and all the valour of the troops destined to attack. Realizing this, the men of the 13th watched the aerial combats with deep concern, groaning in spirit when a British plane was worsted, but cheered immensely by the fact that, even when this occurred, vengeance frequently overtook the Hun before he could turn his initial victory to practical account.

Following the six days at Maison Blanche, the Battalion moved up on March 12th and relieved the Canadian Scottish (16th Battalion) in trenches opposite the Argyll and Paris groups of mine craters, "A" and "D" Companies occupying the left and right front, with "C" and "B" in left and right support. This position was held by the 13th for the regulation six days, the tour proving by no means uneventful. At 4 o'clock on the morning of the 13th the enemy commenced a heavy bombardment with 5.9's, 4.1's and .77's, smashing in several trenches on the left front, badly damaging Douai Communication Trench and severing connection between the supporting companies and the front line. With the first crash of the barrage, Capt. W. S. M. MacTier, of "C" Coy., endeavoured to get through by telephone to Battalion Headquarters and the companies in the front line, only to find that his wires were cut. Eventually, however, he got in touch with Major I. M. R. Sinclair, of "A" Coy. and through him with Major N. M. MacLean, of "D" Coy., both of whom reported that they did not require immediate assistance, but that the situation was not yet clear. What actually developed was an attempted enemy raid. Ten minutes after fire had opened a party of twelve Germans approached a sap running into No. 4 of the Paris group of craters. Bombs were exchanged between this party and the Canadian post in the crater and one of the Highlanders was killed.

Lieut. Christie, who was in command at this spot, thereupon withdrew his men from the sap and was in the act of setting up a Lewis gun at its base, when the man carrying the gun slipped and fell into a water filled trench. Christie, however, rescued the gun and opened fire, one of the enemy being seen to fall and the remainder effecting a retreat, leaving a number of stick bombs behind them.

Meanwhile, in reply to the enemy barrage, the Canadian artillery opened on the Hun trenches, smashing them in badly and, judging from shouts, whistles and confused noises, causing a number of casualties. Fire on both sides continued till 4.45 a.m., when the Germans set off a rocket which, soaring up, divided into two green lights and was apparently a signal to their artillery that the show, from their point of view, was over.

Apart from this raid and the activity of the Canadian artillery during the days that followed, the chief feature of the tour was provided by the air pilots, who continued their ceaseless fight for supremacy. One German plane with red wings and body was conspicuous and rather disconcertingly successful. It seems probable, though by no means certain, that this plane was piloted by Captain Baron von Richthofen, the German ace, who was a thorn in the side of the Allied Air Forces for a long time and who was shot down by a Canadian pilot some months later.

By March 18th, when the tour in the front line terminated, three men of the 13th had been killed and ten wounded. In addition to these, Major W. E. Macfarlane, M.C. had received his third wound of the war, but on this occasion his injury was not serious and did not keep him away from duty for long.

When the Royal Highlanders had handed over the front line to the 15th Battalion, they retired to familiar billets at Bois des Alleux and remained in this position for the next ten days, training,

VIMY RIDGE

drilling, checking deficiencies and providing night working parties to carry ammunition from Maison Blanche to the front line. During this period Capt. F. S. Mathewson, who had recovered from his wounds, returned to duty with the Battalion. On March 24th the enemy shelled the town of Mont St. Eloy and the neighbouring camps, causing losses to personnel and destroying a number of horses. This shelling was repeated on the 25th and came so close to the Bois des Alleux Huts that Lieut.-Col. McCuaig ordered the men to scatter. In spite of this precaution, two men were killed, but because of it, heavier losses were undoubtedly avoided.

During the ten days at Bois des Alleux, one party, composed of Major I. M. R. Sinclair, Lieut. G. H. Hogarth, Lieut. W. D. C. Christie and sixty-seven other ranks, took no part in the general training, but devoted themselves to preparations for a raid on the enemy's trenches. This raid was planned for the night of March 28th and the spot chosen for the venture was just behind Nos. 1, 2 and 3 of the Paris group of mine craters. The Canadian front in this area was held by the 14th Battalion, Royal Montreal Regiment, which was to conduct a simultaneous raid at a different spot.

On the morning of the 28th the 13th Battalion left Bois des Alleux and proceeded to Estrée-Cauchie, the raiding party separating from the main body and moving up to Brigade H.Q. Here the day was spent in putting last touches to the preparations and in waiting for the hour to go over. Late at night the party moved up and was in readiness when the artillery opened fire, shortly before dawn. The barrage was perfect and the raiders got through the enemy wire with little difficulty. Leaping into the German front trench and making their way into the support line, the Highlanders quickly disposed of such opposition as was encountered and blew up several dugouts with large tubes of explosives brought over for the purpose. Everything went well and all objectives had been attained when, at the end of fifteen minutes, the recall signal was set off. A number of the enemy had been accounted for, several dugouts had been blown up, identifications had been secured and the Highlanders themselves had escaped with a casualty list of two men wounded, this including an injury to Lieut. Hogarth which did not compel him to leave duty. For their work in this well executed little operation, Major Sinclair and his men were warmly commended by General Currie.

ROYAL HIGHLANDERS OF CANADA

II

From March 28th until April 5th the 13th Battalion remained at Estrée-Cauchie, carrying out a definite programme of training in preparation for the assault on Vimy Ridge. As a rule the greatest secrecy was maintained in these matters, but on this occasion the opposite policy was adopted and all ranks were informed of the exact task that lay before them. Only the day and hour of the attack were unknown.

It is probable that in the history of war up to this time no troops ever rehearsed their parts as thoroughly as those who were about to take part in the Battle of Vimy Ridge. At Estrée-Cauchie the 13th Battalion found a whole area laid out to resemble the German positions in every particular that was possible. Tapes represented the enemy trenches and communication trenches, sign posts showed the whereabouts of dugouts and unit headquarters, while all obstacles such as wire and ditches were clearly indicated. Over this area the men advanced again and again, carrying full battle equipment and familiarizing themselves with every detail of the terrain. On several occasions the whole 3rd Brigade worked over the ground, so that each battalion became aware, not only of what its own part was to be, but of the part to be taken by the units with which it would be associated. In addition to the practices over the taped-out area in the open, a large coloured map of the German positions was prepared at Battalion Headquarters and, using this to illustrate their remarks, Lieut.-Col. McCuaig and Major Perry lectured to various groups and parties until it seemed that every contingency had been foreseen and provision made to cope with it.

While the various brigades and battalions were engaged in this training, the country for miles around was the scene of endless activity of a different nature, but all working towards the same end. Motor lorries swarmed on all roads and the great munition dumps beside the highways grew and grew until they reached amazing proportions. Never in their wildest dreams had the troops imagined such enormous supplies of shells. Brother Boche, it appeared, was in for a bad time and the veterans of "the days of bitter fear," when the Germans had plenty of shells and the British daily ration was about three rounds a gun, smiled with grim satisfaction at the prospect. Indeed, the bad time for the Boche had actually

VIMY RIDGE

begun, for already the great guns were shelling his positions and lines of communication, tuning up, as it were, for the roar of artillery that would herald the actual assault.

The tremendous traffic required by these preparations tore up the roads and made maintenance work urgent in the extreme. On one occasion an Engineer officer of the First Army Staff came to Battalion Headquarters and requested that a fatigue of 50 men be detailed to lay half-round logs over a stretch of road that had become well nigh impassable. He stressed the point that the work was urgent, so Lieut.-Col. McCuaig ordered out a party of 200 men and instructed them to "clean up the job" without delay. Acting on these orders, the party worked like the proverbial beavers and had the road open for through traffic in a surprisingly short time, much to the delight of the Chief Engineer and the Army Commander, General Horne, both of whom dropped in on the following day to express satisfaction.

On April 4th Lieut. C. D. Craig, acting in his capacity as Adjutant, issued, in its amended and final form, the operation order covering the Battalion's part in the coming battle. Much to the disappointment of the 13th, this confirmed the announcement that the Battalion was not to form part of the first wave of the attack, but was to advance in close support, consolidating the positions gained, ready to render assistance should this be required and performing a variety of necessary services. Some idea of these services can be gained from the summary of the operation order which follows:

(1) In conjunction with the Third Army, the Canadian Corps will take the Vimy Ridge and form a defensive flank.

The 1st Canadian Division will capture the high ground S. and S.E. of Thelus.

The 3rd Canadian Infantry Brigade will take the following:

(a) First Objective—The Black Line, or Zwolfer Weg.

(b) Second Objective—The Red Line, or Swischen Stellung.

The 2nd Canadian Infantry Brigade will attack on the right and the 4th Canadian Infantry Brigade on the left.

(2) "B" and "D" Companies will consolidate the Black Line.

(3) Battle Formation:— The Battalion will attack on a two company front, each company on a two platoon front, with a half company, 1 Colt gun and 4 Lewis guns in support.

ROYAL HIGHLANDERS OF CANADA

Frontages:—Company—150 yards.
          Platoon — 75 yards.
Distances:— 15 yards between lines of waves.
           25 yards between waves.

(4) Plan of Attack:— The Battalion will go forward at zero hour, as close to the last wave of the 14th Battalion as possible until No Man's Land has been crossed. It will then move at a slow rate until there is an interval of 150 yards between the leading wave of the 13th and the rear wave of the 14th Battalion.

The role of the Battalion is to give additional power to any one of the attacking battalions should the strength of any of the latter be insufficient to attain its objectives.

The Battalion will not be merged into the attack, unless requested by one of the attacking battalions.

The Battalion will not go through to the Black Line until the attacking battalions resume their advance to the Red Line at zero plus 75, and in the meantime will occupy the Eisner Kreuz Weg.

When the advance to the Red Line is resumed, the Battalion will move up to the Black Line, "B" and "D" Companies extending to the right and left to cover the Brigade frontage. This line will be consolidated and the Battalion will be prepared to send forward reinforcing platoons if necessary.

During the pause at Eisner Kreuz Weg "B" Coy. will hold three platoons in hand, ready to move forward to the Red Line if required, i.e. one platoon as a first reinforcement to each attacking battalion.

The Colt gun and four Lewis guns will remain near the advanced Battalion Headquarters as a reserve.

After the Red Line has been consolidated, the 14th Battalion will be withdrawn from this Line, and the 13th and 14th will then become Divisional Reserve.

(5) Barrages:— At zero plus 35 minutes the barrage will lift off the Black Line.

From zero plus 35 minutes to zero plus 38 minutes, it will stand 100 yards East of the Black Line.

From zero plus 38 minutes to zero plus 75 minutes, it will form a standing barrage 200 yards East of the Black Line.

During the pause from zero plus 35 to zero plus 75, units will be sorted out, casualties among officers and N.C.O.'s replaced, and

VIMY RIDGE

any new commanders made known to their command; liaison will be effected with units on the flanks and communication opened up with Battalion and Brigade H.Q's.

(6) The Battalion will move from Bois des Alleux huts on Y/Z night, under orders to be issued later.

(7) Communication Trenches:
In —Claudot, Bentata.
Out—Paris, Douai, Sapper.

(8) Subways:— The Bentata Subway runs from Claudot Avenue to the front line, between Roger and Claudot Trenches. This will be used as a covered route during bombardments previous to zero hour and after zero hour for runners. At the top and bottom of each entrance are notice boards showing to whom the entrance is allotted, and where each entrance or exit leads to.

(9) Inter-Communication and Intelligence:— The Battalion O.P. will be with the 14th Battalion O.P. off Bentata. Two runners will be stationed there on Zero Day. They will reconnoitre it on Y. Day.

The O.P. will watch the progress of the advance and will keep the Brigade Report Centre in touch with the situation by means of telephone or runner. Forward of this station communication will be maintained by visual signalling, carrier pigeons, runners and Aeroplane Contact Patrols. The Intelligence Officer with his Section, six signallers and four runners, carrying signal fans, ground sheet, carrier pigeons and two signalling lamps, will follow in the rear of the last wave and make for a dugout in Eisner Kreuz Weg. It will be the duty of the Intelligence Officer to collect and communicate all messages received from his observers and the company officers to Battalion Headquarters. This forward report centre will plant a red and blue flag.

The first thing to be done on arrival at the forward report centre will be to call up the Brigade O.P. by visual, and report the progress to this point, using the B.A.B. Code.

It must be impressed on all ranks that communication with the contact aeroplane is of the utmost importance.

All runners will move in pairs.

All messages must be numbered, bear the time, date and place, and be written on the back of maps which have been struck off

ROYAL HIGHLANDERS OF CANADA

and which show the German trenches. At the time of writing each message the officer will chalk in his position on the sketch. These will be issued as follows:

To Company Commanders—12.

To Platoon Commanders — 8.

Each Company Commander will detail two men with sandbags, into which all papers found will be placed and forwarded by runner to Brigade H.Q.

(10) Liaison:—Capt. F. S. Mathewson will report to Brigade H.Q. for liaison duty.

(11) Carrying Parties:— The Relay System:—

A. Line Dumps—Battalion Dumps.

B. Line Dumps—Lille-Arras Road.

C. Line Dumps—Red Objective.

"A" Coy. and two platoons of "C" Coy., less Lewis guns, will be assembled in the support line and Rocade. Two platoons will be detailed to carry for each of the three attacking battalions. These parties will work under the Brigade Grenade Officer. As soon as the situation permits, these parties will commence to carry forward from the A. Line Dumps to the B. Line Dumps. They will then return to the Brigade Dump and carry forward the material to the B. Line Dumps. As soon as the Red Line is captured, "C" Coy. will detail one half of a platoon for each of the attacking battalions and carry the material forward from the B. Line Dumps to the C. Line Dumps. All carrying parties will report to the Battalion in the Black Line as soon as they have finished their work.

(12) Escorts for prisoners will be provided in the proportion of 15%. Escorts should, as far as possible, consist of slightly wounded men. Prisoners and escorts will march overland and not by communication trenches.

(13) The wounded will be taken to the Battalion Aid Posts.

(14) All ranks must have their water bottles filled prior to the attack. There are water taps at (map locations given).

(15) Equipment:—The haversack will be carried on the back. Both the Box Respirator and Tube Helmet will be carried.

Ammunition—120 rounds, except for bombers, signallers, scouts, runners and Lewis gunners, who will carry 50 rounds.

Mills Grenades—2, one in each top pocket. These will be collected in dumps in the Black Line.

VIMY RIDGE

Ground Flares—2, one in each bottom pocket. These will be collected in dumps in the Black Line.

Sandbags—5, carried across the back.

Tools—4 picks and 12 shovels per platoon.

The six carrying platoons will not carry Mills grenades, ground flares, sandbags or tools.

(16) Salvage:— All arms and equipment found in the area between the Eisner Kreuz Weg and Old German Front Line will be dumped at junction of Claudot and Bentata with old British Front Line. For this purpose parties of 10 other ranks each from "B" and "D" Companies and one officer from "D" Coy. to take charge will be detailed. These parties will work back from Eisner Kreuz Weg.

(17) The 13th Battalion is responsible for the burial of all dead between Eisner Kreuz Weg and the Old British Front Line. Lieut. J. L. Atkinson is detailed to supervise the clearing of the battlefield in the above area. He will report at Battalion Headquarters before dawn and will work in conjunction with, and under the orders of, the Divisional Burial Officer.

Further orders were issued at various times before the attack, but as these did not materially alter the Battalion's task, it is unnecessary to quote them here, the original (amended) order giving a comprehensive idea of the duties to be performed by the 13th in its capacity as Brigade Support Battalion.

At 4 p.m. on April 5th the Royal Highlanders left the training area at Estrée-Cauchie and moved forward to the huts in the Bois des Alleux. Owing to the tremendous amount of traffic on the roads, progress on this occasion was slow, the troops being forced to advance in single file and frequently to take the ditch to allow the hurrying motor lorries free passage.

During the two days that the Battalion remained in the Bois des Alleux all ranks were extremely busy with arrangements for the engagement that was now imminent. Momentary interest in the outside world was aroused by the announcement that the United States had declared war on Germany. Inasmuch as this fact was likely to have little effect on the coming battle, however, such interest as the men displayed was more or less academic and soon the news was almost forgotten in the rush of seemingly more important matters connected with the business immediately in hand.

ROYAL HIGHLANDERS OF CANADA

For the Vimy Battle the 13th Battalion was divided into two sections, the main body, which consisted of 25 officers and 760 other ranks, under Lieut.-Col. G. E. McCuaig, D.S.O., carrying out the operations mentioned above, while a smaller body, totalling 17 officers and 264 other ranks, under command of Major K. M. Perry, D.S.O., remained at Bois des Alleux, ready to reinforce should the forward section be overtaken by some unforseen disaster. As well as being up to strength, the Battalion was fortunate at this time in having on its roster a fine body of men, both physically and in every other way, while the officers were experienced for the most part, many of them having rejoined after recovering from wounds received during the previous year. The companies were to be led into action by Major I. M. R. Sinclair, Capt. W. S. M. MacTier, Capt. A. R. Gibson and Major N. M. MacLean.

On April 6th stripes of different colours were painted on the men's haversacks, so that the waves of the attack could be recognized at a glance and proper distances maintained. Everyone was pleased with this arrangement, except the men of the third wave, whose distinguishing stripe was yellow. Only repeated assurance that the colour was fortuitously chosen and was in no way a reflection on their personal courage, satisfied the men of the yellow wave and enabled them to stand the jibes of the 1st and 2nd waves, whose respective stripes were red and green.

Last touches were put to the preparations on April 8th and at 5.45 p.m. the Battalion paraded ready to move into the line. Before the order to march was given Lieut.-Col. McCuaig inspected the men and immediately afterwards ranks were broken to form a semi-circle around the padre, Capt. E. E. Graham, who held a short service of intercession for the success of the undertaking. Following this Lieut.-Col. McCuaig addressed the men in a soldierly speech which was received with a roar of cheers. Ranks were then re-formed and the band struck up the tune of "Highland Laddie," the attacking section of the Battalion moving off amid cheers and shouted good wishes from those disappointed ones who were left behind.

III

Darkness was falling when the 13th marched off the parade ground at Bois des Alleux and started down the Arras road. In all directions troops were on the move and the scene was extra-

VIMY RIDGE

ordinarily impressive, particularly as the machinery of concentration seemed to be running on well oiled wheels. In the gathering dusk battalions could be seen resting in sheltered spots near the roadside and, as the Royal Highlanders passed along, they and the men of these units would exchange greetings and good wishes. "There go the 13th! Good old 13th!" would be met with "It's the Umpty-ninth! Good luck, Toronto!", or "Winnipeg," or "Vancouver," or "Halifax," as the case might be. For the first time the four divisions of the Canadian Corps were attacking side by side and the men were keyed up with excitement and anticipation of victory. As one officer recorded his impressions, "Never have I seen the fighting spirit of the troops more in evidence. You could tell before the show started what the outcome would be."

As an evidence of the minute care that had gone into the preparation of this battle, it is of interest to note that at the point where the Royal Highlanders left the Arras Road to take an overland route, they found a series of luminous stakes which led them unhesitatingly to a spot in the communication trenches where guides were waiting to take them forward to the assembly positions, which had been carefully reconnoitred.

So well had all plans been worked out in advance, that the Battalion found itself in position shortly after midnight, or some five hours before "zero." This eliminated the confusion that is inevitable when troops must come forward, hurriedly distribute themselves in strange jumping off trenches and be ready to attack within a short space of time. The only drawback is that, should the enemy become aware of the concentration, he can bring his artillery into play and nullify the attack before it is even scheduled to begin.

No disaster such as this overtook the 13th, although at one point "B" Coy., under Capt. MacTier, encountered an enemy barrage which threatened to prove serious. All during the delay caused by this shelling, the Regimental Chaplain, Capt. E. E. Graham, who was experiencing his first tour in the line, exhibited a fine disregard for his own safety, moving about and encouraging the men in a manner that won their respect and admiration. "D" Coy. also encountered some shelling on the way up, Lieut. Christie's platoon suffering one or two casualties, but, as in the case of "B" Coy., the delay was not serious.

The night was cold and the company cooks had been sent forward to the assembly position to have hot soup ready when the troops arrived. Unfortunately, the cooks did not share in the good

ROYAL HIGHLANDERS OF CANADA

luck of the Battalion, several of them losing their lives from shell fire on the way up. The remainder pushed on and did the best they could, their courage on this occasion being much appreciated by those who got hot soup and almost equally by the still larger number for whom, owing to the casualties, they were unable to provide.

During the wait before zero hour, Battalion Headquarters was established in one of the several tunnels specially built for the occasion. These tunnels started at a point several hundred yards behind the front line and ran out into No Man's Land, the last few yards of earth being removed only a short time before the attack. The tunnels were electrically lighted and numerous chambers off the main passages provided excellent assembly points for all sorts of special parties.

The weather all this time was cold and dreary, but at 4 a.m. an issue of rum warmed the men up and reduced their discomfort. For a few minutes before zero the silence that reigned over the whole area was almost uncanny. Then a single gun, a little off schedule, opened up, followed in a few seconds by a crash of gunfire such as, with all their experience, the Canadian troops had never heard before.

With the first thunder of the guns, which opened fire at 5.30 a.m., the four Canadian Divisions and the British Divisions on the flank went over the top. So devastating was the rolling barrage and so completely were the German batteries smothered by the British and Canadian big guns, that the advance, in its early stages, met little opposition.

Rain and snow were falling by this time and No Man's Land was a mass of shell holes and churned up soil. Following closely in the wake of the 14th Battalion, however, the men of the 13th pushed steadily forward. It was still fairly dark, but direction was not hard to maintain, for the German trenches were marked by the flashes of hundreds of bursting shells.

As the barrage moved back, the waves of the 14th and 13th advanced, crossing the German front line trenches, which were almost completely obliterated. Here the 13th paused, in accordance with instructions, to allow the waves of the 14th to get well ahead. Continuing their advance toward the German support line a few minutes later, the Highlanders came under heavy machine gun fire, which caused numerous casualties. One of the first to fall was Capt. W. S. M. MacTier, commanding "B" Coy., whose thigh was

VIMY RIDGE

badly shattered. This was MacTier's second appearance on the casualty list, he having suffered previously in the spring of 1915. His injury on this second occasion proved serious and incapacitated him for several years. Further to the right, Lieut. D. S. Grieve, a gallant officer, who had won his commission in June of the previous year, was struck and killed, while many N.C.O's. and men also fell. "B" Coy. was most unfortunate in this respect, losing 17 N.C.O's. of whom nine were killed, among these being Sergt. T. Goodwin, an "original," who had rendered splendid service and who was regarded as one of the most efficient N.C.O's. in the Battalion. Even earlier than this Major N. M. MacLean, commanding "D" Coy., had suffered his second wound of the war.

In spite of these casualties, the Battalion continued to advance most steadily, maintaining the pace laid down in orders and reaching the various objectives absolutely on time. Even at this early stage it could be seen that the attack was going well. No call for support came to the 13th from the three battalions forming the front waves, these reporting that they were maintaining their schedules and were not meeting with serious opposition. At many other points along the wide British and Canadian front the attack, in its early stages, swept forward with equally few casualties. On the extreme left, however, the 4th Canadian Division encountered stiff opposition from the moment the men left their trenches and elsewhere, even at points where the first waves had but little trouble, fighting developed as the attack bit deeper and deeper into the German lines.

By 7 a.m. the battalions of the 3rd Brigade had advanced over a mile and had reached the point where orders called for a halt to allow the 1st Brigade to pass through. Even before this time the Highlanders had begun the consolidation of the Black Line, while the platoons acting as carrying parties were doing extremely well. By early afternoon these platoons, which had suffered less severely than expected, had brought forward all the material entrusted to them and had dumped it at the points selected on the Lille-Arras Road.

Meanwhile, Battalion Headquarters had been established in a large German dugout, which rejoiced in the name of Neuberger Haus. Here the Herr Commandant had just celebrated his birthday, the walls being festooned with wreaths of evergreen, while enshrined amongst these was an ornate sign, "Zum Geburtstag." Soda water bottles were much in evidence, but the only food that the curious Highlanders could discover consisted of some very filthy looking sausages and a large quantity of "kriegsbrot," which resembled saw-dust and which the Canadians found utterly unpalatable.

All day the 13th remained in this position, the men busy with the thousand and one tasks that fell to their lot, while Battalion Headquarters and the Signalling and Intelligence Sections worked at top speed transmitting to Brigade the messages that arrived back from the front line. Owing to the failure of certain direct lines of communication, the 13th acted as a report and relay centre and managed at all times to get messages through without appreciable delay.

By nightfall the attack had been pushed forward nearly three miles in all and had swept down the far side of Vimy Ridge to the railway running through Farbus Village. Elsewhere along the wide front things had gone equally well. The prisoners' cages in the rear, which had so tickled the fancy of the Highlanders weeks before, were now filled to overflowing, while large numbers of enemy guns and a vast amount of material had passed into British and Canadian hands.

In addition to the intrinsic and strategic value of what he had lost, the Hun's pride had received a nasty blow. He had boasted that no troops could take Vimy by frontal attack, but Vimy had been taken in spite of his boast and the wound rankled and smarted. Knowing all this, the Canadian Corps did not waste too much time in rejoicing over the victory, but set to work to prepare for the shrewd knocks that the indignant Hun would undoubtedly attempt to administer as soon as he recovered his second wind.

NOTE:—In addition to the casualties mentioned in the text Major I. M. R. Sinclair, commanding "A" Coy. and Capt. A. R. Gibson, commanding "C" Coy. were wounded during the Vimy engagement, as was Lieut. D. H. Burrows. This was Major Sinclair's third appearance on the casualty list.

CHAPTER XIII

Thélus, Farbus, Arleux and Fresnoy

> Boom of thunder and lightning flash—
> The torn earth rocks to the barrage crash;
> The bullets whine and the bullets sing
> From the mad machine-guns chattering:
> Black smoke rolling across the mud,
> Trenches plastered with flesh and blood.
> —Crosbie Garstin.

I

DAWN on April 10th found the 13th Battalion at work improving the Black Line, or Zwolfer Weg. Vimy Ridge by this time was a scene of great activity. The weather was atrocious, with a high wind and frequent snow falls, but these seemed only to spur the troops to work harder. Roads and light railways sprang up in all directions, while huts and shelters, growing as it seemed by magic, changed the landscape from hour to hour.

Burial and salvage parties were busy all this time and the clearing of the battlefield, so far as the area allotted to the 13th was concerned, was completed during the day. Long before nightfall the Canadian big guns were creeping forward over roads that had not been in existence when the day dawned. For their assistance in building these roads several parties of the 13th received special commendation from the officers of the Artillery and Engineers.

At 5 p.m. on the 10th, the Royal Highlanders moved back from Neuberger Haus to a point in the Old British Front Line, with Headquarters at Poste de Lille. Difficulty was experienced in finding the dugouts that were to be used as billets owing to the damage done by shell fire during the attack. Such trenches as were left more or less intact were flooded with water and deep in mud, but even so the men were glad to get a chance to remove the heavy equipment which they had been carrying for two days and nights.

At Poste de Lille the Battalion remained until April 13th. Technically the time was spent in resting; actually all ranks, including the reserve section of the Battalion, which had come for-

ROYAL HIGHLANDERS OF CANADA

ward from Bois des Alleux, were busy cleaning and repairing equipment, salvaging material and preparing for the next tour in the line.

All afternoon on the 13th the Battalion "stood to," ready to move, but orders did not arrive until nearly 9 p.m. As the companies were moving off in obedience to these belated instructions, an unfortunate incident occurred when someone kicked a Mills bomb which lay concealed in the mud. This exploded and wounded nine or ten men, among these being Major K. M. Perry, D.S.O., who was wounded in the neck, Capt. G. R. Johnson, the attached Medical Officer, who was wounded in the leg, Lieut. H. H. Chanter, slightly wounded for the second time, the Signalling Sergeant, who was struck in the back and a Pioneer, who suffered injuries from which he died in hospital two days later.

After the casualties of this accident had been attended to, the companies of the 13th marched off, via the Corduroy Road, to the Lens-Arras Road and thence overland, past the famous Nine Elms, to a support position in the Blue Line, south-east of the ruins of Thélus village and behind Farbus Wood. This move was carried out with the greatest difficulty, as all landmarks had been obliterated and in the pitch darkness of the night direction was hard to maintain. One company took the whole night to advance a distance of approximately two miles, arriving at its destination just at dawn.

In the Blue Line the Battalion spent two uncomfortable days. Shelling on both sides was brisk and, although casualties were not heavy, there was scarcely a moment when the German shell fire was not distinctly threatening. Movement during the day was almost impossible, owing to enemy observation balloons, and for the same reason cooking was considered inadvisable. At night, however, when the ration parties came up, all ranks made up for lost time and thoroughly enjoyed the hot food and drink that the cooks provided.

At dusk on April 15th the Battalion moved forward from support by platoons, to take over a section of the front line opposite Arleux. Moving down hill to the bottom of the Ridge, it seemed that the men must be in full view of the German lines and anxiety was felt, particularly when the enemy dropped a series of shells close enough to suggest that the platoons of the 13th were the target. Apparently this was not the case, or the Hun's shooting was bad, as the platoons reached the front line without serious losses.

At this point the front line ran along the Sunken Road, near

THELUS, FARBUS, ARLEUX AND FRESNOY

Willerval, and consisted of shallow pits providing a bare minimum of shelter. As the German artillery had the line of the road ranged to perfection, the next three days were extremely unpleasant and casualties mounted to a considerable total.

On the first morning in the line, Lieut. P. E. Corbett took a patrol for several hundred yards along a shallow trench, which crossed No Man's Land, to determine if the enemy still occupied Arleux Loop. By exposing himself at well chosen spots and at judicious intervals, Lieut. Corbett drew enemy fire, which convinced him that the trench in question was strongly held. Bombs were exchanged with a party of Huns, who were encountered, but, so far as the Canadians were concerned, no damage was done and the party returned safely at about 8.30 a.m.

Owing to the long carry for rations, the 13th left a detail for this purpose near Farbus Wood. Unaware that the approach to the front line was under observation, this detail, about 100 strong, advanced cheerfully towards the line in broad daylight, giving all the appearance of a miniature attack. Somewhat surprised, it is to be imagined, at this extraordinary manœuvre, the Hun opened up on the party with artillery and treated them to a blast of gunfire from which they were fortunate to escape without heavy losses. Needless to say this daylight bringing up of rations was not repeated.

After being relieved on April 18th, the Royal Highlanders moved back to a comparatively quiet spot in Farbus Wood. Here three days were spent, the men keenly enjoying the fact that nearby a battery of captured German guns was in action against its former masters. The Canadian Artillerymen who manned these guns also seemed to delight in their task, each shell being entrusted with blood curdling messages to deliver in the German trenches.

From Farbus Wood the 13th moved back on April 21st and spent the next five days at a point between the Lens-Arras Road and the Old British Front Line. Working parties were the chief feature of this period, these being employed to repair dugouts with a view to converting them into regular billets. On April 23rd a different task was accomplished when each company detailed 1 officer and 85 other ranks to bury cable. These parties proceeded independently to Nine Elms, where they were combined into one large party, under the command of Capt. D. B. Donald, who reported to an officer of the 1st Divisional Signal Coy.

At this time the 73rd Battalion, Royal Highlanders of Canada,

ROYAL HIGHLANDERS OF CANADA

of the 4th Canadian Division, passed out of existence, the personnel being drafted to the 13th and 42nd Battalions. This reorganization was caused by the fact that Montreal was over-represented by battalions at the front in proportion to the total of her enlistments and ability to maintain reinforcements. The passing of the 73rd, which had gained an enviable reputation, was deplored by the officers and men of the 13th and 42nd, who none the less welcomed the splendid drafts that came as a result of the dissolution. One group allotted to the 13th included the entire 73rd Pipe Band, this addition bringing the strength of the 13th Pipe Band up to nearly fifty, a formidable number when the authorized establishment was six. To celebrate the union of the two battalions, the combined bands attempted an entertainment on April 23rd, but this was not an entire success, as the enemy rudely dispersed the performers with some well placed shells.

Before the tour in this area was completed, Lieut.-Col. G. E. McCuaig was evacuated, suffering from a severe attack of laryngitis and trench fever, brought on by the exertions and exposure of the previous fortnight. On his departure, command of the Battalion was assumed by Major J. Jeffery, M.C., who handed over to Major K. M. Perry, when the latter returned from hospital on the evening of the 26th. Just previous to Major Perry's return the 13th had moved back to Pendu Huts, not far from the Bois des Alleux Huts, with which the men were so familiar. This was the first occasion on which the Battalion had been back out of the fighting area since the assault on Vimy Ridge on the morning of April 9th. Casualties during the 17 days had totalled 186, a number that was reasonable, considering the nature of the work accomplished. All ranks were congratulating themselves on this good fortune and preparing to settle down for a period of training when, on the afternoon of April 28th, Brigade advised that the village of Arleux had been captured and ordered the 13th forward into support.

Leaving a reserve of 12 officers and 180 other ranks under Major Jeffery, Major Perry led the main body forward to a position in the Bois de la Ville, stopping at the Nine Elms en route, where Lieut. Renahan distributed bombs, sandbags and ground flares. Some time after arriving at Bois de la Ville, the Battalion moved forward again and relieved the 5th Battalion (Western Cavalry), in the front line.

IN RESERVE NEAR LENS.

Canadian Official, Copyright.

FARBUS, MAY, 1917.

Canadian Official, Copyright.

THELUS, FARBUS, ARLEUX AND FRESNOY

The "line" at this particular point was found by the 13th to be a name rather than a reality. "D" Coy., under Major W. E. Macfarlane, who had with him Lieuts. H. A. Johnston, A. S. MacLean, J. S. Ireland, W. D. C. Christie and F. C. Smith, was selected to occupy the actual front, with the other companies in fairly close support. Macfarlane, accordingly, took over and found that his position was in a most uncertain state. On the right flank was the 15th Battalion, but between this unit and the 13th was a gap nearly 200 yards wide. The left flank was even worse, being "in the air," as the adjoining battalion of the 2nd Division could not be found in the location where it had been reported. As a result, Macfarlane found that the front which his company, with a bayonet strength of about 130, was expected to hold was nearly a mile in width. Heavy shelling complicated his situation, as his wires to Battalion Headquarters were constantly being cut, while communication by runners was difficult owing to the weight of the enemy barrages.

Becoming aware of all these difficulties and noticing that the terrain was well suited to a German counter-attack, Major Perry ordered Macfarlane to take no chances, but to touch off an S.O.S. should the enemy show the slightest sign of aggressiveness. Meanwhile, Perry undertook to get in touch with the 2nd Canadian Division and straighten out the obscure situation on the left flank, while Capt. F. S. Mathewson, of "B" Coy., who had two platoons directly in front of Arleux village in support of "D" Coy., made dispositions with his remaining platoons to protect this same danger point.

All day on the 29th and again on the 30th, the companies of the 13th were subjected to heavy shelling, but, while this was unpleasant for all, "D" Coy., owing to its exposed position, and "B" Coy. in support got much the worst of it. In "D" Coy. casualties were numerous, while, as a result of concussion, such men as were otherwise uninjured were dazed and shaken almost beyond endurance, this condition being accentuated by the fact that no food or water could be sent through to them.

Meanwhile the Canadian artillery was active, shelling Fresnoy Village, Fresnoy Wood and the wire that protected these locations, in preparation for an attack by the infantry. In order to make sure that the wire was well cut and that the Canadian battalions, when the time came, would not be hung up and slaughtered as at

ROYAL HIGHLANDERS OF CANADA

Regina Trench, Lieut. P. E. Corbett and a party of 10 men conducted a daring daylight reconnaissance, as a result of which the exact condition of the enemy wire was made known to those who were to control the attack. In addition, this reconnaissance assisted in clearing up and rectifying the obscure position on the left flank.

At dusk on May 1st the left platoon of "D" Coy. caught sight of several bodies of the enemy filtering into a sunken road, obviously massing for something more serious than a patrol. Accordingly, in obedience to Major Perry's explicit orders, Major Macfarlane set off an S.O.S. which, on this occasion, consisted of three red Very lights. The reply of the Canadian artillery to this message was magnificent, both as regards promptness and volume. Actually before the last of the lights had died away, a terrific barrage fell on the area and the Hun attack, if such had indeed been planned, was smothered before it had a chance to develop. Afterwards a Highland patrol found three German dead and three badly wounded men whom their comrades had abandoned.

Later that same night an Engineer officer arrived at the front and, under his supervision, the 13th prepared jumping off trenches several hundred yards in advance of their position and close to Fresnoy. From these, units of the 1st Brigade, which relieved the 13th early on the morning of May 1st, launched the assault which brought Fresnoy into Canadian hands two days later.

After relief by the 1st Brigade, the 13th moved back to the Red Line of the Vimy Battle, Battalion Headquarters being in a dugout, called "Wittelsberger," or "Wittelsbacher" Haus. Working parties cleaned up this area on May 2nd, but on the following day unexpected orders took the Battalion forward to the Brown Line once more, the advance being made in small parties to escape enemy shelling.

After holding this new position for 24 hours, during which time the artillery on both sides displayed activity, the 13th was relieved by the 1st Devons of the 95th British Infantry Brigade. This unit had suffered severely in the recent fighting and was in no shape to take over an important part of the line. Morale was good, but the unit was very weak numerically, consequently it was no surprise to the Canadians, though a great disappointment, when news was received that the Germans had counter-attacked and retaken the

THELUS, FARBUS, ARLEUX AND FRESNOY

ground which the 1st Canadian Infantry Brigade had bought so dearly.

With this one day tour in the Brown Line, the part played by the 13th Battalion, Royal Highlanders of Canada, in the so-called Battles of Arras, 1917, comes to an end. Under date of May 3rd, Lieut.-Gen. Sir Julian Byng, K.C.B., K.C.M.G., M.V.O., who had commanded the Canadian Corps through all these engagements, issued the following special message:

"The brilliant operations during the last month, culminating in the capture of Arleux and Fresnoy, seem to give me the opportunity of expressing to all ranks the pride I feel in commanding the Canadian Corps.

"Since the 9th April, when the offensive against the Vimy Ridge began, till the morning of May 3rd, when Fresnoy was captured and consolidated, it has been one series of successes, only obtained by troops whose courage, discipline and initiative stand pre-eminent.

"Nine villages have passed into our hands. Eight German Divisions have been met and defeated. Over 5,000 prisoners have been captured and booty, comprising some 64 guns, 106 trench mortars and 126 machine guns, are now the trophies of the Canadians.

"The training undergone during the winter has borne fruit, and it is this training, coupled with the zeal and gallantry which are so conspicuous in all ranks of the Corps, that will continue to gain results as potent and far reaching as those which began with the capture of Vimy Ridge."

This message to the troops of the Canadian Corps was followed shortly by the announcement that, in recognition of gallantry during the period in question, honours had been granted to a number of officers and men. On this list appeared the names of Capt. W. S. M. MacTier and Lieut. P. E. Corbett, of the 13th, who received the Military Cross, while the Military Medal was awarded to Sergt. W. T. Hornby, Sergt. W. W. Ireland, Sergt. J. Robertson, Corp. J. Tupper, Lance-Corp. R. G. Bell, Private A. W. Crawford and Private F. S. Nelles.

II

Following the termination of the Vimy battles, the 3rd Canadian Brigade was withdrawn for nearly a month to Corps Reserve, during

ROYAL HIGHLANDERS OF CANADA

which time the 13th Battalion occupied billets, first at Chateau de la Haie, where the accommodation was excellent, and then for a longer period at Gouy Servins, where billets were inferior, but where the men were interested in meeting again many of the French inhabitants with whom they had struck up acquaintance in November of the previous year.

Immediately on reaching the Reserve Area, the Battalion, whose strength at this time totalled 1077 all ranks, started an extended programme of training. Realizing the value of morale in connection with training, the first parade held was to the Divisional Baths, where the men, in addition to enjoying the luxury of hot water, received clean underclothing and socks that were very welcome.

The next move on the programme was the renewal of the anti-typhoid inoculation, this being followed by an inspection to see that all men had their tunics cut in Highland fashion, or if they had not, to get this defect remedied. All other ranks then passed through the hands of the regimental barbers and had their hair cut, while the regimental shoe-makers were put to work repairing faulty boots. Considerably smartened as a result of these attentions, the Battalion presented a fine appearance on May 9th when the 3rd Brigade carried out a ceremonial parade before the Divisional Commander, Major-Gen. A. W. Currie, and also on May 10th when the Brigade was inspected by the Corps Commander, Lieut.-Gen. the Hon. Sir Julian Byng.

During this period a Sergeants' Mess was organized and a Battalion concert party came into being, both these organizations in their respective fields helping materially to make the stay in Corps Reserve agreeable. The officers, too, re-established their Mess and were able to offer hospitality to a number of their friends in units stationed nearby. With a view to offsetting any tendency to slackness that might arise from war conditions, it was understood that suitable attire would be expected in the evenings and the ordinary etiquette of Mess routine observed at all times.

As was to be expected, sports took up the men's time when they were not employed in drilling and training. Baseball games between companies and platoons were numerous, while the Battalion football team practised faithfully and indulged in several contests with success, bowing, however, to a team from the 15th Battalion after a game that was a thriller from start to finish. Some consolation for this defeat was obtained when a 13th rifle team shot against

THELUS, FARBUS, ARLEUX AND FRESNOY

a team from the 15th on the latter's ranges and came away winners by a score of 988-876.

Battalion sports were held on May 12th and aroused the usual keen interest, the pillow fight on the greasy pole being one of the most popular items on the programme. For this event, which was won by Lance-Corp. W. Armstrong, of "A" Coy., a large water tank was placed to receive the defeated entrants, whose puffings and splashings pleased the spectators immensely. Brigade sports followed in due course and in these the men of the 13th distinguished themselves by winning first place in six out of the twelve events contested. In a baseball match for the "Championship of France," which brought the sports to a close, the Royal Highlanders were also winners, gaining the decision by a score of 9-1. As one member of the Battalion remarked in a letter home, "I won 125 francs on the sports and 200 francs on the baseball game, so it wasn't a bad day's work at all." Later in the month Brig.-Gen. G. S. Tuxford, C.M.G. was invited to judge a competition between the four best platoons in the Battalion, the decision to be based on efficiency and smartness of appearance. This competition was close, but eventually the prize was awarded to No. 15 Platoon, of "D" Coy., under command of Lieut. J. S. Ireland.

On May 13th the battalions of the 3rd Canadian Infantry Brigade attended a special service of thanksgiving for the victory granted to Canadian arms at Vimy Ridge. This service, though simple, was most impressive and was attended by the Army Commander, General Horne, and many other officers of high rank, who had taken part in the operations.

All during the time in Corps Reserve the services of the pipe band of the 13th were in great demand. The massed bands of the Brigade played at the Brigade Sports, which were held at Chateau de la Haie, and again at Army Headquarters at Ranchicourt, on May 26th. On May 29th an even more ambitious programme was carried out at Camblain l'Abbé, when the massed bands of the whole Canadian Corps, consisting of 162 pipes and 105 drums, played at Corps Headquarters before an audience which included Field-Marshal Sir Douglas Haig, G.C.B., G.C.V.O., Commander-in-Chief of the British Armies in France, Gen. Sir H. S. Horne, K.C.B., Lieut.-Gen. Sir Julian Byng, K.C.B., Major-Gen. A. W. Currie, C.B., Prince Arthur of Connaught and many other officers on the Corps, Divisional and Brigade Staffs. The great success of the proceedings on these occasions was in no small measure due to the painstaking work of Pipe-Major D. Manson, of the 13th Royal Highlanders, who was in supreme control.

The health of the troops at this time was good. Sixty-seven men were sent to hospital during the month of May for one cause or another, but the great majority of these cases were of a minor nature and many reported back for duty after undergoing a few days treatment, so that, with the addition of two drafts, totalling 113 men, the strength of the Battalion when the period in Corps Reserve came to an end, had crept up to 1113 all ranks.

On May 29th, in preparation for a move, an officers' party, consisting of Major J. Jeffery, Major I. M. R. Sinclair, Capt. Melrose, Capt. Bennett and Lieut. Corbett, reconnoitred the series of trenches which the Battalion was destined to occupy on its next tour in the line. Simultaneously another party, composed of Lieut. E. Appleby, Lieut. J. S. Ireland and ten other ranks, reported to No. 16 Squadron, Royal Air Force, for one day's instruction in co-operation between Infantry and Aircraft.

Two days later the Battalion marched from Gouy Servins, passed the night in tents at Berthonval, proceeded on the next day to Thélus Cave and, after dark, moved over the top of the ridge to relieve the 21st Canadian Battalion in the front line between Acheville and Mericourt, with the support companies at Mont Forêt Quarries. As had now become the established custom, a percentage of officers and men was left out of the line to form the Battalion reserve.

The position occupied by the 13th was rather a novel one. The ground was not much broken up by shell fire, the trenches were new and quite small, no dugouts existed, nor was there any wire out in front, conditions consequently resembling to some extent those of open warfare. Curiously enough, the 13th was warned on taking over this position that the enemy was master of No Man's Land and it was suggested that the Battalion govern itself accordingly. Accepting this information rather in the nature of a challenge, strong patrols of the 13th prepared to contest the Hun superiority. Although these patrols swept No Man's Land over and over again, their free progress was never even disputed.

For five days the 13th held this section of the line, the task being a difficult one, owing to the fact that the enemy had direct observation from a position on the left and made use of this to

THELUS, FARBUS, ARLEUX AND FRESNOY

enfilade the trenches with machine gun fire. Casualties from this and other causes totalled 16, amongst the wounded being Lieut. H. H. Chanter, who was struck in the leg on June 2nd while coming forward to rejoin the Battalion after a temporary absence. This was the third occasion on which Lieut. Chanter had suffered wounds.

During this tour the Battalion endured its first experience of that horror of the war's latter stages—night bombing from aeroplanes. On this occasion the Battalion Transport got knocked about, while several men in the front line were injured as a result of bombs dropped from an enemy plane. Gas shelling was another feature that made the tour unpleasant. On the night of June 5th, when the Battalion was relieved, the move back was accomplished under a barrage of gas shells. In spite of respirators, some of the men caught a whiff or so of gas, which caused them to retch miserably, while the great majority suffered no ill effects from the gas itself, but had a hard time to see where they were going, the night being dark and progress much obstructed by old trenches, ditches and barbed wire entanglements.

For the next five days the 13th remained in a reserve position not far from Vimy Station, whence parties fared forth nightly to work in or near the front line. The chief event of this period was a competition at the Transport Lines between the four battalions of the 3rd Brigade, in which prizes were offered for the best Cook-Kitchen, Water-Cart, Limber and Pack Cob. There was great rejoicing in the Battalion when it was found that the 13th had won first prize in all four classes, Lieut. Johnston, the Transport Officer, and his men receiving warm congratulations.

After the tour near Vimy Station, the Royal Highlanders moved back, under shell fire that killed two men, and spent a fortnight in Brigade Reserve, first at Paynesley and later at Fraser Camp, near Mont. St. Eloy. At both these places a stiff programme of training was carried out, special attention being paid to grenade work, under Lieut. Renahan, and Lewis Gun operations, directed by Lieut. G. Millar. Entertainments by the Battalion Concert Party were successfully held on several occasions, while an innovation appreciated by all the men was the serving of hot tea immediately after reveille and before the morning's physical drill.

On June 25th the Battalion moved forward and at night took over the same section of front as had been held early in the month. A week was spent in the front line, the tour being marked by two events of some importance. The first of these occurred on June 28th, when the Battalion staged a "Chinese attack," with the object of diverting the enemy's attention from another part of the line where more serious operations were contemplated.

To carry out the "Chinese" attack, the men of the 13th built a jumping off trench in front of their own line, knowing full well that this work would not escape the attention of the vigilant Hun. Dummy figures were then secretly placed in the trench and strings with which to work them run back to the front line. At the moment of the "attack" these strings were jerked, the dummies bobbing around in response and the trench, from a distance, looking as if crowded with eager troops awaiting the signal to go over the top. Half a minute later a smoke barrage hid the dummies from view, lest some German observer with powerful glasses, or unusually quick intuition, should penetrate the deception and give the whole show away. The appearance of the dummies a few seconds in advance of the smoke would, it was hoped, be taken by the Germans as a failure on the part of the Canadians to synchronize things properly. The ruse worked well on this occasion and the German artillery, quick to answer their infantry's S.O.S., concentrated on the poor dummies and blew them out of existence. The danger in an "attack" of this sort lies in the fact that the enemy does not confine his attention to the dummy trench, but shells the whole area, including the front line and communication trenches. Knowing this, the Royal Highlanders took the obvious precautions and escaped without losses, while the Canadian artillery, seeing that the Hun had swallowed the bait, shelled his lines heavily in the hope of catching troops whom he might rush up to meet the threatened assault.

At one point observers noticed that the enemy shelled a portion of his own line and this fact was duly reported to the powers that be, who evidently found in the information something that puzzled them not a little. Rumours had reached them that the Hun was contemplating a retirement on this front and the fact that he shelled his own front line may have suggested that the retreat had actually begun, despite the fact that the forward battalions found nothing in the quality of their opposition to support such a belief.

The point was an important one, however, and the 13th received orders to push a patrol into the enemy lines to investigate. On the night of June 28th, in obedience to these orders, Lieut. J. F. Smith,

THELUS, FARBUS, ARLEUX AND FRESNOY

the Patrol Officer, and a party of eight other ranks, proceeded across No Man's Land and worked their way in through the enemy wire.

Suddenly a bomb was thrown at them and simultaneously a machine gun opened fire at close range. Realizing that he had encountered a strong enemy post, Lieut. Smith ordered his men to retire to their own lines, while he himself with one man remained to cover the movement. The party suffered several minor casualties during the withdrawal, but eventually reached the front line in safety. After receiving the report of the party and waiting in vain for Smith's return, Major F. S. Mathewson and Sergt. W. T. Hornby went out to discover what was amiss.

Half way across No Man's Land Mathewson and Hornby found the man who had remained with Smith when he ordered the party to retire. This man reported that a bomb had struck Smith and, presumably, killed him. He himself had started at once to the officer's aid, but had been struck down and seriously wounded before he could reach the spot where the latter fell. Realizing his inability to be of assistance to Smith, the man had started to crawl to his own lines, dragging his shattered leg behind him. As day was breaking by this time, Mathewson and Hornby were unable to push further forward. Between them they carried the wounded man, who had reached the extreme limit of his endurance, back to safety in the 13th lines. That night Sergt. Hornby took out a large patrol to the spot where Smith had last been seen but, in spite of an exhaustive search, no trace of the latter could be found. With little hope therefore and with deep regret this brave officer's name was added to the Battalion's roll of "missing."

During the remainder of the tour in the front line, patrols at night were frequent and No Man's Land was combed with a thoroughness that brought to light many important items as to the disposition of the enemy and the state of his wire. Aeroplanes were also active during this period, and one daring Hun flew low over the front trenches, engaging in a battle with the Highlanders' machine guns and coming off a winner by wounding two men and, so far as could be judged, escaping uninjured himself.

On the night of July 3rd, "B" Coy., part of "A" and "C" Companies and Battalion Headquarters were relieved by the 3rd Canadian Battalion, command of those sections which remained in the line passing temporarily to the 16th Battalion, Canadian Scottish. These sections were relieved by the 14th Battalion on the following night and rejoined their own unit, which had moved to a reserve position a little south of Vimy Station.

As was always the case in reserve, working parties in and about the front line at night kept a large number of the men busy. The duties of these parties were hard and tiring, but in no way exceptional, consisting chiefly of digging and wiring trenches, carrying forward materials, rations and trench mortar ammunition, and other tasks of a similar character.

On the evening of July 8th, after dusk, the 13th Battalion moved up and relieved the 16th Canadian Battalion, in the support area around Saskatchewan Road. This position had been reconnoitred by parties of the 13th on the previous day, the officers and N.C.O's. of "A" Coy. having had a miraculous escape when a salvo of field gun shells landed amongst them and exploded without causing a single casualty. Observers of the incident have commented that the miracle of the escape was at least equalled by the miracle of speed shown by the party in leaving the unwholesome spot behind.

For five days the 13th remained in the Saskatchewan Road support position, supplying working parties at night with unfailing regularity. These parties, however, found their task somewhat less monotonous than usual, as they were engaged well out in No Man's Land in front of Mericourt, digging and wiring a new front line trench. Covering parties lay still further out to protect the workers from any sudden attack, but none such occurred, the only casualties suffered being caused by long range machine gun fire, this in spite of the fact that the moon was unusually bright and the danger correspondingly increased.

During this period a large wooden cross was constructed at the 13th Transport Lines and erected in the Cemetery at Nine Elms, as a memorial to officers and men of the Battalion who had given their lives in the spring engagements at Vimy Ridge. This cross was brought to Canada after the war and now stands in the grounds of the Royal Military College, Kingston.

Somewhat unexpectedly, the Royal Highlanders were relieved by the 11th Battalion of the East Lancs. on the night of July 13th, the platoons marching back to the "Rhine and Elbe" area and reaching their destination at an early hour in the morning. Here the pipe band joined the Battalion and in the afternoon the companies, each with its quota of pipes and drums, moved back to Ottawa Camp in the Bois des Alleux.

THELUS, FARBUS, ARLEUX AND FRESNOY

This was familiar territory to the men of the 13th, but the scene had altered since their last visit. Then all was bustle and activity and mud; now the Bois was a peaceful, almost idyllic, spot, pervaded by a sense of calm and with wild flowers growing everywhere in great profusion.

No parades for drill were held on the one day that the Battalion remained in this location, but rifles were inspected, as were kits, while a part of the unit paraded for pay and another for bathing purposes. The greater part of the time, however, was given to the men to rest, officers being anxious that the latter should be in good condition to march early on the following morning.

CHAPTER XIV

Hill 70

No easy hopes or lies
Shall bring us to our goal,
But iron sacrifice
Of body, will, and soul.
—RUDYARD KIPLING.

I

REVEILLE sounded at 5 a.m. on July 16th and at 7 a.m. the companies moved off, preceded by the cook-kitchens, which had a hot lunch ready when the troops reached a point near Verdrel. After lunch the march was continued, Headquarters finally halting with "A" and "B" Companies at Fosse 7, "C" Coy. billeting at Barlin and "D" Coy. at Ruitz. Here the Battalion remained for some 24 hours, the men bathing and amusing themselves in the evening by visiting the local stores and estaminets. After dinner on the 17th, Battalion Headquarters and the four companies paraded and marched to a camp on the outskirts of Noeux-les-Mines, where the men billeted in some of the most comfortable and well equipped huts that had up to this time fallen to their lot.

Moving from these commodious quarters on the afternoon of the 18th, the Battalion proceeded, via Sains-en-Gohelle and Bully Grenay, to billets in les Brebis and Maroc, "C" and "D" Companies continuing on to a position in support trenches further forward. Considerable shelling of Maroc and neighbourhood occurred at night, but the men of the 13th, occupying cellars, escaped without casualties. One man was killed and several injured, however, while engaged on a working party carrying ammunition.

On July 20th Lieut.-Col. McCuaig and a group of officers went forward to reconnoitre trenches on the slight rise just to the east of the village of Loos. This was Hill 70, famous as the tragic spot where the Territorial Highland Regiments had suffered such disastrous losses in the autumn of 1915. Lieut.-Col. McCuaig and his party were informed by the Brigadier that the task of avenging

HILL 70

these losses and of capturing the Hill had been entrusted to the Canadian Corps, which would begin preparations immediately.

Many of the officers of the 13th had some acquaintance with this district, but the secret of the coming assault sharpened their interest in the topography of the country, a sound knowledge of which was now essential. Field glasses were accordingly unslung, maps eagerly consulted and every effort made to gather all information possible. As secrecy was an important element in the plan for the capture of Hill 70, the officers of the 13th on returning from the reconnaissance made no mention of what was in the wind even to the most trusted of their N.C.O's., preferring to wait till the Battalion had retired to the training area, when there would be less chance of harm from a careless remark, or an ill judged confidence.

Relief occurred on the afternoon and night of July 22nd, the Highlanders reaching their destination, which proved to be Noeux-les-Mines, early on the morning of the 23rd. In some extraordinary way the civilian population, as was so often the case, seemed well aware of matters regarding which the troops themselves were ignorant. On this occasion the arrival of the Highlanders in Noeux-les-Mines evoked considerable quiet enthusiasm, the citizens greeting them affectionately as, "the brave Canadians, who were soon to drive the dirty Boches far away."

From the 24th of July until the end of the month the 13th Battalion trained intensively, devoting every effort to perfecting the moves to be undertaken in the coming operations. First of all a party of officers and N.C.O's. visited the area at Aix-Noulette where, as had been the case during the preparations for the Battle of Vimy Ridge, a facsimile of the enemy's trenches had been taped out. On the following day actual training began, the platoons of the Battalion receiving individual attention and rehearsing over the taped area. As soon as the platoons had mastered their parts, work by companies commenced, this being succeeded in turn by Battalion rehearsals and finally by Brigade operations on an elaborate scale.

In these operations the troops moved forward behind a line of men carrying small flags, who represented the barrage. Hill 70 was duplicated in every possible feature and at one point it seemed that the Engineers in their eagerness to render the contours exact had committed a dangerous error, as the troops on pushing over the top of the hill found that the latter stage of their advance was under direct, though distant, observation from the German lines. The explanation of this seeming mistake lay in the fact that the area in question was the only one where operations on such a scale could be conducted without alienating the friendship of the local population by trampling down the growing crops, which every Frenchman regarded as of vital importance. What the distant German observers thought of the solemn row of little figures, each waving a tiny flag, and of the denser rows which followed so determinedly, no man will ever know. Perhaps they were too busy with their own affairs to be interested. At any rate, the Canadian rehearsals were quite undisturbed, for which all ranks were devoutly thankful.

Every private was expected to familiarize himself with the taped area and to study large coloured maps prepared for the purpose. Officers took pains, too, to answer questions and encouraged the men to make suggestions on matters which immediately concerned them. Lectures were delivered to all ranks and officers were instructed to visit and examine a specially prepared plasticine model of Hill 70, which revealed every feature that the keen eyes of aerial cameras could detect. All this time the Intelligence Section of the 13th was in the front line studying the actual ground to be fought over, with the assistance of a huge telescopic periscope captured at Vimy, collecting information, piecing this together and keeping Battalion Headquarters informed regarding all developments of consequence.

Meanwhile changes in the higher command of the Canadian Corps had taken place. Sir Julian Byng, in recognition of his striking success at Vimy Ridge, had been promoted to the command of the Third Army. His place as Corps Commander had been taken by Lieut. Gen. A. W. Currie, a Canadian born civilian soldier, whose distinguished record throughout the whole war clearly entitled him to this post of importance and honour. In turn, General Currie's position as Commander of the 1st Canadian Division had passed to Major-Gen. A. C. Macdonell, C.B., C.M.G., D.S.O., whom the troops had known as a Brigade Commander and news of whose appointment to higher rank was received with universal satisfaction. It was in his new capacity as Divisional Commander that Major-Gen. Macdonell inspected and addressed the men of the 13th on the afternoon of July 30th, complimenting them on what they had done

HILL 70

in the past and expressing confidence in their ability to continue the good work in the future.

Bad weather during the next few days rendered living conditions at Noeux-les-Mines miserable in the extreme and only strenuous work by draining parties prevented the huts from being badly flooded. It was not with much regret, therefore, that the Battalion vacated the camp on August 2nd and moved up into the forward area, "C" and "D" Companies and Battalion Headquarters taking over billets at les Brebis, whilst "A" and "B" Companies proceeded to support positions in the Village Line.

Three days later "A" and "B" Companies were relieved and rejoined the main body of the Battalion in les Brebis. Here five days were spent, the time passing agreeably enough in daylight when, for some reason or other, the enemy artillery was not particularly active. At night, on the contrary, shelling was too brisk for comfort and the men on more than one occasion were roused from sleep and forced to take refuge in the cellars or surrounding fields. Many narrow escapes occurred, but actual casualties were avoided, as was the case with numerous working parties provided by the Battalion during this period.

On August 10th the Battalion moved back to Barlin, spent two days there and returned to les Brebis on August 13th, Headquarters moving up to Meath Trench after dark, "C" Coy. to forward trenches and "B" Coy. to the Village Line. The following night "A" and "D" Companies moved up and the whole Battalion assembled in jumping off trenches for the Battle of Hill 70.

Operation Order No. 112, dealing with the duties that would fall to the lot of the 13th, was now about to be carried out. Roughly, the plan was that the 1st and 2nd Canadian Divisions should attack, with the 1st Division on the left. Each Division was to use two Brigades in the assault and, in the case of the 1st Division, the 2nd and 3rd Brigades were those chosen, the 3rd Brigade being on the left. In the 3rd Brigade the attacking battalions, from left to right were the 15th Battalion (48th Highlanders), the 13th Battalion, Royal Highlanders of Canada and the 16th Battalion, Canadian Scottish. The 14th Battalion, Royal Montreal Regiment, was to mop up and carry, a role which the 13th had played at Vimy Ridge.

As will be seen from the above, the 15th Battalion was on the extreme left of the attack, with the 13th Battalion coming next. As the objectives assigned to the units farther to the right were at

ROYAL HIGHLANDERS OF CANADA

a greater distance from the jumping off trenches, the attack was really a pivotal one, with the 15th occupying the hinge position.

So far as the 13th Battalion was concerned, orders called for an attack in two stages, with objectives named respectively the Blue Line and the Green Line.

The Blue Line was to be attacked by two companies, "D" Coy. on the right and "B" Coy. on the left. During this stage of the operation "A" Coy. was to act in support of the whole front, while "C" Coy. was to mop up and carry supplies. After the capture of the Blue Line "A" Coy. was ordered to replace "B" Coy. on the left front of the attack and await the lifting of the barrage. When this occurred "A" and "D" Companies were to advance against the final, or Green, objective.

"B" Coy. in the meantime was ordered to consolidate the captured Blue Line, while three platoons of "C" Coy. continued the work of carrying material and mopping up. The remaining platoon of "C" Coy. was ordered to move forward with "A" and "D" Companies to wire the Green Line as soon as possible after its capture.

Some idea of the immense quantities of stores that the Battalion was to use in the attack can be gathered from the tables attached to the Operation Order. From these lists one picks items such as the following:

66,000 rounds of rifle ammunition.
   700 rounds of pistol ammunition.
 1,500 rounds of blank cartridges to propel rifle grenades.
 4,100 bombs.
   870 Very lights.
   666 ground flares.
   334 shovels.
   134 picks.
 6,750 sandbags.
   135 sheets of corrugated iron.
   135 long screw pickets.
   400 short screw pickets.
    14 infantry foot bridges.
    14 trench ladders.
    70 coils of barbed wire.
     7 steel shelters.

MEMORIAL CROSS, ERECTED BY THE BATTALION AT NINE ELMS, VIMY RIDGE, MAY, 1917.

(This Cross now stands in the grounds of the Royal Military College at Kingston.)

HILL 70

All this material, together with nails of various sizes, pit props, wire cutters and other articles too numerous to mention, was in possession of the Battalion before the day of the attack actually dawned.

II

On the night of August 14th the Royal Highlanders, as already stated, moved up into trenches whence the assault on Hill 70 was to be launched. Battalion Headquarters was in Meath Trench, slightly in rear of the left front, and here gathered the various infantry and artillery liaison officers and all the connecting links so vital in the conduct of a great battle. In this dugout, too, Lieut.-Col. McCombe, of the 14th Royal Montreal Regiment, established his advanced headquarters.

Assembly was complete by 2.40 o'clock on the morning of the 15th, an hour and three quarters before the attack was due. Taking advantage of this, Lieut.-Col. McCuaig called a conference of his company commanders to make certain that each had thoroughly grasped the details of his task. "A" Coy. was to be led by Major I. M. R. Sinclair, "B" by Major F. S. Mathewson, "C" by Capt. H. D. Ives and "D" by Capt. W. H. D. Bennett. Each of these stated that his company was ready and showed that he himself had mastered every detail of his orders. Satisfied, therefore, that the companies would not fail through any fault in leadership, Lieut.-Col. McCuaig dismissed the conference and the four officers proceeded to their commands.

For the next half hour silence reigned over the whole area. Thousands of men were packed in the front line, yet a few yards away in No Man's Land an observer, had there been such, might easily have fancied himself alone in a desolate and deserted country. Only the occasional crack of a rifle and the even less frequent boom of a big gun would have told him that his solitude was more fancied than real.

About 3.55 a.m. Lieut.-Col. McCuaig and several other officers moved out into No Man's Land and lay down to await the zero hour. The strictest silence was maintained during this move, nevertheless a vague warning of approaching disaster seemed to permeate the enemy lines. Under its influence a few of his batteries came to life and laid a light barrage along the Canadian line. His infantry, too, became uneasy, as if fearing something, but unaware of what they feared. Thus, at 4.20 a.m., two double red

ROYAL HIGHLANDERS OF CANADA

signal lights blazed suddenly in the German lines, followed a minute or two later by a rocket, which soared up into the blackness of the night and burst into a shower of golden rain. Exactly what these signals meant the Highlanders never knew, for half a minute after the rocket had gone up the Canadian machine gun barrage started and five seconds later the air was torn and split as the artillery joined in.

With "D" Coy. on the right, "B" on the left and "A" in close support, the waves of the Royal Highlanders started for their first objective. No time was lost in pushing forward, as all ranks realized that in a matter of moments the German counter barrage would fall and in all probability the target chosen would be No Man's Land and the trenches from which the attack had come. Until certain of what had happened the enemy would hesitate to shell his own front line, so that was a spot to be reached as fast as was consistent with discipline and good order.

In the darkness of the night the attack of "D" Coy. had at first a tendency to bear to the right, but this was quickly overcome, largely through the gallant and devoted effort of Capt. W. H. D. Bennett, an original 13th N.C.O., who, although mortally wounded, continued to direct his men until no longer able to speak. A second factor which assisted in correcting direction at some points, although it dazzled the men and had the opposite effect at others, was a great sheet of red and yellow flame, which sprang up on the left flank and burned with extraordinary brilliance. At the moment the troops had no explanation of this phenomenon, but later it was discovered that a special party of the Royal Engineers had used trench mortars to throw cylinders of blazing oil and thus put out of action a German strong point, known as "Puits No. 14-bis." The red light from this blazing oil, flashing and glittering on the long lines of bayonets was a sight to fire the imagination. There was something grim and symbolic about it, as if the bayonets had done their work and were running red in consequence.

On reaching the German front line system, the Royal Highlanders picked up some 25 prisoners and swept forward without serious opposition, reaching their first objective, the Blue Line, on scheduled time and just as the grey light of early dawn changed to the full white light of day.

At this point the Battalion halted, in accordance with the

HILL 70

Operation Order, and effected the arranged changes in dispositions. "A" Coy. moved up and took over the left front from "B" Coy., while "D" Coy. reorganized on the right front and "C" Coy. carried on with its programme of mopping up. Simultaneously with these moves, Lieut.-Col. McCuaig arrived up and established his Headquarters in the dugout which aerial photographs had enabled him to select in advance. A party of the enemy were hiding in this dugout, but surrendered when called on to do so. Unfortunately, a member of a mopping up party of another battalion came along at this moment and, seeing the trench full of Germans, opened fire, killing a 13th Battalion runner, wounding two signallers and narrowly missing the C.O. himself. Curiously, the German prisoners escaped without a scratch.

Following this incident, Lieut.-Col. McCuaig sent a message to Major W. E. Macfarlane, his acting Second-in-Command, to come forward and bring with him the various liaison officers and other Headquarters personnel. This little party, laden down with pots, pans, rations and signalling equipment, had a rather adventurous trip up through the barrage, but arrived eventually, after one or two of its members had fallen.

Meanwhile, the position of the Battalion had become decidedly uncomfortable. The Blue Line at this point ran along the top of the hill and the men could be seen by the German snipers in Hugo Trench down the forward slope, also by various observers who controlled the fire of the enemy guns. Under these circumstances the 40 minute delay to allow the whole attack to reach its objectives and reform for the second stage seemed almost endless.

Shells poured on the line and, to add to the distress, one of the covering batteries was firing short and delivering salvo after salvo right at the Battalion's centre, where "A" Coy. joined up with "D." To avoid this fire, both companies were forced to shift to their respective flanks and direct contact was temporarily severed. Annoying as this fire was, however, casualties from it were easily avoided, but there was no escape from the deadly bombardment inflicted by the Hun.

Just at this time, when all ranks were feeling the strain of remaining inactive under galling fire and when casualties had mounted to over 100, a skirl of the bagpipes was heard and along the 13th front came a piper of the 16th, Canadian Scottish. This inspired individual, eyes blazing with excitement and kilt proudly swinging to his measured tread, made his way along the line, piping as only a true Highlander can when men are dying, or facing death, all around him. Shell fire seemed to increase as the piper progressed and more than once it appeared that he was down, but the god of brave men was with him in that hour and he disappeared, unharmed, to the flank whence he had come.

At last the 40 minute pause in the Blue Line came to an end and the Royal Highlanders were ordered forward to the Green objective. As the waves were about to move off, Major Mathewson, of "B" Coy. discovered that, in addition to Capt. Bennett, "D" Coy. had lost two subalterns, Lieuts. J. S. Ireland and A. S. MacLean. Lieut. Ireland was seriously wounded, while Lieut. MacLean, who had suffered wounds at the Somme in the autumn of 1916, had gone down this time with injuries that were mortal. This left Lieut. J. E. Christie as the only surviving officer of the Company and, as he was at the extreme left of the line and probably quite unaware of what had happened, Mathewson promptly turned "B" Coy. over to his second-in-command and himself led "D" Coy. forward.

Between the Blue Line and the Green Line, which was their final objective, the men of the 13th encountered stiff opposition. On the left "A" Coy., under Major Sinclair, pushed forward across fairly open country, using such shell holes as were available for shelter and beating down the enemy fire as they went. At Hugo Trench they met with serious resistance, the enemy garrison fighting stubbornly until the majority were killed or wounded. A dozen or so fell unwounded into the hands of the Canadians and a somewhat larger number made their escape down Humbug Communication Trench, but as this avenue of retreat brought them again under the lash of the British barrage, it is not likely that they reached safety.

Pausing only a few moments in Hugo Trench, which was at least eight feet deep and in excellent condition, Sinclair led "A" Coy. on to the Green Line a hundred yards ahead, reporting to Battalion Headquarters at 6.05 a.m. that the Line was in his possession and that he was consolidating. What he did not report was that he was having a hard time to make his men halt and dig in. Their blood was thoroughly up and ahead of them the barrage had crashed on Hercules Trench, disturbing a swarm of Huns who

HILL 70

were buzzing about like so many bees. The sight of these individuals was almost more than the men of the 13th could stand. They longed to charge with the bayonet and only stern orders forced them to be content with seeing the enemy fall under the barrage and rifle fire.

Meanwhile, on the right front "D" Coy., led by Major Mathewson, had advanced through a shattered wood, known as the Bois Rasé. The Company was considerably under strength as a result of the casualties suffered in the Blue Line and the broken underbrush, some three feet high, rendered the ground ideal for defence, nevertheless, the waves pushed steadily on until they approached Hugo Trench. Here, as in the case of "A" Coy., the enemy offered determined resistance, coming out of their trench, standing up behind it to get a better view, and opening a withering fire.

With his diminished numbers, Mathewson decided that an attempt to rush the position would be dangerous. Accordingly, he ordered the men of "D" Coy. to stalk the enemy, creeping ever nearer and nearer, firing all the time and closing in until a rush would seem advisable. Although these tactics involved a slight loss of time, they succeeded admirably. Noticing that a few of the enemy had started to retreat, Mathewson decided that the psychological moment had arrived and gave the order to charge. Responding with a yell, the Highlanders plunged forward and took the trench with the bayonet, killing or wounding many of the garrison and capturing a round dozen of unwounded prisoners.

With this position cleared, Mathewson had little trouble in advancing to the final, or Green, objective. At 6.10 a.m. he reported to Battalion Headquarters that the position was in his hands and that he was in communication with Sinclair on the left. On receipt of this message, Lieut.-Col. McCuaig and the officers at Battalion Headquarters heaved a sigh of relief. The Bois Rasé, it had been felt, might conceal machine gun nests, or other strong points, against which the waves of the attack would beat in vain. Now this apprehension had been removed and, despite considerable losses, the Battalion was at all points holding its objectives. Apparently the Battle of Hill 70 was going well.

While these events were taking place on the fronts of the attacking companies, the platoons of "C" Coy., under Capt. H. D. Ives, were carrying out the arduous duties assigned to them. Lieut. E. B. Q. Buchanan was wounded at an early stage of the engagement,

ROYAL HIGHLANDERS OF CANADA

while leading his platoon forward to the Blue Line. Lieut. Plante's platoon suffered from the German barrage, one section, under an N.C.O., being caught by an intense burst of fire and practically annihilated. Machine gun fire also caused the platoons of "C" Coy. some trouble, especially at one point where a stubbornly fought gun continued firing until Lieut. Plante shot down the gunners manning it. Meanwhile, Lieut. R. M. Hebden, with No. 10 Platoon, accomplished much good work, while No. 11 Platoon, under Sergt.-Major Morrison, carried out its allotted tasks with courage and devotion. From 11 o'clock on the morning of the attack until the Battalion was relieved on the night of August 16th, "C" Coy. was employed in carrying ammunition, burying dead and evacuating wounded. In all these tasks, accomplished under heavy fire, the conduct of the men was admirable.

When Major Mathewson had seen "D" Coy. established in the Green Line, he returned to the Blue Line and reassumed command of his own company, Major Macfarlane, accompanied by Lieut. Renahan, proceeding up from Battalion Headquarters and taking over "D" Coy. On arrival in the front line, Macfarlane found that scattered bodies of the enemy in shell holes were still giving trouble. Several stiff little fights ensued before these parties could be overcome and in one instance Lieut. Christie had a narrow escape when a Hun, who had surrendered, suddenly leaped at him with a knife. Only the watchfulness of Corp. Macdonnell saved Christie from death, or serious injury. Quick as a flash the N.C.O. swung his rifle and crashed the butt on the German's head.

All this time the Green Line was being heavily shelled and accordingly Macfarlane, to avoid losses, moved nearly all his effectives into the outpost line, 200 yards in advance, leaving only a skeleton platoon, under Company Sergt.-Major Jones, in the front line proper.

About 11.50 a.m. Sinclair notified Macfarlane that he could see a counter-attack massing in Hercules Trench on the latter's immediate front. Macfarlane had already become aware of this menace and a few minutes previously had sent notice of it to Battalion Headquarters. Sinclair also reported to Headquarters and the latter, as communications further back were cut, forwarded the report to 1st Divisional H.Q. by carrier pigeon.

Apparently this bird, on whose safe arrival depended the lives of scores of men, flew swiftly to her destination. Possibly, on the

HILL 70

other hand, her arrival merely confirmed reports from other quarters. Be that as it may, the Canadian artillery received news of the danger that threatened and, having made special arrangements for just such a contingency, concentrated a weight of gun-fire on Hercules Trench and the Bois Dix Huit and prevented the attack from moving forward. At 12.15 p.m. the enemy again massed near the Bois Dix Huit and an attack in some strength developed. Once more, however, the German effort was withered by the blast of shell fire that greeted it. Undeterred by these failures, the enemy pushed forward another attack at about 1.15 p.m., but this, too, was dealt with by the Artillery, assisted by rifle fire from the outpost line.

On Sinclair's left, and practically at right angles to his position, ran the Bois Hugo. This wood was rendered untenable by the Canadian heavy artillery, so that to launch a counter attack from this direction and at the same time avoid a great area of marshy ground, which would have impeded his advance, the enemy was compelled to make use of a narrow and exposed neck of land. All afternoon on the 15th the Germans endeavoured to drive home a counter attack from this location. Battalion after battalion was seen to march up in column of route and try to deploy under terrific shell fire. As each effort failed the retiring remnants brought confusion to those forming up, and the Canadian gunners were presented with a target such as they never had before and in all probability have never had since. As the guns were well served and ammunition plentiful, they took full advantage of the opportunity and the German losses at this point alone must have been staggering. At a later stage it came to the knowledge of the Royal Highlanders that the Field Artillery, which gave such wonderful support in repulsing the counter-attacks, had been heavily shelled with gas and had worked all the time under most trying conditions.

Meanwhile on "D" Coy's front considerable activity was prevailing. At 3 p.m. Major Macfarlane found to his anxiety that his rifle ammunition was down to 10 rounds per man, even after every possible cartridge had been collected from casualties. Finding that the officer in command of the company of the 16th Battalion on the right flank was facing a similar shortage, he agreed with the latter that no further firing should take place, except at close range and in the event of a most determined attack. A few minutes later an attack developed up Humbug Alley, a communication trench connecting the Green Line with Hercules Trench. In accordance with the agreement, no rifle fire was used to check this attack, No. 14 Platoon going over to meet the Hun with the bayonet and one section, filled with more zeal than discretion, pursuing the defeated enemy right back to Hercules trench.

During some of the enemy counter-attacks the bravery and fearlessness of certain small parties of Germans aroused the Highlanders' respectful admiration. On one occasion a party of about 20, led by an officer with a shattered arm, kept right on when the attack of which they were part had failed and forced their way into the Canadian trenches. It was almost with regret that the Highlanders shot these brave men down, but there was no alternative as only a few of them would even consider surrender.

About 4 o'clock in the afternoon a carrying party of "C" Coy. arrived at the Green Line with small arm ammunition and the order to withhold all rifle fire was accordingly modified. Shelling became less intense as evening drew on and the Germans, for the time being, abandoned their counter attacks. The night was spent in further consolidation of the front line and in strenuous efforts to evacuate the wounded, this work entailing much hardship on the supporting companies, as the rear areas, through which all stretcher-bearers had to pass, were shelled persistently. During the night the 1st Canadian Pioneer Battalion started work on a communication trench across the former No Man's Land, but this was not completed at the time when the 13th stretcher parties were busiest.

When morning broke on August 16th it seemed that the Hun was about to renew his efforts to recapture the ground torn from his grasp. At 6 a.m. a small party approached the 13th front and was driven off by rifle fire. At 7 a.m. a more determined effort was made, apparently with the object of overcoming a block the Highlanders had established in Humbug Alley and thus clearing the way for a counter attack in strength from Hercules Trench. When this effort was thrown back with appreciable loss, the enemy evidently decided that the game was not worth the candle and no further attacks were launched. During all this period the arduous and dangerous work of the Battalion Signal Section, under Lance-Corp. Hayden, was performed with commendable courage and perseverance.

About 10 a.m. a German officer and two or three men approached to within 50 yards of the Highlanders' outpost line and were shot

HILL 70

down by a Lewis gun. Speculation was aroused by the strange behaviour of these individuals and, as their advance could hardly have been an "attack," it was presumed that they had lost their way and wandered unintentionally towards the Canadian line.

All day on the 16th, "A" and "D" Companies held the new front, suffering considerably from shell fire and exhaustion. "D" Coy. was in a particularly bad way and "A" was only relatively better, while "B" Coy. in the Blue Line and "C" Coy. and H.Q. in the old German front line were harassed sharply by persistent shelling. Rest was quite impossible, of course, and the strength of all ranks was taxed to the limit. In "D" Coy. the shortage of officers was keenly felt. Lieut. Christie did excellently, as did Lieut. Renahan, though the latter was really ill and not fit to be on duty. Company Sergt.-Major Jones, too, was a tower of strength all during this trying day. Just at dark this plucky N.C.O. had an eye put out by a flying piece of shell. Some minutes later Major Macfarlane came along and found the wounded man carrying on as usual. In the darkness Macfarlane was unaware that Jones was injured and discussed with him several matters that concerned the Company. Later when Macfarlane discovered that Jones had lost an eye and insisted on his retiring, the latter did so only after repeated protests and assurances that he was quite fit to carry on.

During the night the Battalion Chaplain, Capt. E. E. Graham, arrived in the Green Line and said that he had come forward to bury the dead, as the 13th was to be relieved before morning. A rather sharp barrage was falling at the moment, but if the work was to be done it must be done immediately and all agreed that it behoved them to give their dead such burial as was possible, rather than leave the task to strangers. Accordingly all bodies that could be found were collected and buried in several large shell holes, the padre noting with care the identity of each individual and the location of his grave. When this task was finished, Capt. Graham removed his steel helmet and recited the lines of the burial service, a small group of officers and men standing motionless and bareheaded while he did so. Thus, in the soil they had captured, with enemy shells still bursting overhead, but with their own Regiment as mourners, the men of the 13th Royal Highlanders who died in the Green Line were left sleeping with Hill 70 well behind them.

CHAPTER XV

Passchendaele

British soldier, once again
You are marshalled on the plain
By our fathers' blood renowned:
You are treading sacred ground!
Harken, harken as you pass,
To the voices in the grass!
—Lord Gorell.

I.

EARLY in the morning on August 17th the companies of the 13th Battalion were relieved by parts of the 2nd and 3rd Battalions and retired to les Brebis, the movement being accomplished under a harassing shell fire which caused several casualties. In spite of extreme fatigue the stretcher cases were brought out at once by carrying parties of "C" Coy. The men of all companies were weary and limping along silently when, just at daybreak, the red brick houses of their destination came in sight. Automatically ranks closed, step was picked up and someone started a song. Breakfast was ready when they reached billets, but few took the time to eat. Bed on a heap of straw was waiting and nothing in all the world seemed quite so desirable.

With the arrival of the Battalion in billets checking of casualties and deficiencies began. The battle had been a success, all objectives had been attained, approximately 1500 prisoners captured and heavy losses inflicted on the enemy. Such a victory, however, can be purchased only at a price. In the 13th, roll call showed that approximately 40% of those who had gone over with the attack were casualties. In addition to losses already mentioned Capt. J. P. Melrose had been wounded, as had Lieut. A. A. McArtney and Lieut. C. D. Llwyd, while amongst other ranks 34 had been killed, 34 were missing, probably killed, and 186 wounded.

After two days of rest at les Brebis the Battalion paraded on the afternoon of August 19th and moved to billets at Barlin, proceeding

PASSCHENDAELE

on the following day to Allouagne, not far from Lillers. Allouagne is a name that brings pleasant memories to those officers and men of the 13th Battalion who enjoyed its temporary hospitality. After the hard fighting at Hill 70 the excellent billets and the opportunity for recreation provided just the tonic the men required. The inhabitants were friendly and of a superior class, so that it was not uncommon to see a huge and brawny private acting in the capacity of nursemaid, while madame prepared him a tasty meal, or to behold a smart N.C.O. with his sleeves rolled up doing his utmost to assist a smiling demoiselle with the problem of the week's laundry.

The officers, too, enjoyed themselves immensely and on one occasion organized a game of polo, using the Battalion's horses, and sticks that some enthusiast found in Lillers. While the form displayed was not up to that of international polo, the contest was spirited none the less and ended only when all sticks but one had been broken. As the tired players guided their equally weary horses off the field, they found to their surprise that the Corps Commander was amongst the laughing spectators on the side lines. He had arrived during the game, but, as his business was not urgent, had refused to have play interrupted and had apparently enjoyed the fun almost as much as the players themselves.

One night, too, the officers staged a concert in the local theatre, all the talent being drawn from their own roster. By sacrificing his moustache, Lieut.-Col. McCuaig scored a tremendous hit in a charming female role, while Capt. A. W. Appleton, the Paymaster, distinguished himself as Salome.

During the fortnight that the 13th remained in Allouagne training of a routine nature was carried out and on two occasions the Battalion paraded for inspection. Major-General A. C. Macdonell and Brig.-Gen. G. S. Tuxford reviewed the unit on August 22nd, and on August 27th the whole Brigade was honoured by a visit from Field Marshal Sir Douglas Haig. Unfortunately, the Commander-in-Chief's inspection was marred by a downpour of rain, nevertheless the men made a good showing and Sir Douglas expressed his gratification and his pride in what the troops had recently accomplished.

On September 2nd the rest and training period came to an end and the Battalion accomplished a long march to the Bouvigny-Boyeffles area. Here the billets proved a sharp contrast to those the men had just left, as once more the Battalion was up in the area where few houses could boast a roof and four solid walls.

On the night of the 3rd the Battalion advanced again and relieved the 49th Canadian Battalion in Cité St. Pierre, moving up again on the following night and relieving the 52nd Canadian Battalion in the front line. Three days were spent in this location, during which the men of the Battalion were comparatively inactive by day and extremely busy by night, large working parties being sent forward to assist in the construction of a new front line. This whole sector had been badly battered in the August fighting, with the result that many trenches which appeared on the maps had been blown entirely out of existence, or rendered indistinguishable. Under these circumstances it was unusually difficult to conduct the working parties to the scene of their labours and on many occasions much time was lost searching for routes, or communication trenches, which seemingly existed only in the imagination of those enthusiasts who had prepared the maps. During the tour there was a certain amount of shelling and machine gun fire, but casualties were light, 1 man being killed and 2 wounded.

Relief took place late on the night of September 7th and the Battalion moved back to Marqueffles Farm early on the morning of the 8th. Three days were spent here, during which shortages were checked, damaged gas helmets replaced and the men given an opportunity to bathe. Then, on the night of September 10th, the Battalion moved forward once more and occupied billets in Cité St. Pierre, as Brigade Reserve.

On the following night a party of 450 officers and men went forward to work on the construction of the new front line. Apparently the enemy became aware of what was happening, for up from his trenches rose a signal rocket to which his artillery responded with heavy shelling. The Canadian Artillery endeavoured to check this fire, but could not do so in time to protect the party of the 13th, which suffered sharply, among the casualties being Lieuts. J. M. Morphy and L. C. Monkman, both severely wounded. In spite of his injuries, Lieut. Monkman did excellent work in getting his men under cover and set a splendid example of coolness in a sudden emergency. Lieut. Morphy's injuries were more serious and he died after being removed to hospital. By his death the 13th lost a most promising and capable officer.

Shelling continued to be brisk for the next four days and the

PASSCHENDAELE

ration parties of the 13th had trying times, as the dumps from which they drew supplies seemed to be the Hun's choicest targets. Casualties during this period mounted to a total of 22, five killed and 17 wounded.

On the night of September 16th the Royal Highlanders moved from reserve into support, but as the support billets were also in Cité St. Pierre, the move was short. Here six days were spent, artillery activity rendering difficult the task of the large working parties, 450 to 500 strong, which toiled nightly at the construction of the new front line. The back areas also received their full share of shell fire and ration parties had a rather nasty time, while one runner, who was delivering a message to Brigade H.Q., was hurled from his bicycle and had a leg blown off by the burst of a heavy shell.

Heavy shelling occurred at dawn on the 21st, the straffe spreading rapidly until it assumed the proportions of a general engagement. For an hour the 13th "stood to" awaiting developments, but eventually matters quieted down and news was received that the Germans had attempted a big raid somewhat to the right and had been driven off.

After dusk on the night of September 22nd, the 13th was relieved by the 9th Battalion of the Norfolk Regiment. Quiet prevailed during the movement and the Highlanders reached billets in the Coupigny Huts without incurring losses. Casualties during the whole tour were 2 killed and 16 wounded.

All morning on the 23rd the Battalion Transport was busy moving stores and equipment from Sains-en-Gohelle to Gauchin-Légal, the Battalion proper marching to the latter place during the afternoon. Here the Highlanders spent twelve days, carrying out a programme of training, with special classes for N.C.O.'s, directed by Lieut. Carstairs, Battalion Sergt.-Major Butler, Sergt.-Major Evans and Sergt. Stone. During this period, too, much time was devoted to gas drills. Lectures on various phases of this subject were delivered and all box respirators tested and, where necessary, renewed. In his eagerness to accustom the men to wearing the helmets, the Gas N.C.O. on one occasion ordered a route march of the men of "A" Coy. at 8 p.m., his idea being that a march in the dark with helmets on would provide realistic practice. Unfortunately, the men refused to take this experiment seriously and the parade degenerated more or less into a game of "Blind Man's Buff," the troops, like overgrown children, enjoying hugely both their own horse play and the efforts of the distracted N.C.O. to restore some semblance of order.

On October 4th the Battalion paraded at 1 p.m. and marched from Gauchin-Légal, via Estrée-Cauchie, to familiar huts at Chateau de la Haie. Rain poured during this march, consequently the troops found the camp at their destination in a fearful state of mud. There being no attraction outside, the majority of the men retired as soon as possible, though a few of the more enterprising visited Petit Servins to see some of their old friends and acquaintances.

Next morning the Battalion moved again, marching to Souchez Huts in Zouave Valley. Here the remainder of the day was spent and at night the unit moved up to relieve elements of the 46th, 47th and 50th Canadian Battalions in the front line, Headquarters being situated at a point midway between the villages of Givenchy and la Coulotte.

Mud was the feature of the five days that followed. Shelling was not heavy and the enemy was otherwise inactive, but rain fell steadily and the trenches were soon knee deep in mud and water, this necessitating the calling out of large working parties every night and on several occasions in the daytime. Fuel was scarce and dry clothing almost unobtainable, so it was without regret that the Battalion received orders to hand over the area to the 15th Battalion on the night of October 10th. This relief was accomplished without incident, and the Highlanders retired to a position on the so-called Red Line, sending out working parties on the two following days and withdrawing again on the night of the 13th to take over from the 4th Battalion of the Leicesters at the old billets in Souchez Huts. A day only was spent here, the Highlanders moving on the afternoon of the 14th to Estrée-Cauchie, where they spent a week in training of a routine nature, the only outstanding incident being a review at Verdrel, by the Commander of the First Army, General Sir H. S. Horne.

II

During October Sir Douglas Haig selected the Canadian Corps as the instrument with which he would bring to a close the great battle that had been raging at Ypres for many weeks. The German Army was flushed with victory at this time, as the result of triumphs

PASSCHENDAELE

in Russia and Italy. The French Army, on the other hand, was for the first time showing signs of lowered morale, accordingly for political as well as strategic reasons, a striking British success was desirable.

Every effort had been made to achieve this success and some of the finest Corps in the British Army had been flung into the Ypres battle, with the result that the German line had been driven back for a considerable distance. Passchendaele Ridge, however, had up to this time defied all efforts to capture it, and several large scale operations against it had been bloodily repulsed. Realizing that the season for operations was fast drawing to a close and that, in consequence, he must succeed in his next effort, or admit definite failure, Sir Douglas Haig laid his plans with the greatest care. Under these circumstances he paid a splendid tribute to the Canadian Corps in selecting it to act as the spear head of his assault and summoning it from the Lens district for the purpose.

So far as the 13th Battalion was concerned, the move to the scene of the new operations began on October 20th, when the unit marched from Estrée-Cauchie to Bruay. Continuing the march on the following day, the Highlanders passed through the familiar towns of Marles-les-Mines, Allouagne and Lillers and billeted for the night in Manqueville. Boeseghem proved to be their destination on the 22nd and on the 23rd they reached Hondeghem, a few miles from Hazebrouck. Reveille sounded at 3 a.m. on the 24th and the Battalion paraded in time to reach the church at Staple by 6 o'clock. Here busses were waiting, and the men were conveyed, via Flêtre, Caestre, Bailleul, Locre and Kemmel, to a position on the outskirts of Ypres.

It was not without deep feeling that the veterans of 1915 and 1916 surveyed the country through which the route led. Flêtre recalled their earliest days in France, while Ypres brought to mind a thousand memories of the splendid men of the Battalion who had laid down their lives in the shadow of its walls.

Leaving the busses at the head of the road which leads to Dickebusch, the Royal Highlanders halted to await further orders. About 2.30 p.m. they proceeded through Ypres in single file, then north along the Canal bank and eastwards to a position in a field about half way between Ypres and St. Jean. No billets were available at this spot, but canvas bivouacs were rigged up and in these the men settled down for the night, obtaining some shelter from the driving rain. Had fires been permitted, they might have cooked themselves a hot meal, but these were strictly forbidden, owing to the fact that German bombing planes came over every night and it was not advisable to assist them in discovering their target.

After a miserable night, during which rain continued and most of the bivouacs were flooded, the men of the Battalion spent the day in drawing off the surface water and in cleaning their equipment. At night German planes came over and bombed the roads and rear areas on a scale such as the men of the 13th had never previously witnessed. Starting soon after 9 p.m., these raids continued at intervals throughout the night, but fortunately for the Highlanders, their canvas bivouacs were not the object of the enemy's attention.

Early on the morning of October 26th the first stage of the operations against Passchendaele began, when, in conjunction with a British and French offensive, the 3rd and 4th Canadian Divisions advanced against the Bellevue Spur. Rain poured during the day and the fighting in the resultant mud was unbelievably bitter, nevertheless the attacking troops attained their objectives and brought the Spur into British hands.

While the Royal Highlanders took no part in the actual attack, they were of necessity involved in its ramifications. At 2 a.m. on the 26th a working party, consisting of practically every available man in the unit, reported at Spree Dump and there obtained materials to relay and repair a corduroy road, the sole route by which supplies could be sent into the forward area. That night parties, totalling 400, were again employed on the corduroy road, which was constantly being torn to pieces by shelling and the great volume of traffic which flowed over it. Much work, too, was done in the neighbourhood of the camp on the Ypres-St. Jean Road, where drainage ditches were dug and a hut built to take the place of an orderly room.

Working parties continued on the following day and the whole Battalion was employed in regular eight hour shifts. On the morning of the 28th the camp was thoroughly cleaned up and handed over to the 15th Battalion, the men of the 13th marching back by platoons to Kruisstraat Dump, whence busses conveyed them, via Vlamertinghe and Abeele, to Steenvoorde, thence over the hill through Cassel and on to a point about two miles from Staple.

At dawn on October 31st the second stage of the battle for

MARCHING BACK TO REST BILLETS AFTER THE CAPTURE OF
HILL 70, AUGUST, 1917.

Canadian Official, Copyright.

MARCHING FROM HILL 70, AUGUST, 1917.

Canadian Official, Copyright.

PASSCHENDAELE

Passchendaele began and the Canadian line was pushed forward for 1200 yards on a front of 3000 yards. No mere recital of yards gained, or prisoners captured, can convey any idea of the task accomplished. The mud was appalling and the fighting for every foot of ground was so bitter as quite to defy description. Men died by the score to capture a miserable concrete "pill box," only to have their comrades find that somewhere in the awful mud ahead lay other "pill boxes" which resolutely blocked the way to victory. No praise is too high for the courage of the men, who, at terrible cost, pounded these miniature fortresses into submission, nor, indeed, for that of the German garrisons, who fought until the last possible moment and, in nine cases out of ten, died fighting rather than yield.

On November 6th the final stage of the operation was undertaken. By this time the weary 3rd and 4th Divisions had been replaced by the 1st and 2nd Divisions and it was these fresh troops who swept over the crest of the Ridge, through Passchendaele itself and down the slopes beyond. Once again the Canadian Corps had been called on to accomplish a hard task and had not failed, though the victory cost the four Divisions a casualty list that was appalling. Small wonder that in Canada, as elsewhere throughout the Empire, the Ypres Salient is looked on as a place both sacred and accursed.

While the 13th Battalion was not used in any of the actual assaults at Passchendaele, the work of the unit throughout the whole series of operations was arduous in the extreme and was not accomplished without losses. At 1.30 o'clock on the morning of October 31st a runner from Brigade Headquarters reported at the Battalion Orderly Room, at Staple, with orders for the unit to entrain at Ebblinghem, two and a half miles away, at 6 a.m. Runners were immediately despatched to the billets of the various companies, but, as these were widely scattered, it was nearly 3 o'clock before all had received their orders. Parading at 4 a.m., without waiting for breakfast, the unit marched to Ebblinghem and entrained at the appointed time, only to have the train wait for over an hour before moving off.

At noon the train reached Ypres Station and the platoons of the 13th, marching in Indian file, proceeded through the town and up Infantry Track No. 5 to the crest of the hill at Wieltje, where a halt was called and the companies each given a section of ground in which they were told to make themselves as comfortable as possible.

ROYAL HIGHLANDERS OF CANADA

On reaching this forward area the men of the Battalion soon found that aerial activity, which had been so marked a feature of their previous tour, was still prevailing. Hardly had they arrived when a British plane crashed down in the midst of them, the pilot and observer having been killed in a battle somewhere far above their heads. Shortly afterwards a huge Gotha bomber, escorted by eleven smaller planes, sailed majestically over the 13th lines, dropped a bomb, which killed two men, and then proceeded to spread death and destruction in the camps between Wieltje and Ypres. That night little sleep could be had, owing to the frequency with which enemy planes bombed the area, though, fortunately for the 13th, the majority of the raiders concentrated their attention on the roads and camps nearer Ypres.

Early on the morning of November 1st shelling became troublesome, two men being killed and two wounded when a 5.9 scored a direct hit on a shallow dugout in "C" Coy's. area. Shortly after 2 o'clock in the afternoon the Battalion left the position at Wieltje and moved up, via No. 5 Infantry Track, to Pommern Castle, which, despite its aristocratic name, was only a captured "pill box." Shelling was brisk during this move and the Battalion suffered 10 casualties, a sergeant being killed and nine other ranks severely wounded. That casualties were not more numerous was fortunate, as the watery mud made it impossible for the troops to leave the narrow "bath-mat" track, of whose existence and exact location the enemy was well aware.

On reaching their destination, the men of the 13th took shelter in such shallow dugouts as were available; in "pill boxes," of which there were several, and in some cases under derelict tanks. These provided reasonably good protection from enemy artillery fire, which continued all night.

Dull and misty weather prevailed on the following day, a condition welcome to the troops, as it freed them from aerial observation and served to limit the enemy's bombing raids. Large working parties were employed throughout the day in carrying "bath-mats" and using these to repair No. 5 Infantry Track. The mud was as bad as ever and progress was slow in consequence, but, as the work was of vital importance, all ranks put their hearts into it and much was accomplished. On returning from a working party one small group of men bivouacked under a stranded tank and were filled with

PASSCHENDAELE

indignation when a salvage party from the Tanks Corps effected some repairs and, cranking up, drove their shelter away.

On November 3rd the Battalion furnished working parties in the morning, moving forward in the afternoon to Abraham Heights, where Headquarters was established in a large concrete "pill box" at Otto Farm. Numerous batteries had their gun pits near this farm and the enemy artillery, in searching for the guns, shelled the whole area freely. In contrast to this, the areas further forward in which the companies were situated, were not shelled nearly so briskly. At 11 p.m. "D" Coy. moved up into close support and passed for the time being under the command of the 16th Canadian Battalion, with Headquarters at Bellevue.

Artillery was active on the 4th of the month and in the afternoon a high velocity gun, directed by an aeroplane, shelled the area in which the 13th Battalion Transport Lines had been established. This same gun, or one of a similar type, opened again at 11 p.m. and caused a good deal of damage. The first two shells failed to detonate, but the third scored a direct hit on an ammunition dump, which exploded with a terrific roar and hurled fragments of steel in all directions. Fortunately, the two shells that did not explode had given a warning and many of the troops had vacated their canvas bivouacs to take shelter in nearby dugouts. Serious casualties were avoided in this manner, though Lieut. Plante and Corp. Cowan received painful injuries of a minor nature. Damage to material was considerable. The Canteen was completely wrecked and havoc was created amongst the officers' kits piled nearby, some garments of an intimate nature being later recovered from the position they were jauntily holding in the branches of a neighbouring tree.

Meanwhile, forward at Abraham Heights, the main body of the Battalion remained in support. Early in the evening "A" Coy. moved forward and joined "D" Coy. in close support. Many dead were passed by "A" Coy. during the move, among these being a number from the 42nd Royal Highlanders, the Sister Unit to the 13th having lost heavily in the gallant assault which captured the Bellevue Spur.

On November 5th the Battalion experienced heavy shelling and suffered appreciably. Late in the afternoon the companies moved back to Pommern Castle. Grim evidence of the heavy bombardment that had occurred were to be seen all along the route. In many places the Infantry Track itself was damaged, while everywhere were strewn the dead of the battalions which had pushed forward.

Halting at Pommern Castle, the 13th awaited orders for some hours, moving back when these were issued at 1.30 a.m. to a position near Wieltje. Enemy bombing planes were active in this neighbourhood in the hours that preceded dawn, but the men of the Battalion were tired and, as the bombs did not strike their particular area, they gave them little attention.

The weather was dull and poor for observation on November 6th, a comforting state of affairs to the Royal Highlanders, who spent the day at Wieltje, resting and preparing for another move forward to relieve the troops who had finally captured Passchendaele and the Ridge.

About noon on the 7th this move began, the companies following No. 6 Infantry Track to the vicinity of Gravenstafel Ridge, whence, after a halt of several hours, they moved up towards the left sector of the front line. Little information was available as to the best route forward, but Lieut.-Col. McCuaig decided to proceed along Track 6 and sent Lieut. P. E. Corbett ahead to reconnoitre. Later this officer met the head of the Battalion with the information that it would be necessary to proceed south across country to Gravenstafel Cross Roads. As there was no help for it, the men left the Track and floundered through the mud to the point mentioned. From here the distance to the front line was about a mile, but progress was rendered extremely slow by the fact that the road up, the only one available, was packed with troops, not only of the 13th Battalion, but of the 14th and of two battalions of the 1st British Division, which had to use the same road to reach the Canadians' left. Two anxious hours were consumed in advancing that one mile, anxious because of the fact that the troops could not advance except by the road, while many dead bodies strewn about warned them that the Germans had marked the route down and might shell it at any moment. No such disaster occurred, however, and the Battalion reached the front safely, but in a thoroughly exhausted condition.

On reaching the front line, it was found that accommodation was very limited, a state of affairs which, in the event of heavy shelling, would mean serious casualties. In consequence, it was considered

PASSCHENDAELE

advisable to hold the line with less strength and a number of men were sent back to the Transport Lines.

The front line at this point was in bad shape and bore eloquent testimony to the bitter fighting which it had recently witnessed. The mud was in many places waist deep, torn and twisted wire lay everywhere, water filled shell holes were numerous, while all about lay the bodies of the dead, the whole area presenting a picture of desolation and horror hard to equal and impossible to surpass.

Little could be done by the men in the front line during the one day that the Battalion held this position, but the support companies assisted in the task of evacuating the endless stream of wounded. Herculean efforts were required in this work, as the appalling mud was worse than the Canadians, with all their varied experience of mud, had ever encountered before.

The artillery on both sides was active during the afternoon, consequently all those whose duties permitted were ordered to keep under cover as much as possible. Towards evening the shell fire, which had assumed barrage intensity, moderated, a fortunate matter, as the 13th was being relieved by the 8th Canadian Battalion. On completion of relief, the Royal Highlanders moved back, via Wieltje, to the camp near St. Jean.

Here two days were spent in comparative inactivity. Aerial bombing continued to be an unpleasant feature and several men were killed in the next battalion, but the 13th escaped without losses. Rain poured during the two days, until the camp became a veritable swamp and the troops assumed the appearance of having lived in mud all their lives. Under these circumstances, the pleasure the men derived from a visit to the baths was even keener than usual, in spite of the fact that on this occasion no change of underclothing was available.

Starting at 12.30 p.m. on November 11th the companies of the 13th moved away from St. Jean, followed Infantry Track No. 6 to the bank of the Ypres Canal, thence through Ypres itself to the Station. Several narrow escapes were experienced in passing through the town, as the enemy was shelling the ruins with persistence. No actual misadventures occurred, however, and the Battalion entrained at 2.30 p.m., reaching Derby Camp, near Brandhoek, before dark.

So far as the 13th was concerned, the period in camp at St. Jean brought the series of tours in the Ypres Salient to an end. The

ROYAL HIGHLANDERS OF CANADA

Canadian Corps had been brought to the Salient for a very definite purpose—to attack and capture Passchendaele Ridge. This purpose had been accomplished and the Corps was about to move back to the Lens area, whence it had come. It was without regret that the men bade the Salient good-bye. Although he spoke for himself alone, one veteran, who had fought at Ypres in 1915, in 1916 and again in 1917, voiced a sentiment that was shared by all, "I hope to God," said he, "that I never see the cursed place again!"

CHAPTER XVI

The Third Winter in France

> But No Man's Land is a goblin sight
> When patrols crawl over at dead o' night.
>
> . . . . .
>
> When the "rapid," like fireflies in the dark,
> Flits down the parapet spark by spark,
> And you drop for cover to keep your head
> With your face on the breast of the four months' dead.
> —JAMES H. KNIGHT-ADKIN.

AT noon on November 12th the Royal Highlanders climbed into a long line of motor busses which whirled them to Merville, passing through Ouderdom and Bailleul on the way. At Merville the men got out and marched some two kilometres to Neuf Berquin, reaching this spot at about 6 p.m. Returning to Merville on the following morning, the men again took busses and enjoyed a two hour run to Bethune, where they were to remain over night. As they had plenty of time at their disposal, they were instructed to clean up and be properly dressed with kilt, belt etc., before visiting the town. Another bus journey took place on November 14th, the route on this occasion passing through Noeux-les-Mines and Bracquemont and terminating at Noulette Huts, in the Hersin-Coupigny area.

Two days were spent in this position and at 4.30 p.m. on November 16th the Battalion moved up to relieve the 2/5th South Staffordshire Regiment in support, Headquarters, with "A" and "D" Companies, being stationed in Red Trench, "C" Coy. at Givenchy-en-Gohelle and "B" Coy. in a trench across the Lens-Arras Road. Relief was completed about 1 a.m. Moving up again twenty-four hours later, the 13th took over the right front line, Avion-Lens Sector, from the 2/6 South Staffordshire Regiment, "C" and "B" Companies occupying the front line proper, with "D" Coy. in support and "A" Coy. in reserve.

For eight days the Battalion held this front. Inter-company reliefs occurred on the night of November 21st and an extension of the line to the right on the night of the 23rd. Owing to the nature of the front, which consisted largely of semi-detached strong posts, communication patrols were busy at night, while, in view of the battle which Sir Julian Byng was waging with the Third Army at Cambrai, other patrols were out constantly to obtain immediate information should the enemy start to retire.

Considerable rain fell during the tour and this, of course, necessitated working parties to keep the trenches in a reasonable state of repair. The enemy artillery was comparatively inactive, but his trench mortars kept up a troublesome bombardment, which cost the 13th a price. Particularly was this the case on November 24th, when a working party of "C" Coy. was badly caught and had 11 men killed and 3 severely wounded. In this instance the party saw the projectile coming and attempted to escape down the narrow trench, but without success. On the same date "D" Coy. had 3 men killed and 1 wounded by a Minenwerfer which struck in the front line. With a total of 14 killed, this day was the most unfortunate the Battalion had experienced for some time.

Relief occurred on the following evening and the 13th marched back to la Coulotte, entraining there and reaching Alberta Camp about 10 p.m. Here the Battalion remained until December 2nd, resting, cleaning equipment and training. On November 27th the baths at Carency were allotted to the 13th and the men also received a change of underclothing. Following the bathing parade all N.C.O's. and men marched to the Q.M. Stores and exchanged the kilt and hose tops for trousers and puttees in preparation for the winter. This equipment was thoroughly inspected on the 28th and on the same day all men with damaged boots were paraded to the Battalion Shoemaker to have them repaired.

No parades were called on the 29th, but during the day all ranks, under special arrangements, polled votes for candidates in the General Election which was taking place in Canada. Apart from this novel experience, the chief event of the Battalion's stay occurred on December 1st when a working party, consisting of 7 officers and 400 other ranks, under command of Major J. Jeffery, proceeded to the forward area to bury cable. This party, having accomplished good work, returned to camp at 10 p.m. On the following day the Battalion moved to Gouy Servins.

In the early part of December, 1917, Lieut.-Col. G. E. McCuaig, D.S.O. left the 13th Battalion at Gouy Servins and proceeded on

THE THIRD WINTER IN FRANCE

several months leave to Canada. All parades were cancelled on the morning of his departure, as officers and men were anxious to give him a send-off that would leave no doubt as to the place he held in their esteem. Lining the road along which his car would pass, the men waited till he made his appearance and cheered him until out of sight. On his departure temporary command of the Battalion passed to Major K. M. Perry, D.S.O., but, as the latter was attending the Senior Officers' School at the time, Major J. Jeffery, M.C. took over his duties.

For a week after McCuaig's departure the Battalion remained at Gouy Servins, moving up on the night of December 11th and taking over the Right Sub-Section (Lens Sector) of the front line from the 5th Canadian Battalion.

The tour that followed lasted four days and was by no means uneventful. At the very beginning the Battalion nearly lost its Officer Commanding when a "pine-apple" fell within three feet of Major Jeffery and killed the man to whom he was speaking. Another incident occurred early in the tour when Lieut. J. B. Beddome, the Intelligence Officer, turned out a patrol with the intention of harassing an enemy post. So excellently did this patrol conduct its little operation that Lieut. Beddome received the congratulations of the 3rd Brigade Staff.

Then, early in the morning of December 13th, a special company of the Royal Engineers projected 600 drums of gas into the enemy line from a point in the Highlanders' trenches. This operation required careful preparation. For example, notice of whether the operation would take place or not had to be given to all troops concerned some three hours before "zero," so that such posts as would be endangered by a slight change in the wind could be withdrawn to a place of safety. It was not considered advisable to write or telephone these messages, so a code was arranged in advance. Thus, if an officer received a message consisting of the single word "Elm," he knew that conditions for the projection were considered favourable. If his message was "Spruce" it informed him that conditions were unfavourable and that his troops, in consequence, could be moved back to the posts from which they had been withdrawn. When he received the message "Oak" it meant that the attack was over and that the gas was no longer a source of danger. He then had to decide whether immediate re-occupation of his posts was advisable, considering the amount of daylight prevailing.

ROYAL HIGHLANDERS OF CANADA

In retaliation for this projection of gas the enemy bombarded the Highlanders' front with trench mortars and, in retaliation for the retaliation, the Canadian artillery put on a heavy "shoot" with guns of all calibres. So things continued up to the night of the 15th when the Battalion moved back to the support area at Liévin.

After four days in support, during which all available men were employed on working parties, the 13th moved up to the front line once more. Heavy artillery fire and concentrated "shoots" were the features of the next four days, some of these being carried out by guns of all calibres and some by light and heavy Trench Mortars. All these "shoots" involved work on the part of the Infantry, as in most cases troops had to be withdrawn from exposed positions, while, even when this was not necessary, the enemy retaliation usually smashed down some trenches which had to be repaired.

Apart from the work of the trench mortars and artillery, the tour was marked by activity of the Battalion's snipers and machine gunners. One foggy morning the mist lifted momentarily and disclosed a party of 12 Germans at work on a slag heap, known as the Green Crassier. "D" Company's gunners promptly opened fire on these individuals, killing one outright and apparently wounding several others. Later a sniper picked off a Hun who was firing from a window in a ruined building and still later another party of Germans was discovered on the Green Crassier, two being killed without a doubt and three others wounded, according to the claim of the Highlanders' machine gun crew.

At 8.45 p.m. on December 23rd the 13th was relieved by the P.P.C.L.I. and moved back to billets in Gouy Servins. Here the Royal Highlanders celebrated their fourth Christmas on active service and their third in France. Christmas Day, so far as the weather was concerned, was typical of many the men had passed at home in Canada. Snow had fallen a day or two before and this, combined with bright sunshine and sharp frost, rendered the whole countryside very clean looking and attractive. Only the forlorn billets, some of which lacked roofs and others walls, served to remind the men that they were not in Canada, but in a less happy land, much of whose soil was still under the foot of a foreign invader.

On account of the cold weather and to distinguish the day, an issue of rum was served to the men first thing in the morning. After breakfast voluntary church parades were held and Holy

THE THIRD WINTER IN FRANCE

Communion was celebrated for all who desired to attend. For the Roman Catholics Mass was celebrated in the Village Church.

The men had a light lunch at noon and sat down to Christmas dinner at 4.30 p.m. Officers visited their men during dinner, exchanging good wishes and joining in the expressions of hope that the next Christmas would be spent under happier circumstances. All ranks then proceeded to celebrate the evening as joyously as possible. On the following evening the Warrant Officers, Staff Sergeants and Sergeants held a dinner of their own. Many of the officers attended this merry party, which brought to a close in a fitting manner the Battalion's Christmas celebrations.

Owing to a thaw, the billets at Gouy Servins became uninhabitable and the 13th moved to Petit Servins for New Year. Lieut.-Col. Perry rejoined the Battalion on the day this move occurred and took over the command which had been held in his absence by Major Jeffery.

New Year's celebrations were not as elaborate as those at Christmas, nevertheless the senior officers, viewing the unit with a kindly eye on the morning after New Year's Eve, decided that a sharp route march in the keen, fresh air would do the men more good than the regular training. The afternoon was given over to games.

During January the Battalion remained in billets behind the lines and carried out a programme of training. The first week of the New Year was spent at Petit Servins, the period from the 7th to 23rd at Houdain and the final week at Bracquemont.

At Houdain a newly organized unit, the Tump Line Section, was given a great deal of training, while the companies and all specialists, such as the Lewis Gun Section, the Intelligence Section, the Rifle Grenadiers, the Communication Section, the Signallers and Bandsmen, worked hard to perfect themselves in their respective spheres.

On January 12th all ranks were pleased by the announcement that the Battalion Chaplain, Hon. Capt. E. E. Graham, and Capt. A. S. Plante had been awarded the Military Cross, while Major F. S. Mathewson and Sergt.-Major Butler had been "Mentioned in Despatches" for valuable services rendered. Two days later it was announced that the Distinguished Conduct Medal had been awarded to Company Sergt.-Major Evans, "B" Coy., whose work had been of an extremely creditable nature.

ROYAL HIGHLANDERS OF CANADA

Competitions of various kinds were numerous during the month. On January 13th the four battalions of the 3rd Brigade each entered a platoon in a contest on a basis of 30 points for smartness of appearance, 60 points for way platoon commander disposes of his platoon so as to bring maximum fire on enemy, 120 points for method of advance and of covering advance by fire, 60 points for handling of Lewis Gun Section, and finally a rifle match in which one-quarter of a point was scored for every target hit and three points deducted for every target missed. In this competition the platoon from "B" Coy. of the 13th, commanded by Lieut. A. N. Sclater, led in each of the first four phases, only to fail dismally in the shooting, and to drop in consequence to third place in the competition as a whole. Under the supervision of Major Jeffery, strenuous measures were immediately taken to correct in the whole Battalion the weakness in shooting which the platoon competition had shown up so glaringly.

As an offset to the defeat in the platoon competition, the Battalion Transport scored 291 points out of a possible 300 in a Brigade contest, leading the other entrants by a comfortable margin and winning on the score sheet the only "excellent" that was granted. By this victory the 13th retained the whip presented by the G.O.C. the Division and symbolic of Transport supremacy.

Sports of one kind and another occupied much of the men's spare time. On January 19th the officers played the other ranks at football and won by a narrow margin. A week later that Battalion football team played against the team of the sister unit, the 42nd Royal Highlanders of Canada, and lost a keenly contested game 1-0. On several occasions during the month the Battalion concert party, the "Red Hackles," entertained officers, men and a limited number of guests with excellent vaudeville performances. The audience enjoyed the shows immensely and the applause was loud and insistent, the performers acknowledging the tributes by many clever encores.

About the 20th of the month the Pioneers of the Battalion began to paint the men's steel helmets, a gentle reminder that the period behind the lines was drawing to a close. When the Battalion marched on January 23rd, however, it was not to the front, but to Bracquemont, where another week was spent in training. During the march the Battalion was inspected by the Corps and Divisional

THE THIRD WINTER IN FRANCE

Commanders, "C" Coy. receiving General Currie's compliments for its smart appearance and march discipline.

On the night of January 31st the 13th Battalion relieved the 8th Canadian Battalion, which was acting as Brigade Reserve, in the Hill 70 Sector. The Royal Highlanders, for this relief, were divided into two parts, "A" and "D" Companies taking over billets in Loos, while "B" and "C" Companies and Headquarters moved to Mazingarbe. During the week that followed working parties were supplied with unfailing regularity at night, these on each occasion totalling approximately 8 officers and 315 men. Their work consisted of digging and wiring a series of new trenches and widening, or otherwise improving, trenches that already existed. Lieut. T. B. D. Tudball and two other ranks were wounded during the tour.

On the night of February 7th the Royal Highlanders relieved the Royal Montreal Regiment in the Right Sub-Section, Hill 70 Sector, of the front line, "A" Coy. taking over the right front and "D" Coy. the left front, while "B" Coy. and "C" Coy. moved into right and left support. Considerable machine gun and trench mortar fire prevailed during the relief, 2 men being killed and 4 wounded near "D" Coy's. Headquarters. The next four days were marked by activity on the part of the enemy's artillery and trench mortars. Machine gun fire was also brisk, but, though narrow escapes were many, casualties totalled only four or five slightly wounded. Inter-company reliefs took place on the night of the 11th, "B" and "C" Companies relieving "A" and "D" Companies, while a patrol, consisting of one N.C.O. and five O.R. lay out in No Man's Land to cover the movement. Company commanders were instructed to warn their men that this patrol was out and to notify Battalion Headquarters that relief was complete by use of the code word "Helen."

During the tour in the front line the 13th Battalion, in conjunction with the 14th Battalion, planned a raid on the enemy's trenches, the object being, as stated in the Special Operation Order, "to secure identifications, to kill Huns and to destroy dugouts and gun emplacements." In the same Order, Lieut. J. Young and Lieut. D. L. Carstairs were named to accompany the expedition, which, so far as the 13th party was concerned, was to consist of 5 N.C.O's. and 35 other ranks. The 14th Battalion party was to raid the

ROYAL HIGHLANDERS OF CANADA

enemy front at a point somewhat to the south and it was hoped that the two parties would effect a junction in the enemy lines.

In elaboration of the general plan, the raiders of the 13th were sub-divided into four minor parties, "A" "B," "C" and "D," and each was carefully instructed in its particular role. Bayonets and buttons were dulled and faces blackened, lest some unexpected flash of light should betray the party and warn the Germans of what was coming. Strict orders were issued that casualties were in no case to be abandoned, but, whether dead or wounded, were to be brought back to the Canadian lines. As a further precaution against the enemy securing identifications, officers and men were ordered to remove all badges and colours and all pencilled numerals on steel helmets, clothing, tunics and equipment. Private correspondence was also ordered removed and each man warned that, if by mischance he were taken prisoner, the only information the enemy could legitimately demand was his name, rank and regimental number.

During the night of February 12th Lieut. P. E. Corbett and a party from the Battalion Intelligence Section laid guiding tapes for the raiding party to a gap in the enemy wire, which had been cut by the Canadian Trench Mortars. Then, at 3 a.m. on the 13th, all watches having been synchronized most carefully, the raiders moved forward on their dangerous mission.

In spite of all the care taken, the raid was not an entire success. The enemy wire had been well cut, but through some error the barrage did not strike on the appointed place at the appointed time and, in consequence, the troops in pushing through the gap came under sharp machine gun fire. Notwithstanding this, every effort was made to carry out the pre-arranged schedule and one party, entering the enemy trench, bombed a troublesome machine gun and fired on a group of Huns who ran back to their support line.

Having done as much damage as was possible and finding himself in danger of being cut off, Lieut. Carstairs abandoned the effort to secure prisoners and reluctantly gave the order to withdraw. To carry this out was no easy matter, as the enemy had become thoroughly aware of what was happening and his machine guns were sweeping No Man's Land at all angles, paying particular attention to the gap in his wire, which provided the sole avenue of retreat.

At this stage of the affair two Rifle Grenadiers, Privates J. Given and R. D. Hall, gave a splendid exhibition of courage and

THE THIRD WINTER IN FRANCE

devotion to duty, remaining behind and covering the retreat of the party by engaging as many as possible of the hostile machine guns. Having performed this vital service with skill and success, the stout hearted pair retired themselves. Very unfortunately, Private Hall was killed in No Man's Land. His body was recovered and brought back to the Canadian lines.

When the raiders returned to their jumping off trench, a careful check showed that Lieut. J. Young and 4 other ranks had been wounded, while Lieut. P. E. Corbett, M.C., who, though not officially attached to the party, had rendered valuable assistance, had also been wounded. All these had been brought in safely.

During the next three days the Royal Highlanders suffered some 10 casualties, while, on the evening of the 15th, the enemy made a projector gas attack, which involved the right company and necessitated the wearing of respirators, but failed to do serious damage. At about 7 o'clock on the same evening a German party was discovered attempting to cut the wire in front of No. 6 Post, and some two hours later another party approached the front and threw several bombs. This party was dispersed by a Lewis gun and afterwards Lieut. M. L. Brady, with one other rank, went out and found a wounded Hun caught on the wire and abandoned by his comrades. This individual was brought in a prisoner.

At 9 p.m. on the 16th, the Royal Highlanders were relieved by the 1st Canadian Battalion and marched back to familiar billets in Bracquemont, where they remained until the 25th. During this period routine training was carried on and special attention given to work with gas masks and respirators. On the 18th it was announced that the Belgian Croix de Guerre had been awarded to Coy. Sergt.-Major G. P. Morrison, of "C" Coy., and to Sergt. H. E. Copeman, of the Intelligence Section. Unfortunately, Sergt. Copeman did not live to receive this honour, he having been killed in No Man's Land, where his decoration had been bravely won.

With Major Jeffery in command during the temporary absence of Lieut.-Col. Perry, the Battalion moved forward on February 25th and relieved the 8th Canadian Battalion in Brigade Support in the Cité St. Emile Section, "A" and "B" Companies taking over billets in Cité St. Edouard, "C" and "D" Companies in Cité St. Pierre and Headquarters occupying the same dugout in Cité St. Pierre as in the previous September. Working parties were the chief feature of the tour in support, which lasted nine days. Lieut.-Col. Perry

ROYAL HIGHLANDERS OF CANADA

re-assumed command on March 3rd and on the 6th of the month the Battalion took over the front line from the 14th Battalion. Lieut. Mowry, United States Army, was attached to the Royal Highlanders for instruction at this time and created a favourable impression by his keenness. The officers of the 13th were interested to hear from him of the speed with which American troops were being brought to France and of the preparations that the United States was making to fill an adequate part in the war.

During the tour that followed the Canadian heavy artillery carried out several concentrated "shoots," while the light and heavy trench mortars were also active. The enemy was by no means slow in retaliating for the punishment inflicted upon him, and the Highlanders suffered a casualty list of 1 killed and approximately a score wounded. Owing to the excellence of the klaxon warning system, however, and the speed with which the men donned respirators when necessary, losses from a large number of gas shells which the Hun sent over were entirely avoided. Fears were entertained one day that a case of spinal meningitis had broken out in the Battalion and prompt measures were taken to isolate all contacts. Later the afflicted man was found to be suffering from a malady of a less serious nature.

Summer time came into effect during the tour and all watches were advanced one hour. On the night of March 13th the 38th Canadian Battalion relieved the Highlanders, who retired to reserve, "A" and "D" Companies to billets in Boyeffles, "B" and "C" Companies and Battalion Headquarters to Petit Sains and Sains-en-Gohelle. A week was spent in these locations, uneventful for the most part, but marked on the 18th of the month by manœuvres, in which the Battalion practised an attack in liaison with aeroplanes and tanks. Routine drills, rifle practice and special training of all sorts occupied the other six days of the week, while off duty time was filled by a varied programme of sports, with baseball and football matches predominating. The "Red Hackles" appeared on two occasions and gave clever exhibitions, while the Battalion Orchestra assisted at Divine Service at Fosse 10 on St. Patrick's Day, Sunday, March 17th. Previous to this it was announced that the Military Medal had been awarded to Corporal C. H. Camm and Private J. Given, both of whom had rendered conspicuous service during the raid on the early morning of February 13th.

In addition to the training mentioned above, the Royal High-

AVION, SEPTEMBER, 1917.

Canadian Official, Copyright.

PASSCHENDAELE, NOVEMBER, 1917.

Canadian Official, Copyright.

THE THIRD WINTER IN FRANCE

landers during their stay in the Boyeffles-Petit Sains area supplied working parties to an Australian Tunnelling Company and to the Canadian Engineers, these totalling on an average about 120 men a day. On the 20th of March the week in this district, came to an end and the 13th moved to familiar billets in Bracquemont, where they relieved the 4th Canadian Battalion as Divisional Reserve.

CHAPTER XVII

Anxious Days

> What of the fight? Or well or ill,
> Whatever chance our hearts are sure;
> Our fathers' strength is with us still
> Through good or evil to endure.
>
> Our spirit, though the storm may lower,
> Burns brighter under darkening skies,
> Knowing that at the appointed hour
> The glory of the dawn shall rise.
>   —CLAUDE E. C. H. BURTON.
>   ("Touchstone")

I

WHEN spring arrived in 1918 it brought the certainty that a German offensive on the Western Front was imminent. Even earlier than this it had been realized that the power to choose the time and place for battle had passed temporarily from Allied hands and that the next great move would be Germany's. Exactly when and where this blow would fall no one knew for certain, though the British General Staff gave as their opinion a date and location which proved amazingly accurate and showed that they possessed a lively appreciation of the strategical situation that existed. As early as the previous November, on their return to Lens from Passchendaele, the men of the Canadian Corps began to strengthen the defences of the vital Vimy area, which was entrusted to their care. Sir Douglas Haig has noted in his despatch of July 8th the characteristics of this district which rendered it so important. Behind Vimy, he says, "lay the northern collieries of France and certain tactical features, which cover our lateral communications. Here—little or no ground could be given up."

All during the winter and spring of 1918 the Canadian Corps toiled to render this district quite impregnable. Under the supervision of the Engineer Staff, the Field Companies of Engineers, the Tunnelling Companies, the Pioneer Companies and huge working parties from the Infantry battalions created a vast fortress, such

ANXIOUS DAYS

as the mind of the layman can hardly conceive. Line after line of trenches were dug and wired, with switch lines to protect the flanks. Special "defended localities" were brought into being, each a miniature fortress, with trenches, dugouts and machine gun emplacements; tanks for water, shelters for ammunition, tunnels for communication, and every other improvement that experience had shown to be of value.

It is to be presumed that the German Intelligence Department was not unaware of the tremendous strength with which the Vimy area had been endowed. Be that as it may, it is certain that when the time came for the enemy to launch his great assault, he avoided the district as he would the plague, in spite of the fact that at no spot on the Western Front would a comparatively short advance have yielded him greater benefits. When, later in the year, his vast effort had expended itself and the tide of victory was turning against him, the British centre, with Vimy as its chief bastion, was the only part of the line which stood firm on the ground it had occupied in 1917. For this fact the defensive work installed by the labours of the Canadian Corps must, at least in some measure, be held responsible.

On March 21st, 1918, the Germans attacked on a 50-mile front from Arras to la Fère. So tremendous was the force of this blow that the Fifth British Army reeled and gave ground somewhat alarmingly. Only when the attack had advanced some 35 miles to a point almost in the shadow of Amiens was its progress definitely stayed. Then, on April 9th, another drive was launched in Flanders and forced the British back, until Ypres and the Channel ports were once more in danger. At this time Sir Douglas Haig issued the Special Order in which he said, "Every position must be held to the last man. There must be no retirement. With our backs to the wall, and believing in the justice of our cause each one of us must fight to the end." How splendidly the Army responded to this Order is known to all who followed the progress of the war.

Having delivered two mighty blows against the British and having fallen short of the tremendous victory of which he dreamed, the enemy, on May 27th, shifted his point of attack and struck hard at the French front between Soissons and Rheims, following this a fortnight later by a drive on the front between Noyon and Montdidier.

Meanwhile, the first of these great attacks had penetrated some

ROYAL HIGHLANDERS OF CANADA

32 miles and had been brought to a halt by French troops, aided by American Marines and Regulars. By the 1st of July the United States had landed nearly 1,000,000 men in France; many of these were lines of communication troops and many others were not ready to take their place in the line, but those who had reached the front were rendering excellent service and showing what might some day be expected of the remainder. To hasten that day every effort was being made to shorten and intensify their period of training.

By July 15th the great German drive in the south had been brought to a standstill and on the 18th of the month Marshal Foch, who previous to this had been given supreme command of all the Allied Armies on the Western Front, launched a counter offensive, which achieved immediate success and marked the turning point in the campaign of 1918.

While these great engagements were taking place to the south and north, the Canadian Corps was having a comparatively quiet time. During the winter and early spring the Corps, as has been described, held and fortified the great Vimy bastion, which formed the centre of the whole British line. Then, on May 7th, the Corps, less the 2nd Division, which was temporarily attached to the VI British Corps, was withdrawn from the front line to form part of a special striking force, known as "G.H.Q. Reserve."

On several occasions previous to this it had been suggested that the Corps should be broken up and one, or all, of its divisions attached to other corps and thrown into the bitter fighting to the north or south. This was the counsel of despair and wiser heads realized that the Corps, owing to certain advantages, was capable of delivering a heavier blow than any other, and that in time the opportunity for such a blow would certainly come. The advantages the Corps possessed were several. Firstly, it was the strongest Army Corps in Europe, with adequate reserves to keep it so. Secondly, and contrary to the custom prevailing in the British Army, it had preserved its identity throughout, its divisions, when serving with any other corps, never by any chance considering themselves as incorporated in that unit, but invariably speaking and thinking of themselves as "attached." This had brought about an esprit de corps and a sense of confidence on the part of every unit towards every other that was of the utmost value in time of stress and emergency. Thirdly, in its auxiliary services the Corps had built up an organization that was unique, while, in the matter of the

ANXIOUS DAYS

higher command, it was served and guided by a staff of marked ability. When the great day finally came, it more than justified the policy that kept it intact in the face of strong pressure to break it up and fling its divisions hither and yon to meet the immediate need.

II

When the first great German drive began on March 21st, the 13th Battalion, Royal Highlanders of Canada, was in billets at Bracquemont. Two days later the Battalion moved to Fosse 10 and there experienced the first effect of the distant battle, when a warning message was received from Brigade stating that the Battalion was to hold itself in readiness to move at one hour's notice on receipt of the order, "stand to." With the possibility of this order arriving at any moment, nothing much could be done during the remainder of the day, but all spare kit was eliminated and arrangements made to store the surplus in Bruay. In the afternoon the officers played the officers of the 16th at "indoor" baseball and won their match by a considerable margin. No "stand to" order was received during the day, but an officer was posted at the telephone all night so that, should the order arrive, not a moment would be lost in calling up the sleeping men.

At 10.30 o'clock on the following night, March 25th, a priority message was received ordering the Battalion to "stand to" from 5.30 a.m. on March 26th. It was confidently expected that this would be followed by a message ordering the Battalion forward, but such was not the case and even a move into another area, which had been arranged, was cancelled.

Early on the morning of the 27th, however, the Battalion paraded and marched to Chateau de la Haie, near Gouy Servins. In the evening the "Red Hackles" appeared in a sketch entitled "Gipsy Love" and, at the conclusion of the performance, Brig.-Gen. G. S. Tuxford, commanding the 3rd Brigade, informed the audience that at about midnight the 3rd Brigade would move to an unnamed destination, presumably to take its part in the latest and most vigorous "push" of the war.

At 11 p.m. definite orders were received and at midnight the whole Battalion was drawn up in the grounds of the Chateau, awaiting busses, which did not arrive till 1.30 a.m. The ride which followed was a long one, half the Battalion leaving the busses near

ROYAL HIGHLANDERS OF CANADA

Doullens and marching 10 kilometres to Humbercourt, while the other half, which was scattered owing to motor troubles, finally debussed at Merieux, rested for a few hours, then embussed again and proceeded to Humbercourt, which was reached at about 5 o'clock in the afternoon. Picking up the first half of the Battalion at this spot, the busses continued to Wanquetin, whence the men marched some 7 kilometres to huts at Agnes-lez-Duisans, arriving at about 9 p.m. As it rained during the march and as the Battalion had been on the move, with only a few hours rest, since the previous midnight, the weary men thoroughly appreciated the hot tea and ration of rum that was issued when billets were reached.

At 2 o'clock on the following morning the men were roused from sleep and at 3.30 a.m., after a hurried breakfast, the Battalion moved to Arras, Headquarters, with "C" and "D" Companies, billeting in the Grande Place, while "A" and "B" Companies occupied a section of the famous Ronville Caves and passed temporarily under the command of the 16th Canadian Battalion. In the afternoon these companies rejoined the main section in the Grande Place and the whole Battalion went into Brigade Support.

On March 30 the Royal Highlanders "stood to" in the morning, but, as no call was made for their services, the remainder of the day was spent in resting. At night on the 31st the entire Battalion, with the exception of a few Headquarters details, was employed in digging reserve trenches west of Arras. On the following day, April 1st, the unit moved into the western end of Ronville Caves.

In these underground passages, hewn out of the chalk and extending for miles, the Battalion remained for five days, together with a trench mortar battery and a machine gun unit, who were also using the Caves as a temporary home. Cooking was done in cellars and dugouts overhead, as no fires were permitted in the Caves themselves, where ventilation was a problem. The men were not allowed out of the Caves during the day for fear of observation, so time hung heavily on their hands. At night, however, parties went forward on several occasions and worked under the supervision of the Engineers. Particularly good work was accomplished on the night of April 2nd when Major W. E. Macfarlane took forward a party which included almost the entire Battalion personnel. In a report regarding the work performed, Major E. F. Lynn, commanding the 2nd Field Company, Canadian Engineers, wrote to Brig.-Gen. G. S. Tuxford as follows:

ANXIOUS DAYS

Sir:

I have the honour to report that the work now being done by the 3rd Canadian Infantry Brigade — is going on very satisfactorily —. I am writing specially to express my appreciation and pleasure of working with the 13th Canadian Infantry Battalion.

The work carried out last night was accomplished with keenness and thoroughness by every officer, N.C.O. and man. Lieut. Bate, officers and sappers of this unit are keen to praise the spirit in which the men took hold and completed the task which was given them to do.

I have the honour to be, Sir,
Your obedient servant,
(Sgd.) E. F. LYNN,
Major, C.E.
Comm'd'g. 2nd Field Company, C.E.

On April 4th Lieut.-Col. G. E. McCuaig returned from his extended furlough and took over command of the Battalion from Major K. M. Perry, who had acted as C.O. during his absence.

At 8.45 p.m. on April 5th the Royal Highlanders left the Ronville Caves and relieved the 2nd Canadian Battalion in Brigade Reserve near Beaurains. Right at the exit from the Caves the Battalion suffered a severe loss, when a 5.9 shell burst on the cobbled pavement in the midst of a platoon of "C" Coy., killing ten men, wounding twenty-one severely and leaving but two uninjured. Amongst the dead was Capt. E. W. Waud, who had been wounded in June, 1916, and who, on recovering from his injuries, had returned to the Battalion and rendered devoted service. Together with those killed by the same shell, Capt. Waud was laid to rest in the Military Cemetery at Duisans, all officers and men of the Battalion's rear details attending the burial to pay their regretful respects.

Considerable shelling accompanied the Battalion in its progress forward to the reserve position, the majority of the sections being forced off the road into the adjoining fields where, in the pitch blackness of the night, they had a bad time with barbed wire entanglements, progress being made still more difficult by gas shelling, which forced them to wear respirators. Lieut. R. N. Morewood was slightly wounded during the relief, which was completed about midnight. On reaching their destination the men billeted in corrugated bivouacs which, while better than nothing, provided little shelter against heavy artillery fire.

On the morning of April 7th the rear details of the 13th, 14th,

ROYAL HIGHLANDERS OF CANADA

15th and 16th Battalions were organized into a special emergency attacking battalion, under the command of Lieut.-Col. C. W. Peck, D.S.O. So far as the 13th was concerned, the rear details were organized into a regular company, with Capt. A. W. Ruston as O.C., Capt. D. B. Donald as second-in-command and Lieuts. B. G. Field, K. G. Blackader, F. S. Stowell and W. D. C. Christie as platoon commanders. The personnel of the company was made up of all Headquarters details, the Battalion Concert Party, all tailors (except the Master Tailor), all shoemakers (except the Master Shoemaker), the band (except the Pipers), all Q.M. details and Transport men who could possibly be spared, all batmen, police and prisoners, cooks and specialist instructors. Each of the other battalions in the 3rd Brigade turned out a company similar to that of the 13th, with the result that the Brigade found itself in possession of a spare battalion, which, while by no means to be compared with the front line units, was none the less well officered and quite capable of dealing a shrewd blow, should necessity arise.

On the evening of the 7th the Royal Highlanders were relieved by the 1/13th Battalion of the London Regiment and moved back to huts at Dainville. At noon on the following day the Battalion received orders to relieve the West Riding Regiment in the right front line of the Feuchy-Fampoux Sector. At 3.30 p.m. busses arrived to convey the advance party to their destination, the remainder of the Battalion following in busses later. Relief began at 8.30 p.m. and proceeded apace, except in the case of "D" Coy., whose officers had some difficulty in securing information as to the exact location of their outposts and the position occupied by the enemy, a perturbing state of affairs as the front had very little protecting wire. By 10 p.m. the 13th Signallers, under the direction of Sergt. Bonner, had, according to their invariable custom, established telephone communication from Battalion Headquarters to all the company H.Q's., much to the surprise of the outgoing battalion, who regarded this feature of the relief as an extraordinary example of Canadian enterprise. The Canadians were equally surprised to hear that the British regiment had not been in telephone communication with their companies during their whole tour in the front line, but had relied on other means, which the Canadians regarded as obsolete, but which the less impetuous Britishers apparently found quite satisfactory.

Dawn on April 9th, the anniversary of the Battle of Vimy Ridge,

[232]

ANXIOUS DAYS

found the Highlanders' front blanketed in heavy mist. Aided, or possibly bewildered, by this curtain of fog a party of three Germans approached "D" Coy's. front and were fired on by No. 1 Lewis Gun post, which was commanded by Lance-Corp. Loiselle. One man was killed and another wounded, the latter escaping with the third man, who was uninjured. Later Lieut. J. E. Christie with a small party went out and examined the body of the dead Hun, who proved to belong to the 28th German R.I.R.

Still later in the day Lieut. Christie, aided by the mist, made a daylight reconnaissance across No Man's Land, entered the enemy line and, discovering a vacant post stocked with captured British bombs and German stick grenades, de-detonated these and restored them to their positions, with a view to attacking the post when it was occupied and possibly capturing, or killing, the garrison, who would be horrified to find their bombs worthless.

At 6 p.m. Lieut. A. N. Sclater, the Battalion Patrol Officer, led a party of eight men forward and visited the post which Christie had discovered, but found it still unoccupied. Continuing investigations, this patrol worked along the German line for some 400 yards, without encountering any opposition. Eventually the party decided that they had progressed quite far enough and started to retire. On reaching the unoccupied post, they laid a trap and were rewarded about half an hour later when three Huns walked into it. Being covered with revolvers, these individuals surrendered without further ado and the patrol, having achieved a brilliant little success, returned forthwith to their own lines, whence the Germans, all members of the 28th R.I.R., were sent back to Brigade H.Q. for interrogation.

Further patrols of an interesting nature were carried out on April 10th. Lieut. Christie proceeded to the enemy post, the scene of the previous day's coup, and once more found it unoccupied. Accordingly, he salvaged the bombs which he had de-detonated, re-detonated them and issued them to his platoon. Later in the day Lieut. M. L. Brady and six men took up a position in enemy territory and awaited developments. In about half an hour two Germans approached, but became suspicious and, after pausing for a moment, started to run. Fire was thereupon opened by the Highlanders, but the latter could not claim definite hits. As a result of these patrols it became obvious that the enemy's main line of trenches was situated along the top of Monchy Hill, which rose

ROYAL HIGHLANDERS OF CANADA

a little to the rear, and that at night he occupied advanced posts along the foot of the Hill, retiring to his main line in the morning.

Trench mortar activity marked the morning of April 11th and in the evening aerial battles above the lines were numerous, one man of the 13th suffering a painful wound when a stray bullet from one of these encounters tore a jagged hole in his foot.

An unfortunate incident occurred on the 13th front at about noon on April 12th, when a strange officer, accompanied by a private, passed one of the Highlanders' advanced posts and disappeared in the direction of the enemy's line. Presuming that the officer knew where he was going, the men in the advanced post made no effort to stop him, but reported the incident as a matter of routine. Later it developed that an officer of the 16th Battalion was missing and the obvious conclusion was that he and the officer who had passed the 13th post were one and the same. Apparently he had been unaware of his actual position and had imagined that the front line still lay ahead, as it would have had he been a little further north.

The same night Lieut. Sclater, Lieut. Brady and four other ranks moved across No Man's Land to pay the enemy another visit. Five Huns were sighted at one spot and fire was opened on them. One was seen to fall and a Mills bomb was thrown and seen to burst amongst the remainder. The Highlanders' party then withdrew to their own lines.

During this tour stringent orders were issued to the troops to be on guard against German spies masquerading in British uniforms. One day Maj.-Gen. A. C. Macdonell entered a dugout in the front line and asked some questions of a canny Scot, who had joined the Battalion a few days before and who did not know the Divisional Commander by sight. If these lines ever meet General Macdonell's eyes he will learn, possibly for the first time, that he was suspected of being a spy on this occasion and that for over a quarter of an hour he was continually covered by the canny Scot's concealed revolver.

On the night of April 13th the Royal Highlanders were relieved by the 2nd Canadian Battalion and moved back to billets in St. Aubin. Shelling occurred during the relief and one man of No. 3 Platoon was killed, seven others being severely wounded. This brought the casualty list for the whole tour up to a total of 39 all ranks, 10 having been killed and 29 wounded.

ANXIOUS DAYS

Meanwhile, the rear details of the four 3rd Brigade battalions, forming the special counter-attacking battalion, had paraded under the command of Major Plow, M.C., M.M., of the 14th Battalion, and had marched to rejoin their respective units. The 13th company broke off at St. Aubin and was already in billets at this place when the Battalion proper arrived back from the front line.

During the week that the 13th remained at St. Aubin in Corps Reserve, large working parties, under Major I. M. R. Sinclair, reported to the Engineers on three occasions and were employed on the never ending task of digging reserve trenches. Kilts were re-issued in the early part of the week and, as if to celebrate the occasion, the companies began to give more attention to training in open warfare, events on other parts of the front having demonstrated that the long years of trench warfare were probably coming to an end.

An incident of this period was a quarrel between "Flora Macdonald," the Battalion goat, and her masters of the pipe band. It was the pride of "Flora's" life to march and counter-march with the pipers, and her skill in wheeling at the exact moment when a turn was required was the envy and admiration of all units whose mascots could not be trained to do likewise. "Flora" got well smeared with tar one day and bitterly resented the efforts of the pipers to clean her coat, so much so that for the first time in her three years' service she utterly refused to parade, though obviously yearning for her accustomed place at the head of the column. How the quarrel was adjusted no one knows, but eventually her heart was softened by some skilled philanderer and the incident of the tar forgotten.

At night on April 21st the Battalion advanced and relieved the 5th Canadian Battalion in support. Working parties were the chief feature of the tour that followed. Significant of the times, however, was the placing of small demolition parties on two bridges over a railway cutting in the Battalion area, with instructions to blow these should a sudden German attack force the Canadians to withdraw. Some shelling occurred during the tour and one man was killed while on a ration party, but on the whole working and other parties were not seriously interfered with.

On the morning of April 28th the 13th Battalion acted as support to a highly successful raiding operation, carried out by the Royal Montreal Regiment and the Canadian Scottish. Some 12 officers and 240 other ranks took part in this little engagement, which resulted in the capture of 1 German officer, 54 other ranks, 3 machine guns and 1 "pine-apple thrower." In addition, the raiders inflicted sharp casualties on the enemy with the bayonet and bombs, while they themselves escaped very lightly. Considering all these facts, Sir Arthur Currie, the Canadian Corps Commander, complimented the two battalions concerned and stated that this had proved one of the most successful minor operations in some time.

On the night following the raid the 13th Battalion moved forward and relieved the 14th in the front line. Early on the morning of May 1st Corp. T. G. Gilchrist accompanied a sergeant out into No Man's Land to inspect a gap in their own wire. They proceeded further than ordered, and Gilchrist was hit by an enemy bomb. The sergeant thereupon returned to the Highlanders' front line and reported what had happened. Lieut. J. Kerry immediately took a patrol to the spot the sergeant had indicated and searched the ground thoroughly. No trace of Gilchrist could be found, unfortunately, and it was presumed that the party which had thrown the bomb had taken him prisoner. Lacking more definite information, he was posted on the Battalion's records as "wounded and missing."

On the 3rd and 4th of the month visibility was unusually good and the Battalion observers were able to report to the artillery the location of several large parties in the enemy's back areas. On one occasion 250 Huns were observed in the vicinity of Square Wood, these being shelled by the Canadian 4.5's as soon as their presence was reported. On another occasion Lieut. B. G. Field reported that the enemy had dug two gun pits in Square Wood and had dragged a light field gun into one of them. To deal with this situation a special "shoot" was arranged by the Canadian 4.5 howitzers.

Special precautions against surprise attacks were taken on the night of May 4th, in view of information regarding an impending movement secured from two escaped British prisoners. Strong defensive patrols lay out in No Man's Land all night, but no attack developed. Late on the following night, or well on in the morning of the 6th, to be more exact, the Battalion was relieved by the 13th Battalion, Royal Scots, and retired to billets in a single large house in Arras.

Shelling of Arras that day caused no little anxiety, owing to the fact that one large shell striking the house in which the whole Bat-

ANXIOUS DAYS

talion was billeted might easily bring about losses approximating those of a major engagement. In consequence, it was with relief that the Battalion, during the afternoon, moved out of Arras to familiar billets in St. Aubin.

CHAPTER XVIII
G. H. Q. Reserve and Arras

Light green of grass and richer green of bush
Slope upwards to the darkest green of fir
How still! How deathly still! And yet the hush
Shivers and trembles with some subtle stir,

. . . . .

"Behold all Europe writhing on the rack,
The sins of fathers grinding down the sons,
How long, O Lord!" He sends no answer back,
But still I hear the mutter of the guns.
—Sir Arthur Conan Doyle.

I

ON May 6th, 1918, the Canadian Corps went into G.H.Q. Reserve, consequently it was almost three months before the Royal Highlanders saw more fighting. During the first two weeks of this period the Battalion remained at St. Aubin, where, on the 7th of the month, it was announced that the Military Cross had been awarded to Lieut. A. N. Sclater and the Military Medal to Lance-Corp. E. Hest, for the services that they had rendered in the brilliant patrolling operations at Feuchy-Fampoux during the early part of April. Simultaneously it was announced that the Italian Bronze Medal for Military Valour had been awarded to Sergt. S. Chandler, of the Intelligence Section, who, throughout the three years of the Battalion's work in France, had rendered courageous, constant and faithful service.

Apart from routine, the work of the Battalion at this time consisted of special training in open warfare, with particular attention paid to the attack. Several whole days were spent in manœuvres of this type and on at least one occasion aeroplanes co-operated to train the men in effective methods of liaison. At the end of the day's work, the men derived a great deal of pleasure from the proximity of the River Scarpe, which afforded them the opportunity,

G.H.Q. RESERVE AND ARRAS

rare on active service, for bathing and swimming to their hearts' content.

Sports of all varieties occupied much of the spare time. Brigade sports were held at Etrun on the 15th of the month and the Battalion attended in a body. Quite the most sensational number on the programme was the "chariot" race in which the entrants "drove wild" while seated on the front limber of a G.S. wagon. This contest provided the spectators with a thrill, which even the ever-popular greasy-pole event could not rival. The day's sports were brought to a close by a baseball match in which the 13th went down to defeat before the superior playing of the 15th by a score of 12-6. On May 13th Major K. M. Perry, D.S.O., who had acted as Commanding Officer during the absence of Lieut.-Col. McCuaig in the winter and who, since the latter's return, had served as Second-in-Command, left the Royal Highlanders to assume command of the 87th Battalion, Canadian Grenadier Guards. While it was with regret on both sides that the separation took place, Major Perry was the recipient of hearty congratulations and sincere expressions of good will. Judging from their own experience, all ranks felt that the Guards had secured a commanding officer who was capable of handling a battalion with the best. Previous to his departure Major Perry was the guest of honour at a lively party in the Officers' Mess. The "ladies" of the Battalion Concert Party in their smartest frocks helped by their dancing and singing to make the affair a howling success.

On May 19th the Royal Highlanders said farewell to St. Aubin and moved to Izel-lez-Hameau. Special training in the attack was a feature of the five days spent at this spot. On several occasions Brigade manœuvres were held and one night the Brigade bivouacked in a wood near the Avesnes-le-Comte-Frévent Road. With camp fires blazing in all directions and with groups of officers and men gathered around, singing and telling stories, the scene was one that all present will long remember. Somehow it seemed as if the hands of time had been turned back, for bivouacs and camp fires in a pleasant wood were familiar to the soldier of 1918 more from his childhood memories of highly coloured prints than from actual experience.

The next morning further manœuvres were carried out with the assistance of contact aeroplanes. An interesting feature of the day was a series of experiments in producing localized smoke screens

ROYAL HIGHLANDERS OF CANADA

with specially prepared rifle grenades. Considerable enthusiasm was displayed by the troops in this new sport, with the result that the hide of one referee's horse was badly singed, while a hay-stack which sheltered an imaginary machine gun was so successfully screened that it took fire and was totally destroyed. When the resulting bill for damages was presented by the honest farmer who owned the land, this particular hay-stack, which had seemed about the same size as its fellows, was discovered by the astonished Highlanders to have dwarfed these as Gulliver dwarfed the Lilliputians.

After five days at Izel-lez-Hameau the 13th moved to Bailleul-aux-Cornailles. Anti-typhoid inoculation marked the first day at this spot, while on the second day, which was a Sunday, the men were permitted to rest. On the 29th of the month Brigade manœuvres were carried out, the 15th Battalion acting on the defensive, while the other three units practised the attack in liaison with contact aeroplanes and tanks. On this occasion the 15th was called the "British" force, while the 13th, 14th and 16th became "Germans." Lieut.-Col. McCuaig became General von Quaig for the day and issued ferocious operation orders to Colonels Hans der Pecksburg and Fritz von Wortle, who seemed strongly to resemble Lieut.-Cols. Peck and Worrall, the distinguished commanding officers of the Canadian Scottish and Royal Montreal Regiment. Keen rivalry was displayed between the opposing forces and many stratagems and tricks were resorted to. The 16th Battalion before daylight concealed two spies, with a heliograph, in some trees in the area the 15th was to defend. These were discovered and hauled ignominiously from their position by the triumphant "British," the feat being accomplished to the enthusiastic applause of a pair of simple French farmers who appeared on the scene from nowhere in particular. Long hours afterwards the "British" discovered to their chagrin that the honest sons of the soil before whom they had so cleverly captured the spies were themselves disguised members of the attacking forces.

Inter-company baseball and football games were numerous during this period and on several occasions the Battalion engaged in contests with other units with varying degrees of success. On the evening of June 8th the officers of the 13th entertained the Matron and Nursing Sisters of No. 3 Canadian Casualty Clearing Station at dinner. A large marquee was erected for the occasion and the services of the Battalion Concert Party retained to provide a cabaret

WINTER, 1917-1918.

Canadian Official, Copyright.

IN THE TRENCHES NEAR LENS, DECEMBER, 1917.

Canadian Official, Copyright.

G.H.Q. RESERVE AND ARRAS

for the guests. After dinner the whole company proceeded to the local chateau, where the floor of the Battalion Orderly Room had been prepared for dancing. If the guests enjoyed the party as much as the officers, and they claimed to have done so, there is no doubt they will long remember the evening as one of the most agreeable spent in France.

Some days after this party a list of honours appeared in which Lieut.-Col. G. E. McCuaig, D.S.O., was awarded the C.M.G., while he, as well as Major (A/Lieut.-Col.) K. M. Perry, D.S.O., and Lieut. W. F. McGovern, were listed as "Mentioned in Despatches." In view of the excellent party which he had so recently supervised, Lieut.-Col. McCuaig has always maintained that either the C.M.G., or at very least the "Mention in Despatches," must have been awarded for proficiency in entertaining under difficult circumstances. The earnest seeker after the truth, however, will find that both these awards were made for the skill with which the Battalion had been handled under McCuaig's command.

On June 16th the Battalion left Bailleul-aux-Cornailles and moved to Anzin. Here the unit continued its programme of training, while the men in their spare time were again able to enjoy swimming in the River Scarpe. Organized aquatic sports were held on one occasion, with prizes for swimming races, fancy diving, high diving and all the other items of a regulation meet. On June 17th the 1st Canadian Division held a sports day at Tinques, at which the 13th officers' "indoor" baseball team won their match, advancing a step in the eliminations for the Corps championship. Numerous other contests of one sort and another occurred during the fortnight the Battalion remained at Anzin, but these were never allowed to interfere with training for the grim business that lay ahead.

From the 24th to the 26th of the month, inclusive, and on several other occasions the Battalion rose at 5.30 a.m. and proceeded to Ariane Dump on the Lens-Bethune Road to work on the construction of reserve trenches. Influenza became prevalent at this time and a number of men were quarantined in consequence. These did not accompany the working parties, of course, but remained in their billeting area, where they were kept busy with routine drills and training. During this period it was announced that for work such as the name of the decoration indicates, the Meritorious Service Medal had been awarded to Sergt. D. S. Fraser and to Regimental Quartermaster-Sergeant C. Millward.

ROYAL HIGHLANDERS OF CANADA

Reveille sounded at 4.45 o'clock on the morning of June 30th and at 7 a.m. the Battalion moved off, passing through Mont St. Eloy, Camblain-l'Abbé and Cambligneul and completing the 18 kilometres to Caucourt by 11 a.m. Influenza had increased to such an extent by this date that fully a quarter of the Battalion's strength made the move to Caucourt in ambulances. Fortunately the cases were mild and of short duration.

Dominion Day, July 1st, was a holiday on which all men who desired were permitted to attend the Corps sports at Tinques. Practically the whole Battalion personnel availed themselves of this privilege, and few missed the splendid entertainment. In a field between the Arras-St. Pol Road and the Railway a huge arena had been prepared, with grandstands and pavilions on the one side and a hill which formed a natural grandstand on the other. Flags and bunting were used for decorations and these, in combination with the green grass and the white of the numerous tents that served as dressing rooms, presented a most attractive sight. Numerous brass bands were distributed throughout the grounds, while the massed pipe bands of the 1st Division were also present, lending a Highland touch to the scene. Thousands of troops gathered for the event, while the Corps numbered amongst its guests H.R.H. the Duke of Connaught, Sir Robert Borden, General John J. Pershing, the American Commander-in-Chief, and many other distinguished soldiers and civilians. Aeroplanes hovered in the distance throughout the day, protecting spectators and contestants alike from any danger of enemy bombing. As for the programme, it included track and field events of every conceivable nature, as well as matches in lacrosse, football, baseball, "indoor" baseball, tennis, volley ball and so on. The officers' team of the 13th won the Corps championship at "indoor" baseball, while the 3rd Field Company, C.E., won the "outdoor" title. The 1st Canadian Division won the highest aggregate of points. The whole memorable day was brought to a conclusion by the "Volatiles," the First Divisional Concert Party, who staged their latest and best revue, "Take a Chance."

On the day following the Corps sports the 3rd Canadian Infantry Brigade was reviewed at Béthonsart by the Corps Commander, who was accompanied by Sir Robert Borden. Following the review, Sir Robert addressed the troops, who afterwards marched past and tendered him the salute while on the way to billets.

G.H.Q. RESERVE AND ARRAS

Routine training continued for some days, then, on July 6th the Battalion marched to the scene of the Corps sports to attend a "Highland Gathering" conducted under the auspices of the 3rd Canadian Infantry Brigade. All Highland units were invited to attend, or send representatives, to this gathering and as the 15th (Scottish) and 51st (Highland) Divisions were in the neighbourhood, there was a gathering of the clans and a display of tartans varied enough to delight the heart of any loyal Scot. The programme on this occasion included dancing, wrestling, hammer throwing, tossing the caber and a tug-of-war, as well as piping contests and a competition amongst the pipe bands. The feature of the day was "Retreat," played by 24 massed pipe bands, with 284 pipers and 164 drummers participating. As the bands marched up and down in parallel files, the swing of the tartans was a martial sight worth going many miles to see. At the head of the centre column, bursting with pride, and keeping in time to the fraction of a second, marched "Flora Macdonald," the 13th Battalion goat. And well she might be proud, for no such gathering of pipers had ever taken place before. To complete the day, the 13th and 16th Battalions' Concert Parties gave a vaudeville entertainment that was much appreciated by a large audience.

Extensive manœuvres took place on the 8th of the month under the supervision of the Corps, Divisional and Brigade Commanders. On the completion of these operations, Sir Arthur Currie addressed the troops and informed them quietly that the days of training were coming to an end and that before long the Canadian Corps was once more going into battle. Cheers greeted his announcement and it added interest to the somewhat monotonous programme of training that continued for a few days thereafter.

On the evening of July 8th Canon Scott, Chaplain of the 1st Canadian Division, and an old friend of the 13th, paid the Battalion a visit and lectured to a large number of the men who gathered in a field for the purpose. The Canon told about a visit to Rome, where his British uniform had received a tumultuous welcome, both for its own sake and by reason of the fact that some of the populace took his small party to be the advance guard of a large force. The story of his adventures on this trip was full of interest for the men of the 13th, who, when he had concluded his tale, expressed their appreciation by spontaneous and long continued applause.

Somewhat less scholastic in nature was the entertainment on

another occasion when the officers of the 13th accepted the challenge of the officers of the 15th for a cocking main. Few of the 13th officers knew much about cock fighting, nevertheless a sum of money was hastily raised and the surrounding country searched for a suitable champion. At last someone found a bird which rejoiced in the name of "The Pride of Ruitz." When the great day arrived the 13th backed "The Pride" to a man, but, alas, the confidence was misplaced. He made an indifferent showing and the 15th bird won easily. As a disgusted backer was heard to observe when the battle was over, "That 'Pride of Ruitz' must have won his name in an egg laying contest. If he got it in a fight, all I can say is that Ruitz is easily pleased."

At 5 p.m. on July 13th the Royal Highlanders paraded at Caucourt and marched to "Y" Camp, near Etrun. From this point a party of 9 officers and 400 other ranks moved off for work near Maroeuil on the following day, while the rest of the Battalion remained in camp, attending Divine Service in the morning and playing games in the afternoon. In the early evening the officers of the Battalion defeated the men at "indoor" baseball by a score of 6-5, reversing the verdict of a game on the previous day when the men won by 15-13.

More working parties and more sports marked the next few days, while on the 16th the chief event was a parade of the Brigade for Major-General S. C. Mewburn, Canadian Minister of Militia, who was accompanied by the Hon. C. C. Ballantyne, Minister of Marine and Fisheries, and by Major-General E. W. Wilson, G.O.C. No. 4 Military District in Canada.

II

Two days after the review by the distinguished visitors from Canada, the 13th Battalion paraded in battle order and proceeded to relieve the 19th Canadian Battalion in Arras. This city was reached about 9.30 p.m. and the men were deeply interested to note that it had suffered much damage since their visit in the spring. Billets were secured in the rue d'Amiens and towards midnight considerable shelling took place in the immediate vicinity. Two nights later a 5.9 shell crashed into a house where the officers of "B" and "D" Companies were sleeping, but, apart from a rude awakening for the officers in question, no harm was done.

Owing to the damaged and unprotected condition of many of

G.H.Q. RESERVE AND ARRAS

the stores in Arras, troops were confined to billets during the stay in the town, but small parties of 15 at a time, under the supervision of an officer, were permitted to visit a swimming pool, part of the old moat, just outside the city. Soon it was discovered that Arras, while convenient in many ways, was not an entirely desirable place to billet a reserve battalion and accordingly the Royal Highlanders, on July 22nd, moved out of the city and proceeded to an area west of Beaurains. Meanwhile, a special counter-attacking battalion had been formed out of the rear details of the Brigade, similar to that which had existed in the spring and which had passed out of existence when the Brigade withdrew from the forward area. Command of this unit was given to Major R. O. Bell-Irving, M.C.

While in reserve at Beaurains, working parties of the 13th went forward nightly to improve an important communication trench known as North Alley. No casualties occurred during these operations, but on the night of the 22nd, or rather in the early morning hours of the 23rd, the Battalion proper had a narrow escape when a change in the wind blew back gas from the front line. Box respirators were quickly adjusted, however, and no harm was done.

On the night of July 26th the 13th Battalion moved forward and relieved the Royal Montreal Regiment in the Telegraph Hill sector of the front line. Relief was delayed somewhat owing to the fact that 15 officers and 400 other ranks of the 2nd Canadian Infantry Brigade were raiding the enemy's line at 9 p.m. and it was considered advisable not to begin the relief until the artillery fire brought about by this operation had died down. The Highlanders, accordingly, did not move into the line until nearly midnight.

Rainy weather marked the first day of the tour in the front line and working parties were employed to keep the trenches in good condition. At ten minutes to one on the morning of July 28th, 9 officers and 150 other ranks of the Canadian Scottish, on the Royal Highlanders' immediate left, raided the enemy's trenches for the purpose of obtaining identifications and inflicting casualties. This operation was called the "Llandovery Castle Raid" and was planned, not only for the purposes already mentioned, but also as a reprisal against the Germans for the black and unspeakable crime of sinking His Majesty's Hospital Ship, "Llandovery Castle," together with many Canadian Nursing Sisters. Combined with the bombing of Canadian hospitals, this dastardly crime had stirred the men of the Canadian Corps to a feeling of intense bitterness towards the Hun, unequalled, perhaps, since the days of the first gas attacks at Ypres.

The defence scheme in the Telegraph Hill Sector had been worked out by the French and was a novel one to the Canadians. Long rolls of French wire were strung along the edge of the front and support trenches. In the event of an attack the garrisons of these trenches were supposed to pull this wire into the trench, set off an S.O.S. and retire to the reserve line in rear. The artillery would then pound the front trenches where the enemy was presumably floundering in the rolls of wire. In the case of the battalion to the left of the 13th this arrangement would so work that when a shift had been made battalion headquarters would be in No Man's Land. However, as the contingency seemed remote and as the quarters were comfortable, no one worried much about it.

On the whole the tour in the front line passed uneventfully. Enemy shelling was intermittent and casualties negligible. A party of seven Huns approached one of "C" Coy's posts on the 29th, but was driven off with bombs. Later Lieut. J. Kerry took out a patrol in an effort to capture prisoners, but no enemy was encountered. That same night a slight change in the disposition of the companies was made to conform with a shift in the Battalion boundary. A rather pathetic story was revealed during the tour by the finding of the body of an 18th Battalion man who had been missing since early in the summer. Some old equipment marked the spot where he had received death wounds and from this point he must have crawled over 200 yards back towards the Canadian line. Then, when almost safe, he had been too weak to make a way through his own wire and had died with comrades just too far away to hear his calls for assistance.

Early on the morning of August 2nd the 13th Battalion was relieved by the 2nd and 16th Battalions of the London Regiment and moved back to Dainville, whence, after a few hours sleep, the men were conveyed by light railway to Lattre St. Quentin. Here details were received of an air raid on Izel-lez-Hameau on the night of July 31st, as a result of which Private W. H. Hutchinson, of the Battalion Concert Party, had been killed and a fellow actor, Private J. P. Allen, wounded. The remainder of the party, who had just given an entertainment, were badly shaken up, but not otherwise injured.

CHAPTER XIX

The Battle of Amiens

> E'en now their vanguard gathers,
> E'en now we face the fray—
> As Thou didst help our fathers,
> Help Thou our hosts to-day!
> —RUDYARD KIPLING.

I

ON August 8th, 1918, Sir Douglas Haig struck the blow which, to quote General Ludendorff, resulted in the Germans "losing hope for a military victory." In many ways the Battle of Amiens, as the engagement has been named, was the greatest surprise attack of the war. As early as July 20th Sir Arthur Currie was informed of the operation and notified that, for the occasion, the Canadian Corps would be attached to the Fourth British Army, under General Sir Henry Rawlinson. On July 28th the First French Army, under General Debeney, was placed by Marshal Foch under Sir Douglas's orders and it was arranged that this distinguished force should co-operate.

On the following day the Canadian Divisional Commanders were taken into the secret, but were instructed to discuss the matter with no one, not even with their brigadiers, while to deceive the enemy they were ordered to continue preparations for an attack on Orange Hill, east of Arras. In a further effort to mislead the enemy, news was allowed to leak out that the Corps was going north to Flanders, and two battalions, the 27th, of the 2nd Division, and the 4th C.M.R.'s, of the 3rd Division, were actually put into the line on the Kemmel front, where care was taken to see that the enemy identified them. Lest the German Intelligence system had developed unusual stupidity, two Canadian Casualty Clearing Stations were also moved north, as was a Buzzer Section of the Signal Corps, to send messages which the enemy could pick up and decipher without too great difficulty. An amusing result of these deceptions occurred when a number of foreign officers, temporarily attached to the Corps, were "taken in" and hurried north to secure good billets for themselves while such were still available. The indignation of these individuals when the Corps went elsewhere was unbounded, but, as was pointed out, their move northward had not been prompted by any responsible member of the Corps Staff, but was the result of listening to estaminet gossip, which on the face of it was quite "unofficial."

On August 3rd the men of the 13th Battalion, Royal Highlanders of Canada, utterly unaware of where they were going, but suspecting strongly that something big was in the wind, started their move toward the scene of the forthcoming operations. At 10.30 a.m. the Transport Section moved off by road for Frévent. At 12.45 p.m. "A" Coy. proceeded to Fosseux, thence by busses to Frévent, a point whither the remainder of the Battalion followed some hours later. Here the 13th entrained, Lieut.-Col. McCuaig being handed a package of sealed orders shortly before the train pulled out at 9.30 p.m. Capt. D. B. Donald, two officers and sixty other ranks of "A" Coy. travelled by an earlier train to act as a detraining party for the 3rd Brigade group.

Proceeding southward, the long string of the famous "40 hommes, 8 chevaux" box cars jolted along throughout the night. Early on the morning of the 4th a halt was made to water the horses and to give the men a cup of tea and a chance to stretch their cramped legs. Continuing, the train proceeded through beautiful and well cultivated country until about 11 o'clock, when the Battalion detrained at Vieux-Rouen-sur-Bresle. Delaying at this point for breakfast and a rest and, on the part of some, a plunge into the cool waters of the Bresle, the Battalion marched at 2 p.m. and proceeded some 14 kilometres to Epaumesnil.

Reveille sounded at 6 o'clock on the following morning and at 8 o'clock the Battalion marched to an area to practise the attack in co-operation with the newest and fastest tanks. From this point Lieut.-Col. McCuaig rode to Brigade Headquarters to attend a conference of C.O.'s, and while there heard with a deep regret, later shared by all his officers, of the death of Lieut.-Col. Bartlett McLennan, D.S.O., the Commanding Officer of the Sister Battalion, the 42nd Royal Highlanders of Canada.

Returning to billets after an interesting morning's work, the men of the 13th rested until 8.30 p.m., when, in disagreeable weather, the Battalion marched about 10 kilometres to a point where ensued a long and tedious wait for busses. At midnight,

THE BATTLE OF AMIENS

the men boarded the busses and travelled all night, debussing at 7.30 a.m. on the 6th and marching some 9 kilometres to Boves, a roundabout route being necessary to avoid crossing the sky line of a ridge, which was under enemy observation.

Boves proved to be a medium sized town and in fairly good condition, though evacuated by the civilian population. Comfortable billets were secured by the 13th in the rue Victor Hugo, where the tired and hungry men were immediately provided with a hot meal by the Battalion Field Kitchens, which had preceded them.

At 4.05 p.m. Lieut. A. T. Howard, the Acting Adjutant, issued an operation order which informed the troops that the Battalion would move forward in battle order at midnight. In accordance with this order, the Battalion advanced to the reserve area at the time mentioned, leaving the rear party, under Major I. M. R. Sinclair, M.C., in billets at Boves.

Operation Order No. 193, which laid down the task to be accomplished in the forthcoming battle, may be summarized as follows:—

(1) General Plan:—The 3rd Canadian Infantry Brigade will attack on the morning of the 8th instant with the following dispositions:—

16th Canadian Battalion—On the right.
13th Canadian Battalion—In the centre.
14th Canadian Battalion—On the left.
15th Canadian Battalion—In centre support.
5th Canadian Battalion—In right support.

(2) Objectives:—The 13th Canadian Battalion will capture Hangard Wood West, all of Hangard Wood East and Croates Trench. The Battalion will consolidate on the Green Line.

(3) Formation:—"B" and "C" Companies will attack on the right and left, each with a two platoon frontage, with "A" and "D" Companies in right and left support respectively, who will do any necessary mopping up.

(4) Relief:—"B" and "C" Companies will take over the line from the 49th Australian Battalion and will post necessary covering patrols.

(5) Direction:—Intelligence Section will detail parties of four men each to maintain touch with 14th and 16th Battalions on flanks.

ROYAL HIGHLANDERS OF CANADA

(6) Tanks:—The following tanks will co-operate:—
   3 on left company frontage.
   4 on right company frontage.
For these the Intelligence Section will supply 7 observers.

(7) Aeroplanes:—Contact aeroplanes will call for red ground flares, if these are available for issue.

(8) Trench Mortars:—Two trench mortars, under Lieut. Bain, will be attached to 13th Battalion Headquarters.

(9) Communications:—3rd Brigade will maintain communications with Battalion Headquarters as it advances. Battalion Headquarters will operate a power buzzer with Brigade. Companies will endeavour to maintain visual communication with Battalion Headquarters.

(10) Synchronization of Watches:—A runner from each company will report at Battalion Headquarters at 7.30 p.m. with a watch, and companies on reporting that they are in jumping off positions will again send a watch for synchronization at new Battalion H.Q.'s.

(11) Zero Hour:—will be communicated by message at 7.30 p.m.

The advance of the Royal Highlanders into the line on the night of August 6th-7th was not entirely uneventful. The roads were jammed with traffic of all description and the roar of numerous exhausts was so loud that it seemed impossible the enemy could fail to hear it. Low flying aeroplanes were used in an attempt, apparently successful, to drown the noise, for the Germans gave no sign that it had reached them, though they did shell to some extent, particularly at Taza Alley, where the burst of a 5.9 caused the Battalion its first losses, Lieut. C. E. Hyde being instantly killed and two other ranks wounded.

During the day that followed fine weather proved a boon to the men, who lay around in shell holes and communication trenches, keeping all movement carefully concealed. No fires were permitted and a strong force of aeroplanes patrolled all day to prevent the enemy from observing the assembly. As two brigades were crowded into an area that would ordinarily accommodate one battalion, it was a literal fact that officers, in some cases, had to walk over the men while arranging dispositions.

THE BATTLE OF AMIENS

Parties from the four companies and Battalion Headquarters reconnoitred their jumping off positions during the day, receiving every courtesy and much assistance from the officers and men of the 49th Australian Battalion, who were holding the line. As a result of this reconnaissance, Lieut.-Col. McCuaig discovered that there was a great deal of wire in Hangard Wood West, also a number of German strong posts. Accordingly it was arranged to have one of the tanks go through this section of the wood to assist in clearing these obstructions out of the way.

At dusk the companies of the 13th began to move into their jumping off trenches in Hangard Wood West, completing the move and reporting themselves ready by 1.45 a.m. on the 8th instant. The Battalion was short of bombs and rifle grenades and had no ground flares, Very lights, or S.O.S. rockets. These deficiencies were regrettable, but were not likely to prove vital and in any case nothing could be done about them, as no supplies were available.

At 2 a.m. Battalion Headquarters moved up into the front line to a quarry in Hangard Wood West and reported to Brigade that all was in order. Throughout the night the German artillery was active. Possibly they suspected a relief, but more probably they were the victims of that vague uneasiness by which some sixth sense so often conveys a warning to those in imminent danger.

At 4.20 a.m. the barrage opened and immediately the men of the Canadian Corps, together with the Australians on their left, started out on their great adventure, while the French to the right began the shelling which preceded their attack. In speaking of the advance that ensued, the correspondent of the London "Times" wrote as follows:—"In structure it was chiefly a Canadian battle. It was their advance on the Luce that was the core and crux of the operation, and on their progress depended the advance of both the Australians on their left and that of the successive French armies on their right, each of which was thrown in only as the advance above it prospered."

In the first few minutes of the attack it was seen that visibility was going to be bad. A light ground mist prevailed and soon this was thickened by the dense smoke of the barrage until it was difficult to see more than ten or fifteen yards. This greatly hindered the work of the tanks detailed to co-operate with the 13th, as the crews could not see where the Infantry were having trouble.

ROYAL HIGHLANDERS OF CANADA

Very tragically, the first losses amongst the Royal Highlanders were caused by one of the supporting guns firing short, this being accounted for by the fact that, in order to keep the secret of the attack, many of the batteries had not been permitted to register on their targets before "zero." Some thirty casualties occurred from this cause, Capt. Campbell, the Battalion Medical Officer, and Capt. Boules, attached Machine Gun Officer, being wounded and Capt. N. M. MacLean, who had twice previously suffered wounds and whose career with the Battalion had been a distinguished one, being instantly killed.

In clearing Hangard Wood the 13th ran up against several machine gun nests, which caused serious trouble. Lieut. A. N. Sclater, M.C., was killed whilst attacking these, as was Lieut. E. Creighton, while Capt. R. L. Calder, Lieut. N. A. McLean, Lieut. R. H. Morewood and Lieut. M. L. Brady were wounded. Lieut. Brady set a fine example of courage and endurance on this occasion, suffering three distinct wounds before he would admit himself hors-de-combat.

Many of the rank and file gave splendid exhibitions of bravery and skill during the fighting in the Wood. The shortage of bombs was sharply felt in attacking the machine gun nests, the men being compelled to outflank these instead of using the quick and effective method of smashing them up with bombs and rifle grenades.

A splendid piece of work of this nature was performed by Private J. B. Croak of "A" Coy., who, single handed, attacked a machine gun nest in Ring Copse, silenced the gun with a well directed bomb from the scanty supply available and took the whole crew prisoners. Shortly after this Croak was severely wounded in the right arm, but his fighting blood was thoroughly up and he refused point blank to retire from the line. In the course of the advance that followed, his platoon encountered another strong point, from which several machine guns were firing with disastrous effect. With no bombs available, Croak organized a rush and was the first to reach the objective. Once at grips with the enemy, the little party of Royal Highlanders overcame all resistance. A moment of fierce work with the bayonet and all was over, three machine guns and several prisoners falling into the attackers' hands. Very unfortunately, Private Croak was again wounded, this time fatally, in the moment before the last resistance was overcome. He died within a few minutes.

THE BATTLE OF AMIENS

Somewhat similar and equally fine was the work of Corporal J. H. Good, of "D" Coy., who, alone, charged a nest of three machine guns and killed or captured the crews. Later, when the advance had penetrated deep into the German lines and was pushing forward to its final objective, this same N.C.O. discovered a battery of 5.9-inch guns, in action and pounding the Canadian advance and rear. To charge a battery of 5.9's with a force which consisted of himself and three privates might seem the act of a madman, but Corp. Good realized that the gun crews were not trained in hand-to-hand fighting and that, once at grips, he and his stout-hearted companions would have an advantage sufficient, possibly, to offset their appalling inferiority in numbers. Accordingly he and his party charged. What the German gunners thought when this assault was launched, no man will ever know. Perhaps in the drill and text books they had studied no instructions were given as to procedure when four Canadian Highlanders charged a battery with the obvious intent of doing bodily harm. Be that as it may, the battery surrendered and the four Highlanders found themselves owners of three excellent guns and masters of a good sized batch of prisoners.

Soon after zero hour, Lieut.-Col. McCuaig decided that he would move his Battalion Headquarters forward, as the fog rendered visual signalling impossible and he was anxious not to lose touch with the advance. The wisdom of this course soon manifested itself, for by map and compass he was able to keep the attack of his own Battalion headed in the right direction and at the same time to redirect many parties from other units whom the dense mist had led astray.

Having surmounted the obstacles presented by the machine gun nests in Hangard Wood, the attack of the 13th swept victoriously forward, capturing prisoners, killing those who resisted and taking several batteries of enemy guns. The list of these, compiled when the engagement was over, presented a gratifying total, comprising as it did, four 3-inch field guns, four 4.1-inch guns, four 4.1-inch howitzers, four 5.9-inch howitzers, three 8-inch howitzers, four 3-inch light trench mortars, four 6¾-inch medium trench mortars and thirty-one machine guns.

When the attack of the Royal Highlanders reached Croates Trench it was held up for forty-five minutes by a series of machine guns whose crews fought most stubbornly. In their efforts to overcome this resistance the men of the 13th were greatly handicapped by the lack of bombs. Rifle fire was ineffective and two tanks, which went forward in response to the Infantry's request for aid, were put out of commission as soon as they got astride the trench and before they could deal with its occupants. Eventually, two Stokes' guns were brought up and opened fire. After a few rounds from these had burst in the enemy position, a shirt, once white, appeared on the end of a rifle and the German garrison surrendered.

By 8 o'clock in the morning the assault of the 3rd Brigade had penetrated 5,000 yards into the German positions and had reached its objective, the so-called Green Line. Halting at this point in accordance with orders, the 13th Battalion consolidated and reformed its ranks, while the Infantry of the 2nd Canadian Brigade passed through to carry the attack on. Then, wonder of wonders, up from the rear in jingling array came squadron after squadron of British Cavalry.

Long before night had fallen it was clear that the Battle of Amiens had resulted in a great victory. At the close of the day's operations the troops engaged had completed an advance of between six and seven miles; ten thousand prisoners had been captured, nearly one hundred and fifty guns had been taken, while booty, consisting of vast stores of ammunition and supplies of all kinds, had fallen into the victors' hands.

"The brilliant and predominating part taken by the Canadian and Australian Corps in this battle," says Sir Douglas Haig, "is worthy of the highest commendation. The skill and determination of these troops proved irresistible and at all points met with rapid and complete success."

II

Meanwhile, the 13th Battalion in the Green Line was busily employed in evacuating its wounded and burying its dead. In both of these tasks the Battalion Chaplain, Capt. E. E. Graham, M.C., assisted the Tump Line Section with tireless energy.

Following a comparatively quiet night, the Battalion advanced at 9 a.m. to a position in Claude Wood, moving forward again in the afternoon to a wood east of Beaucourt-en-Santerre. At this point the Battalion found accommodation in a series of German huts, that occupied by Headquarters being a particularly elaborate

THE BATTLE OF AMIENS

affair, with stained glass windows, which the gentle Hun had undoubtedly looted from one of the neighbouring churches. At 9 p.m. the Battalion moved forward into close support of the 2nd Brigade, east of Warvillers Wood, reaching this position and digging in shortly before 3 o'clock in the morning.

August 10th was marked by heavy fighting on the part of the 3rd and 4th Canadian Divisions and on the part of the 32nd British Division, which had passed under the command of the Canadian Corps the previous night. Little effect of this fighting was felt by the 13th, which remained quietly in the position east of Warvillers Wood, resting and preparing for whatever further service might be required. A marvelous view of the 4th Division's attack was obtained by a small group of officers who mounted to the top of a 70-foot observation tower in the centre of the Wood, but this did not last long, for a low flying German plane spotted the group and drove them to earth with a few rounds from a machine gun.

August 11th also passed quietly, though in the afternoon a large number of enemy planes appeared and succeeded in bringing down a British observation balloon in flames, a stray machine gun bullet, presumably from this attack, wounding one of the Highlanders' signallers. At 9 p.m. the Battalion moved forward a short distance to a position where dugouts and shelters were occupied for the night.

Beautiful weather, which had marked the period from the opening of the battle, continued on the 12th. This day was comparatively uneventful for the Battalion, except for the fact that a draft was received, consisting of Lieuts. H. H. Chanter, W. T. Hornby, W. A. Ramsay, W. E. Dunning and H. G. Lawton, together with 118 other ranks. Lieuts. S. T. Barratt and H. H. Nobbs followed this draft on the 13th and 14th of the month respectively.

On August 13th Sir Arthur Currie issued a "Special Order," which read in part as follows:

"The first stage of the Battle of Amiens is over, and one of the most successful operations conducted by the Allied Armies since the war began is now a matter of history. The Canadian Corps has every right to feel more than proud of the part it played." On August 8th "the Canadian Corps—to which was attached the 3rd Cavalry Division, the 4th Tank Brigade, the 5th Squadron R.A.F.—attacked on a front of 7,500 yards. After a penetration of 22,000 yards the line to-night rests on a 10,000 yards frontage.

ROYAL HIGHLANDERS OF CANADA

Sixteen German Divisions have been identified, of which four have been completely routed. Nearly 150 guns have been captured, while over a thousand machine guns have fallen into our hands. Ten thousand prisoners have passed through our cages and casualty clearing stations, a number greatly in excess of our total casualties. . . . .

"From the depths of a very full heart I wish to thank all Staffs and Services—and to congratulate you all on the wonderful success achieved. Let us remember our gallant dead, whose spirit will ever be with us, inspiring us to nobler effort, and when the call again comes, be it soon or otherwise, I know the same measure of success will be yours."

On the 13th and 14th of the month the Royal Highlanders remained in their reserve position, deeply interested in all that went on around them and in the news from the fighting line, whence they awaited a call. At 3.30 p.m. on the 15th orders were received that the Battalion would proceed forward at night to relieve the Sister Unit, the 42nd Royal Highlanders of Canada, which, under the command of Lieut.-Col. R. L. H. Ewing, had been engaged in a dashing and highly successful, but costly, series of operations near Parvillers. Preparations for this relief were at once begun, the rear details, who previously had moved up to a position not far from that occupied by the Battalion proper, moving back to where the other rear details of the 3rd Brigade were stationed. At 9 p.m. the main section of the Battalion started forward. The march on this occasion was rendered extremely unpleasant by the appalling smell from scores of dead cavalry horses which lay scattered over the fields en route; also by the threat from enemy bombing planes, which were active over the whole area. No misfortune occurred, however, and relief of the 42nd was completed about midnight.

III

Having taken over the new sector, which lay about 1,000 yards north of Parvillers, the Royal Highlanders quickly familiarized themselves with their surroundings and prepared for all eventualities. Early on the morning of August 16th two French prisoners of war who had escaped from a German prison camp made their way into the Highlanders' lines. Food and drink were at once given to these men, who, after they had expressed their thanks

A Trophy. Amiens, August 8th, 1918.

Canadian Official, Copyright.

The Drocourt-Queant Line, September, 1918.

Canadian Official, Copyright.

THE BATTLE OF AMIENS

and appreciation, were forwarded to Brigade H.Q. Later in the morning the Battalion received a visit from Brig.-Gen. Tuxford, who was accompanied by Brig.-Gen. W. O. H. Dodds, of the Canadian Artillery. While these visitors were looking over the front and discussing questions of mutual interest with Lieut.-Col. McCuaig, General Tuxford was called to the telephone and informed that a German retirement on the Canadian front was considered possible on account of a successful attack which the French were even at the moment pushing against Roye. As a result of this information, General Tuxford ordered the Battalion to push out battle patrols against the village of la Chavatte, in an attempt to judge from the character of the opposition encountered whether the suggested German withdrawal was seriously contemplated.

Accordingly, after fifteen minutes' preliminary bombardment, two patrols of 30 men each, under Lieut. J. Kerry and Lieut. W. T. Hornby respectively, moved forward. Having progressed some distance, Lieut. Kerry halted his party and advanced up a communication trench with four companions, driving in a small German outpost en route. Heavy fire was then opened by the enemy, at least seven machine guns being in action at the same time, as well as a number of rifle grenadiers. The fact that the German line was held in considerable strength having been definitely established and several men having become casualties, Lieut. Kerry, who had been slightly wounded by a grenade, issued orders for the party to withdraw.

Adopting tactics similar to those employed by Kerry, Lieut. Hornby led his party to the outskirts of la Chavatte, where strong opposition was encountered and Hornby painfully, but not seriously, wounded in the head by an enemy machine gun. In face of this opposition it was quite useless to proceed and the patrol was accordingly withdrawn.

From 4.30 to 4.53 p.m. the village was subjected to heavy artillery fire, but patrols which reconnoitred immediately afterwards reported that the enemy was still holding the position in strength. Again at 7 p.m. the artillery opened up and fired till 7.30, but still the bombardment produced no weakening of the enemy's hold. About 9 p.m. Brigade reported that troops of the 2nd Canadian Division had advanced and were established in Posen Trench to the north of la Chavatte. Patrols from "D" Coy. checked this report, confirmation of which was duly sent to Brigade.

By this time it had become obvious that the enemy had no intention of retiring voluntarily from la Chavatte and that measures more strenuous than battle patrols would be required to make him do so. Accordingly, Lieut.-Col. McCuaig called a conference of his company commanders to arrange an attack. Disposition of the companies at this time was as follows: "D" Coy., under Major W. E. Macfarlane, M.C., held the left front, while "A" Coy., under Capt. D. B. Donald, held the right front. In support on the left was "C" Coy., commanded by Lieut. C. D. Llwyd, M.C., while "B" Coy,, with Lieut. J. B. Beddome in command, was in support on the right.

As a result of the conference arrangements were made for an enveloping operation to take place on the following day. Before dawn on the 17th "A" and "D" Companies went forward in accordance with these arrangements, the former up Sottises Alley, a communication trench which lay to the right of la Chavatte, and the latter up Peloponese Alley, a similar trench which lay to the left, "B" and "C" Companies immediately occupying the front line positions which "A" and "D" vacated. At 4.30 a.m. the attacking companies commenced to envelop la Chavatte from the south and north, each company at the same time sending one platoon up communication trenches to attack the position frontally. "D" Coy. pushed through la Chavatte Village from the north and continued its advance to a point in Sottises Alley, up which "A" Coy. was making its way. Here in a brilliant little operation, from which "D" Coy. emerged without a single casualty, three men of the 56th German R.I.R. were killed and about a dozen, together with several machine guns, captured.

Meanwhile, Lieut. O. B. Krenchel, with a party from "D" Coy. pushed up Rothard Alley, which ran past the village on the north and was in effect a continuation of Peloponese Alley, up which "D" Coy. had originally advanced. In the course of his move forward Lieut. Krenchel took two prisoners and established a strong post in Rothard Alley at a point previously selected. When this task was accomplished, he took forward a small patrol to reconnoitre Oberon Trench and a railway track, which crossed the line of the Highlanders' advance. This position he found to be strongly held.

THE BATTLE OF AMIENS

By this time the main bodies of "A" and "D" Companies had completed their enveloping operation and had effected a junction in Sottises Alley. Lieut.-Col. McCuaig then came up to look over the situation and distributed the platoons of "A" and "D" Companies to hold the ground captured in the strongest possible manner. After dark that same night "A" and "D" Companies dug in posts of sections at intervals from Sottises Alley on the right to the Divisional Boundary on the left, thus rendering the captured area safe from anything less than a counter attack in strength. In view of the neat success which had been achieved and of the fact that casualties had been held to a minimum, the Battalion had every reason to be content with the result of the day's operation.

Early on the following morning Lieut. W. T. Hornby took out a patrol and surprised a small German post, whose garrison promptly retired. Entering the post, Hornby secured three packs and brought them back to the Canadian lines, where, on examination of the contents, it was discovered that the owners belonged to the 2nd Jaeger Battalion, a fact which the Canadian Intelligence was glad to have confirmed.

The night of the 18th and early morning of the 19th were spent by the Royal Highlanders in connecting up and otherwise strengthening the series of posts established after the capture of la Chavatte. The enemy was quiet all night and the work, in consequence, made rapid progress. About 10.30 o'clock in the morning Lieut. H. H. Chanter advanced with a patrol up the continuation of Sottises Alley and drove off the garrison of a German post. Returning to this same spot at about 5 p.m., accompanied by Private Kamal Khan, a Gurkha, who by some queer turn of fate had enlisted in the Canadian Forces and been forwarded to the Royal Highlanders in a draft, Lieut. Chanter entered the post and discovered that the enemy had once more forgotten their packs. From three, which he and Kamal Khan brought back and which were forwarded at once to Brigade, identification of the 56th German R.I.R. was secured.

During the period under review the 13th Battalion was supported by the 5th Canadian Divisional Artillery, which had been formed in England some time previous to this, but which had never before the Battle of Amiens taken part as a unit in any great engagement. The Royal Highlanders have stated in their official records that the support received at this time was well up to the high standard which the work of the other Divisional Artilleries had led them to expect.

At 9.20 p.m. German shell fire became heavy in the forward area and observers at Battalion Headquarters reported that an S.O.S. had gone up on the front of the 4th Canadian Division to the left. Five minutes later an S.O.S. rose to the right, but, as telephone communication to the front line companies had been cut, it was not clear at Battalion Headquarters whether this had risen from a point in the 13th lines, or from the lines of the 16th Battalion on the flank. In any case no harm would be done by laying down a barrage, so Lieut.-Col. McCuaig called on the artillery for S.O.S. fire. After several minutes of this, he requested the guns to drop to "slow," until the exact situation could be ascertained. At 9.53 p.m. runners from the two front line companies reported that the affair seemed to have no particular significance and that nothing in the nature of an attack was developing on their respective fronts, although a few casualties had occurred from the shelling. Judging from this that support was not needed, the Colonel, at 9.55 p.m., requested the artillery to "cease fire." Early on the morning of the 20th a deserter from the 56th German R.I.R. made his way into the Highlanders' line. On being questioned, this individual stated that his Regiment had planned to raid the front line on the previous night, but that enthusiasm for the project had waned when the Germans saw the promptness and heard the crash of the Canadian S.O.S. barrage.

During the whole tour the enemy kept dropping an occasional gas shell into the Highlanders' area, increasing the number at night. As no gas proof dugouts were available and as it was impossible to wear helmets at all times, this caused great inconvenience to all ranks and gas casualties mounted to a total of nearly 40, amongst those who suffered being Lieuts. J. E. Christie, J. S. Buchanan, and L. C. Drummond. Not including these, battle casualties incurred between the 8th and 21st of August totalled 275 all ranks, 56 of these being killed, 217 wounded and 2 missing.

Patrols were out again on the morning of August 21st, checking up the situation on the front in preparation for a relief. At dusk the 4th Canadian Division on the left took over a section of the 13th front and when this movement was complete, the 112th Regiment of French Infantry relieved the Royal Highlanders, who moved back to bivouacs in an orchard near Beaufort. Consid-

THE BATTLE OF AMIENS

erable significance attached to the fact that the French were taking over the area, as it indicated to thoughtful observers that the Canadian Corps was being withdrawn and was probably off on another high adventure. Where, or when, this would take place, no one knew. All that seemed certain was that the Corps, flushed with victory and at the top of its form, would not wait long for an opportunity to test its mettle again.

CHAPTER XX

The Second Battles of Arras, 1918

> But hark! a heavy sound breaks in once more,
> As if the clouds its echoes would repeat:
> And nearer, clearer, deadlier than before,
> Arm! Arm! it is—it is—the cannon's opening roar.
> —BYRON.

I

WHEN the Canadian Corps was withdrawn from the scene of its triumph at Amiens, the task placed before it was nothing less than the smashing of the immensely strong Hindenburg line in front of Arras. On August 22nd the plan was communicated to Sir Arthur Currie, who describes it, in outline, as follows:—

"The Canadian Corps, on the right of the First Army, was to attack eastwards astride the Arras-Cambrai Road, and by forcing its way through the Drocourt-Quéant Line south of the Scarpe to break the hinge of the Hindenburg System and prevent the possibility of the enemy rallying behind this powerfully organized defended area."

"The four main systems of defence," continues the Corps Commander, "consisted of the following lines:—

(1) The old German front line system east of Monchy-le-Preux.
(2) The Fresnes-Rouvroy Line.
(3) The Drocourt-Quéant Line.
(4) The Canal du Nord Line.

"These, with their subsidiary switches and strong points, as well as the less organized but by no means weak intermediate lines of trenches, made the series of positions to be attacked without doubt one of the strongest defensively on the Western Front."

Little time could be given to Sir Arthur Currie to prepare for this vast operation, which it was obvious would involve sustained fighting such as even the Corps, with all its proud record, had never up to this time encountered. Three days only he had, but much was accomplished in that short time and it was with every

THE SECOND BATTLES OF ARRAS, 1918

hope of success that the 2nd and 3rd Canadian Divisions opened the battle on the morning of August 26th. Nor was this hope of success denied realization, for by night, as the result of dour fighting, Monchy-le-Preux, Guémappe, Wancourt Tower and the top of Héninel Ridge were in Canadian hands. Renewing the attack at 4.55 a.m. on August 27th, the 2nd and 3rd Divisions pushed doggedly forward, the former capturing Chérisy and crossing the Sensée River, while the latter captured the Bois du Vert and the Bois du Sart and drove its assault to the outskirts of Haucourt, Remy, Boiry Notre-Dame and Pelves. It was during the bitter fighting on this and the following day that Lieut.-Col. W. H. Clark-Kennedy, an original officer of the 13th Battalion and at the time Commanding Officer of the 24th Battalion, Victoria Rifles of Canada, led his unit with a display of personal bravery that aroused the admiration of all who witnessed it and won a well deserved V.C.

It had been intended to withdraw the 2nd and 3rd Canadian Divisions after the fighting of the 27th and to renew the assault on the 28th with the 1st Canadian and the attached 4th British Division, but this was found impossible and the divisions in the line were ordered to "carry on." Accordingly the 3rd Division drove forward once more, capturing Boiry and Pelves before being relieved at midnight by the 4th British Division. Meanwhile the 2nd Division also attacked, but encountered opposition of the very strongest character and made but limited progress. Casualties were very heavy, particularly in the 5th Brigade, which in two days fighting lost over 100 officers and 2,500 men. In the 22nd French-Canadian Battalion, every officer engaged was killed or wounded, while in several other battalions casualties were almost as heavy. At night the 2nd Division was relieved by the 1st Canadian Division.

II

With the entry of the 1st Canadian Division into the Second Battles of Arras, 1918, it seems fitting to turn back a few days to follow the fortunes of the 13th Battalion which, at the end of the previous chapter, had just concluded its part in the Battle of Amiens.

After relief by the French, the Royal Highlanders marched back, as previously mentioned, and spent the night of August 21st in bivouacs in an orchard near Beaufort. On August 22nd the whole trench strength of the Battalion bathed at Beaufort and le Quesnel and removed the sweat and grime of the long tour in the line. At 9.05 p.m. the companies left their bivouacs and marched steadily, through Beaucourt-en-Santerre, where they narrowly missed a bombing attack; through Demuin, where the moonlight emphasized the pitiful aspect of stark rafters and shell torn walls; and on to Morgemont Wood, where the men found shelter for the night, some under derelict tanks, some actually inside these monsters, but the majority on bare ground in the shadow of the trees.

Following a day of rest and comparative idleness, the Battalion paraded at 8.30 p.m. and marched back in battle order to comfortable billets in the rue Victor Hugo, in Boves. Here another quiet day was spent, many of the men enjoying a bathe in one or other of the various pools just outside the town.

"D" Coy., acting as an entraining party for the Battalion, moved off to Saleux at 7.30 a.m. on August 25th, the Transport following at midnight and the Battalion proper at 3 o'clock on the morning of the 26th. At the very moment when the Royal Highlanders marched from Boves, far away to the north the 2nd and 3rd Canadian Divisions were plunging across No Man's Land in the opening engagement of the Second Battles of Arras.

Breakfast was waiting for the men of the 13th when they completed the eight mile march to Saleux Station and dinner was also eaten at this spot. Shortly after dinner the men entrained and at 1 p.m. the train moved off to Aubigny, whence busses conveyed the men to Dainville. From this point the Battalion marched to Achicourt, reaching its destination at about 2.30 a.m. on the 27th.

After a few hours sleep preparations were made to move at noon, but these orders were cancelled at the last minute and the men spent the afternoon in preparing comfortable sleeping quarters for the night. Alas! this work was useless for, in obedience to later orders, the Battalion marched at 7.30 p.m. to a position in the Neuville Vitasse area. Here a quiet day was spent and at night the Battalion moved forward to relieve elements of the gallant 5th and 6th Brigades in the front line, the rear details, under Major Sinclair, also moving forward and occupying old trenches and dugouts near Beaurains.

On August 29th Major-General A. C. Macdonell, commanding the 1st Canadian Division, was informed of the plans of the Army Commander for an assault on the Drocourt-Quéant Line. This

THE SECOND BATTLES OF ARRAS, 1918

extensive operation was to have taken place on the morning of September 1st, but at the last moment plans had to be changed and zero hour postponed till the early morning of September 2nd. Meanwhile, in preparation for the great attack, minor assaults, involving severe fighting, had to be carried out at various points on the Corps front, to straighten the line and provide satisfactory jumping off positions. On the front of the 1st Canadian Division, these operations were entrusted for the most part to the 1st Brigade, with elements of the 2nd Brigade also involved. Reliable as always, these fine troops accomplished the tasks allotted to them, in spite of the fact that the Germans, alarmed by the way the attacks were uncovering vital defences, fought bitterly and threw into the fray a considerable number of reserves.

With "A" and "D" Companies in the front line and "B" and "C" in close support, the 13th Battalion spent the 29th of August in definitely locating the line held and in consolidating the area. Four other ranks were killed by shell-fire during the day and seven wounded. The Battalion Medical Officer, Capt. H. A. Cochrane, was also wounded, but remained on duty, while Major E. E. Graham, M.C., the Battalion Chaplain, together with his batman, gave a splendid exhibition of courage and devotion by carrying to the Regimental Aid Post, under heavy fire, a number of men of the 22nd Battalion who had been wounded in the fighting of the previous day.

Following the operations of the 1st Canadian Infantry Brigade on August 30th, reconnoitring parties of the 13th Battalion went forward and examined the ground captured. Later "A" and "D" Companies moved up into the captured area, with "B" and "C" also advancing in support. Capt. D. B. Donald was wounded on this date.

Further adjustment in the disposition of the companies took place on August 31st. Then, at 4.50 a.m. on September 1st, the 14th Royal Montreal Regiment and the 15th (48th Highlanders), Toronto, in conjunction with units of the 171st British Brigade on the right and the 2nd Canadian Brigade on the left, advanced the line of the 3rd Canadian Brigade, completing preparations for the assault on the Drocourt-Quéant Line. During the advance of the 14th and 15th Battalions on September 1st, the 13th and 16th Battalions followed in close support.

Late on the afternoon of September 1st, details of the attack which was to take place on the following morning were explained to the 13th company commanders. Unfortunately, no means could be found of giving the men anything but the scantiest outline of the plan, as they were scattered in shell holes and dugouts and no assembly was possible. Even the officers were forced to study the plan hastily, as maps did not arrive till after dark, nor final orders till 11 p.m. In spite of these grave drawbacks, the spirits of the men, who had been living on cold food and in most uncomfortable surroundings for four days, rose splendidly at news of the assault and it was a confident Battalion that awaited the word to go "over."

In outline, the plan of attack was as follows:—

The 1st Canadian Division was to attack on a two brigade frontage, the 2nd Brigade on the left and the 3rd Brigade on the right, with the 1st Brigade in Divisional Reserve. To the right of the 3rd Brigade was the 57th (West Lancs) T. Division. The 3rd Brigade was to attack on a front of two battalions with the 16th Canadian Scottish on the right and the 13th Battalion, Royal Highlanders of Canada, on the left. The 14th and 15th Battalions were to follow in support. When the 13th on its front had smashed the Drocourt-Quéant Line and had reached the Drocourt-Quéant Support, the 14th Battalion was to "leap-frog" the 13th and drive the attack through the village of Cagnicourt and against the Buissy Switch Line, the 13th following in close support and mopping up where necessary. "A" and "D" Companies, under the command of Lieut. W. D. C. Christie and Major W. E. Macfarlane, M.C., respectively, were selected to lead the assault of the 13th with "B" and "C" Companies following immediately behind.

Late on the night of September 1st, the companies moved up into their jumping off positions. There was little shelling on this occasion and the night was clear, consequently assembly was reported complete at 2 a.m. on September 2nd.

Three hours later the blast of the rolling barrage struck the German trenches and in its wake the companies of the Royal Highlanders moved forward. As was so often the case, casualties in the first few minutes of the attack were light. The German barrage was slow in falling and little machine gun fire was encountered in the front line, accordingly this obstacle was speedily surmounted and the attacking waves pushed on towards the support line. On approaching this position, which was the Battalion's

THE SECOND BATTLES OF ARRAS, 1918

first objective, Major Macfarlane took advantage of the shelter provided by a small ridge to line up his company for the charge, he himself leading the assault and bayoneting three of the enemy who contested his advance. At 7.10 a.m. he sent up three white flares as a signal that the trench was definitely in his possession. Simultaneously Lieut. Christie on the right led his company into the first objective.

Casualties in the 13th up to this time had been surprisingly light. "D" Coy. had suffered only ten and the other companies had also escaped easily, in spite of the fact that they had captured and sent to the rear some hundreds of German prisoners. This state of affairs was quite too good to last and soon machine gun fire from the front and right flank began to cause sharp losses.

At this stage of the battle, while the 13th was waiting in the German reserve line for the 14th Battalion to "leap-frog," a battalion of the Royal Munster Fusiliers was discovered to have missed direction and to have penetrated over 1,000 yards across the Canadian frontage. This unit, which had lost heavily, was uncertain as to its whereabouts, but Lieut.-Col. McCuaig redirected it towards its objective on the exposed right flank.

At 8 a.m. the 14th Battalion passed through the Royal Highlanders and advanced against the village of Cagnicourt, followed closely by the companies of the 13th. This stage of the advance was hotly contested and both battalions suffered severely. Machine gun fire was very heavy, especially from the neighbourhood of Villers lez Cagnicourt on the left and from points on the right flank. In addition, a battery of German field guns was firing at point blank range on the left front, while shells were also crashing into the advance from the right flank.

Heavy casualties amongst officers of the 13th and 14th as a result of this shelling and enfilade fire brought about some confusion. Accordingly, Lieut.-Col. Worrall, of the 14th, went forward to see for himself just how the situation lay. Lieut.-Col. McCuaig also went forward and, meeting Worrall, who was making his way back, the two established joint headquarters at a point somewhat to the left of Cagnicourt Village. Orders were then forwarded to the men of the 13th to "stand fast" until the situation could be cleared. At the time these orders were received "D" Coy. was in captured gun pits and trenches northeast of the village, while the remaining three companies had advanced some

ROYAL HIGHLANDERS OF CANADA

1200 yards further and were extended between the Bois de Loison and the Bois de Bouche.

About 3 p.m. orders were received for the attack to be pushed against the Buissy Switch Line. Accordingly, the troops moved forward between the woods and drove their assault up a long communication trench, known as Queer Street. Heavy fire was encountered during this move and eventually the attack was brought to a standstill, but fresh troops took over the assault and carried the operation to a successful conclusion.

When the Highlanders were relieved by troops of the 1st Brigade, they moved back to a position in the Drocourt-Quéant support line, arriving at 3 o'clock on the morning of September 3rd. Here the men rested for a few hours and then undertook the work of strengthening the position in case of counter attack. Previous to this, attention had been given to the evacuation of the wounded and burial of the dead.

In the support position the Battalion had its first opportunity to check the result of the previous day's operations. On the debit side of the account was a casualty list of approximately 230. Lieut. O. B. Krenchel had been killed, together with 32 other ranks, while Major W. E. Macfarlane, M.C., Lieuts. W. D. C. Christie, J. B. Beddome, H. Newman, H. H. Chanter, I. L. Ibbotson, S. T. Barratt, H. G. Lawton and approximately 150 other ranks had been wounded. Of the officers who appeared on this list, Major Macfarlane and Lieut. Chanter had each suffered wounds on three previous occasions.

While the loss of so many experienced officers and men was serious, the other side of the account presented an appearance satisfactory in a high degree. Above all else the Drocourt-Quéant Line had been broken utterly, and approaches gained for an attack on the Canal du Nord. Thus the Canadian Corps, assisted by the splendid 4th British Division, was the first of the Allied Armies to breach the supposedly impregnable Hindenburg system of defence which, once broken, crumbled rapidly before the hammer strokes subsequently launched against it.

While all the advantages of the victory were not clear to the Royal Highlanders on the morning of September 3rd, every moment emphasized the extent of the German rout on their particular front. Far exceeding the 230 casualties in the 13th was the number of prisoners the Battalion had captured. No exact count

THE SECOND BATTLES OF ARRAS, 1918

of these had been kept, for as fast as they were gathered in the Battalion had bundled them off to the rear, but it was certain that their number exceeded 750 and probably approached 1,000. In addition to prisoners, the 13th had captured twelve 77 mm. field guns, as well as a large number of machine guns and a considerable quantity of enemy stores. With regard to the prisoners it is of interest to note that some of these, according to their own statements, were peacefully sleeping 45 kilometres behind their line when the battle opened. They were rushed forward in all manner of conveyances, thrown into the battle in a desperate effort to stop the Canadian advance, and found themselves prisoners and on the way to the Canadian rear before the sun crossed the meridian.

After two fairly quiet days in the Drocourt-Quéant support position, the Royal Highlanders marched back to a point near Chérisy on the afternoon of September 4th and proceeded thence by bus to Dainville, where they remained for a fortnight. The two weeks at Dainville were devoted to routine training, training of all specialists, such as Signallers, Machine Gunners, Rifle Grenadiers, Tump Line Section, Intelligence Section and Stretcher Bearers, and also to refitting and preparing for the next tour in the line. Several drafts of officers and men were taken on strength and distributed to the various companies in proportion to the casualties suffered in the recent engagements.

Of great interest to all ranks was a series of lists announcing the award of honours and decorations gained by officers and men during the operations at Hangard Wood on August 8th. Heading one of these lists, to the great satisfaction of the whole Battalion, was the name of Lieut.-Col. G. E. McCuaig, C.M.G., D.S.O., who received a Bar to his D.S.O. Next on this same list came Lieut. W. D. C. Christie, who was awarded the D.S.O. Christie had been wounded in the more recent Battle of Arras, and was at this time fighting gamely for his life in hospital. It was with regret that the Highlanders heard on September 17th that the odds had proved too strong and that this brave officer had succumbed to his injuries. In addition to the honours to Lieut.-Col. McCuaig and Lieut. Christie, it was announced that the Military Cross had been awarded to Capt. R. L. Calder, Capt. H. A. Johnston, and to Lieuts. M. L. Brady, K. G. Blackader, J. Lothian and L. C. Drummond, while the Distinguished Conduct Medal had been granted to eleven other ranks and the Military Medal to forty-three, amongst these last being Sergt. L. G. Woodward, of "D" Coy., who had previously won the D.C.M. A Bar to the Military Medal was awarded to Corp. W. Hamilton, of "A" Coy.

On September 12th the Battalion received a visit from Sir Arthur Currie, who was accompanied by Brig.-Gen. G. S. Tuxford. Both these expressed themselves as satisfied with what they saw of the Highlanders' training and congratulated the unit on its general bearing during the march past. Two days later Lieut.-Col. G. E. McCuaig, C.M.G., D.S.O., left the 13th Battalion to assume command of the 4th Canadian Infantry Brigade. While all ranks were pleased to see the Colonel receive such well deserved promotion, they realized with regret that the honour, of necessity, meant the severance of his connection with the Battalion which he had served so long and faithfully and led so well. On his departure, command of the unit was assumed by Major I. M. R. Sinclair, M.C., an officer who had joined the Battalion in Canada and whose record since that time gave assurance that the chain of distinguished leadership which the Royal Highlanders had enjoyed from the beginning was not now to be broken.

CHAPTER XXI

The Canal du Nord

The roll of honour stretched from sea to sea,
The loyal lands that bred them—
The gallant souls that led them—
The deaths they died that Britons might be free.
—*From St. James' Budget.*

I

DURING the month of September, 1918, the Allied Armies delivered blow after blow against the combined forces of Germany, Austria, Bulgaria and Turkey, increasing these in force as the enemy showed signs of cracking under the strain and as victory, without another weary winter of trench warfare, became a distinct possibility. Simultaneously with the victory of the Canadian Corps at Arras, British and Australian troops swept across the old battlefields of the Somme, wresting Bapaume and Péronne from the German grasp and capturing thousands of prisoners. By the middle of the month the British were close to St. Quentin, while the French had driven their assault to the outskirts of la Fère. Further to the east the American Army had wiped out the St. Mihiel Salient and restored 150 square miles of French territory, held by the Boche since 1914.

Farther afield, too, it appeared as if the various campaigns were approaching a climax. In Palestine General Allenby had captured Nazareth and driven forward to a great victory over the Turks, of whom 40,000 had been captured and many thousands killed or wounded. Later in the month Bulgaria was routed by an Allied Army, which included troops from Britain, France, Serbia, Italy and Greece, and was thus the first of the Central Powers to be "counted out."

In his account of the position of affairs on the Western Front early in the month, Sir Douglas Haig states:

"The details of the strategic plan—were the subject of careful discussion between Marshal Foch and myself. Preparations were already far advanced for the successful attack by which the First

ROYAL HIGHLANDERS OF CANADA

American Army, assisted by certain French Divisions, drove the enemy from the St. Mihiel Salient—"

"Ultimately it was decided that as soon as possible after this attack, four convergent and simultaneous offensives should be launched by the Allies as follows:—

"By the Americans west of Meziéres.

"By the French west of Argonne, in close co-operation with the American attack and with the same general objectives.

"By the British on the St. Quentin-Cambrai front in the general direction of Maubeuge.

"By the Belgian and Allied forces in Flanders in the direction of Ghent.

"The results to be obtained from these different attacks depended in a peculiarly large degree upon the British attack in the centre. It was there that the enemy's defences were most highly organized. If these were broken, the threat directed at his vital systems of lateral communications would of necessity react upon his defences elsewhere."

On September 15th Sir Arthur Currie received the details of the large operations by the Third and Fourth British Armies, in which the Canadian Corps was to co-operate by crossing the Canal du Nord and capturing Bourlon Wood and the high ground to the northeast of it, to protect the left flank of the attack. The 11th British Division and the 7th Tank Battalion were to be attached to the Corps for the occasion.

"This attack," says Sir Arthur, "was fraught with difficulties. On the Corps battle front of 6,400 yards the Canal du Nord was impassable on the northern 3,800 yards. The Corps had, therefore, to cross the Canal du Nord on a front of 2,600 yards and to expand fanwise—to a front exceeding 15,000 yards. This intricate manœuvre called for most skilful leadership on the part of commanders, and the highest state of discipline on the part of the troops.

"The assembly of the attacking troops in an extremely congested area, known by the enemy to be the only one available, was very dangerous," but "careful arrangements were made by the counter battery staff officer to bring to bear a specially heavy neutralizing fire on hostile batteries at any moment during the crucial period of preparation. These arrangements were to be

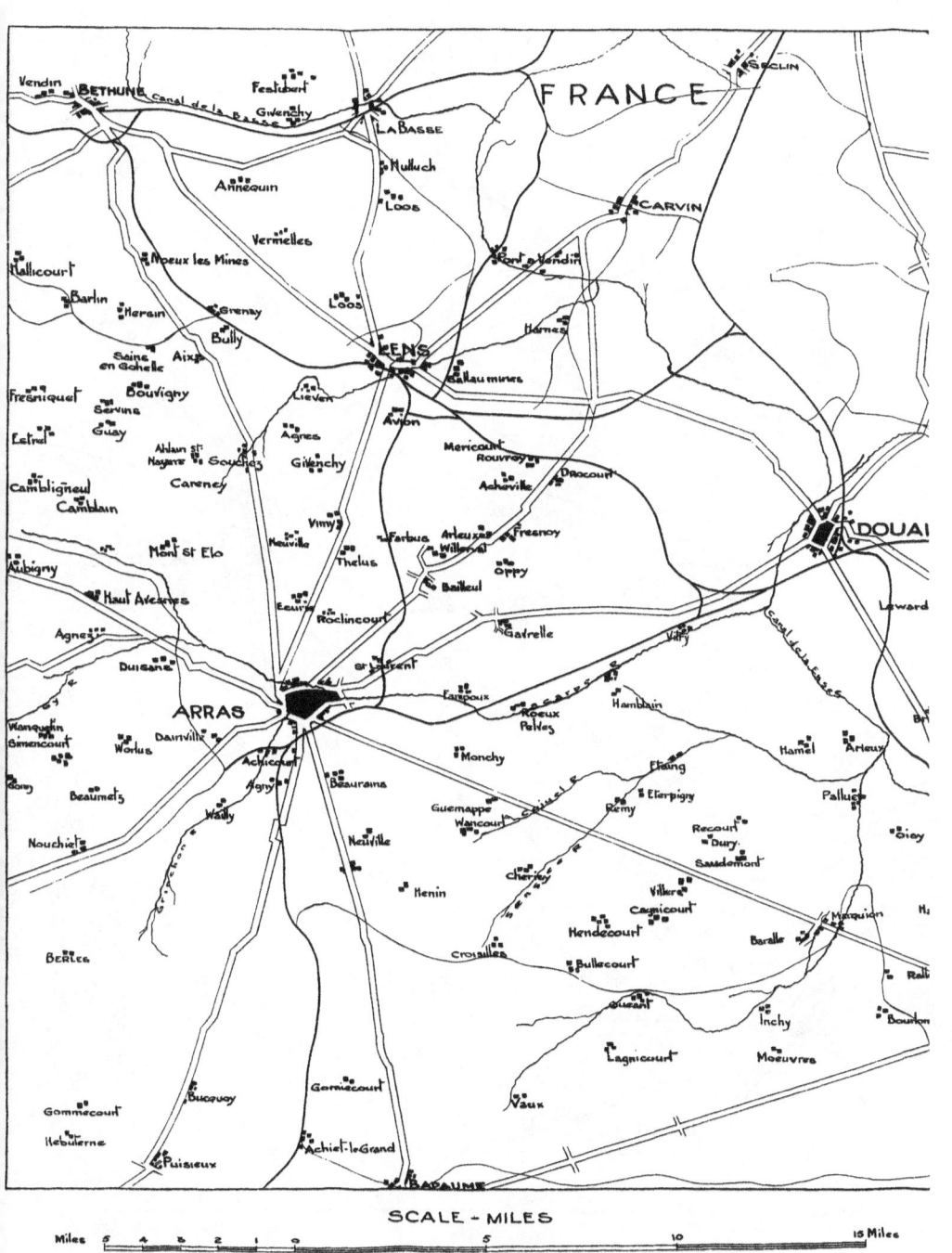

ARRAS AND CAMBRAI

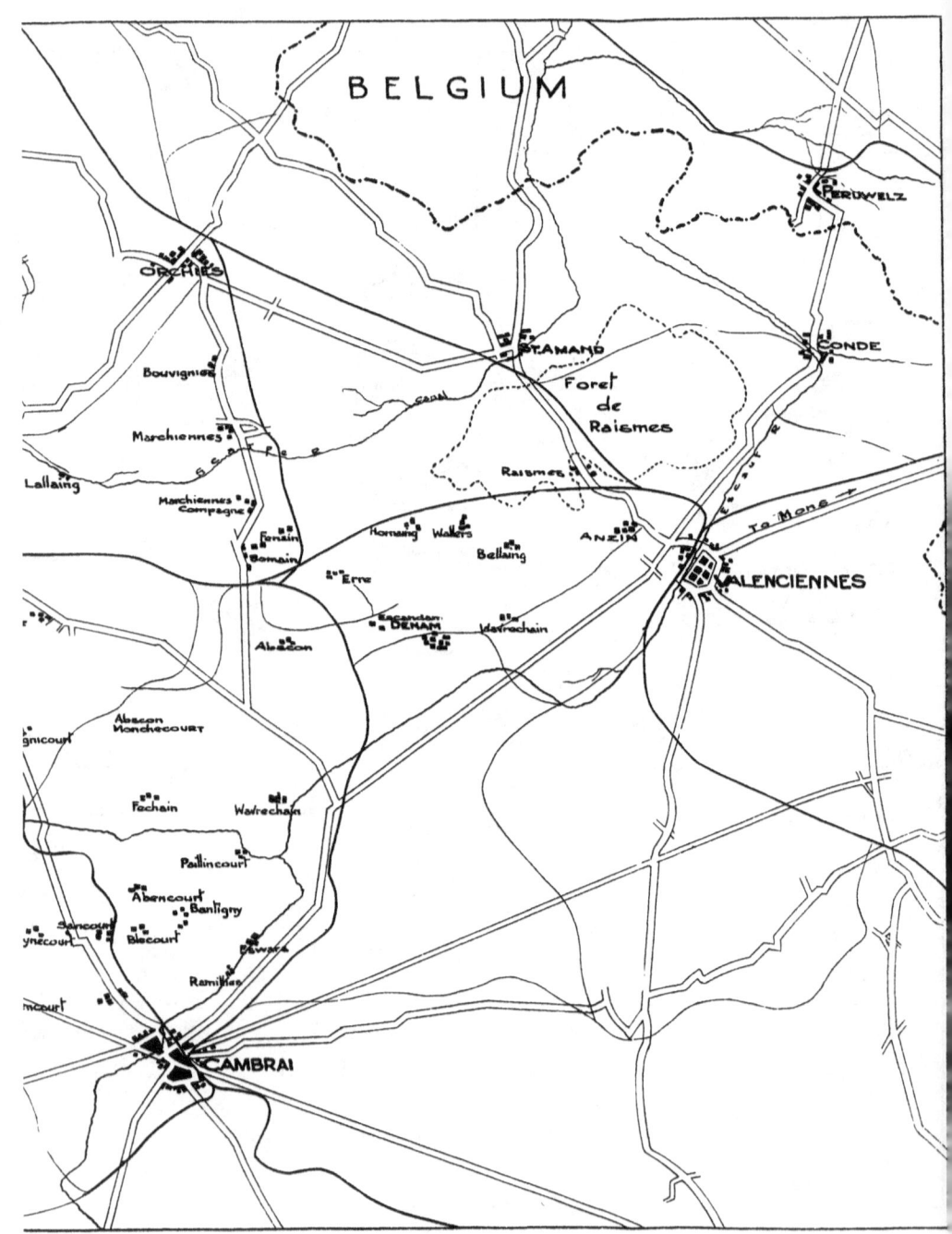

THE CANAL DU NORD

put into effect, in any case, at "zero" hour, to neutralize the hostile defensive barrage on the front of the attack.

"With the exception of the 2nd Canadian Division, which—would be in Corps Reserve at the time of attack, every resource of the Canadians was to be crowded in that narrow space."

Sir Julian Byng, the former Corps Commander and at this time Commander of the Third British Army, is reported to have visited Corps Headquarters to discuss the attack on the Canal and to have stated, when informed of the plan, that it was feasible in his opinion, but was the most difficult manœuvre attempted by any troops since the great offensive began.

II

On September 19th the companies of the 13th marched from Dainville to Tilloy. From this point Major Sinclair, accompanied by the Intelligence Officer, went forward on the 20th to reconnoitre the Buissy area and to select suitable assembly positions for the Canal du Nord attack. Further reconnaissances were made on the 21st and on this same date the strength of the Battalion was increased by the arrival of a draft of men, under the command of Lieuts. S. H. Browning, F. L. Hayden, E. Mather, L. E. Wells and R. A. C. Young.

On the following day, Sunday, a drumhead Church Service was conducted by Major Graham for the main body of the Battalion, the Roman Catholics parading separately, under the command of Lieut. Reaume. Reconnoitring parties went forward on Sunday afternoon and again on the following day, which was devoted by the main section of the unit to company training, bombing instruction and musketry practice. On this same date information was received by wire that "His Majesty the King has awarded the Victoria Cross to Corp. H. J. Good and to the late Private J. B. Croak," these awards having been won in the Hangard Wood operation already described. The deep gratification of the Battalion in this signal honour was marred only by regret that Private Croak had not lived to enjoy the reward so bravely earned.

The morning of September 24th was spent by the Battalion in preparations for a move to the forward area. While these were in progress several enemy planes flew high over the district and dropped leaflets with propaganda for peace. A few of these were recovered by the Highlanders and created a deep impression, in-

ROYAL HIGHLANDERS OF CANADA

asmuch as they convinced the men that Germany was weakening and that consequently their great sacrifices in the recent battles had not been made in vain.

At 2.50 p.m. orders for the move to the forward area were issued. In accordance with these the Transport divided into two sections, the first marching almost at once with the men's packs, while the second section, including the cook kitchens, remained till the men had had their evening meal.

The Battalion proper paraded at 6 p.m. and marched to Arras Station. Here a tiresome wait ensued, no pleasure being added to this by German aeroplanes which circled high over the town, dropping brilliant flares. These floated down most beautifully and were followed by heavy bombs whenever the enemy saw, or thought he saw, a suitable target. Several bombs burst in the neighbourhood of the station, but no direct hits were scored and, so far as the 13th was concerned, no damage done. At last a string of box cars appeared on the scene and Capt. Conroy, who was in charge of the entraining, soon had the men distributed. Box car traveling is never a luxurious business and this occasion provided no exception to the general rule. However, the move was made in safety and early on the morning of September 25th the men, supervised by Lieut. C. D. Craig, tumbled out of their cramped quarters and moved into dugouts and shelters in the Drocourt-Quéant Line. Here the Battalion remained all day, moving forward in full battle order at 8.40 p.m. to relieve elements of the 18th Canadian Battalion in the Buissy Switch Line. The rear details of the 13th were for this occasion placed under the command of Capt. R. E. Heaslip.

Previous to the move into the jumping off line, Operation Order No. 203 had been issued, with details of the task the Battalion was to perform. In outline this order stated that:—

(1) On a date and at a time to be notified later the 3rd Canadian Infantry Brigade will attack across the Canal du Nord, as part of an operation by the Canadian Corps. The Corps attack will be to form a defensive flank, facing northeast, to protect a major attack by the Third and Fourth Armies. The 3rd Brigade will attack on a one battalion (14th Royal Montreal Regiment) front. The 13th R.H.C. will in turn attack (north and east) through the 14th, and the 15th Battalion (48th Highlanders) and the 2nd Canadian Infantry Brigade will leap-frog the 13th Bat-

THE CANAL DU NORD

talion, attacking north and northeast respectively. The 16th Battalion (Canadian Scottish) will be in Brigade Reserve.

(2) Assembly:—On zero-minus-one-night, the 13th Battalion will move up behind the 14th and assemble for the attack in positions to be prepared. "B" Coy. will lead and the others will follow in order "C"-"D"-"A."

(3) Move:—At zero hour the 14th Battalion will attack across the Canal on a 500 yard front immediately south of Lock No. 3. As they advance the 13th Battalion will follow close behind on a one company front. Companies will be on a two platoon front, with sections of half platoons in file.

(4) Leap-Frog:—The 13th Battalion will take up the attack through the 14th Battalion on the Red Line.

(5) Barrage:—A barrage map will be issued separately, but the general idea is as follows:—

General rate of progress—5 minutes per hundred yards. Barrage halts—45 minutes at Red Line and 30 minutes at Green Line. A standing barrage will be held on the eastern outskirts of Sains until the Red Line is captured.

(6) "B" Coy., which will move quickly across the Canal, will then get into attack formation and follow close behind the 14th Battalion. On the 14th capturing the Red Line, "B" Coy. will prepare to pass through the Red Line, following behind the barrage and attacking to the Green Line—making good all ground between the right boundary and the light railway on the left. On this being done the O.C. Coy. will put up a signal of three white Very lights. The exact Green Line must be held by each company by a line of posts, though the main line of consolidation may be placed to the rear of this at the O.C. Coy's. discretion. "C" Coy., keeping in touch with "B" Coy., will pass through "B" Coy's. left flank and attack due north behind the barrage, establishing the Green Line on their right flank and front. On completion of the capture of its area, "C" Coy. will also put up a signal of three white Very lights. "D" Coy. (plus No. 1 Platoon of "A" Coy.), following close on "C" Coy's. left rear in order not to lose the barrage, will attack the town of Marquion from the southeast. They will attack through the town to the Green Line. No. 1 Platoon will follow close in and will be responsible for mopping up all the town to the south of the Arras-Cambrai Road. On this being completed No. 1 Platoon will be withdrawn to its own Com-

pany area. Signal for "Operation complete" will again be three white Very lights.

"A" Coy.:—The remaining three platoons of the Coy. will follow up "D" Coy. to the area just west of Chapel Corner, where two platoons and Company Headquarters will take cover from shell fire and act as Battalion Reserve. The third platoon will at once move eastward, through Keith Wood towards the Canal, dealing with any possible trouble in that area, will sweep north to the Arras-Cambrai Road and will then rejoin its Company.

Many further details were dealt with in Operation Order No. 203, but sufficient has been quoted to make clear the difficult nature of the task which the Royal Highlanders had before them. In effect their attack, from the moment they crossed the Canal behind the 14th Battalion, was to spread like a fan, a most complicated manœuvre and one wherein certain of the troops found themselves attacking towards the Canal from what they had been wont to consider the German side.

At 4 a.m. on September 27th the Battalion assembled for the attack in the meadows to the S.W. of Paviland Wood, without interference. 5.20 a.m. was "zero" and as this hour approached things became unusually still. Just to the rear of "C" Coy. was a battery of field guns, so close that every word of the commands that prepared the guns for action was clearly audible. Suddenly came the shrill blast of a whistle, followed by the sharp command, "Fire No. 1 Gun!" The Battle of the Canal du Nord had begun.

III

Immediately in front of the position from which the Royal Highlanders started their advance was a stream, some three to five feet deep and fifteen to twenty feet across. This was to have been bridged previous to the attack, but time had not permitted, so, with their kilts floating the men waded through, encouraged by a lively tune played by Piper G. B. Macpherson. Shell and machine gun fire was brisk at this point and several casualties occurred before the obstacle was negotiated.

Little difficulty was encountered in crossing the Canal itself, which was quite dry, but once the far bank was reached machine gun fire became severe and reorganizations had to be hurriedly carried out in consequence. Even with the delay cut to a minimum,

THE CANAL DU NORD

the Battalion suffered considerably during the halt, amongst the casualties being several tried and experienced N.C.O.'s.

Meanwhile, the 14th Battalion had pushed its attack forward and was at all points in possession of the Red Line. In moving up to take over the assault, the Highlanders encountered certain difficulties. Chief among these were broad belts of wire which at some points forced the men into narrow lanes, where progress was advisable only in single file and at the double. By adopting this method of advance casualties were kept down, though from the multitude of sparks caused by machine gun bullets striking the strands of wire it appeared as if heavy losses were a certainty. Once clear of the wire, little difficulty was encountered in advancing to the Red Line, though machine gun and shrapnel fire continued to be troublesome and caused several casualties, amongst these being Company Sergt.-Major Kelly, of "C" Coy., badly wounded.

As was so often the case, the pause at the first objective resulted in numerous casualties and gave the enemy an opportunity to reorganize. Opposition was consequently stiff when the time came for the 13th to resume the attack. As arranged in advance, "B" Coy., under Capt. H. A. Johnston, M.C., led the renewed assault, attacking due east and driving forward in the face of obstinate resistance. At one point Lieut. Reaume, who was accompanied at the moment by a party of only a half dozen men, encountered several large groups of the enemy, who, having fought well as long as it was a matter of machine guns, surrendered when the Canadians approached to close quarters. In all, the prisoners captured by this officer and his men totalled over 70. After an advance of a mile, the Company reached its objective in the Green Line and promptly consolidated.

Attacking due north from "B" Coy's left flank, "C" Coy., under command of Capt. R. M. Hebden, encountered opposition almost from the beginning, shell fire from the direction of Bourlon Wood striking the Company in the flank and rear and machine gun fire from the direction of Marquion causing serious losses. Amongst the first to fall was Lieut. W. A. Ramsay, who was knocked unconscious by a 5.9 inch shell, which burst a few feet in advance of his platoon. Shortly after this Lieut. K. R. Townsend was hit in the arm by machine gun fire and simultaneously a number of N.C.O.'s and men also fell. By this time the barrage had got ahead of the troops, who were having a very hard time, struggling forward through a vast amount of uncut wire, while to add to the seriousness of the situation a masked battery of field guns was firing point blank from a spot some 250 yards forward on the right flank.

Casualties continued, and the attacking strength of the Company was further reduced by the disorganization consequent on men getting separated from their platoons while making their way through the wire. Accordingly Capt. Hebden sent a runner to Battalion Headquarters stating that his advance was in danger of being brought to a standstill and asking for reinforcements. No reply to this message was received and Hebden realized that the runner had not got through, or that no reinforcements were available. Accordingly he prepared to carry out the operation as originally planned. In this attempt, which involved an advance across open ground towards Marquion, Lieut. G. H. Hamilton was fatally wounded and Sergt. Hannaford also became a casualty. This left the Company without any of its platoon commanders, and apparently a lance-corporal was the senior N.C.O. unwounded. With this depleted force progress to the final objective became impossible and the advance was accordingly halted.

Meanwhile, "D" Coy., which had followed close to "C" Coy's. left rear, was driving its assault in a northerly direction against the village of Marquion. As in the case of "C" Coy., great belts of barbed wire presented almost insuperable difficulties, and the Highlanders looked back in despair for the four tanks which were supposed to assist at this stage of the operation. At last these monsters arrived on the scene and the Highlanders, breathing a sigh of relief, prepared to advance behind them. The explanation of what happened next is not clear. Some say that the tanks found themselves running out of gasoline, others that they received orders to report for even more urgent service elsewhere. Be that as it may, the tanks approached the wire, then, despite "Come to our help" signals and personal appeals from Lieuts. R. A. C. Young and J. E. Christie, they turned and moved off in the direction of Sains.

With the departure of the tanks the men of "D" Coy. turned doggedly towards their objective and began the heart-breaking task of cutting through the wire by hand. As had happened to "C" Coy., the delay caused by the wire had allowed the barrage

THE CANAL DU NORD

to get far ahead, a fact which permitted the enemy machine gunners to come up from their cellars and dugouts and offer the stoutest opposition. In the face of this the Company made slow and painful, though determined, progress. Lieut. G. W. Megan, who had acted splendidly throughout, was killed and Lieuts. J. Young and J. E. Christie, M.C., wounded, but Lieut. E. Appleby, who was himself suffering from minor wounds, continued to lead the Company forward. Foot by foot ground was gained, but at last, on reaching a great belt of wire which ran west from Chapel Corner and along the south of the village of Marquion, the advance was definitely checked.

"A" Coy. considerably weakened by casualties, came forward at this juncture, and, together with the right company of the 15th Battalion, prepared to continue the assault. Just as this movement was getting under way, up came a battalion of the Manchester Regiment, 11th British Division. With the arrival of these splendid troops the fate of the action in this vicinity, which had been trembling in the balance, was definitely settled and the whole line swept irresistibly forward. Almost at once the back bone of the German defence was broken and the village itself, together with the territory beyond up to the Green Line, was captured and consolidated. In reporting on the capture of the village, Major Sinclair of the 13th wrote as follows:—"The Commanding Officer wishes to express the admiration of all ranks of this Battalion at the magnificent way in which the Manchesters' attack went forward. In spite of very heavy fire, the whole battalion behaved as if carrying out a field day practice."

This brought to a conclusion that phase of the battle in which the Royal Highlanders were directly interested, as other troops took up the burden and carried the line forward. In so far as the 13th was concerned, Major Sinclair had every reason to be proud of the way the men had behaved when fighting for the first time under his command. In the face of serious obstacles, they had carried out the difficult fan attack called for; had met and defeated three German Battalions, of the 62nd and 189th Regiments; had captured three 77 mm. field guns, one anti-tank gun, two trench mortars and nineteen machine guns; and had advanced over a mile on a front of two miles. Then, when the force of their attack had spent itself, they had maintained every inch of the captured ground and had charged forward with the reinforcements to the capture of the final objective.

All this had not been accomplished without paying a price. In addition to the officer casualties already mentioned, Capt. H. A. Johnston, M.C., had been wounded, as had Lieuts. D. C. McEachran, C. L. Cantley, K. G. Blackader, M.C. and L. C. Drummond, M.C., while Capt. A. G. C. Macdermot and Lieut. R. A. C. Young had been wounded, but were able to remain at duty. Amongst the other ranks 33 had been killed, 8 were missing, and 169 had been wounded. Together with the losses in the Arras battle, this brought the Battalion's casualty list for the month of September up to a total of 24 officers and 432 other ranks.

For two days after the conclusion of the attack on September 27th the 13th Battalion remained in Divisional Reserve. Fierce fighting, meanwhile, was carried out by other units of the Corps, which, in the face of strong counter-attacks, was exploiting to the utmost the success of the daring "fan" assault already described. Realizing that they would soon become involved if the fighting continued, as seemed likely, the 13th hastened to re-organize and prepare for further action, no easy task with so many experienced officers gone and with staggering losses amongst the trained and trusted N.C.O.'s.

CHAPTER XXII

The Beginning of the End

> Stand fast and forget not the sign that is given,
> Of the years and the wars that are done,
> The token that all who are born of the blood
> Should in heart and in blood be one.
> —SWINBURNE.

I

THE last days of September, 1918, found the Canadian Corps, bloody and not a little weary, still driving with all its force against the Hun. Already the attack across the Canal du Nord and the capture of Bourlon Wood had resulted in a direct threat to Cambrai, and, as possession of that city was vital to him, the enemy was defending it with the courage born of despair. Almost recklessly he withdrew troops from other parts of his line and threw them into the Cambrai battle in an effort to stop that appalling advance, which, together with Allied advances at other crucial points, seemed like the fateful writing on the wall. If only the hand that wrote could be stayed, even momentarily, somehow, anyhow, he would hold out till the winter and then negotiate a peace on the basis of a draw. And so he fought with all the strength he could muster and all the cunning he could command, giving ground easily where the loss was of no vital importance, holding it with dogged courage if to yield were a matter of real concern.

"On September 29th," says Sir Arthur Currie, "the 3rd Canadian Division, the 4th Canadian Division and the 1st Canadian Division all made progress in the face of severe opposition." On the 30th further advances were made, but, as the result of savage counter attacks and a destructive enfilade fire, some of the captured territory had to be yielded again. "The net gains for the day," to quote Sir Arthur, "were the capture of Tilloy and some progress on the right of the 3rd Canadian Division from Neuville St. Remy south."

At 6 p.m. on September 30th the 13th Battalion moved forward from Divisional Reserve into Divisional Support. At 7 p.m. Major I. M. R. Sinclair, M.C., the Commanding Officer, was summoned to a conference at Brigade Headquarters and informed that the Battalion would attack before daylight on the following morning. Returning to Battalion Headquarters with all possible speed, Major Sinclair called his company commanders together and told them of the forthcoming operation, instructing them to inform their officers of the details and to see that these in turn passed as much information as possible to the N.C.O.'s. Owing to the exceedingly short time before zero, there was no way of letting the men know what was expected. For them it was a case of obeying orders and doing the best they could.

At 12.30 a.m. in pouring rain the Battalion moved forward to its jumping off position. Nine guides were picked up at an appointed spot on the Arras-Cambrai Road, but as only one of these really knew where he was going, the whole Battalion was forced to advance in single file, a tedious business which resulted in the unit's arriving in position, immediately behind the 85th Canadian Battalion's outpost line, with little time to spare before zero. Battalion Headquarters was established in a dugout in the centre of Sancourt, and almost immediately the "show" began.

The barrage, as was only to be expected considering the hasty arrangements, had at least one battery firing short, and the Highlanders suffered a few casualties from this cause at the very beginning. In spite of these, "B" Coy. on the left and "D" Coy. on the right, each on a front of 500 yards, advanced steadily into the darkness, dealing with such Hun posts as they encountered and capturing a number of prisoners. "A" Coy. advanced behind the attack as support, "C" Coy. being held in Battalion Reserve. During this fighting in the dark it was inevitable that a good deal of confusion should take place, but much to the credit of the troops concerned, the attack through the pitchy blackness of the night was driven forward most courageously. "B" Coy., however, did not quite achieve its purpose and suffered serious losses. Lieut. A. P. Nason was killed in effecting the capture of a machine gun nest, which was defending the railway embankment northwest of Blécourt, and, as all the company officers became casualties, Regi-

THE BEGINNING OF THE END

mental Sergt.-Major F. Butler took command. The Company then consolidated the embankment and prepared it for defence against counter attack.

Meanwhile, "D" Coy. on the right had had less trouble. Enemy posts were encountered frequently, but these were quickly dealt with and did not serve to check the advance, which reached its objective, the Blue Line, without much loss.

Advancing behind "D" Coy. as support until the diagonal railway was reached, "A" Coy. swung half left, taking over "B" Coy's area and carrying the assault on that front the remaining distance through Blécourt to its final objective. "A" Coy., however, did not accomplish this task without paying a price. During the advance it lost all its officers, with the exception of Capt. A. G. C. Macdermot, and a considerable proportion of the reduced strength with which it had entered the engagement. Then, just as it was driving forward to the Blue Line, a Hun, who came forward apparently to surrender, shot Macdermot dead. This individual was, of course, immediately disposed of, but the damage had been done and the Royal Highlanders had lost a brave and capable officer who had twice previously been wounded and whose presence could ill be spared. Following the death of Capt. Macdermot, "A" Coy. dug in on the Blue Line, command being taken over by Capt. E. Appleby, of "D" Coy., who also retained command of his own men. This completed the operation as far as the 13th was concerned, the 14th and 16th Battalions leapfrogging and carrying the assault forward.

Shortly after day had broken and just when it appeared that the attack of the 3rd Brigade had been an entire success, Major Sinclair received a report from Capt. Appleby, O.C. the 13th front line, that the enemy had appeared in large numbers on his left flank and were firing heavily with rifles and machine guns; also that a field battery had come into action against him and was firing at close range from the direction of Abancourt. To this Capt. Appleby added that he had been unable to get in touch with the 1st Canadian Brigade, which he had expected to find on his left flank, and asked if this Brigade had as yet come forward. As it was vital to protect the flank and rear of the 14th and 16th Battalions, which had gone forward, Major Sinclair ordered Appleby to withdraw from the exposed hillside where he found himself to a sunken road which provided good shelter and was well situated to protect the flank and rear of the forward battalions. "C" Coy. was sent forward at this juncture to reinforce Appleby's weakened line.

During the next hour the Stokes guns attached to the 13th did excellent work in holding back the enemy infantry, but their range was insufficient to reach the German field guns, which were harassing the 14th and 16th, as well as the 13th, from the direction of Abancourt.

By 9 a.m. the situation had become serious, and Major Sinclair reported by pigeon that the ground on the left must be attacked by reinforcements, or the 3rd Brigade was in danger of being badly cut up. By this time the 13th had all been faced to the left flank to meet the threatened danger. The 14th and 16th, meanwhile, had occupied the sunken road along the east side of Blécourt and were suffering severely from the enfilade. Realizing that a partial victory was infinitely better than a possible stinging defeat, Lieut.-Col. Peck, D.S.O., the veteran and experienced commander of the 16th, who had come up and appreciated the situation, ordered the 14th and 16th to withdraw to a line behind Blécourt and some 600 yards in advance of the jumping off position. Simultaneously, or nearly so, the two front companies of the 13th were withdrawn into the sunken road to escape the enfilade fire. There they remained until the Battalion was relieved on the following morning.

Altogether it was a somewhat unsatisfactory finish to an attack, which, starting under serious disadvantages, had progressed for a while amazingly well. Defeat had been avoided, but victory had escaped the Canadians' grasp, though, in compensation for losses suffered, the 3rd Brigade had maintained a considerable portion of the ground captured, had taken many prisoners and had killed or wounded an even larger number of the enemy.

In the 13th Battalion casualties had been particularly severe amongst the officers and N.C.O.'s. In addition to Capt. Macdermot and Lieut. Nason, killed, Capt. C. D. Llwyd, M.C. and Lieut. J. S. Reaume were wounded and missing, while Lieuts. R. A. C. Young, L. E. Wells and H. H. Hobbs had been wounded, as had the Battalion Chaplain, Major E. E. Graham, M.C., an officer who, from the time he joined the Highlanders just before the Battle of Vimy Ridge, had played a courageous part in every engagement where the unit had seen fighting. Lieut. L. Armstrong had also been wounded, but was able to remain on duty. Amongst the other

THE BEGINNING OF THE END

ranks 14 had been killed, 61 were wounded and 7 missing. For some time hope was entertained that Capt. Llwyd and Lieut. Reaume had survived. Both had served the Battalion faithfully and well, and it was with great reluctance that the Highlanders considered the possibility that they had been killed. Eventually, however, Lieut. Reaume's body was found and given burial. Capt. Llwyd's body was not found, and his name was added to the roll of that gallant company who are listed simply as "missing."

II

Following the relief on the morning of October 2nd, the 13th Battalion moved back to familiar territory near Keith Wood. Here the rear details rejoined and reinforcements were received to fill the depleted ranks. In common with all units of the Canadian Corps, the Royal Highlanders were feeling keenly at this time the loss of experienced officers and N.C.O.'s. Accordingly the call was sent forth and many whose wounds and other services entitled them to occupy less strenuous posts hastened to forego the privileges so dearly won and report back for Regimental duty.

On October 3rd, Sir Arthur Currie issued a Special Order to the Corps with reference to the engagements in which the troops had just taken part:—

"I wish to express to all troops now fighting in the Canadian Corps my high appreciation of the splendid fighting qualities displayed by them in the successful battle of the last five days. The mission assigned to the Corps was the protection of the flank of the Third and Fourth Armies in their advance, and that mission has been carried out to the complete satisfaction of the Commander-in-Chief. As you formed the flank, you suffered enfilade and frontal artillery fire all the way, and the hundreds of machine guns captured testify to the violence of the opposition from that source.

"Every evidence confirms the fact that the enemy suffered enormous casualties. He fought stubbornly and well and for that reason your victory is more creditable. You have taken in this battle over 7,000 prisoners and 200 field and heavy guns, thus bringing the total captures of the Canadian Corps since August 8th of this year to 28,000 prisoners, 500 guns, over 3,000 machine guns and a large amount of stores of all kinds.

"In the short period of two months the Canadian Corps—to

ROYAL HIGHLANDERS OF CANADA

which were attached the 32nd (British) Division for the Battle of Amiens, the 4th and 51st (British) Divisions for the Battle of Arras, and the 11th (British) Division for this Battle of Cambrai—has encountered and defeated decisively 47 German divisions; that is nearly a quarter of the total German forces on the Western Front. I am proud of your deeds and I want to record here my heartfelt thanks for your generous efforts, and my unbounded confidence in your ability to fight victoriously and crush the enemy wherever and whenever you meet him."

Shortly after the promulgation of this message, the 13th Battalion was gratified by the publication of a list of honours and awards in which officers and men of the unit figured conspicuously. For his courage and valuable services during the la Chavatte operations in August, Lieut. O. B. Krenchel, who previously had won the D.C.M. while serving in the ranks, was awarded the Military Cross. Very unfortunately, this brave officer did not live to receive his decoration, he having been killed during the operations on September 2nd. Lieut. W. T. Hornby, who had won the Military Medal previous to his gaining commissioned rank, was also awarded the Military Cross for his work at la Chavatte. For conspicuous bravery and devotion to duty during the Cagnicourt operations on September 2nd, a Bar to the Distinguished Conduct Medal was awarded to Sergt. F. A. D. Sorby, of "D" Coy., while for similar reasons a Bar to the Military Medal was awarded to Lance-Corp. C. C. Smith, of Headquarters Company, to Sergt. M. H. Mills, of "A" Coy. and to Sergt. W. P. C. Kelly, of "C" Coy. In the same list Private S. Edwards, of "D" Coy., received the D.C.M., while the M.M. was granted to 29 other ranks.

After several days spent in reorganization and training, the Battalion paraded on the morning of October 5th and marched to the Vis-en-Artois area, where dugouts, bivouacs and other shelters were occupied. Here the 13th remained for a little over twenty-four hours, passing a quiet Sunday morning and afternoon, but missing the presence of the Battalion Chaplain, who had been wont to honour the Sabbath with Divine Service whenever conditions permitted. At 6 o'clock on Sunday evening the companies of the 13th paraded in battle order and moved off to relieve the 2nd Battalion of the Lancashire Fusiliers in the front line. Guides were met in Boiry Notre-Dame at 7 p.m. and the relief was completed without incident three hours later.

THE BEGINNING OF THE END

The position in which the Battalion now found itself was peculiar. Its right and left flanks rested on land which had been inundated, while its front conformed roughly to the windings of the Trinquis River, beyond which was the village of Sailly-en-Ostrevent, heavily wired and acting as an outpost to a northern extension of the strong Drocourt-Quéant Line. On moving into this area, 13th Battalion Headquarters was located in a central position to the south of Boiry Notre-Dame, "C" Coy., under Lieut. E. Mather, was distributed on the left, "D" Coy., under Capt. R. E. Heaslip, in the centre, "A" Coy., under Capt. E. Appleby, on the right and "B" Coy., under Capt. J. L. Atkinson, in Battalion Support. The actual front was held for the most part by a series of day and night posts at strategic locations, one or two of which the Lancs. had established in the far bank of the stream.

After a quiet night in this position, some excitement was caused at about 8 a.m. when a low flying German plane attempted to "shoot up" "D" Coy's. outposts. No particular damage was caused on this occasion, nor did the Battalion suffer much as the result of enemy shelling, which was intermittent throughout the day, and included a proportion of gas shells.

During the morning Major Sinclair attended a meeting of battalion commanders at Brigade Headquarters, near Monchy-le-Preux, where details of a minor operation to be undertaken on the 8th were discussed and settled. This little operation, which was to be carried out by "D" Coy., involved crossing the Trinquis River and establishing a new line on the left front some distance beyond. As "D" Coy's. total strength at this time was down to 124 all ranks, a platoon of "C" Coy. was attached to act as support. The intention of the attack was to occupy the new line as described, but also to divert the attention of the Hun from other sections of the front, where larger operations were planned.

At 5 o'clock on the morning of the 8th the Highlanders beat off a German patrol which came nosing forward, but which, fortunately, did not see any of the preparations for the attack, these having been carried out while darkness was still complete. Half an hour later the barrage, a rather feeble affair, opened up and the attack got under way. The first difficulty was the crossing of the Trinquis River, which on this front varied from 20 to 50 yards in width and which was spanned by a rickety little one-man bridge. Another bridge was to have been provided previous to the attack, but this had not been done, so the one span remained the sole means of communication between the two banks. To protect the advancing troops against the danger of a shell burst cutting the bridge and leaving them stranded, adequate supplies of ammunition and entrenching tools of all kinds had been moved across previous to zero.

Having crossed the bridge in safety, Capt. Heaslip and Lieuts. Ferguson, Dunning and Hayden led the attack forward. On the right little opposition was encountered and objectives were reached without much difficulty. On the left resistance was firmer, and the men on this flank captured three enemy machine guns and some 25 prisoners, including one officer, all members of the 363rd German Regiment, 214th Division.

The German barrage on the occasion of this attack did not fall until twenty minutes after the operation began, consequently casualties in the 13th were held to a minimum and totalled only four, Lieut. S. H. Browning and 3 other ranks being wounded. When the Germans did lay down their barrage, it fell with considerable weight on the line of the River and the meadows beyond, but the only casualties it caused were amongst prisoners who were being conducted to the rear. By 7 o'clock the artillery on both sides had quieted down, and Capt. Heaslip reported that he was at all points holding his objectives and that the situation was quite satisfactory.

Throughout the day German trench mortars were active against the new line that "D" Coy. had established, and at 8 o'clock in the evening a strong enemy party raided one of the posts and was expelled only after sharp hand to hand fighting. Two men of "D" Coy. were killed in this encounter and six wounded, while the raiders also suffered losses and left one wounded corporal in the Highlanders' hands. This individual was found to be a member of the 50th German Infantry Regiment.

On the morning of October 9th the enemy shelled the 13th outpost lines with 5.9's and 4.1's, and treated the neighbourhood of Battalion Headquarters to a sprinkling of gas shells, which caused considerable inconvenience. Gas shelling on the outpost lines a little later in the day caused a good deal of suffering. Four men in one of "D" Coy's. posts were caught in a concentration of what appeared to be Blue Cross (Diphenylchlorarsine) gas and were in a deplorable condition when darkness made it safe for them to attempt to retire. Runners from Battalion H.Q. found these

THE BEGINNING OF THE END

four groping their way back, almost blind and suffering in a manner that was pitiable.

In the evening orders were received from Brigade instructing the 13th to push out battle patrols at 2 a.m. on the 10th instant, to try to capture Sailly-en-Ostrevent and enter the Drocourt-Quéant Line. This movement was to be carried out in co-operation with the 15th Canadian Battalion on the left and the 2nd Canadian Infantry Brigade on the right. Major Sinclair's operation order gave details of the attack to those concerned and may be summarized as follows:—

"It is intended that the 13th Battalion will move forward on the morning of October 10th to follow up a suspected retirement of the enemy. The Battalion will advance on a one company front, "A" Coy. will be the leading company, followed by "C", "B", "D" in that order. "A" Coy. will send forward one platoon around the south of Sailly-en-Ostrevent and one around the north. The third platoon will act as support and will move to the north of the village. The attitude to be adopted by the patrols will be:

(a) If opposition is slight—drive in and overcome it.

(b) If the enemy is still holding the position in force—our patrols will stand fast, report back and await orders to withdraw. It is not intended to attack heavily if the enemy has not retreated.

The leading platoon of "A" Coy. will advance from our line at 2 a.m.

"C" Coy. will "stand to" ready to move from 2 a.m. onwards. They will only move on the command of Battalion Headquarters. In case an advance is not found feasible, all units will be ordered to withdraw and will then move back to their positions as at present."

Promptly at 2 a.m. Capt. Appleby, O.C. "A" Coy., sent his patrols forward, each with scouts in advance. Lieut. E. B. Q. Buchanan's platoon proceeded up the light railway to the south of Sailly-en-Ostrevent, while Lieut. Armstrong led his men around the enemy wire to the north. Lieut. Dunning followed in support, with the additional duty of mopping up Sailly-en-Ostrevent. At 3.25 a.m. it was reported that the mopping up platoon had entered the village. Sounds of bombing and machine gun fire were then heard, but fifteen minutes later "A" Coy. reported that Lieut. Dunning's platoon had been unable to force its way through.

Meanwhile, the platoons on the right and left had pushed forward without much difficulty and had entered the Drocourt-Quéant

ROYAL HIGHLANDERS OF CANADA

Line. Each patrol, on attaining its objective, at once endeavoured to establish communication with the troops whom it expected to find on its flanks. In neither case, however, were these efforts successful, the 15th Battalion on the one flank and the 2nd Brigade on the other, having encountered opposition which prevented their making the junction.

Seeing that all had gone well with his own flanks and that Sailly-en-Ostrevent could probably be reduced without a great deal of difficulty, Major Sinclair ordered "C" Coy., under Lieut. Mather, to move forward. With the assistance of a platoon from this Company the village was quickly captured, together with some 30 prisoners. Shortly after this all the forward platoons reported themselves O.K.

Daylight was now approaching and Major Sinclair, in consequence, had to decide whether to hold the position gained or to withdraw his troops to the original line. He consulted with Major A. D. Wilson, D.S.O., Brigade Major of the 3rd Brigade, and, as the battalions on both flanks had been held up, it was decided to withdraw. Accordingly, the "recall" signal was sent up by Capt. Appleby and repeated by Battalion Headquarters.

Shortly after this Lieuts. P. O. Ferguson and E. B. Q. Buchanan, the officers of the right patrol, reported back. They had encountered little resistance, but had killed one German, whose shoulder strap bore the number of the 363rd German Regiment.

Some three quarters of an hour later Lieut. L. Armstrong reported that a part of "C" Coy., approximately 50 strong, was in the Drocourt-Quéant Line and could hold it, provided adequate reinforcements were sent up. This party was under the command of Lieuts. E. Mather, I. A. Ross and J. H. Molson. "B" Coy. was ordered forward on receipt of this information and had started with one platoon when Lieut. Mather arrived at Battalion Headquarters with news of a strong enemy counter attack, heavy casualties and a considerable number of his men taken prisoner. This distressing news changed the situation instantly. Accordingly, "B" Coy's. orders to advance were cancelled and the original jumping off line was immediately manned.

The explanation of the misfortune that had befallen the party of "C" Coy. lay in the simple fact that no one had seen the three white Very lights signalling the recall. Failing to see these, the party held its ground, according to orders, until day had broken.

THE BEGINNING OF THE END

Somewhat later Lieut. Mather, feeling strongly that all was not well, decided to return to Battalion Headquarters for orders. After his departure, Lieut. Molson stood his ground until it became obvious that he was in immediate danger of being surrounded. He then started to retreat along the German line, evacuating his wounded with him and leaving a guard at each communication trench to protect the main body against an attack from the rear. Soon, however, it became apparent that the end was not far off. Large bodies of the enemy manoeuvred to cut his retreat, which was hampered by the necessity of carrying the wounded. Lieut. Ross rendered valuable assistance throughout the operation, but there was really nothing that could be done. Molson himself was wounded over the eye, but carried on with his efforts to get his men out of their danger. At last ammunition gave out and this party, 2 officers and 30 men, thereupon surrendered. The determined stand of Lieuts. Molson and Ross and their men was of great assistance to such of the wounded as were able to care for themselves. An odd dozen of these escaped the Germans and, by many and devious routes, reached their own lines in safety during the day, or after dark that same night.

As a result of the operation the Royal Highlanders had definitely established the fact that the Drocourt-Quéant Line was held, at least at some points, in strength. Two officers, two N.C.O.'s and 45 other ranks of the enemy had been captured and a considerable number killed or wounded. To offset these gains the 13th had suffered a total of 145 casualties, many of these from gas. Four officers, Capt. R. E. Heaslip, Lieut. T. B. D. Tudball, Lieut. F. Hayden and Lieut. W. E. Dunning suffered from this cause, as did some 79 other ranks. Eight other ranks were killed, five fatally wounded, ten less seriously wounded and forty-three, including those known to be prisoners, were listed as missing.

In this operation, as in previous engagements, the men showed no little courage, but at the same time it was obvious that only the stern necessity which existed could justify the policy of filling up the depleted ranks of a battalion with untrained, or partially trained, men and sending them into action under officers and N.C.O.'s. who were themselves in some instances lacking, not in courage and resourcefulness, but in the finer degree of leadership which can be gained only by long experience. In the circumstances that existed there was no help for this condition. Every

ROYAL HIGHLANDERS OF CANADA

battalion in the Canadian Corps was similarly handicapped, and such senior officers as remained were alternately filled with admiration for the way in which the new men went at their work and depressed by the loss of the tried and experienced veterans whose shoes it was so difficult to fill.

CHAPTER XXIII

The Last of the Fighting

Till having backward rolled the lawless tide
Of trusted treason, tyranny and pride,
Her flag hath brought, inflexible as fate,
Charter of freedom to a fettered state.
—ALFRED AUSTIN.

I

WHILE the 13th Battalion was engaged in the series of operations described in the previous chapter, events had taken place on the Corps front that were of the utmost importance. Chief among these was the capture of the city of Cambrai. In his report dealing with the operations which brought this prize to Canadian arms, Sir Arthur Currie writes as follows:—

"The period from October 3 to 8 passed without any material changes on the Corps front. Many patrol encounters took place, in which some prisoners were captured and our artillery and machine guns kept the enemy under continual harassing fire day and night. Plans for further operations having been formulated to take place on the Third Army front, the Canadian Corps was ordered on October 5 to co-operate by forcing the crossing of the Canal de l'Escaut north of Cambrai. The Third Army had been successful in crossing the Canal de l'Escaut, south of Cambrai, between Crevecœur-sur-l'Escaut and Proville. The operation now contemplated had for object the capture of Cambrai by envelopment. This was to be carried out in two phases. In the first phase the XVII Corps was to capture Awoignt by attacking from the south; the Canadian Corps was to co-operate by an artillery demonstration. In the second phase the Canadian Corps was to cross the Canal de l'Escaut and, advancing rapidly, capture Escadœuvres, joining hands with the XVII Corps northeast of Cambrai. At 4.30 a.m. October 8, the Third Army attacked and at the same hour an artillery demonstration was carried out on the Canadian Corps front. The XVII Corps on the right did not reach Awoignt, but in the evening they were ordered to continue their advance

ROYAL HIGHLANDERS OF CANADA

on the morning of October 9 to capture this town; concurrently with this advance the Canadian Corps was to secure the crossings of the Canal de l'Escaut. In spite of the darkness of a rainy night the assembly was completed and the attack was launched successfully at 1.30 a.m. October 9. Rapid progress was made, and at 2.25 a.m. the 2nd Canadian Division had captured Ramillies and established posts on the Canal there, and patrols were pushing out to the northeast. By 3.35 a.m. our Infantry were well established on the eastern side of the Canal. The 3rd Canadian Division had cleared the railway, and their patrols were pushing into Cambrai, while the Engineers were commencing work on the bridges. By 8 a.m. the 2nd Canadian Division had captured Escadœuvres and had established a line—to the north and east. Detachments of the 3rd Canadian Division had by this time completely cleared Cambrai of the enemy. An air reconnaissance at dawn indicated that the enemy had withdrawn from the area between the Canal de l'Escaut and Canal de la Sensée, and that all bridges over the latter had been destroyed. Brutinel's Brigade, passing through the Infantry of the 2nd Canadian Division, seized the high ground at Croix St. Hubert and pushed cavalry patrols into Thun Leveque. The 2nd Canadian Division, east of the Canal, progressed towards the north and occupied Thun Leveque. Thun-St. Martin, Blécourt, Cuvillers and Bantigny, and the 11th Division occupied Abancourt and reached the outskirts of Paillencourt. The 3rd Canadian Division was moved on the following day to bivouacs in the Inchy-Quéant area to rest and refit after twelve days of battle. The attack was continued at 6 a.m. October 10, by the 2nd Canadian and 11th (British) Divisions, and good progress was made. At 9 a.m., October 11, the Canadian Corps resumed the attack, with the 49th Division on the right and the 2nd Canadian Division on the left. After fierce fighting, however, our attack made good progress, the 49th Division gaining the high ground east of Iwuy and the 2nd Canadian Division capturing Iwuy and the high ground to the north. Meanwhile, on October 7-8, the 1st Canadian Division had relieved the 4th (British) Division, (XXII Corps), on the frontage between Palluel and the Scarpe River, and passed under the command of the G.O.C., XXII Corps. At 5 p.m. October 11, I handed over command of the Corps front (less the 11th Divisional section) to the G.O.C., XXII Corps, and the 2nd Canadian and the 49th and 51st Divisions

THE LAST OF THE FIGHTING

were transferred to the XXII Corps. At the same hour I assumed command of the former XXII Corps front and the 56th and the 1st Canadian Divisions were transferred in the line to the Canadian Corps. During the night of October 11-12 the 2nd Canadian Division was relieved in the line east of the Iwuy-Denain railway by the 51st (Highland) Division, and on completion of the relief I assumed command of the remainder of the 2nd Canadian Divisional front, extending from the Iwuy-Denain railway (exclusive) to the Canal de l'Escaut. The Battle of Arras-Cambrai, so fruitful in results, was now closed. Since August 26 the Canadian Corps had advanced twenty-three miles, fighting for every foot of ground and overcoming the most bitter resistance.

In that period the Canadian Corps engaged and defeated decisively 31 German Divisions, reinforced by numerous Marksmen Machine Gun Companies. These Divisions were met in strongly fortified positions and under conditions most favourable to the defence.

In this battle 18,585 prisoners were captured by us, together with 371 guns, 1,923 machine guns and many trench mortars. Over 116 square miles of French soil, containing 54 towns and villages, and including the city of Cambrai, were liberated. The severity of the fighting and the heroism of our troops may be gathered from the casualties suffered between August 22 and October 11, and which are as follows:—

	Officers	Other Ranks
Killed	296	4,071
Wounded	1,230	23,279
Missing	18	1,912
Totals	1,544	29,262

II

Following the operation at Sailly-en-Ostrevent on October 10th, the 13th Battalion held the line for the remainder of the day, expecting an enemy counter-attack, or at least prepared to meet a counter-attack if one should develop. The Hun, however, made no move against the Highlanders' front, being pleased enough, apparently, to have retained his position in the northern extension of the Drocourt-Quéant Line.

ROYAL HIGHLANDERS OF CANADA

Late at night the 13th was relieved by the 16th and moved back to old trenches near Monchy-le-Preux. Here the men rested during the morning that followed, but at 4.10 p.m. "B" and "C" Companies were ordered forward to the position they had vacated the night before. On further orders being received the remainder of the Battalion also moved forward, arriving in the old position at 7 p.m. The 16th Battalion, meanwhile, had advanced their line almost to Noyelle-sous-Bellonne.

At 2.15 a.m. on October 12th a message was received from Brigade, which stated that the 15th and 16th Battalions were to attack at 6 a.m. and that the 13th Battalion would advance in close support. As there was no time in which to prepare written orders, Major Sinclair gave his company commanders, Capt. Appleby, Capt. Atkinson, Major J. D. Macpherson and Lieut. Stowell, verbal orders over the telephone. Assembly positions were in the Drocourt-Quéant Line and on reaching these each company commander was given a map marked with the boundaries and dispositions to be followed.

At 6 a.m. the 15th and the 16th Battalions started forward and the 13th followed according to instructions. No opposition was encountered by the forward battalions for some time, but at last the Canal de la Sensée, in front of Ferin, was reached and here the retreating Hun had evidently decided to make a stand. While the 15th and 16th Battalions tested out the Hun line, the companies of the 13th dug in as support. During the afternoon the 4th Canadian Battalion took over the support position and the Royal Highlanders moved back to an area near Eterpigny. Through some error no billets were available at this spot and, as a cold rain fell heavily, an uncomfortable night followed.

October 13th was spent by the troops in locating suitable billets and in resting. On the following morning the men bathed at St. Rohart Factory, near Vis-en-Artois, and paraded for pay in the afternoon, Lieut. A. T. Howard officiating as Paymaster in the absence of Capt. Appleton, who was on leave.

On this date Lieut.-Col. K. M. Perry, D.S.O. returned to assume command of the Battalion. It will be remembered that he had left the 13th in May to command the 87th Battalion, Canadian Grenadier Guards. At that time Perry had stipulated that if the command of his own unit should become vacant he would be permitted to return. When Lieut.-Col. McCuaig had been given com-

THE LAST OF THE FIGHTING

mand of a brigade Perry could not be spared by the 87th and the higher command, knowing that in Sinclair the 13th had an efficient and experienced officer, delayed putting Perry's re-transfer through until his place with the Guards could be satisfactorily filled. After handing over to Perry, Sinclair, who had led the Battalion through exceedingly difficult times, went on leave to England. This leave, incidentally, was long overdue, but Sinclair's duties with the Battalion had been quite too arduous for him to consider taking it. Now, however, he could do so with a free conscience.

Three more days were spent at Eterpigny, officers and men drilling hard to take advantage of the short period before they would be called on again to move up into the line. During this period there appeared a list of honours "for conspicuous gallantry in the Cagnicourt operations of September 2nd." Five officers were named in this list, Major W. E. Macfarlane receiving a Bar to his Military Cross, while the Military Cross was awarded to Capt. H. A. J. Cochrane (Medical Officer) and to Lieuts. F. S. Stowell, J. B. Beddome and D. L. Carstairs. The Distinguished Conduct Medal was granted to Regimental Sergt.-Major T. Sim, Coy. Sergt.-Major A. Watson, Sergt. T. Imrie, Sergt. A. Fernie, Sergt. J. Dickie and to Private C. Raine.

On October 18th the Royal Highlanders paraded at 7.45 a.m. in heavy marching order and proceeded, via Etaing, Lecluse and Tortequenne, to Estrées. The roads were muddy and congested with traffic, nevertheless Estrées was reached about noon and dinner promptly served. Billets here were satisfactory, but the Highlanders were only a few hours in occupation when orders were received to move again. This time a two hour march brought the men to Roccourt, where they settled down for the night.

III

In accordance with Operation Order No. 213, the Royal Highlanders moved forward early on the morning of October 19th and advanced in support of the 14th Battalion, Royal Montreal Regiment, which was pursuing the retiring Hun. No opposition was encountered, and at 10 a.m. "C" Coy., on the left front, reported Bruille les Marchiennes clear of the enemy. Battalion Headquarters passed through Somain at 1 p.m.

The advance of the Canadian Corps had by this time brought the troops far back of the "War Zone" to which they had become accustomed and into a district where the capture of a town or village did not mean the occupation of a few evil smelling cellars with a mass of debris overhead, but implied the liberation of territory almost untouched by shell fire and the freeing of French civilians who had spent weary years in virtual captivity.

Just as no one other than a soldier can perfectly visualize a modern battle, or the ghastly monotony and physical exhaustion of long days and nights in flooded trenches, so no one who has not suffered the experience can really appreciate the mental anguish that the French and Belgian civilians must have endured while their every going and coming was controlled and directed by an unscrupulous enemy, the foulness of whose actions in occupied territory constitutes a record in infamy for civilized nations.

The men of the 13th Battalion will never forget the scenes in Somain on the 19th of October. Old men and women crowded about them, eager to press on them gifts of food and flowers and cups of coffee, while every once in a while from some heart overflowing with emotion would arise a shout of "Vive la France!" At this the townspeople would look fearfully around, forgetful for the fraction of a second that the iron heel of the invader had been definitely lifted, then with full remembrance would come tears of thanksgiving, more shouts of "Vive la France!" and blessings on the heads of the brave Canadian troops who had effected the town's deliverance. Midst all the excitement that prevailed several French flags, concealed for years against the day when the vile Boche should rule no more, were produced from their secret hiding places and given proudly to the breeze. The Highlanders, however, could not delay their advance to take much part in the rejoicings. Fritz was on the run, but only continued and relentless pressure would keep him moving. Accordingly the advance was not allowed to halt, and by 3.15 p.m. Battalion Headquarters had been established near Hornaing.

At this point Lieut.-Col. Worrall, of the 14th Battalion, advised Lieut.-Col. Perry that the 14th and 16th Battalions would halt for the night on the line they had reached, joining up with the 1st Canadian Infantry Brigade on their left. As the 4th Canadian Division had not come up on the right, the 13th Battalion was placed for the night to form a defensive flank.

At 7 o'clock on the morning of October 20th the 13th Battalion passed through the 14th Battalion on the right of the 3rd Brigade

THE LAST OF THE FIGHTING

front, the 15th Battalion passing through the 16th Battalion on the left. The advance of the Brigade was then continued. Forty minutes later Capt. A. W. Ruston, O.C. "B" Coy., which was on the right flank, reported that his men had passed through the village of Wallers. Two or three machine guns were offering some opposition to his further advance. Lieut.-Col. Perry rode through Wallers at 10 a.m., in order to keep closely in touch with the progress of the advance. At 10.50 a.m. "C" Coy., on the left front, came under heavy machine gun fire and also under the fire of field guns at short range, whereupon the Colonel returned to Battalion Headquarters and reported to Brigade that his companies were temporarily held up.

It appeared at this time that the advance of the 3rd Brigade had momentarily outstripped that of the 4th Division on the right. Accordingly a halt was made and cyclist patrols despatched to discover just how the situation lay. During the day the Battalion suffered several casualties. The majority of these were not serious, but to the regret of those with whom he had come in contact and of those who had known him personally in other spheres, Lieut. W. Stewart, who had joined the Battalion less than a fortnight before, was killed in action.

By nightfall the 13th was in touch with the 15th on the left flank and the 54th Battalion, of the 4th Canadian Division, on the right. Preparations were accordingly made for continuing the advance on the morrow. At 4 o'clock on the morning of the 21st Lieut.-Col. Perry issued an operation order with instructions for the day's advance. "A" and "D" Companies were to carry out the move, with "B" Coy. in support and "C" Coy. in reserve. The 14th and 16th Battalions were to pass through the 13th and 15th when the advance had progressed a specified distance. Emphasis was given to the order that the advance was to be carried out only if the opposition was slight. Officers were instructed to see that heavy casualties were avoided.

Shortly after this order had been distributed, Lieut. J. Kerry took a patrol forward and, returning at 7 a.m., reported that the village of Aremberg had been evacuated by the enemy. The advance of the 13th was to have begun at 9 a.m., but at 7.30 a.m., Brigade telephoned and instructed the Battalion to move forthwith. By 10 o'clock "A" Coy. had reached its objective and some time later Battalion Headquarters was advanced to near Aremberg.

ROYAL HIGHLANDERS OF CANADA

During these moves five British planes circling overhead were seen to draw fire from hostile artillery. A German plane which came forward, flying low in an effort to establish how far the Canadians had advanced, was driven off by a battery of anti-aircraft guns, mounted on trucks, which kept pace with the forward movement of the Infantry. At 5 p.m. an outpost line was established east of Aremberg and the remainder of the Battalion was withdrawn into the village. No sounds of firing were heard during the night and everything indicated that the enemy was quite unable to make a stand and was retiring rapidly.

At 9 o'clock on the morning of October 22nd a battalion of the 9th Infantry Brigade, 3rd Canadian Division, passed through Aremberg and took up the pursuit of the enemy, the Royal Highlanders remaining at Aremberg during the forenoon and marching to billets at Fenain immediately after midday dinner. Casualties during the tour in the line totalled 26 all ranks. One officer and four men were killed, while Lieut. J. J. Marshall was slightly wounded. Twenty other ranks were wounded.

Leaving Aremberg, the route followed by the Battalion led through Wallers, Hornaing and Erre. In each of these little towns and villages the troops were enthusiastically greeted, amid scenes of emotion on the part of the civilians whose joy in their deliverance remained unabated. Evidence of the eagerness of these poor people to assist the Canadian advance in any way and to help in the undoing of the Boche was furnished at numerous road crossings, where the retreating enemy had blown large mines. Into the resulting craters the civilians had flung all manner of bulky articles, even mattresses and furniture, with a view to assisting the Engineers to bridge the yawning gaps, lest the hated masters of yesterday should escape the retribution that was treading on their heels.

At the beginning of the march to Fenain, "Flora Macdonald," the Battalion goat, occupied her usual proud place at the head of the Regiment. She seemed in good spirits and swung into step as soon as her beloved pipes struck up one of the tunes she knew so well. But, alas, it was Flora's final appearance! She sickened on the march and died within a few minutes. One wonders if she knew that her task was finished, that the Battalion she had served so faithfully and loved so well was never again to fire a shot in action nor charge against the trenches of the enemy in grey. If

THE LAST OF THE FIGHTING

so, she knew more than the Royal Highlanders themselves even suspected. To them the move to Fenain meant merely a period of training preparatory to further effort against the Hun.

No time was lost in starting to train. Cleaning of equipment and replacing shortages in kit occupied the time of the men on October 23rd, but on the following day drills commenced at an early hour in the morning and continued without intermission till noon. The afternoon was devoted to games, these proving of tremendous interest to the civilian population, who, although their knowledge of the finer points was scant, entered thoroughly into the spirit of the play and applauded vociferously at frequent intervals.

During the remainder of October, life was very agreeable for the men of the 13th. They worked hard, but not too hard, and when work was finished for another day they sauntered about the streets of the little town, making friends and exchanging amenities with the townspeople. The fact that the troops and their hosts spoke different languages provided no serious obstacle to mutual understanding. Where words failed, gestures and expressive facial contortions seemed to convey all the sense that was required. So the villagers learned of the glory that was Vimy; of the horrors of the Somme; and of Canada across the sea, while the Highlanders listened with ever growing indignation to tales of how the Hun had acted during his long years of mastery.

On October 24th all ranks of the Battalion were pleased by the announcement that Major E. E. Graham, M.C., the Regimental Chaplain, had been awarded the Distinguished Service Order for gallantry in rescuing wounded under heavy fire at the beginning of the Battle of Arras in August. Late in September Major Graham had been wounded and sent back to hospital, where he was recovering from his injuries at the time the above award was made.

At 3 p.m. on November 1st, the 13th Battalion, including the Transport, paraded and, together with the other units of the 3rd Brigade, was inspected by Major-General A. C. Macdonell, G.O.C., the 1st Canadian Division. Just as the inspection commenced, H.R.H. the Prince of Wales, who at this time was attached to the Staff of the Canadian Corps, arrived on the scene and accompanied the Divisional Commander through the ranks. Afterwards His Royal Highness took the salute as the Battalion marched past.

ROYAL HIGHLANDERS OF CANADA

As November wore its way along, the troops, for the first time, began to take seriously the talk of a cessation of hostilities. Always before the possibility had seemed remote, but now, with Austria, Bulgaria and Turkey definitely defeated and with the German armies reeling back before the heavy blows of the combined French, Belgians, Americans and British, the likelihood of such a development became obvious. On November 9th news was received that German delegates, under the white flag, had arrived at some unnamed spot seeking terms for an armistice. Would they get terms, or would they not? Opinions differed, some maintaining that no terms were possible till Germany had been crushed and invaded, others insisting that Germany was already crushed and could be made to accept whatever terms the Allied peoples might care to impose.

Meanwhile, far in advance of the line which the 13th had handed over on the morning of October 22nd, troops of the 3rd, 4th and 2nd Canadian Divisions, in co-operation with the British forces, were flinging the Hun from one position after another. As a result of heavy fighting, Valenciennes was entered on November 1st and cleared of the enemy by November 2nd. Steady progress continued from this point and, early on the morning of November 11th, patrols of the 42nd Battalion, Royal Highlanders of Canada, entered Mons.

Thus when the 11th hour of the day arrived and the Great War came to an end, the British Army stood fast on the ground where the "Old Contemptibles" had given of their glorious best when first they met the onrushing Hun four weary years before. Outnumbered and outgunned, but never outgamed, the "Old Contemptibles" had been forced out of Mons and back to the Marne—not a tremendous distance if measured in miles—but one which the British Army covered and retraced only at the cost of a million British lives and a toll of sacrifice too great for the mind of man to conceive. But the price had been paid; Mons was again in British hands and its inhabitants, free at last, heard again the skirl of the pipes and witnessed the march of khaki battalions, some kilted, as had been the case in 1914, others in the familiar trews and puttees, till it seemed to the Belgians that the very men of 1914 were back in Mons again. Such was not the case. The "Old Contemptibles" had died on the road to the Marne, on the Aisne, at Ypres and at Neuve Chapelle, bequeathing a tradition of

THE LAST OF THE FIGHTING

indomitable courage when faced with appalling odds that was an inspiration to the troops who followed, not least to those with "Canada" on their shoulders whose final effort had effected the recapture of Mons, a city which, together with Ypres, will hold a significant place in the hearts of the British and Canadian peoples as long as the generation which knew the men of the Great War shall endure.

CHAPTER XXIV

The March to the Rhine

March, march, Ettrick and Teviotdale,
Why the deil dinna ye march forward in order?
March, march, Eskdale and Liddesdale,
All the Blue Bonnets are bound for the Border.
—Sir Walter Scott.

I

TO the men of the 13th Battalion in billets at Fenain, news of the capture of Mons and the signing of the Armistice brought a sense of bewilderment and anti-climax. What, under such circumstances, did a battalion do? Did it continue to train for battle, or did it in some mysterious way prepare for peace? The men discussed these questions interestedly, but, as no definite answer was forthcoming, they shrugged their shoulders and, with true fatalism, decided to wait and see. What would be, would be.

Meanwhile, the civilian population had decked the streets with bunting and were celebrating to the best of their ability. At night a huge bonfire was lighted on the parade ground between Fenain and Somain and around this gathered the population of the two villages and the troops billeted in the vicinity. In an effort to make the occasion memorable from a scenic point of view, large numbers of Very lights and signal rockets were sent up into the sky. Viewing these with an approving eye, one veteran N.C.O. was heard to observe that he had never seen a Canadian S.O.S. signal look attractive before.

Very aptly, a lengthy honours list appeared in the day's orders, Sergt. W. Hannaford, D.C.M., M.M., receiving a Bar to his Military Medal, as did Sergts. G. Dunmore and C. H. Camm. The Military Medal was granted to 26 other ranks, among the recipients being Sergt. D. Simard and Private J. M. Buick, both of whom had previously won the Distinguished Conduct Medal.

On November 12th all doubt as to what the Battalion would do in the immediate future was set at rest when it became known

THE MARCH TO THE RHINE

that the Canadian Corps, (consisting, as arranged later, of the 1st and 2nd Canadian Divisions), was to join in the long march of the British Army to the Rhine.

In accordance with Operation Order No. 218, the Royal Highlanders paraded in battle order at 7.30 a.m. on November 13th and marched to the Aubry-la Sentinelle area, which was reached some few hours later. On the following day the route lay along the northern outskirts of Valenciennes, thence, via the Mons Road, to Quiévrain and Elouges, this latter point being reached about 3.45 p.m.

November 15th was fine and cool and the Royal Highlanders, parading at 9 a.m., reached Quaregnon in three and a half hours without difficulty, though the roads were congested by hundreds of civilians who, with all their worldly goods on small push carts, were returning to the homes whence the Hun had driven them.

No move was made by the Highlanders on November 16th and 17th. On the former date some reorganizations were carried out. a number of men attached to Battalion Headquarters being returned to duty with the companies, and the Trench Mortar Section being disbanded, its personnel also returning to duty with the companies. On Sunday, November 17th, Divine Service was held at 10 a.m. for the main body of the Battalion, the Roman Catholic party, under Capt. R. L. Calder, M.C., having proceeded to the celebration of Mass in the local church an hour earlier. In the afternoon the Pipe Band of the 13th proceeded to Jemappes to take part in a special liberation celebration.

The following morning was cold and wet, nevertheless the Battalion paraded at 6.25 o'clock and moved forward, crossing the Armistice Line at 11 a.m., halting for lunch north of the Jurbise-Soignies Railway and completing a 15 mile march to Chaussée-Notre-Dame-Louvignies by 2.30 p.m. Being the first British troops to enter Chaussée-Notre-Dame-Louvignies, the men of the 13th received an enthusiastic welcome.

Two days were spent here, and on the morning of November 21st the advance was continued. Marching at 7.40 a.m., the Highlanders passed through Soignies, a large town where the inhabitants lined the streets and cheered the Canadians vociferously. Braine-le-Comte was the next town en route, after which came a stretch of wooded and hilly country that was most attractive. Ronquières was passed through and finally, after a march of about

ROYAL HIGHLANDERS OF CANADA

26 kilometres, the Battalion reached Nivelles. "A" Coy. proceeded beyond the town that night to mount guard over a large dump of enemy war material. The men of the other companies, in spite of the fatigue of the day's march, joined the civilians in a celebration in the Town Square which lasted far into the night.

Two days were spent at Nivelles, the troops resting on November 22nd and parading in full marching order for inspection by the Commanding Officer on the 23rd. Several parties of officers took the opportunity to visit the historic battlefield of Waterloo, only a few kilometres away. Reveille sounded at 4 o'clock on the morning of November 24th and three hours later the Battalion, with "C" Coy. acting as vanguard, moved forward. At the first halt outside Nivelles the company pipers were brought together and marched thereafter as a full band in the centre of the column. About 10 a.m. Bonaire was reached and the companies settled down in billets, the vanguard, under command of Major J. D. Macpherson, M.C., proceeding forward and establishing examining posts on all roads leading into the Brigade area.

Five miles was all that the men were asked to march on November 25th. Accordingly the start was not made until 2 p.m. Roads were muddy and the weather disagreeable, but good time was made and Mellery reached in due course. Here the Battalion remained on November 26th, the companies spending the morning in light training. Mounting the guard in the afternoon provided the civilian population with a spectacle which they enjoyed keenly, the Pipe Band arousing many favourable comments.

With a long march of 35 kilometres ahead of them, the men of the 13th rose early on November 27th and got away soon after daylight. A drizzling rain and cold wind made the morning's march anything but agreeable and spoiled the pleasure of the midday halt. Consequently it was a tired and "fed up" Battalion which arrived at Waret la Chaussée at 6 p.m.

If the march on November 27th was disagreeable, that on the following day was more so. Great difficulty had been experienced in keeping the forward troops supplied with rations, but on this date, for the first time, rations definitely failed to appear. Accordingly, at 8.20 a.m. the troops marched without any breakfast. Rain fell heavily during the day, but in spite of this the inhabitants of Petit Waret turned out en masse to cheer the Battalion through the town. After a march of 15 kilometres, the hungry troops

THE MARCH TO THE RHINE

reached Couthuin at 1.30 p.m., hoping that in some mysterious way rations would have arrived before them. Visions of a hot meal faded during the afternoon, but just when hope had been abandoned and the troops were preparing to go supperless and blanketless to bed, supplies arrived and the men received their first meal of the day.

Orders were issued for a short move to Bas Oha on November 29th, but, owing to continued difficulty in bringing forward rations, this move was postponed until the morning of the 30th. At Bas Oha, a beautiful little village on the banks of the Meuse, the 13th Battalion remained for two days. Proceeding again on December 2nd, the Royal Highlanders crossed the Meuse at Huy and, after a march of 23 kilometres through mountainous and heavily wooded country, reached Jenneret at half past three in the afternoon.

Fine weather prevailed on December 3rd when the Battalion, in battle order, continued the march at 11.15 a.m. Ten kilometres was the distance set for the day and billets at Hamoir were reached shortly after 1.30 p.m. The march on December 4th provided an entirely different set of conditions, as the weather was bad, the roads ankle deep in mud and the distance to be covered 28 kilometres. Starting at 8.45 a.m., the men toiled up the long hill leading to Filot and slogged steadily along until 10 kilometres had been left behind, when a halt was made for dinner. Resuming the march, the Battalion reeled off 18 kilometres in three and a half hours, a very creditable performance considering the heavy and ploughed-up condition of the roads.

At Basse Bodeux and Haute Bodeux, which were the destinations on December 4th, the Battalion rested on the day that followed. The difficulty in connection with rations had been overcome by this time and the troops were served full meals at the regular hours. Tobacco supplies were short, however, as the Y.M.C.A. and similar canteens where the men had been wont to augment their rations, had been unable to keep pace with the forward battalions.

On December 6th a march of 22 kilometres was accomplished to the village of Petit Thier. This brought the Royal Highlanders to within a few miles of the German border and well within that section of Belgium where German influence had, even before the war, been paramount. The difference was noticeable in all the little towns and villages through which the Battalion passed. Above the public buildings and over many of the private houses the Belgian flag floated in the breeze, but in the streets there were no demonstrations of enthusiasm and no shouts of warm hearted greeting. Instead the townspeople were polite, with that frigid and studied courtesy which might well conceal intense dislike. Accordingly, it was no surprise to the Canadians to find on the village notice boards a warning to the inhabitants from Sir Douglas Haig that all acts of hostility against His Majesty's Forces, or any wanton destruction of roads, railways or telegraphs, would be regarded as a serious offense punishable by death.

On the morning of December 7th, considerable excitement prevailed amongst officers and men of the 13th, for the day's march would carry them over the German border. Extra pains were taken to see that the Battalion was at its smartest, with the result that, when the men paraded in full marching order at 9 a.m., a critical inspection would not have disclosed much amiss.

On reaching the Frontier, at Poteau, at 9.30 a.m., the Band of the Royal Highlanders swung to the right and played the Battalion across the Line to the stirring tune of "Blue Bonnets over the Border." For all ranks the moment held a deep significance. Almost it seemed as if marching by their sides were those gallant officers and men, a full battalion of them, who, at the sacrifice of their lives had helped to bring this hour about.

Continuing the march, the 13th passed through the villages of Recht and Amel, where children with close cropped heads stared curiously from the roadsides, their elders keeping discreetly out of sight and contenting themselves with a view of the troops through half closed doors and windows. Eventually, after a march of 18 kilometres, the men of the 13th were billeted in Möderscheid.

Very appropriately, the entry of the Battalion into German territory was marked by the appearance in orders of a list of honours won during the great battles of the autumn. In this list Lieut.-Col. K. M. Perry was awarded a Bar to his Distinguished Service Order, while the Distinguished Service Order was granted to Major I. M. R. Sinclair, M.C., and to Capt. H. A. Johnston, M.C. The Military Cross was awarded to Lieuts. W. F. McGovern and R. H. Hebden, while Private W. Trumper received a Bar to his Military Medal. The Distinguished Conduct Medal was granted to Lance-Corp. J. Junor, who had previously won the Military Medal, and

ENTRAINING AT BENSBERG, JANUARY 5TH, 1919.

Canadian Official, Copyright.

COLOURS PRESENTED IN GERMANY BY H.R.H. PRINCE ARTHUR OF CONNAUGHT, JANUARY 4TH, 1919.

Canadian Official, Copyright.

THE MARCH TO THE RHINE

the Military Medal was awarded to Lance-Sergt. J. T. McGuire, Private G. M. Kelly, Private H. G. Wills and Private F. Borden.

After a day of rest at Möderscheid, the men of the 13th Battalion rose early on December 9th and prepared to march to Hellenthal. Civilian horses and wagons were requisitioned to carry the men's packs and the 29 kilometre march was swung off in six and a half hours. The marching of the men was splendid on this occasion, all ranks feeling the stimulus of marching through enemy country and being anxious to furnish the inhabitants with ocular proof that the Canadian Corps was very different to the German troops who, from the littered appearance of the roadsides, had apparently retreated through the district shortly before the Canadians arrived.

Continuing the move on December 10th, the Royal Highlanders passed through Sistig, Kall and Roggendorf, completing a march of 29 kilometres to Schaven and Gehn about 3 p.m. No rest was given to the men on the following day, but instead orders called for another 30 kilometres march to Pingsdorf. En route the Battalion marched past the 1st Canadian Divisional Commander, who requested the Colonel to convey to all ranks of the Battalion his pride and satisfaction in the showing they had made. At the same time the Colonel announced that the Battalion would proceed to the outskirts of Cologne on the following morning, would have the afternoon to clean and polish equipment and would then, on the next day, take part in the march of the British Army across the Rhine.

In accordance with this arrangement the Royal Highlanders paraded on the morning of December 12th and marched to Rodenkirchen, a suburb of Cologne. In this neighbourhood the whole 3rd Canadian Infantry Brigade was assembled and the afternoon was given over to what in Army parlance is known as "spit and polish," the men being anxious that every button, every buckle and every bit of leather equipment should be shining for the great event of the morrow.

December 13th dawned wet and unpromising, nevertheless the men were early astir and at 8.20 a.m., with the Band leading, and with H.Q., "C", "B"', "A" and "D" Companies and the Transport following in the order named, the Battalion marched towards Cologne. On entering the City, bayonets were fixed and the march continued at the "slope."

ROYAL HIGHLANDERS OF CANADA

The 3rd Canadian Brigade had the honour of leading the 1st Division across the Rhine and, on the toss of a coin, the distinction of heading the Brigade fell to the 14th Battalion, Royal Montreal Regiment, the 15th Battalion (48th Highlanders), of Toronto, the 16th Battalion, Canadian Scottish, and the 13th Battalion, Royal Highlanders of Canada, following in the order named.

It was exactly 9.56 a.m. when Lieut.-Col. Perry led the 13th Battalion onto the New, or Southern, Bridge, the men marching splendidly behind the Band to the familiar tune of "Blue Bonnets over the Border." At the east side of the Bridge Major-Gen. A. C. Macdonell, accompanied by Brig.-Gen. G. S. Tuxford and their respective Staffs and escorted by a squadron of the Canadian Light Horse, took the Battalion's salute. General Sir H. Plumer, G.C.B., G.C.M.G., Commanding the Second Army, arrived at the saluting point during the march past of the Battalion and expressed himself as well pleased with the troops' appearance and bearing.

Thus, on December 13th, exactly a month from the day when the concentration for the march started, the 13th Battalion, Royal Highlanders of Canada, reached and crossed the Rhine.

II

Once across the Rhine, the various units of the Canadian Corps, which was to hold the Right Section of the Cologne-Bonn Bridgehead, unfixed bayonets and marched "at ease" to the towns and villages where billets had been arranged for them.

In the case of the 13th Battalion the village of Heumar was the destination selected. Comfortable billets were secured at this spot and the men settled down almost at once to the ordinary routine of life in peaceful surroundings. Immediately after the arrival of the Battalion a further list of decorations for gallantry in the field was posted. Lieut. J. E. Christie was awarded a Bar to his Military Cross, Capt. E. Appleby, who had won the Military Medal while serving in the ranks, received the Military Cross, while the splendid work of Regimental Sergeant-Major F. Butler was rewarded by the bestowal of the Military Cross and a Bar to his Distinguished Conduct Medal. Later in the month the Military Cross was awarded to Capt. R. E. Heaslip, Lieut. W. E. Dunning and Lieut. J. R. Ferguson.

On December 15th the men of the Battalion were paid in Ger-

THE MARCH TO THE RHINE

man marks for the first time, it being announced that the rate of exchange for the occasion would be on the basis of 5 marks being worth 2/8d, or 3.50 francs. On the following day "A" Coy. proceeded to Cologne to mount guard over enemy war material, while the other companies lined the road through the village to welcome the Commander-in-Chief, Sir Douglas Haig. Something of a ceremony was made of this event, Sir Douglas, who was accompanied by the Canadian Corps Commander, Sir Arthur Currie, and by Major-Gen. A. C. Macdonell, G.O.C. the 1st Canadian Division, alighting from his automobile, greeting Brig.-Gen. Tuxford and Lieut.-Col. Perry and, with his whole entourage, passing through the Battalion lines on foot. During his progress he was greeted by such a roar of cheers that the strains of the Pipe Band, playing "Highland Laddie," were almost drowned out. Afterwards Sir Douglas expressed himself as being much gratified by the warmth of his reception.

Battalion Headquarters moved to a large hotel in Rath on the morning of December 18th, and on the 21st "B" Coy. proceeded to Cologne to relieve "A" Coy. guarding enemy war material. Divine Service was held on the parade ground on the 22nd, and on the 24th the Battalion was inspected by Major-Gen. Macdonell, who took the opportunity to wish the men "a very Merry Christmas." On this same date the Royal Highlanders welcomed back to duty Major F. S. Mathewson, Major W. E. Macfarlane, M.C., and Capt. H. A. Johnston, D.S.O., M.C., all of whom had recovered from their wounds and injuries.

Snow fell during the night of December 24th and Christmas day dawned with a white mantle covering the whole countryside. Holy Communion was celebrated at 10 a.m. for those who desired to attend, while the morning was also marked by a football game against a team from the 16th Battalion. The slippery field militated against good play, but spectators and players enjoyed the fun, the 16th winning the game by a considerable margin.

Although turkeys and similar luxuries were not available, the Battalion cooks displayed commendable ingenuity in their important task and served a Christmas dinner that was unanimously voted excellent. According to established custom, Lieut.-Col. Perry, escorted by his Piper and accompanied by Major Sinclair and Lieut. Smith, his Second-in-Command and Adjutant, visited the Company Messes while dinner was in progress to wish the men good luck. Everywhere his arrival was greeted with much enthusiasm.

Two quiet days followed the Christmas celebrations, then, on December 28th, the Battalion moved by train, "A", "B" and "D" Companies to Loope, "C" Coy. to Vilkerath and Headquarters to an old chateau in Ehreshoven. New Year's Eve was celebrated in keeping with the traditions of a Highland battalion. The officers entertained a number of friends, while the men formed parties of their own and passed the night in suitable revelry. As the bell of the ancient chateau pealed out the Old Year, voices could be heard singing, enthusiastically, even if a little off key, the time honoured greeting, "A Guid New Year to Ane and A'," while the pipers struck up a tune to bid the New Year welcome. And the New Year was welcome in a way that none of its four predecessors had been. Those years had been ushered in, it is true, with merriment and feasting, just as this, but at all previous celebrations there had been one unbidden guest; a guest whose presence was deliberately ignored, but of whose sombre shadow no one could be unaware. But now the shadow had departed and the New Year was full of promise in consequence.

With the advent of 1919, the Royal Highlanders prepared for the ceremony of receiving Regimental Colours. His Royal Highness Prince Arthur of Connaught consented to present these, and the ceremony took place on January 4th in one of the fields of the Castle at Ehreshoven. Prince Arthur, who was accompanied by Major-Gen. Sir A. C. Macdonell and Brig.-Gen. G. S. Tuxford, inspected the Battalion, which was drawn up waiting for his arrival. Major Creegan, Chaplain of the 1st Canadian Division, then blessed the Colours, after which Prince Arthur, with traditional ceremony, handed them to the Battalion for safe keeping. When the presentation was over the 13th Battalion shared with the 14th Battalion, which had received colours an hour before, the rare distinction of having been given colours by a Prince of the Royal House of Windsor on enemy soil. In a speech to the men of the unit after the formal moves had been completed, Prince Arthur referred to the great honour that it was for a battalion to receive colours in such a manner. He mentioned that he had been attached to the Canadian Corps Staff for over two years and was in consequence thoroughly aware of the striking services the 13th had rendered. He then recalled his first visit to the Battalion, at Salisbury Plain,

THE MARCH TO THE RHINE

in 1915, and concluded by stating that if the men carried with them into civilian life the same determination and the same spirit displayed throughout the war, he had no fear for the future of Canada.

CHAPTER XXV

Back from Germany and Home to Canada

The tumult and the shouting dies,
The captains and the kings depart,
Still stands Thine ancient Sacrifice
An humble and a contrite heart.
Lord God of Hosts, be with us yet,
Lest we forget—lest we forget.

—RUDYARD KIPLING.

I

THE presentation of Colours by H.R.H. Prince Arthur of Connaught marked the end of the Battalion's stay in Germany. Parading on the following morning, January 5th, the Royal Highlanders marched to Bensburg, entraining at that point at 2.50 p.m., crossing back over the Rhine at 4 p.m., passing the night on the train and arriving at Huy, Belgium, early on the morning of the 6th. From Huy the Battalion marched a short distance to the village of Wanze, where billets were taken over from the 10th Queen's R.W. Surrey Regiment. These billets being in a friendly country, the order which had prevailed in Germany that officers and men must go armed at all times was cancelled. Simultaneously it was announced that Regimental censorship of letters would no longer be considered necessary.

With the arrival of the Battalion at Wanze, educational classes, under the supervision of Capt. J. B. Beddome, M.C., were made a daily feature of the men's routine. Many of the latter had been on active service for several years and felt that their chances of success in civilian life would be enhanced if defects in their elementary education could be remedied. Every effort was made to help these men, courses being provided in subjects that would almost certainly prove useful. Capt. Beddome also instituted classes for those who thought that a knowledge of the French language would help them, while Lieut. J. M. Moyes taught drawing and similar subjects to those whose tastes lay in that direction.

To provide diversion for the men in the evenings Capt. Walker was appointed "O.C. Entertainments" and drew up a programme

BACK FROM GERMANY TO CANADA

which included dances, concerts and similar forms of amusement. To many of these the men were permitted to bring the demoiselles of the village, most of whom had picked up the "new" dances and all of whom seemed anxious to make the stay of the Canadians as agreeable as possible. To fill the off-duty hours of daylight an inter-company football league was formed and several organizations of a like character were brought into being, these serving in some degree to occupy the attention of the men and to keep them interested during the long wait that of necessity ensued before they could be returned to Canada.

On January 15th it was announced that the Distinguished Conduct Medal had been awarded to Sergt. J. F. McLean, while on the following day an Army Order was issued with regard to the 1914-15 Star. This stated that all ranks who had served in an actual theatre of war previous to December 31st, 1915, might wear the riband of the Star, without waiting to receive the decoration itself or any individual gazetting. A large number of officers and men in the 13th were qualified for this honour and in consequence the red, white and blue riband soon appeared on many tunics. Later in the month it was announced that the Meritorious Service Medal had been awarded to Sergt. J. A. Ayling, Sergt. W. Ganson, Sergt. W. R. Burden and to Lance-Corp. J. C. Sanders. A further announcement of interest was made at the close of the month when it became known that the Divisional Commander's Whip, emblematic of 3rd Brigade Transport supremacy, would remain permanently in the possession of the 13th Battalion, the Royal Highlanders having won this more frequently than any of the other battalions

All during February, 1919, the 13th Battalion remained at Wanze, the time being employed in much the same way as during January, that is to say in the general routine of a battalion in billets, with such diversion as the time and place afforded.

On February 3rd a Composite Company, including in its ranks picked men from every section of the Battalion, entrained at Huy and proceeded to Liège to take part in a great review. The salute on this occasion was taken by Lieut.-Gen. Jacques, K.C.M.G., of the Belgian Army, who afterwards expressed to Major-Gen. Sir A. C. Macdonell, K.C.B., C.M.G., D.S.O., G.O.C., the 1st Canadian Division, his pride in having had this honour. General Jacques stated that in his opinion the march past of the troops was "magnif-

ROYAL HIGHLANDERS OF CANADA

icent." Somewhat later in the month the Composite Company, which was under the command of Major J. D. Macpherson, M.C., paraded together with the Pipe Band and Colour Party and proceeded to Huy, where an inspection of the Canadian Corps was held by Lieut.-Gen. Orth, K.C.M.G., Chief of the Belgian Mission at British G.H.Q. General Orth, who was accompanied by many of the senior Canadian officers, took the opportunity to present the Belgian Croix de Guerre to a number of men who had won this decoration in the field. Amongst these was Sergt. D. K. Miller, of the 13th Battalion.

Considerable interest was aroused towards the middle of February by a series of boxing bouts, held in the theatre at Huy. These were for the Divisional Championship and representatives of the various Brigades and Divisional Troops took part. Privates Veno and Quigley, of the 13th, made an excellent showing at their respective weights, the latter winning through to the finals and disposing of his man by a knockout, and the former also reaching the finals, but losing the decision on points. Many other sporting events occurred during the month, probably the most interesting of these taking place on the 21st when the 13th played a South African team at Rugby football. After an excellent game, which was closer than the score might indicate, the South Africans won by 11-0.

On the afternoon of February 22nd the first definite step towards demobilization was taken when a party of married men, whose dependents in the Old Country wished to return to Canada with them, said good-bye to the Battalion and proceeded to England. On the following day Major I. M. R. Sinclair, D.S.O., M.C., assumed command of the Battalion in place of Lieut.-Col. K. M. Perry, D.S.O., who was leaving to attend the Staff College at Camberley. Meanwhile the Transport, which had been a source of pride to the Battalion, was being broken up, the horses being taken over by representatives of the Belgian Government and the wagons turned in to the Ordnance Corps. By the 25th of the month all that remained was the Medical Officer's cart and one rather dilapidated G.S. wagon. Another step towards demobilization was taken when Major J. D. Macpherson, M.C., Major F. S. Mathewson and Capt. A. W. Appleton were appointed to audit all Regimental accounts.

On February 27th a platoon from "D" Coy., under the com-

LIEUT.-COL. V. C. BUCHANAN., D.S.O. BRIG.-GEN. G. E. McCUAIG, C.M.G., D.S.O.
Jan. 5th, 1916, to Sept. 26th, 1916.   Sept. 27th, 1916, to Sept. 14th, 1918.

MAJ.-GEN. SIR F. O. W. LOOMIS, K.C.B., C.M.G., D.S.O.
Sept. 22nd, 1914, to Jan. 5th, 1916.

LIEUT.-COL. K. M. PERRY, D.S.O.   LIEUT.-COL. I. M. R. SINCLAIR, D.S.O., M.C.
Oct. 14th, 1918, to Feb. 28th, 1919.   Feb. 28th, 1919, to Demobilization.

COMMANDING OFFICERS, 13TH BATTALION, R.H.C.

BACK FROM GERMANY TO CANADA

mand of Lieut. Mather, attended the funeral of a Belgian soldier in the Central Church at Huy. The civilian authorities were in charge of the arrangements, which were simple but impressive, the pipers and buglers of the 13th according military honours. At the conclusion of the service the organist played the British and Belgian National Anthems.

II

Early in March it became obvious that the Battalion's time at Wanze was rapidly drawing to a close. Several small parties left for England, these being composed of men from Prince Edward Island, New Brunswick and Nova Scotia, who did not want to be demobilized in Montreal. All Canada was divided for demobilization into dispersal areas, so that men would not be forced to travel to some distant spot with the unit to which they belonged in France, but could, if they so desired, become attached to some other unit which would demobilize near their homes. By this system the individuals were spared much annoyance and the Government no little expense.

To bid good-bye to the maidens of Wanze and Huy and in acknowledgment of all the hospitality that the troops had received during their stay, a "farewell" dance was given by the Battalion on the evening of March 4th. As several previous "farewell" dances had been given, some of the guests were sceptical about this being the very last, but such it proved, for soon afterwards definite orders were received that the Battalion, plus "E" Coy. composed of several small groups from other units in the 1st Division, would entrain at Huy for Havre on March 8th.

This move duly took place and at 9.30 a.m. the train pulled out of the station. Splendid rationing arrangements were met with during the whole of the journey to Havre, which was reached at noon on March 10th, but in spite of good food and several issues of rum, the men found the trip long and wearisome. Only while passing through the devastated zone of France and the scenes of their own exploits near Arras and Mont St. Eloy was there much in which they were interested.

On arrival at Havre the Battalion moved into huts at the Docks Rest Camp. Here a tiresome week was spent, baths, medical inspections and fumigations occupying a part of the time, while rifle inspections, light drills and a certain number of fatigues filled the

ROYAL HIGHLANDERS OF CANADA

balance. Commissariat arrangements were excellent at this camp and recreation for the troops was provided by several cinema theatres and concert parties.

At 8 p.m. on Sunday, March 16th, the Royal Highlanders embarked on the S.S. "Lorina" and sailed for England. In contrast to the crossing in 1915, the Channel on this occasion was quite smooth and few suffered more than minor qualms of sea-sickness. At 6 a.m. on March 17th the "Lorina" docked at Weymouth and the 13th Battalion, after 49 months of foreign service, found itself once more on British soil.

Entraining at 9 a.m. the Royal Highlanders were conveyed to Liphook, whence they marched to Bramshott Camp, a distance of about two miles. Baths were secured for the men on March 18th and all clothing, blankets and bedding put through what, without equivocation and with no attempt at romance, was frankly called a "steam de-lousing process." A change of underclothes was also provided, so that the men were clean and comfortable and ready to go on leave. Twenty-two officers and 505 other ranks were granted leave on March 21st and on the following day the number of men in camp was reduced to 98, when 140 other ranks also went on leave. By the 25th of the month 5 officers and 12 other ranks alone remained on duty, but this represented low water mark, as on the 26th several individuals whose finances had been unable to stand the strain of extended leave reported back.

Meanwhile medical examination and the preparation of documents for demobilization progressed apace. As regards the former, 26 officers and 652 men had been examined and their condition recorded before the month came to an end. Light drills, sports and the completing of the vast number of demobilization forms filled the time of officers and men during the first week of April. Early in the second week the Battalion paraded and a special alphabetical muster roll was prepared to assist the process of embarkation for Canada which was now imminent.

At the last moment a case of measles broke out in the Pipe Band, with the result that the Pipe-Major and 25 other ranks were isolated and forced to abandon the expectation of accompanying the Battalion when it sailed. This was a great disappointment, not only to those who were left behind, but to all ranks, who had eagerly looked forward to marching through the streets of Montreal with their own band to lead them.

BACK FROM GERMANY TO CANADA

Shortly after midnight of April 9th breakfast was served to the men and at 1.30 a.m. on April 10th the Battalion marched to Liphook Station. At 3.30 a.m. the train pulled out and at 1 p.m. reached Liverpool, where the Battalion embarked on the S.S. "Carmania." Major-Gen. Sir A. C. Macdonell, the 1st Divisional Commander, and Brig.-Gen. G. S. Tuxford, G.O.C. the 3rd Brigade, were both at the dock to bid the troops good-bye. In addition to the 13th, which embarked with a strength of 33 officers and 694 other ranks, the "Carmania" carried the 5th, 7th, 10th and 14th Battalions.

On the whole the voyage that followed was eventless. Sports and concerts were arranged at frequent intervals, while life boat drills and other minor fatigues took up a certain amount of time. The Y.M.C.A., in addition to taking an active part in the organization of amusements, distributed books and magazines which were most acceptable. During the voyage more work was done on documents and pay books. Every man's account was closed by calculating the exact sum that would be due him on arrival in Montreal. In addition to this medical examinations were made in some cases and, where necessary, changes were made in medical history sheets, bringing these up to date. By hard work along these lines the possibility of an enforced stay in barracks was removed and the Battalion prepared for immediate demobilization on reaching Montreal.

At 7 p.m. on April 18th the "Carmania" docked at Pier No. 2 in Halifax and by 9 p.m. the 13th Battalion, which was the first unit off the boat, had boarded a train,—not the 8 chevaux 40 hommes variety—and was on its way westward.

April 19th was spent en route and the morning of Easter Sunday, the 20th, was devoted to "spit and polish" in preparation for the march in Montreal. At 2 p.m. the train pulled into Place Viger Station and the 13th Battalion had arrived home. Inside the station the troops were welcomed by a Guard of Honour, by pipe and brass bands and by many officers of the 5th and 42nd Royal Highlanders, the latter unit having returned to Canada and been demobilized some weeks before.

The greeting extended to the 13th and 14th Battalions inside the station, for all its warmth and cordiality, was as nothing to the fervour of the demonstration accorded to them during their march through the streets. Having saluted the Colours, the men of the 13th, marching with fixed bayonets and wearing with pride the Red Hackle in their bonnets, led the way along Craig St. and across the Champ de Mars, where Major-Gen. E. W. Wilson took the salute. From the Champ de Mars the 13th and 14th proceeded to St. James St., along St. James to Victoria Square and up Beaver Hall Hill to St. Catherine St., the whole route being lined with thousands upon thousands of citizens, who by a great roar of cheering welcomed the men home and paid tribute to the record they had gained in France.

When St. Catherine St. was reached a turn to the left was made and the 13th found itself retracing a part of the route followed when leaving for the war on that August night, almost five years before. Just as on that occasion, the crowd became denser as Peel St. was approached, and the roar of cheering became deafening, but this time the Battalion swung north instead of south and halted at the door of the Peel St. Barracks. Here someone with a sense of the dramatic had suspended a banner on which was inscribed, "The End of the Trail."

Passing beneath this banner the men entered the barracks and were drawn up for their last parade. Major I. M. R. Sinclair, D.S.O., M.C., who had sailed from Canada with the original Battalion as a subaltern, was in command, while the companies were commanded respectively by Capt. A. W. Ruston, Major F. S. Mathewson, Major J. D. Macpherson, M.C., and Major W. E. Macfarlane, M.C., all members of the original Battalion who by reason of their work in France had at one time or another been promoted from the ranks.

Solemnly the men saluted the Colours and awaited the word to dismiss. When this was given the 13th Battalion, Royal Highlanders of Canada, passed out of official existence, until December 1st, 1920, when the Canadian Militia was reorganized and the right to carry the title, "13th Battalion, C.E.F." given to the 1st Battalion, Royal Highlanders of Canada.

Those who served in the 13th ranks and still live share with the reorganized 1st Battalion of the parent Regiment the guardianship of a priceless heritage and an enviable tradition of duty faithfully performed. As for those who served and, serving, died,

"THEIR NAME LIVETH FOR EVER MORE."

Appendices

APPENDIX A.

Honour Roll

KILLED IN ACTION OR DIED OF WOUNDS.

Adams, C.Q.M.S. Arthur.
Adams, Lance-Corp. John B.
Adams, Pte. Thomas.
Addinell, Pte. William R.
Addy, Pte. Frederick.
Adkin, Pte. John D.
Aikins, Pte. Ormal.
Ainslie, Pte. John G.
Ainsworth, Pte. William.
Airth, Pte. David.
Aitchison, Lieut. A. W., M.C.
Aldridge, Pte. Robert.
Allan, Pte. Andrew.
Allan, Pte. William.
Allen, Pte. George.
Allen, Lance-Corp. William.
Alvery, Pte. Owen B.
Ambler, Pte. Leonard.
Ames, Pte. Arnold.
Amon, Pte. Alexander.
Anderson, Pte. Alexander McK.
Anderson, Sergt. John.
Anderson, Pte. John.
Anderson, Pte. Roy W.
Anderson, Pte. William.
Andrews, Pte. Jasper B.
Anthony, Pte. James B.
Arbuckle, Pte. Charles F.
Archibald, Lance-Corp. William A.
Armstrong, Pte. James.
Armstrong, Pte. John D.
Armstrong, Pte. John S.
Armstrong, Pte. Russell.
Armstrong, Lance-Corp. Wellington.
Arrowsmith, Pte. James.
Ash, Pte. Reginald A.
Askin, Pte. Robert.
Atkins, Lance-Corp. Thomas P.

Atkinson, Pte. Joseph.
Atkinson, Pte. Robert C.
Atwood, Pte. Clayton.
Auld, Pte. Alexander.
Ayre, Pte. William.

Babin, Pte. Joseph.
Bailey, Pte. Hugh R.
Bailey, Lance-Corp. J. William.
Bailey, Pte. Joseph.
Baker, Pte. Elvy.
Baker, Pte. Ernest M.
Baker, Pte. Joseph A.
Baker, Pte. William A.
Ball, Pte. Arthur.
Ballard, Pte. Alfred.
Barker, Pte. Thomas H.
Baron, Pte. Oswald.
Barry, Pte. John.
Bartholomew, Corp. Arthur.
Barton, Pte. Frederick W.
Barton, Pte. Oliver.
Bartrum, Pte. Glen A.
Batchelor, Pte. John W.
Batten, Pte. William R.
Baxter, Pte. Robert G.
Bayliss, Corp. Harold.
Beaconsfield, Lance-Corp. James.
Beard, Pte. James.
Bell, Pte. Robert B.
Bellamy, Sergt. William O.
Bennett, Pte. George R.
Bennett, Pte. Joseph A.'
Bennett, Pte. Sam.
Bennett, Pte. Stanley.
Bennett, Capt. William H. D.
Benson, Pte. Lester.
Bentley, Sergt. George M.

ROYAL HIGHLANDERS OF CANADA

Besner, Pte. Avila.
Best, Pte. Thomas.
Bethune, Pte. George B.
Bettinson, Pte. Howard W.
Beveridge, Pte. Robert.
Bingham, Pte. Fred.
Binkley, Pte Allan.
Bird, Pte. Thomas.
Birks, Pte. Harry.
Bishop, Pte. Charles.
Black, Pte. Walter C.
Blain, Pte. John.
Blanchard, Pte. Avariste.
Blevins, Pte. John.
Blount, Pte. James.
Boland, Pte. George.
Boland, Pte. S.
Bond, Pte. John.
Boston, Pte. Thomas.
Boulich, Corp. Anthony.
Bourret, Pte. Thomas.
Bowden, Pte. Jehu.
Bowes, Pte. Edgar A.
Bowie, Pte. John.
Brearley, Pte. Norman O.
Breen, Pte. Joseph.
Brennan, Pte. Andrew.
Brierley, Pte. Philip J.
Brittan, Lieut. Stanley V.
Britton, Corp. Sidney.
Brodie, Pte. Peter.
Brogden, Pte. Fred.
Brooks, Pte. Miles H.
Brown, Pte. Albert.
Brown, Pte. Carl R.
Brown, Corp. Charles A.
Brown, Sergt. Daniel McN.
Brown, Pte. Gerald C.
Brown, Pte. James.
Brown, Lance-Corp. John.
Brown, Pte. John H.
Brown, Pte. Robert H.
Brown, Pte. William.
Bryan, Pte. James E.
Bryanton, Pte. Harry.
Bryson, Lieut. Elmer C.
Buchan, Pte. Thomas.
Buchanan, Pte. Alexander.

Buchanan, Pte. Duncan M.
Buchanan, Capt. Fitz-Herbert Price.
Buchanan, Lieut.-Col. Victor C., D.S.O.
Buchanan, Lance-Sergt. William E.
Buckley, Pte. James.
Bulger, Pte. Louis.
Bullock, Pte. Henry.
Bundy, Sergt. Walter J.
Burke, Pte. John.
Burritt, Pte. Edgar M.
Burrows, Pte. Joseph.
Burt, Sergt. Frank.
Buswell, Pte. Sydney E.
Butcher, Pte. James F.
Byars, Sergt. Henry.

Cahill, Pte. Jerome.
Caine, Pte. Carstairs.
Cameron, Pte. Harry W.
Cameron, Pte. John.
Cameron, Pte. William J.
Camm, Sergt. C. H., M.M. & Bar.
Campbell, Pte. David.
Campbell, Pte. David M.
Campbell, Pte. Douglass.
Campbell, Corp. James J.
Campbell, Pte. John.
Campbell, Pte. Thomas J.
Cann, Pte. Gordon B.
Carley, Pte. John.
Carmichael, Lieut. Kenneth M.
Carrick, Sergt. Robert L.
Carroll, Pte. J.
Carroll, Pte. James.
Carruthers, Pte. John.
Caryer, Sergt. William E. S.
Casey, Pte. Francis J.
Caslake, Sergt. Alfred J.
Catford, Pte. Arthur E.
Chaisson, Pte. Joseph S.
Charles, Pte. Edward A.
Cheesman, Pte. Walter.
Cherry, Pte. Francis S.
Childs, Pte. Henry.
Christie, Pte. William.
Christie, Lieut. W. D. C., D.S.O.
Christman, Pte. Ernest.

HONOUR ROLL

Clarendon, Pte. Alvin, M.M.
Claridge, Pte. George.
Clark, Pte. Charles B.
Clark, Pte. George.
Clark, Pte. William G.
Clarke, Pte. Harold G.
Clarke, Pte. Milton O.
Clarke, Pte. Phillip J.
Clarke, Pte. Stanley H.
Clarke, Pte. Stanley J.
Clarke, Pte. Walter.
Claxton, Pte. Charles A.
Clee, Pte. Charles E.
Clitheroe, Pte. Walter.
Clive, Pte. William.
Cluness, Corp. John M.
Cobb, Pte. Frederick A.
Cockburn, Sergt. John W.
Coldwell, Pte. Francis S.
Coldwell, Pte. James B.
Cole, Pte. Jack E.
Collier, Pte. Eli F.
Collings, Pte. William.
Collins, Corp. Frank.
Conn, Pte. George D.
Connack, Pte. John J.
Connell, Lance-Sergt. Robert.
Cook, Pte. John R.
Cooke, Pte. Thomas C.
Cooper, Sergt. Henry.
Copeman, Sergt. Henry.
Cory, Sergt. John C.
Cossina, Pte. Thomas.
Cossman, Pte. Charles.
Cotton, Pte. Walter J.
Cottrell, Pte. William.
Coulombe, Pte. Arthur.
Courchaine, Pte. Oscar.
Coutts, Pte. James G.
Cowan, Corp. George T., M.M.
Cowling, Pte. Herbert.
Cox, Lance-Corp. Edward J.
Coyle, Pte. Patrick.
Coyston, Sergt. Robert H.
Craig, Pte. George L.
Craig, Lance-Sergt. James.
Craig, Pte. Stewart.
Crampsey, Pte. Patrick.

Crane, Pte. James E.
Crate, Pte. Louis.
Crawford, Pte. Leo.
Crawford, Pte. Michael D.
Creighton, Lieut. Ernest.
Crichton, Pte. George.
Croak, Pte. John B., V.C.
Crocket, Pte. Walter P.
Cronk, Pte. Bruce P.
Crowdy, Capt. C. Hutton.
Crowe, Sergt. Alfred F.
Crowe, Corp. Amos V.
Crowe, Pte. George.
Cryer, Pte. John E.
Culfeather, Pte. Thomas.
Cunningham, Pte. A.
Cunningham, Pte. Bernard.
Cunningham, Pte. Elezar.
Cunningham, Pte. Herbert.
Cunningham, Corp. Lorne E.
Currie, Pte. J.
Currie, Pte. James.
Curwen, Sergt. Francis G.
Cuthbert, Pte. George.
Cyr, Pte. George.

Dale, Pte. Sydney.
Dand, Pte. Matthew G.
Davidson, Pte. Emanuel.
Davidson, Pte. James.
Davies, Pte. Harold L.
Davis, Pte. George.
Davis, Pte. Orville C.
Dawe, Pte. Samuel.
Day, Sergt. Allan W.
Day, Pte. William M.
Daynes, Pte. Duncan.
DeCoste, Pte. Archie N.
Delbrouck, Pte. Gaston.
Denbow, Pte. John C.
Dennis, Pte. Fred B.
Dent, Pte. James W.
DeQuetteville, Lance-Sergt. A. P.
Derrick, Pte. Arthur T. W.
Desrochers, Pte. Henri B.
Devalley, Pte. John.
Deveaux, Pte. John P.
Dewhurst, Pte. Lancelot.

ROYAL HIGHLANDERS OF CANADA

Dick, Pte. Peter.
Dickson, Pte. Alfred J.
Dixon, Pte. William J.
Divers, Pte. Walter H.
Docherty, Lance-Corp. Harry.
Doherty, Pte. William J.
Domingue, Pte. Arthur.
Donaldson, Pte. A.
Dondale, Pte. Karl.
Donohue, Pte. Edward.
Donovan, Pte. Thomas M.
Donoven, Pte. James.
Dorey, Pte. Ottis A.
Doyle, Pte. Lorne.
Drader, Pte. Samuel.
Drinkall, Lance-Corp. George A.
Drummond, Capt. Guy M.
Duff, Lance-Sergt. John.
Duffy, Pte. Stewart R.
Dumas, Pte. Arthur.
Dunbar, Pte. Alexander F.
Dunbar, Pte. Charles.
Duncan, Pte. David.
Duncan, Pte. James.
Duncan, Pte. Joseph.
Dunlop, Pte. James.
Dunlop, Sergt. Matthew B.
Dunmore, Sergt. G., M.M.
Dunn, Pte. Henry A.
Dunning, Pte. John C.
Dunphy, Pte. William.
Dupre, Pte. Thomas.
Dustan, Pte. Edward.

Eadle, Pte. George W.
Edgar, Pte. George.
Edge, Sergt. Albert.
Edge, Pte. A.
Edge, Corp. Frederick C.
Edwards, Lance-Corp. Andrew D.
Edwards, Pte. John.
Edwards, Pte. Stanley W.
Edwards, Lance-Corp. William H.
Element, Pte. George.
Ellis, Lance-Corp. William H.
Ellsworth, Pte. Ernest.
Elston, Pte. Eldon, M.M.
Emerson, Lance-Corp. Phillip S.

Ensor, Pte. William H.
Erickson, Lance-Corp. Gustaf.
Etheridge, Lance-Corp. Alfred.
Evans, C. S. M. Edwin, D.C.M.
Evans, Pte. William (No. 127186).
Evans, Pte. William (No. 193439).
Ewart, Pte. William.
Ewing, Pte. Robert.

Fairley, Pte. Thomas.
Fairley, Pte. William F.
Fancourt, Corp. Alfred G.
Ferguson, Pte. Daniel.
Ferguson, Pte. Donald A.
Ferguson, Pte. Duncan.
Ferguson, Corp. Duncan J.
Ferguson, Pte. Gordon E.
Ferguson, Pte. Leo, M.M.
Ferri, Pte. Angelo.
Fifield, Pte. Malcolm G.
Finch, Sergt. Herbert A.
Findlay, Pte. James B.
Finlayson, Pte. Robert M.
Finn, Pte. Daniel.
Fish, Pte. Charles F. H.
Fisher, Lance-Corp. Fred, V.C.
Fisher, Corp. George.
Fisher, Pte. Walter.
Fitzgerald, Pte. John R.
Fitzpatrick, Sergt. Jack.
Fitzpatrick, Pte. Thomas.
Fitzpatrick, Pte. William H.
Flavelle, Pte. George B.
Flynn, Pte. Owen F.
Fogarty, Pte. Howard.
Forgie, Pte. Hugh.
Forsyth, Pte. William.
Fortier, Pte. Nelson.
Foster, Pte. Alexander R.
Foster, Pte. George S.
Fowler, Pte. Gordon.
Fowler, Pte. James.
Fox, Pte. Melfort F. J.
Frame, Pte. William H.
Fraser, Pte. John B.
Fraser, Pte. Lachlan.
Fraser, Pte. Newton.
Freeman, Pte. Alexander.

HONOUR ROLL

Freeman, Pte. Fred G.
French, Pte. Harry.
Furlong, Pte. James F.

Gaitens, Pte. Rae C.
Gardner, Lance-Corp. Jack.
Garrett, Pte. John.
Geal, Lance-Corp. John A.
Geekie, Pte. Stewart.
Gibb, Pte. George.
Gibbs, Pte. George H.
Gibson, Pte. George.
Gibson, Pte. James A.
Giles, Pte. James H.
Gill, Pte. George.
Gill, Sergt. Lorne S.
Gillibanks, Pte. Jonathan R.
Gillis, Pte. Gabriel.
Gillis, Pte. Hector J.
Gillis, Pte. Peter.
Gillooly, Pte. Charles H.
Gilroy, Major Sidney W.
Ginn, Pte. Charles.
Giveen, Lieut. Butler.
Glad, Pte. Konghard.
Glover, Pte. Francis.
Gooch, Pte. Thomas.
Good, Pte. Ernest.
Goodman, Pte. Richard.
Goodwillie, Corp. Charles A.
Goodwin, Pte. Alonzo.
Goodwin, Sergt. Thomas A.
Gordon, Pte. Alexander G.
Gordon, Pte. Joseph.
Gordon, Pte. Thomas E.
Gotell, Pte. Thomas.
Gowans, Pte. Stephen.
Gracey, Lance-Corp. William.
Gracey, Pte. William J.
Graham, Corp. John.
Graham, Pte. J. K.
Graham, Sergt. Thomas, M.M.
Graham, Pte. William H.
Grahamslaw, Pte. William.
Grant, Pte. Jack.
Gray, Pte. Alfred.
Gray, Pte. Angus.
Gray, Pte. Gordon.

Gray, Corp. Hugh.
Gray, Corp. William S.
Grech, Lance-Corp. Robert.
Green, Capt. Carleton C.
Green, Pte. Hugh A.
Green, Pte. Walter W.
Green, Pte. William.
Greenshields, Capt. Melville.
Greenwood, Pte. Thomas.
Gregory, Pte. Ernest E.
Gregson, Pte. James C.
Grey, Lieut. John.
Grieve, Lieut. David C.
Gummels, Pte. George.
Gunn, Pte. Daniel.

Hachey, Pte. George H.
Hadfield, Pte. Thomas.
Haffenden, Pte. Arthur J. F.
Hains, Pte. David A.
Halifax, Pte. Reuben.
Haley, Sergt. Edward S.
Hall, Pte. Alfred.
Hall, Pte. Frederick.
Hall, Pte. Robert D.
Halls, Pte. Frederick C.
Hamilton, Pte. Alexander J.
Hamilton, Lieut. George H.
Hamilton, Pte. Morgan H. C.
Handcock, Pte. Donald K.
Hanley, Corp. William P.
Hanlon, Pte. Clarence A.
Hannaford, Sergt. Wm., D.C.M., M.M. (Bar).
Hannah, Pte. David.
Hannan, Pte. John.
Hape, Pte. William K.
Hardie, Pte. James.
Harding, Pte. Augustus V.
Hardman, Pte. Herbert.
Harkness, Pte. Thomas L.
Harland, Pte. George.
Harpell, Pte. Herbert H.
Harper, Pte. Ernest E.
Harrington, Pte. Archibald.
Harris, Pte. Alexander.
Harris, Pte. Cecil.
Harris, Pte. Charles E.

ROYAL HIGHLANDERS OF CANADA

Harris, Pte. Edward.
Harris, Corp. Thomas.
Harris, Pte. Thomas.
Harrop, Pte. Albert E.
Harvey, Pte. Henry C.
Hawkings, Pte. William C.
Hawkins, Pte. Percy E.
Hawley, Pte. Carlton B.
Hayward, Pte. Stanley A.
Hazard, Pte. Albert.
Healey, Pte. Harold.
Heatherington, Pte. George R.
Henderson, Pte. Cyril.
Henderson, Pte. Ivan.
Henderson, Pte. James H.
Henrich, Pte. Louis.
Herbert, Pte. James.
Herlihy, Pte. Thomas.
Herring, Pte. Reginald F.
Hervey, Pte. Bernard.
Hewitt, Pte. George.
Hewitt, Pte. James.
Hicken, Pte. Edward A.
Hicken, Pte. Stewart.
Hickey, Pte. Samuel.
Hickey, Pte. William L.
Hicks, Pte. Winford C.
Hill, Pte. Arthur.
Hill, Sergt. Edgar H.
Hill, Pte. George.
Hill, Pte. John.
Hill, Lance-Corp. Ruby Charles.
Hinton, Pte. George H.
Hirst, Pte. John.
Hodgkins, Pte. Percy.
Hodgson, Pte. Herbert.
Hodgson, Pte. Samuel P.
Hodgson, Pte. Thomas.
Hollanby, Pte. Albert E.
Holland, Pte. Frederick C. V.
Hollands, Pte. John.
Hollings, Pte. Arthur.
Hooper, Pte. Bertie.
Horne, Pte. Colin H.
Horsey, Lieut. Clifford M.
Horton, Pte. Roy C.
Howe, Pte. Robert.
Howell, Pte. Frederick.

Hownslow, Pte. Albert.
Hudson, Pte. John.
Hughes, Corp. Thomas.
Hull, Lance-Corp. Wilfred.
Hunt, Pte. Henry G.
Hunt, Pte. Louis.
Hurlburt, Pte. David.
Hurshman, Pte. John.
Hutchings, Pte. Harold.
Hutchinson, Pte. Walter H.
Hyde, Lieut. Charles E.
Hyndman, Pte. William.

Imrie, Sergt. George W.
Imrie, Pte. James W.
Innes, Pte. Thomas.
Irons, Pte. Samuel.
Irvine, Pte. Robert.
Isaacs, Pte. Ernest W.

Jackson, Pte. Harry A.
Jackson, Pte. William T.
James, Pte. Harry.
James, Pte. James D. S.
Jaques, Lieut. Maurice A.
Jarrett, Sergt. Edward H.
Jeffery, Pte. Thomas.
Jewers, Pte. Ira Wallace.
Johnson, Pte. Desmond.
Johnson, Pte. M.
Johnston, Lance-Corp. Archibald.
Johnston, Corp. Charles.
Johnston, Pte. Raymond C.
Jolicoeur, Sergt. Ernest E.
Jones, Pte. George.
Jones, Pte. Noel E.
Jones, Pte. Norman.
Jones, Pte. William.
Joyce, Pte. John J.

Kealey, Pte. Chauncey.
Keeley, Corp. Kenneth.
Kellett, Pte. James H.
Kelly, Pte. Patrick.
Kendall, Pte. Arthur H.
Kenna, Pte. Robert.
Kent, Lance-Sergt. George E.
Key, Sergt. Robert.

HONOUR ROLL

Key, Pte. William J.
Kidd, Pte. William.
Kilrea, Pte. Robert.
King, Pte. David.
King, Pte. Frank.
Kirk, Pte. George P.
Kitchin, Pte. Benjamin.
Knapp, Pte. Benjamin M.
Knight, Corp. Herbert J.
Knights, Lance-Corp. Albert.
Krenchel, Lieut. Otto B., M.C., D.C.M.
Krumsei, Pte. Fred.

Lacey, Pte. Frank.
Lagarde, Pte. Joseph O.
Lambe, Pte. John W.
Lancaster, Sergt. James L.
Landry, Pte. Evariste.
Landry, Pte. Harvey.
Lang, Corp. Thomas.
Larin, Pte. Charles.
Laughlin, Pte. Fred A.
Lavery, Pte. Robert.
Lawson, Sergt. John.
Lawson, Pte. William.
Lawson, Pte. William A.
Layer, Pte. William.
Leadbetter, Pte. Robert.
Leary, Pte. Walter.
Leatham, Pte. John S.
Leavitt, Pte. Arthur.
Lee, Pte. Thomas W.
Lees, Capt. Gerald O.
Leger, Pte. Jules.
Legros, C. S. M. Charles, M.M.
Lenener, Pte. John P.
Lennon, Pte. Christopher.
Leonard, Pte. George T.
Lepine, Pte. Alexander.
Lewis, Pte. Arthur N.
Lightbody, Pte. Norman.
Lightizer, Pte. John L.
Lindh, Corp. Bertie A.
Lindsay, Pte. Franklin E.
Ling, Pte. Lawrence.
Ling, Pte. Roy.
Linnell, Pte. Joseph.

Linton, Pte. Harold.
Livingstone, Sergt. George.
Lloyd, Pte. Osman E. B.
Llwyd, Capt. Charles D., M.C.
Lockley, Pte. David.
Love, Pte. John.
Lowe, Lance-Corp. Robert.
Lowery, Pte. Ernest M.
Lunn, Pte. Walter F.
Lynch, Pte. John J.

MacDermot, Major A. G. C.
MacDonald, Pte. Arthur.
MacDonald, Pte. Charles S.
MacDonald, Pte. Kenneth N.
Macdonald, Pte. Neil W.
MacDonald, Pte. Richard F.
MacDougall, Pte. Harold V.
MacGillivray, Pte. Grant.
MacIntosh, Pte. William H.
MacIvor, Pte. Murdie.
MacKay, Pte. Harry J.
MacKay, Sergt. John.
MacKenzie, Pte. Charles R.
MacKinnon, Pte. Daniel.
MacLean, Lieut. Arthur S.
MacLean, Capt. Norman M.
MacLean, Lance-Corp. William S.
MacLucas, Lance-Corp. Kenneth.
MacNamee, Lance-Corp. William H.
MacNeil, Lance-Corp. Donald J.
Macey, Pte. Sylvester J.
Mack, Pte. Frank.
Mackman, Pte. George H.
Magee, Pte. Frank W.
Maguire, Pte. John R.
Malone, Pte. John J.
Maloney, Lance-Corp. Michael.
Manning, Corp. Leonard.
Mantell, Pte. Amos R.
Marceau, Pte. George H.
Marriott, Sergt. Fred.
Marshall, Pte. Harold.
Marshall, Pte. Joseph H.
Marshall, Pte. William D.
Martin, Pte. David G.
Martin, Pte. John C.
Martin, Pte. William.

ROYAL HIGHLANDERS OF CANADA

Masse, Pte. Dieudonne.
Massie, Pte. Charles P.
Matheson, Pte. John A.
Matthews, Pte. Frederick J.
Mayhew, Pte. Arthur.
Mays, Pte. Frank.
Meades, Sergt. Henry M.
Medcroft, Pte. Thomas.
Megan, Lieut. Gerald W.
Meikle, Pte. William.
Meister, Corp. Otis.
Mellowes, Pte. William O.
Melluish, Pte. William A.
Meredith, Pte. Arthur R.
Meredith, Pte. Herbert R. B.
Michelmore, Pte. Francis H.
Mileham, Pte. William.
Millar, Sergt. George.
Miller, Lance-Corp. Albert.
Miller, Pte. Andrew.
Miller, Pte. John.
Miller, Pte. Wilson.
Milligan, Pte. Alexander.
Milne, Lance-Corp. John.
Milne, Pte. Kenneth.
Milne, Pte. Lewis G.
Mills, Pte. Thomas E.
Mitchell, Pte. John.
Mitchell Pte. John G.
Moffitt, Pte. John A.
Monk, Pte. Joseph.
Montanelli, Pte. John.
Mooney, Pte. Albert.
Moore, Pte. Allan.
Moore, Pte. Harold.
Moore, Pte. Marshall B.
Morby, Pte. Arthur.
Morgan, Sergt. Fred B.
Morgan, Pte. Thomas A.
Morphy, Lieut. John M.
Morris, Corp. George W.
Morrison, Pte. Elex.
Morrison, Pte. George.
Morrison, Sergt. William.
Moss, Pte. Edward C.
Mott, Pte. Hubert B.
Muir, Pte. William.
Munro, Pte. Stanley.

Munroe, Pte. Arthur J.
Murney, Lance-Corp. Henry J.
Murphy, Pte. James G.
Myler, Pte. Matthew.
McAfee, Pte. John S.
McAllister, Pte. Frederick.
McAlpine, Pte. David L.
McArthur, John.
McArthur, Pte. Arthur.
McBurnie, Pte. Robert.
McCabe, Pte. Grover C.
McCahon, Pte. Charles P.
McCahon, Pte. George.
McCallum, Pte. James.
McCance, Pte. John.
McCarter, Pte. Andrew R.
McCarthy, Pte. John.
McCleave, Lieut. Harry A.
McCluskey, Pte. Clarence.
McConachie, Lance-Corp. John A.
McConachie, Pte. Raymond H.
McCormack, Pte. Frank.
McCormack, Pte. Joseph M.
McCormick, Pte. Douglas L.
McCormick, Pte. Hugh.
McCully, Pte. Fred A.
McDaniel, Pte. Joseph H.
McDonald, Pte. Alexander J., M.M.
McDonald, Pte. Alexander J.
McDonald, Pte. Archie.
McDonald, Pte. Elmer.
McDonald, Pte. George.
McDonald, Pte. John.
McDonald, Pte. Lewis J.
McDonald, Pte. Robert Alvin.
McDonald, Pte. Ronald J.
McDonald, Pte. William J.
McDonald, Lance-Corp. William M.
McDonnell, Pte. Edward.
McDougall, Pte. Arthur P.
McDougall, Pte. Harry O.
McEachern, Pte. Andrew J.
McFarlane, Corp. Hugh.
McGibbon, Capt. Gilbert D.
McGillivary, Pte. Stephen.
McGrath, Pte. William J.
McGregor, Pte. William.
McGuffin, Pte. William J.

HONOUR ROLL

McIntosh, Pte. Isaac.
McIntyre, Pte. Peter.
McKay, Pte. John B.
McKellar, Pte. Thomas B.
McKenzie, Sergt. Alex., M.M.
McKenzie, Pte. Andrew.
McKenzie, Pte. Dan.
McKim, Pte. William.
McKinnon, Pte. Peter.
McLaren, Pte. Duncan.
McLaren, Pte. Gordon S.
McLaughlin, Pte. William.
McLaurin, Pte. Douglas C.
McLean, Pte. James A.
McLellan, Pte. J.
McLellan, Pte. James.
McLeod, Sergt. Alex., D.C.M.
McLeod, Pte. David R.
McLeod, Sergt. Peter.
McLeod, Pte. Stanley S.
McLeod, Pte. Wallace C.
McLeod, Lance-Corp. William.
McLonney, Pte. William.
McMorran, Pte. Aldron W.
McNab, Pte. John.
McNair, Pte. Robert H.
McNaught, Sergt. John.
McNaughton, Sergt. Harold.
McNeil, Corp. Murdoch A.
McNeil, Pte. Joseph.
McNicol, Pte. Alexander C.
McPhee, Pte. Archibald N.
McPhee, Pte. James B.
McPhee, Pte. Joseph.
McPherson, Pte. John.
McQuade, Pte. James P.

Nash, Pte. Ernest.
Nason, Lieut. Alexis P.
Negus, Pte. Thomas L.
Neil, Sergt. William C.
Newitt, Pte. William.
Newnham, Sergt. Thomas C., M.M.
Nimmo, Sergt. Robert C.
Nolan, Pte. Michael.
Norberg, Pte. Fabian.
Norsworthy, Major Edward C.
Nother, Pte. George.

O'Connor, Pte. John M. J.
O'Donnell, Pte. Bert.
O'Leary, Pte. Harvey.
O'Leary, Corp. Pat.
Oliver, Sergt. Arthur.
Oliver, Pte. George.
Olsen, Pte. Frank T.
Onslow, Pte. Harry V.
Osborne, Pte. John W.
Osborne, Pte. William A.
O'Toole, Pte. James M.
Overson, Pte. James V. S.
Oxley, Pte. William.

Packer, Pte. Richard.
Page, Pte. Sydney.
Palmer, Pte. John J.
Parker, Pte. George K.
Parsons, Pte. George H.
Parsons, Pte. Walter H.
Partridge, Corp. Fred.
Pass, Pte. George.
Payne, Lance-Corp. Robert.
Peacock, Lance-Corp. Charles J. W.
Pearce, Pte. Charles R.
Pearson, Pte. John.
Peffer, Pte. Norman E.
Pegram, Pte. Michael.
Pentland, Pte. William A.
Perigo, Pte. Ira S.
Perley, Pte. Arthur.
Peterkin, Pte. Thomas E. C.
Peterman, Major Wilfred F.
Peterson, Pte. William A.
Petrie, Sergt. Alexander, M.M
Phillip, Pte. William C.
Phillips, Sergt. Ernest.
Phillips, Pte. John D.
Phillips, Pte. Robert.
Piche, Lance-Sergt. James H.
Piche, Pte. Randolph.
Piercy, Lieut. Harold E.
Pigeon, Pte. Georges.
Pilot, Pte. John.
Pitcher, Pte. Alexander.
Pitt, Pte. Edward H.
Plante, Pte. Albert H.
Pollock, Pte. Alexander A.

ROYAL HIGHLANDERS OF CANADA

Poole, Corp. Robert J. M.
Porritt, Pte. John M.
Porter, Corp. James R.
Porter, Pte. Percy R.
Povey, Pte. Joseph.
Powell, Lieut. Haynes R.
Powley, Pte. James W.
Pratt, Pte. Charles H.
Pratt, Pte. Norman.
Pratt, Pte. Thomas G.
Praught, Pte. Dennis P.
Priaulx, Pte. Alfred.
Price, Pte. Frederick.
Price, Pte. Hugh M.
Price, Pte. Samuel.
Price, Pte. Thomas H.
Proctor, Pte. Athol S.
Prosser, Lieut. Arthur D.
Pyper, Pte. John.

Rae, Sergt. Wesley C.
Rafuse, Pte. Willis.
Rainey, Pte. Edmund.
Raynes, Pte. Harry.
Reaume, Lieut. J. Stanley.
Reay, Pte. James.
Redhead, C. S. M. George.
Reekie, Pte. John G.
Reeve, Sergt. Robert.
Reeves, Pte. Joe.
Reid, Pte. Robert S.
Reid, Pte. Wilfred.
Reilly, Pte. William H. L.
Reynolds, Pte. Frederick G.
Rice, Lance-Corp. Arthur G.
Rice, Pte. Jerome.
Richardson, Pte. Albert E.
Richley, Pte. Charlton.
Richmond, Pte. Gavin S.
Rigby, Pte. Fred.
Riley, Pte. George.
Riley, Pte. Roy N.
Ritchie, Corp. George.
Roberts, Pte. Verne D.
Robertson, Pte. Donald A.
Robertson, Pte. George.
Robertson, Pte. Hay.
Robertson, Pte. John W.

Robertson, Pte. Thomas H.
Robinson, Pte. Charles H.
Robinson, Pte. William.
Robson, Sergt. Henry.
Roche, Lieut. Charles J.
Rodgers, Pte. George T.
Rogers, Pte. James S.
Rogers, Pte. Robert.
Rogerson, Pte. Richard G.
Rose, Pte. Gordon S.
Ross, Pte. Archibald.
Ross, Pte. David.
Ross, Pte. Robert J.
Roszel, Pte. George.
Rourke, Pte. James P.
Rowbottom, Sergt. James.
Rowley, Sergt. John.
Russell, Pte. David M.
Rust, Capt. Benjamin Henry.
Ryan, Pte. Charles.
Ryan, Pte. Francis B.
Ryan, Pte. Henry E.
Ryan, Pte. William J.
Ryan, Pte. William P.

Sacritch, Pte. Alexander.
Sadowinski, Pte. Victor.
Sale, Lieut. Gordon N.
Salmon, Sergt. Donald.
Sandford, C. S. M. Richard, M.M.
Saunders, Lieut. T. B.
Saunders, Pte. Thomas.
Saville, Pte. George.
Schofield, Pte. Ralph E.
Sclater, Lieut. Arthur N., M.C.
Scott, Pte. George N.
Scott, Sergt. Samuel.
Scott, Sergt. W. Grahame.
Scott, Pte. William.
Seagram, Pte. John J., M.M.
Seed, Pte. James.
Seivewright, Pte. Henry, M.M.
Selbie, Lieut. Robert J.
Senior, Pte. Walter.
Shannon, Pte. Joseph.
Sharp, Pte. George B.
Sharpe, Pte. Ernest.
Shaughnessy, Sergt. Harold W.

HONOUR ROLL

Shaw, Pte. Edward B.
Shaw, Pte. James.
Shaw, Pte. John.
Shaw, Pte. John H.
Sheehan, Pte. John P.
Shephard, Pte. Wilfred.
Shepherd, Pte. John.
Shepherd, Pte. William R.
Sherwood, Pte. Richard.
Shiell, Pte. John C.
Showman, Pte. Frank F.
Sillitoe, Pte. Arthur.
Simpson, Sergt. James.
Simoneau, Pte. Wilfred J.
Sinclair, Lance-Sergt. Daniel G.
Sinclair, Pte. Donald.
Skeen, Pte. Oswald.
Skuce, Pte. Richard.
Slaven, Pte. Peter.
Sloan, Pte. William.
Sloman, Pte. Herbert.
Small, Corp. William D.
Smile, Pte. Ernest.
Smillie, Pte. William.
Smith, Pte. Albert F.
Smith, Pte. Beverly A.
Smith, Major Charles John.
Smith, Pte. Ernest.
Smith, Pte. Frederick.
Smith, Pte. Howard.
Smith, Pte. James M.
Smith, Lieut. Jeffrey F.
Smith, Pte. J. (No. 414245).
Smith, Pte. John.
Smith, Pte. John W.
Smith, Pte. Stewart.
Snapp, Pte. Simon P.
Sorby, Sergt. Frederick W. D., D.C.M., (Bar).
Southgate, Pte. Lewis M.
Spain, Pte. Henry.
Spencer, Pte. Kenneth.
Spendley, Pte. Arthur.
Spicer, Pte. Russell A.
Splatt, Lance-Corp. William F.
Sprowl, Pte. Perry.
Stamm, Pte. Joseph.
Stansfield, Pte. Israel.

Stark, Sergt. Percival H.
Stedman, Pte. William H.
Stephen, Pte. John L.
Stewart, Pte. Francis.
Stewart, Pte. Norman C.
Stewart, Pte. Sefton I.
Stewart, Lieut. William.
Stirling, Pte. David S.
Stokes, Lance-Corp. Leslie T.
Stracey, Pte. Harold.
Stratford, Pte. Jesse J.
Street, Pte. Richard H.
Stroud, Pte. Richard S.
Strudwick, Lance-Corp. Reginald.
Stuart, Pte. John.
Styles, Pte. Albert G.
Sutherland, Pte. Edgar W.
Sutherland, Lance-Corp. Murray C.
Sutliff, Pte. Neil.
Sweetman, Pte. Carl.

Tait, Pte. John W.
Tait, Pte. Robert A.
Tanner, Pte. Norman J.
Taylor, Lance-Corp. Charles M.
Taylor, Pte. Sydney J.
Taylor, Corp. Richard B.
Taylor, Pte. William E.
Teffer, Corp. Frederick G.
Thomas, Lance-Sergt. Henry.
Thompson, Pte. Engulf.
Thompson, Pte. Ernest.
Thompson, Corp. Fred.
Thompson, Pte. James T.
Thompson, Pte. Lawrence J.
Thomson, Sergt. John H.
Thomson, Pte. Walter.
Thuot, Pte. Eugene.
Tickell, Pte. Isaac.
Toghill, Pte. William T.
Tomlinson, Pte. Ernest.
Tower, Pte. Leonard B.
Towns, Pte. Fred.
Townsend, Sergt. Frank.
Traill, Sergt. Allan D., M.M.
Travers, Lance-Corp. John F.
Trott, Pte. Harry.
Trudel, Pte. Arthur.

ROYAL HIGHLANDERS OF CANADA

Tuckfield, Pte. Francis E.
Twambley, Pte. John B.

Usher, Lance-Corp. Henry.
Ussher, Pte. Robert L.

Valins, Pte. Salem.
Valiquette, Pte. James F.
Vernon, Pte. Oscar D.
Viens, Pte. Arsene.
Vigers, Pte. Frederick.
Vinson, Pte. George J.

Waddicor, Pte. John M.
Wagner, Pte. Bernard G.
Waite, Pte. George.
Wakeling, Pte. Harry.
Walker, Pte. Alexander G.
Walker, Pte. Henry.
Walker, Lieut. James G.
Walker, Pte. John.
Walker, Pte. Michael F.
Walker, Pte. Norman.
Walker, Pte. Sidney.
Wallace, Pte. James.
Wallace, Pte. William B.
Walton, Lance-Corp. Frederick J.
Ward, Pte. Leonard C.
Ward, Pte. Percy.
Ward, Sergt. William, M.M.
Ward, Corp. William.
Ward, Pte. William T.
Warne, Sergt. Owen.
Warrell, Pte. Stanley C.
Warren, Pte. Ernest.
Warren, Pte. Wellington P.
Watson, C. S. M. Alexander C.
Watson, Pte. John.
Watt, Pte. William.
Watt, Pte. William J.
Waud, Capt. Edward W.
Way, Lance-Sergt. Percy, D.C.M.
Webster, Pte. Austin C.
Webster, Pte. John M.
Webster, Pte. Robert L.
Weightman, Pte. William F.
Weir, Lance-Corp. William.

Welch, Pte. Thomas.
Welsh, Pte. William M.
Wentzall, Pte. Joseph H.
Wheaton, Pte. Clarence J.
White, Pte. John.
White, Pte. Melvin F.
Whitehead, Capt. Lionel Ward.
Whitley, Pte. Charles L.
Whitman, Pte. Wilfred.
Whynott, Lance-Corp. Charles S.
Wigmore, Pte. Joseph A.
Wilcox, Pte. Harry J.
Wilkinson, Pte. William.
Williams, Pte. Harry.
Williams, Pte. James Arthur.
Williams, Pte. James W. A.
Williams, Pte. William J.
Willis, Pte. Ernest W.
Willis, Pte. William I.
Willoughby, Pte. Frank.
Wilson, Pte. Adam.
Wilson, Pte. Arthur S.
Wilson, Pte. George E.
Wilson, Pte. George F.
Wilson, Sergt. John.
Wilson, Lance-Corp. Leslie C.
Wilson, Lance-Corp. William G.
Winlow, Pte. Robert S.
Winspear, Pte. Harry.
Winters, Pte. Frank H.
Wise, Pte. Herbert.
Wragge, Pte. Ayrton.
Wray, Sergt. Walter H.
Wright, Pte. Alexander C.
Wright, Pte. Collin M.B., M.M.
Wright, Pte. Fred.
Wright, Sergt. James.
Wright, Pte. Norman H.
Wright, Pte. Percy A.

Yates, Pte. Clement O.
Yates, Pte. James P.
Yensen, Pte. Gustav A.
Young, Pte. George.
Young, Pte. William.
Young, Sergt. William J.

Zinck, Pte. Leo.

HONOUR ROLL

MISSING.

Abbott, Corp. Arthur C.
Armstrong, Pte. William J.
Aston, Pte. Abraham.

Ballantyne, Pte. Albert M.
Beauparlant, Pte. Wilfred, M.M.
Broughton, Pte. Tom W.
Buchanan, Pte. Earl L.
Byrne, Pte. Gerald.

Calvert, Pte. John C.
Campbell, Pte. John L.
Chaters, Pte. John S.
Chisholm, Pte. Charles.
Clarke, Pte. Thomas W.
Clover, Pte. Alfred.
Collins, Pte. James J.
Collins, Pte. Joseph.
Comors, Pte. John.
Coop, Lance-Corp. Henry.
Cornwall, Lance-Corp. Charles W.

Davidson, Pte. Andrew.
Dickenson, Pte. Edwin.
Dickson, Pte. Charles.
Ditrickson, Pte. Henry.
Dixon, Pte. Herbert.
Dixon, Pte. Thomas C.
Dow, Pte. Leslie.
Duncan, Pte. John.
Dykes, Pte. Samuel.

Easson, Pte. John.
Edgington, Pte. Harry.
Evans, Pte. William.

Ferguson, Pte. Archibald.
Ferguson, Pte. James C.
Fisher, Pte. Norman.
Fisher, Pte. William C.
Fitzgerald, Pte. William.
Flin, Pte. Frank S.
Fowlie, Pte. Edward.
Furlong, Pte. Philip J.

Gallagher, Pte. John W.
Gammon, Corp. Earl.
Gibson, Pte. Lorne N.
Gilchrist, Corp. Thomas G.
Goodall, Pte. Josiah.
Goodwin, Pte. James E.

Hagle, Pte. Macklin.
Hall, Pte. Joseph.
Harrison, Pte. John.
Holmes, Pte. Frank.
Homewood, Pte. William.
Hore, Pte. Enos E.
Howard, Pte. Lewis E.
Hurst, Pte. Cuthbert J.

Innes-Brown, Pte. Bernard.
Isherwood, Pte. Richard.

Jahn, Pte. Carl M. C.
Johnson, Pte. Peter.
Jones, Pte. William J.

Keay, Lance-Corp. George N.
Kingston, Pte. Frank.
Knapman, Pte. Herbert C.

Latour, Pte. Emile.
Lecky, Pte. George R.
Ling, Pte. Thomas.
Little, Pte. William W.
Lowry, Pte. William W.
Lynch, Pte. Martin.

MacDonald, Pte. Alexander J.
MacKay, Pte. Stanley.
Magee, Pte. Robert J.
Maltby, Lance-Corp. Charles.
Mathieson, Pte. William R.
Manuel, Pte. Jacob.
Mepham, Pte. Robert.
Marsh, Lance-Corp. Thomas.
Miller, Lance-Corp. James A.
Milne, Pte. James.
Montgomery, Pte. Robert.

ROYAL HIGHLANDERS OF CANADA

Moore, Pte. Thomas G.
Moran, Pte. Edward.
Morrison, Pte. John M.
Mortson, Pte. Alex.
Mount, Pte. George A.
Murdock, Pte. John A.
Murphy, Pte. Fred A.
McCallum, Pte. Ralph A.
McCulloch, Pte. George M.
McGrory, Pte. Frank.
McNeil, Pte. Neil A.
McNulty, Pte. E. J.

Norse, Pte. William.

O'Connors, Pte. John.

Parks, Corp. Stanley.
Paul, Pte. William.
Pearce, Pte. Frederick A.
Petkoff, Pte. Angel.
Pizzy, Pte. Fred.
Pratt, Pte. Charles E.
Purdy, Pte. George.

Quin, Pte. James E.

Rowan, Capt. Frederick John.
Reed, Pte. John J.

Reid, Lance-Sergt. John L.
Richards, Pte. Cecil.
Robinson, Pte. Russell.
Romney, Pte. William.

Smith, Corp. Clifford M.
Smith, Pte. Hughie.
Smith, Pte. Robert H.
Stewart, Corp. James L.
Stewart, Pte. Lawrence D.

Tait, Pte. John.
Tait, Pte. Robert.
Taylor, Pte. Jack.
Thibodeau, Pte. Lorenzo.
Thompson, Pte. Archibald.

Walker, Lieut. Austin H.
Wall, Pte. Michael J.
Watt, Pte. James.
Whetter, Lance-Corp. Richard.
Whitelock, Pte. Henry.
Wilson, Pte. David.
Worsley, Pte. George J.
Wright, Pte. William.

Young, Pte. Walter.

DIED.

Anning, Pte. Harry.
Annon, Pte. John F.
Appleyard, Pte. Albert.
Armstrong, Pte. Francis.
Arsenault, Pte. William J.
Atkinson, Pte. William A.

Bain, Lieut. John S.
Barton, Pte. Allan G.
Bevan, Pte. Owen.
Black, Pte. William F.
Boyles, Pte. Ambrose E.
Butler, Pte. Harry C.

Cann, Pte. William R.
Clarke, Pte. Norman F.

Cooke, S-Sergt. Harry.
Cranfield, Pte. Noble C.
Cuthbert, Pte. David.

Davidson, Pte. Samuel.
Dunlop, Pte. Daniel L.

Elliott, Corp. Frederick G.

Fenn, Pte. Albert S.
Fergus, Corp. William.
Ferguson, Pte. Robert.
Foster, Pte. William H.
Fournier, Pte. Francois.

Gardner, Pte. Ernest J.
Gardner, Pte. William H.

HONOUR ROLL

Goodyear, Pte. William.
Graham, Pte. Norman.
Greens, Pte. William H.
Guyer, Lance-Corp. David, M.M.

Haverly, Pte. Herbert S.
Hueston, Pte. Frank A.

Jessoe, Pte. James L.
Johnston, Pte. Duncan.

Kennedy, Pte. John.

Laing, Pte. Robert.

MacKenzie, Pte. Finlay.
MacNeill, Lance-Corp. Nicolas.
Martineau, Pte. Paul.
Murphy, Pte. Joseph.
McBride, Pte. John.
McEwan, Pte. Frank.
McGuinness, Pte. F. W.

McInally, Pte. Michael.
McKenzie, Pte. Angus D.

O'Dea, Pte. Andrew.

Penfold, Pte. John William.

Racicot, Pte. Theodore.
Robbins, Pte. Norman.
Robinson, Pte. Arthur.

Scott, Pte. James.
Smith, Pte. Samuel H.
Stephens, Pte. Wilfred C.

Taylor, Pte. William T.
Type, Pte. Augustus.

Wardle, Sergt. Joe.
Wilkins, Pte. Charles.
Winter, Pte. George S.
West, Pte. Frank.
Wright, Pte. Charles.

APPENDIX B.
Honours and Awards

THE VICTORIA CROSS.
Lance-Corporal Fred Fisher.
Lance-Sergeant Herman J. Good.
Private John B. Croak.
Lieut.-Col. W. H. Clark-Kennedy. (24th Battalion, V.R.C.)
Lieut. Milton F. Gregg. (Royal Air Force.)

KNIGHT COMMANDER OF THE BATH.
Major-General Sir F. O. W. Loomis.

COMPANION OF THE ORDER OF ST. MICHAEL AND ST. GEORGE.
Major-General Sir F. O. W. Loomis.
Brigadier-General G. E. McCuaig.
Lieut.-Col. W. H. Clark-Kennedy. (24th Battalion, V.R.C.)

COMMANDER OF THE ORDER OF THE BRITISH EMPIRE.
Lieut.-Col. E. R. Brown. (Canadian Army Medical Corps.)

OFFICER OF THE ORDER OF THE BRITISH EMPIRE.
Major John Jeffery.
Major W. J. Taylor, (Paymaster.)

MEMBER OF THE ORDER OF THE BRITISH EMPIRE.
Capt. G. W. R. Simpson.

THE DISTINGUISHED SERVICE ORDER AND BAR.
Major-General Sir F. O. W. Loomis.
Brigadier-General G. E. McCuaig.
Lieut.-Col. K. M. Perry.
Lieut.-Col. W. H. Clark-Kennedy. (24th Battalion, V.R.C.)

HONOURS AND AWARDS

THE DISTINGUISHED SERVICE ORDER.

Lieut.-Col. V. C. Buchanan.
Lieut.-Col. A. G. Cameron.
Lieut.-Col. T. S. Morrisey.
Lieut.-Col. I. M. R. Sinclair.
Major F. S. Mathewson.
Major D. R. McCuaig.
Hon. Major E. E. Graham.
                (Chaplain.)
Capt. H. A. Johnston.
Capt. H. M. Wallis.
Lieut. W. D. C Christie.

THE MILITARY CROSS AND BAR.

Major W. E. Macfarlane.
Lieut. J. E. Christie.
Lieut. W. F. McGovern.
Lieut. Milton F. Gregg. (Royal Air Force.)

THE MILITARY CROSS.

Lieut.-Col. I. M. R. Sinclair.
Hon. Major E. E. Graham,
                (Chaplain.)
Major John Jeffery.
Major J. H. Lovett.
Major J. D. Macpherson.
Capt. Edgar Appleby.
Capt. J. B. Beddome.
Capt. G. W. Brown.
Capt. R. L. Calder.
Capt. H. H. Chanter.
Capt. H. A. Cochrane,
    (Canadian Army Medical Corps.)
Capt. R. M. Hebden.
Capt. R. E. Heaslip.
Capt. H. A. Johnston.
Capt. C. D. Llwyd.
Capt. W. S. M. MacTier.
Capt. C. B. Pitblado.
Capt. A. J. Plant.
Capt. F. S. Stowell.
Capt. H. M. Wallis.
Lieut. A. W. Aitchison.
Lieut. K. G. Blackader.
Lieut. M. L. Brady.
Lieut. D. L. Carstairs.
Lieut. P. E. Corbett.
Lieut. L. C. Drummond.
Lieut. W. E. Dunning.
Lieut. J. R. Ferguson.
Lieut. W. E. Foxen.
Lieut. W. G. Hamilton.
Lieut. W. T. Hornby.
Lieut. O. B. Krenchel.
Lieut. John Lothian.
Lieut. A. N. Sclater.
Reg. Sergt.-Major F. Butler.

THE DISTINGUISHED CONDUCT MEDAL AND BAR.

Lieut. William M. Jones.
Reg. Sergt.-Major F. Butler.
Sergt. F. W. D. Sorby.

ROYAL HIGHLANDERS OF CANADA

THE DISTINGUISHED CONDUCT MEDAL.

Lieut. Ronald C. Bigland.
Lieut. Otto B. Krenchel.
Lieut. John F. MacLean.
Reg. Sergt.-Major Thomas Sim.
Co'y.Sergt.-Major Frank Ableson.
Co'y.Sergt.-Major Eugene C. Brown.
Co'y.Sergt.-Major Charles A. Bulloch.
Co'y.Sergt.-Major Edwin Evans.
Co'y.Sergt.-Major Charles F. E. Hall.
Co'y.Sergt.-Major Neil Osborne.
Co'y.Sergt.-Major Gabriel Watson.
Sergt. William S. Blyth.
Sergt. Percy Bowman.
Sergt. Wallis A. Cooper.
Sergt. Harry Davis.
Sergt. Cecil Doolittle.
Sergt. Harry Fox.
Sergt. Francis T. Fraser.
Sergt. William Hannaford.
Sergt. Robert Hooton.
Sergt. Thomas Imrie.
Sergt. Victor Jenkins.
Sergt. Valentine T. Keough.
Sergt. Emile Latour.
Sergt. Alex. McLeod.
Sergt. William C. Morrison.
Sergt. Edwin J. Moore.
Sergt. David Simard.
Sergt. Leonard Woodward.
Lance-Sergt. John G. Dickie.
Lance-Sergt. Alexander Fernie.
Lance-Sergt. Percy Way.
Corp. Sydney B. Edwards.
Corp. Archibald McWade.
Private John Boutilier.
Private John B. Burnett.
Private Harry Danson.
Private Charles Hopton.
Private John Junor.
Private Terence McGuire.
Private Charles Raine.

THE MERITORIOUS SERVICE MEDAL.

R.Q.M.S. Christopher Millward.
C.Q.M.S. A. H. McGeagh.
Sergt.-Major Derek H. Strutt.
Arm. S.-Sergt. George E. Wright.
Sergt. James A. Ayling.
Sergt. David S. Fraser.
Sergt. William Ganson.
Sergt. Albert G. Ovenden.
Lance-Corp. John C. Sanders.
Private William R. Burden.
Private Frank W. Pyke.

THE MILITARY MEDAL AND BAR.

Lieut. J. S. Buchanan.
Lieut. William Hamilton.
Lieut. Frederick L. Hayden.
Sergt. Charles H. Camm.
Sergt. James A. Glazebrook.
Sergt. William Hannaford.
Sergt. W. P. C. Kelly.
Sergt. Max H. Mills.
Corp. Clarence C. Smith.
Private Patrick Costello.
Private William E. Trumper.

THE MILITARY MEDAL.

Capt. Edgar Appleby.
Lieut. Joseph Bonner.
Lieut. Thorold G. Crossley.
Lieut. M. R. DeLaurier.
Lieut. W. T. Hornby.
Lieut. Percy D. Hoskins.

HONOURS AND AWARDS

Lieut. Walter T. Ibbott.
Lieut. Harold G. Lawton.
Lieut. David Stevenson.
Co'y.Sergt.-Major Henry Gardner.
Co'y.Sergt.-Major Charles F. E. Hall.
Co'y.Sergt.-Major Charles A. Legros.
Co'y.Serkt.-Major Richard Sandford.
Sergt. Kenneth Armstrong.
Sergt. Lawrence F. P. Bell.
Sergt. William S. Blyth.
Sergt. Osborn G. Burtt.
Sergt. Alfred Cartwright.
Sergt. James Davey.
Sergt. Harry Davis.
Sergt. John O. Davis.
Sergt. Albert Dunlop.
Sergt. G. Dunmore.
Sergt. Alexander French.
Sergt. Thomas Graham.
Sergt. A. A. Harper.
Sergt. David J. Hingley.
Sergt. James A. Houston.
Sergt. Edward Hughes.
Sergt. William W. Ireland.
Sergt. William McDonald.
Sergt. James T. McGuire.
Sergt. Alex. L. McKenzie.
Sergt. John F. McLean.
Sergt. George Millar.
Sergt. Thomas C. Newnham.
Sergt. William A. Parsons.
Sergt. Alexander Petrie.
Sergt. Frank G. Petrie.
Sergt. Alfred J. Potter.
Sergt. John Robertson.
Sergt. Henry Robson.
Sergt. John Ross.
Sergt. Norman A. Shields.
Sergt. David Simard.
Sergt. George C. Stronge.
Sergt. Bertram K. Sweeney.
Sergt. Allan D. Traill.
Sergt. Richard Wale.
Sergt. Frederick J. Walker.
Sergt. Harold R. Wall.
Sergt. William Ward.
Sergt. John E. Westerman.
Sergt. Harold W. Williamson.
Sergt. Leonard Woodward.
Sergt. Edward George Wright.
Lance-Sergt. Robert Haxton.
Lance-Sergt. William Hogarth.
Lance-Sergt. William H. A. Preddy.
Lance-Sergt. Thomas Saunders.
Corp. Richard O. Atkins.
Corp. Walter Best.
Corp. Ralph E. Breckon.
Corp. Fred G. Caldicott.
Corp. George T. Cowan.
Corp. John Given.
Corp. Charles A. Goodwillie.
Corp. William S. Hampson.
Corp. Mark W. Heckbert.
Corp. William H. Hill.
Corp. Frank A. Jowett.
Corp. Matthew Lincoln.
Corp. James H. McIntyre.
Corp. John N. Montgomerie.
Corp. Colin Morison.
Corp. James Nicholson.
Corp. William J. Paul.
Corp. Clement A. Randell.
Corp. Henry Reardon.
Corp. Damon W. Ross.
Corp. Cyril T. Tranter.
Corp. Jordan Tupper.
Corp. Reuben N. Watts.
Lance-Corp. Robert Ball.
Lance-Corp. Charles R. Bampton.
Lance-Corp. Emeasy Colpitts.
Lance-Corp. Edward Cunningham.
Lance-Corp. Alexander Florence.
Lance-Corp. Paul B. Gamble.
Lance-Corp. David Guyer.
Lance-Corp. Edward Gyde.
Lance-Corp. William LeBlanc.
Lance-Corp. William D. Love.
Lance-Corp. David McKerrow.
Lance-Corp. Charles Oakley.
Lance-Corp. William F. Somerville.
Lance-Corp. John R. Watts.
Lance-Corp. Zeb. M. Wynn.
Private Joseph W. L. Allen.
Private Arthur Anderson.
Private Robert Anderson.
Private John H. Barbour.

ROYAL HIGHLANDERS OF CANADA

Private Wilfred Beauparlant.
Private Frederick Borden.
Private Frank Bridcott.
Private Frank Brogan.
Private George A. Brown.
Private James M. Buick.
Private Alvin Clarendon.
Private Bradford Collett.
Private Arthur Cook.
Private Thomas Cowhey.
Private Allen W. Crawford.
Private John Crawford.
Private Thomas Crawford.
Private Timothy J. Crowley.
Private John C. Davies.
Private Ambrose W. Davis.
Private John E. Dettmann.
Private John O. Eddie.
Private Eldon Elston.
Private Leo Ferguson.
Private Alexander Gibbon.
Private George Gill.
Private John Grant.
Private Harry C. Gray.
Private Alex. Grossart.
Private Ernest Hest.
Private Lorne A. Higgs.
Private Clarence Hornor.
Private Roland Jack.
Private David F. Jamie.
Private Robert B. Jamieson.
Private John Junor.
Private Ernest Keefe.
Private George M. Kelly.
Private Merton E. Kettredge.
Private Donald A. Kyle.
Private John Land.
Private Fred W. Lee.
Private Clifford Lewis.
Private Charles G. Lewis.
Private Harold Linton.
Private Martin MacDonald.
Private Joseph MacKenzie.
Private James G. McArthur.
Private Alexander J. McDonald. (No. 41158.)
Private John B. McKay.
Private John S. McLeod.
Private George B. McPherson.
Private Louis Miron.
Private Alexander Muise.
Private Steve Nelles.
Private Sangster Peacock.
Private William M. Peterkin.
Private Charles A. Pockock.
Private Jerry Ryan.
Private George R. Sage.
Private John J. Seagram.
Private Harry Seivewright.
Private John Stafford.
Private William J. Stonard.
Private Charles Thompson.
Private Leonard Thompson.
Private John Thornton.
Private Joseph D. Tough.
Private Cecil W. Wheaton.
Private John James Williams.
Private Harry G. Wills.
Private Louis Wood.
Private Daniel Woods.
Private Collin M. B. Wright.
Private Roland Young.

OFFICERS MENTIONED IN DESPATCHES.

Seven times 1
Five times 1
Four times 1
Three times 1
Twice 6
Once 25

OTHER RANKS MENTIONED IN DESPATCHES.

Once 24

HONOURS AND AWARDS

Foreign Decorations

LEGION D'HONNEUR (CROIX D'OFFICIER).
Major-General Sir F. O. W. Loomis.

CROIX DE GUERRE (FRENCH).
Major-General Sir F. O. W. Loomis.
Lieut.-Col. W. H. Clark-Kennedy. (24th Battalion, V.R.C.)
Co'y. Sergt.-Major Frank Ableson.

MEDAILLE MILITAIRE (FRENCH).
Lieut. William C. Pearce.

ORDER OF LEOPOLD (COMMANDEUR).
Major-General Sir F. O. W. Loomis.

CROIX DE GUERRE (BELGIAN).
Co'y. Sergt.-Major Edwin Evans.
Co'y. Sergt.-Major George P. Morrison.
Sergt. Henry Copeman.
Sergt. David K. Miller.

SILVER MEDAL FOR MILITARY VALOUR BY H.M. THE KING OF ITALY.
Sergt. Sidney Chandler.

ORDER OF THE RISING SUN (JAPAN).
Lieut.-Col. T. S. Morrisey. (Siberian Force.)

RUSSIAN MEDAL OF ST. GEORGE (1ST CLASS).
Corp. James J. Campbell.

RUSSIAN MEDAL OF ST. GEORGE (2ND CLASS).
Lieut. Joseph Johnston.

RUSSIAN MEDAL OF ST. GEORGE (3RD CLASS).
Sergt. Alex. McLeod.

RUSSIAN MEDAL OF ST. GEORGE (4TH CLASS).
Sergt. Robert Key.   Private Frank J. Reid.

APPENDIX C.

Statistics

Total of Nominal Roll	5,560
Number of Officers who served	251
Officers promoted from the ranks (not including those commissioned to Imperial Army units)	100
Officers killed	50
O. R. killed	1,055
Officers missing	2
O.R. missing	123
Officers died	1
O.R. died	60
Total All Ranks Dead	1,291
Officers wounded	135
O.R. wounded	3,019
Total Officer casualties	188
Total O.R. casualties	4,257
Total Battalion casualties	4,445
Percentage of Officer casualties to original Officer strength	588
Percentage of O.R. casualties to original O.R. strength	432
Fatal Officer casualties 166% of original Officer strength.	
Fatal O.R. casualties 120% of original strength.	
Percentage of Officers who became casualties	75
Percentage of O.R. who became casualties	76